EDUCATION VOUCHERS:
FROM THEORY
TO ALUM ROCK

EDUCATION VOUCHERS:

FROM THEORY TO ALUM ROCK

Edited by
James A. Mecklenburger
Richard W. Hostrop

AN ETC PUBLICATION

 1972

Library of Congress Cataloging in Publication Data

Mecklenburger, James, comp.
  Education vouchers.

  1. Educational vouchers. 2. Alum Rock Union
Elementary School District. I. Hostrop, Richard W.,
joint comp. II. Title.
LB2342.M38   379'.13
ISBN 0-88280-002-7 $7.50
ISBN 0-88280-001-9 (lib. bdg.) $12.50

Copyright © 1972 by ETC PUBLICATIONS
18512 Pierce Terrace
Homewood, Illinois 60430

CONTENTS

Part II   The EDUCATION VOUCHERS Report

INTRODUCTION

Vouchers, in 1972, replaced conventional methods of assigning students and money, in the Alum Rock School District in metropolitan San Jose, California. Vouchers have been a controversial *idea* for years, but Alum Rock is the first American public school district to operate a voucher system.

Parents of 4000 students, in Alum Rock, received a "voucher" for each student—that is, a certificate said to be worth the cost of one year's schooling. Parents "spent" their vouchers by choosing, for each child, one among several competing elementary school programs. As parents spent their vouchers, so school programs were financed. In effect, schooling was sold to parents as in a marketplace.

Vouchers are neither new nor unique in education. Competition between schools for the customer's dollar antedates the United States. Vouchers differ very little from the circumstance of wealthy parents today who shop among private schools for one to their liking. Vouchers differ very little from "open admissions" policies, in some school districts, where a child may attend any public school of his choice within the district. Vouchers differ very little from the G.I. Bill of Rights under which veterans select schools of their choice while public monies pay the bill.

Precedent or parallels notwithstanding, voucher plans have received nearly universal scorn from spokesmen for American public education. Advocates and critics alike concur in this: *Vouchers, if widely implemented, would make revolutionary changes in American education.* But they disagree on the scope and value of those changes:

* Will competition among schools cause the quality of schooling to improve, or will competition corrupt?

* Will voucher plans be used to revitalize racial segregation?

* Will voucher plans, extended to include private and parochial schools, violate the Constitutional separation of church and state?

* Will voucher plans inspire the growth of alternatives to our failing inner-city schools?

* Will voucher plans serve to destroy teacher organizations, collective bargaining, and teacher job security?

* Will parents make wise choices about their children's education, or will they be hustled by unprincipled hucksters into making foolish or damaging choices?

* Will voucher plans encourage or alleviate inequalities in school finance?

* Will voucher plans result in more money for schools, or act as an excuse not to spend more money?

* Will voucher plans inspire innovation or stifle it?

These emotional questions are at the center of the controversy over vouchers. Until 1972, the argument was heated but the issues were academic. Alum Rock makes the issues vivid and real.

The Alum Rock voucher plan for 1972-1973 is mild and modest in itself. The experiment affects only one-third of the school district and excludes private and religious schools. But the U.S. Office of Economic Opportunity, which is financing the experiment, hopes that 1973-1974 will see the program expand in Alum Rock—to include the entire district as well as private and religious schools. OEO plans voucher experiments in other cities. And, if these voucher experiments appear successful at improving educational opportunity for disadvantaged youngsters, OEO hopes that vouchers will become widespread in the late 1970's and after.

Therefore, Alum Rock will be understood by advocates and critics alike as the stalking horse for radical innovation: Alum Rock will be subject to intense scrutiny, high praise and slashing criticism—as much for what it portends as for what it is. As one spokesman for the American Federation of Teachers, an organization opposed to vouchers, said of the Alum Rock experiment, "It's going to be a hot ballgame, and Alum Rock is just the top of the first inning."

To extend the metaphor, *Education Vouchers: From Theory to Alum Rock* is the record book, line-up and scorecard. Just as a thorough knowledge of baseball teams, their background, strengths, weaknesses, policies, and possibilities, helps baseball fans and commentators to understand and appreciate the action, so reliance upon this book will help observers, educators, reporters, and students of educational change to understand the Alum Rock voucher "ballgame." Moreover, it can be used as a "cookbook" by those school districts who want to provide alternatives via all or components of education vouchers.

The book has four parts:

Part I—The Voucher Controversy Takes Shape traces the history of the current interest in vouchers, introduces its advocates and major critics, and explains OEO's plans.

Part II—The Education Vouchers Report contains the essential portions of the 1970 study by the Center for the Study of Public Policy which was commissioned by OEO and which serves as theoretical justification for OEO's voucher activities.

Part III—The Alum Rock Experiment contains the essential portions of the Alum Rock Feasibility Study conducted in 1971, Alum Rock's proposal to OEO, OEO's 1972 announcement of the project, and the descriptions of the program given to each parent in Alum Rock.

Part IV—Reactions to the Voucher Experiment contains strong views on Alum Rock and subsequent voucher proposals.

Whatever the fate of the voucher experiment, it is the editors' hope that *Education Vouchers: From Theory to Alum Rock* will facilitate informed and factual discussion of the experiment.

PART I

The Voucher Controversy
Takes Shape

VOICES IN THE CLASSROOM

PETER SCHRAG

In 1967, the ideas which have since come to be associated with voucher plans had yet to be called "vouchers." Nevertheless, "proposals for alternatives to the existing public schools" had some intellectual and governmental following.

Competition for the Public Schools

Among the various subterranean phenomena twitching the divining rods of educational dowsers, perhaps the most significant is the growing interest in the study and development of institutions designed to compete with the public schools. Several years ago, the conservative economist Milton Friedman declared that "the imposition of a minimum required level of schooling and the financing of this schooling by the state can be justified. [But] the actual administration of educational institutions by the government, the 'nationalization' of the bulk of the education industry is much more difficult to justify."

Ideas like Friedman's received little attention; to some they looked a little like the recurring schemes for turning the Post Office over to private enterprise on the ground that the government shouldn't operate any kind of business. More important, they seemed to fly in the face of our whole tradition of democratic education. For a century we have prided ourselves on a school system that appeared to offer every child equal opportunities to advance academically, economically, and socially. But in recent years, as we became aware of the inadequacies and inequities of the public schools and of their rigidity against change, proposals have been made for providing alternatives to the established system—alternatives available not only to those affluent enough to afford private education, but also, through public tuition grants, to the children of the ghetto and to anyone else looking for a decent alternative. The wealthy have a choice in private schools, or in moving to the suburbs; the poor have none.

The possibilities for competitive educational programs are almost endless: They include community-operated "public" schools independent of any city-wide board of education, specialized schools of art and music, apprenticeship programs in shops and factories, and formal state-chartered experimental schools with special pedagogical orientations. Some of the suggestions call for financial support through federal tuition grants, others for local tax support channeled to private or semiprivate boards of trustees, others for a combination of public and private foundation funds.

The most recent, and most important, of the proposals for competitive schools came earlier this year from the Task Force on Economic Growth and Opportunity of the United States Chamber of Commerce. The task force, which was headed by Erwin D. Canham, editor of the *Christian Science Monitor* and which included major corporation executives, declared:

> Competition with existing public school systems offers a promising means of improving both public and private education. If all parents, at every income level, could choose between sending their children to public schools and sending their children to approved private schools at public expense, both public and private education would improve as schools attempted to attract and hold pupils. Businessmen should press for the fullest possible consideration of proposals designed to enhance competition in education. Local, state, and federal governments should consider legislation which would enable communities to adopt programs establishing a public-private option for all children.

Similar proposals have come from James S. Coleman, director of the massive United States Office of Education study *Equality of Educational Opportunity,* who suggested that the city of Washington operate competing public school systems; and from critics like Christopher Jencks, Paul Goodman, and Edgar Friedenberg, who feel that a diversity of educational options is the only way to provide healthy alternatives to the conformist rigidities of the established public system.

The response to such declarations is still largely in the talking stage, but the talk is getting serious. In Boston a Committee for Community Educational Development, Inc., was recently awarded a $25,000 Ford Foundation grant (with more expected) to plan an integrated school for children from the ages of three to eighteen. The committee, which includes MIT Provost Jerome Wiesner, physicist Jerrold Zacharias (the man who directed the development of the PSSC physics course), a suburban school superintendent, and Negro leaders from the ghetto of Roxbury, is asking the Massachusetts legislature to authorize the State Education Department to sponsor such a school and to subcontract with a private group to run it. Although no decisions have been made as to who would operate the school, it is at least possible that parents as well as members of the CCED would be involved. The intention of the school, which will not open for at least a year, is to provide opportunities for genuine experimentation in curriculum and other areas.

No one can be certain about the future of such ventures; if the public schools can provide more options, if they offer hope of improvement, then the support and clientele for the experiments may vanish. So far, however, the indicators are pointing in a different direction, and it is likely that there will be increasing talk about providing federal or state tuition support for pupils who want to attend private institutions and escape the monopoly of the public schools. The Chamber of Commerce task force proposed that any school that meets established academic standards should be approved and made eligible to receive payments for publicly financed students, provided Constitutional requirements are met. "The amount of the payment," said the report, "would vary from taxing area to taxing area (much as per-pupil expenditures vary now), but it should not be less than the per-pupil expenditures in the public schools."

The proposals for alternatives to the existing public schools would have been considered quasi-subversive a decade ago. Until recently, democratic education simply meant providing every child with the same resources, no matter what his background. Things like motivation were individual matters; a child who didn't want to learn didn't deserve to learn. But we have now discovered that what we once thought to be equal is in fact equal only for a small range of children, that equality means more than simply providing quantitatively equal resources. We know, moreover, that the alternatives for education and economic advancement that existed fifty years ago—the shop, the farm, the community—are no longer adequate or available. The schools now have a monopoly that they never had before. For all but the very exceptional, they *are* the gates to success. And yet they have not managed to adapt to the variety of backgrounds and problems with which they must deal. The movement to provide alternatives to these schools is therefore not only directed to the development of new educational ideas and of institutions that will be hospitable to minorities, but also toward restoring the choices that a simpler society took for granted. Dropouts become a problem only where the local public school is the only available educational resource—where there is no other place to go.

Peter Schrag is a Contributing Editor to *Saturday Review.*

ALTERNATIVE PUBLIC SCHOOL SYSTEMS

KENNETH B. CLARK

The author asserts that American public education suffers from "pervasive and persistent" inefficiency, particularly in the schools provided for Negro and other underprivileged children. After discussing the obstacles to "effective, nonracially constrained" education, the author proposes a strategy for providing excellent education in ghetto schools in conjunction with efforts to bring about effective school desegregation. Because the present patterns of public school organization are themselves a principal factor in inhibiting efforts to improve the quality of education, it will be necessary, he contends, to find "realistic, aggressive, and viable competitors" to the present public school systems, including such possibilities as industrial demonstration schools and schools operated by the Department of Defense.

It is now clear that American public education is organized and functions along social and economic class lines. A bi-racial public school system wherein approximately 90 per cent of American children are required to attend segregated schools is one of the clearest manifestations of this basic fact. The difficulties encountered in attempting to desegregate public schools in the South as well as in the North point to the tenacity of the forces seeking to prevent any basic change in the system.

The class and social organization of American public schools is consistently associated with a lower level of educational efficiency in the less privileged schools. This lower efficiency is expressed in terms of the fact that the schools attended by Negro and poor children have less adequate educational facilities than those attended by more privileged children. Teachers tend to resist assignments in Negro and other underprivileged schools and generally function less adequately in these schools. Their morale is generally lower; they are not adequately supervised; they tend to see their students as less capable of learning. The parents of the children in these schools are usually unable to bring about any positive changes in the conditions of these schools.

This article was first presented as a paper at the National Conference on Equal Educational Opportunity in America's Cities, sponsored by the U.S. Commission on Civil Rights, November 16-18, 1967.

The pervasive and persistent educational inefficiency which characterizes these schools results in:

(1) marked and cumulative academic retardation in a disproportionately high percentage of these children, beginning in the third or fourth grade and increasing through the eighth grade;

(2) a high percentage of dropouts in the junior and senior high schools of students unequipped academically and occupationally for a constructive role in society;

(3) a pattern of rejection and despair and hopelessness resulting in massive human wastage.

Given these conditions, American public schools have become significant instruments in the blocking of economic mobility and in the intensification of class distinctions rather than fulfilling their historic function of facilitating such mobility. In effect, the public schools have become captives of a middle class who have failed to use them to aid others to move into the middle class. It might even be possible to interpret the role of the controlling middle class as that of using the public schools to block further mobility.

What are the implications of this existing educational inefficiency? In the national interest, it is a serious question whether the United States Government can afford the continuation of the wastage of human resources at this period of world history. Although we cannot conclusively demonstrate a relation between educational inefficiency and other symptoms of personal and social pathology such as crime, delinquency, and pervasive urban decay, there is strong evidence that these are correlates.

Increasing industrialization and automation of our economy will demand larger numbers of skilled and educated and fewer uneducated workers. The manpower needs of contemporary America require business and industry to pay for the added burden of re-educating the mis-educated. This is a double taxation. The burdens of the present inefficient public education include this double taxation in addition to the high cost of crime and family stability and artificial constriction of the labor and consumer market.

Beyond these material disadvantages are the human costs inherent in the failure to achieve equality of educational opportunity. This dehumanization contributes significantly to the cycle of pathology—poor education, menial jobs or unemployment, family instability, group and personal powerlessness. This passive pathology weakens the fabric of the entire society.

Obstacles to the Attainment of Efficient Education

The obstacles which interfere with the attainment of efficient public education fall into many categories. Among them are those obstacles which reflect historical premises and dogmas about education, administrative realities, and psychological assumptions and prejudices.

The historical premises and dogmas include such fetishes as the inviolability of the "neighborhood school" concept which might include the belief that schools should be economically and racially homogeneous. The administrative barriers involve such problems as those incurred in the transportation of children from residential neighborhoods to other areas of the city. Here again the issue is one of relative advantages of the *status quo* versus the imperatives for change.

The residual psychological prejudices take many forms and probably underlie the apparent inability of society to resolve the historical and administrative problems. Initially the academic retardation of Negro children was explained in terms of their inherent racial inferiority. The existence of segregated schools was supported either by law or explained in terms of the existence of segregated neighborhoods. More recently the racial inferiority or legal and custom interpretations have given way to more subtle explanations and support for continued inefficient education. Examples are theories of "cultural deprivation" and related beliefs that the culturally determined educational inferiority of Negro children will impair the ability of white children to learn if they are taught in the same classes. It is assumed that because of their background, Negro children and their parents are poorly motivated for academic achievement and will not only be unable to compete with white children but will also retard the white children. The implicit and at times explicit assumption of these cultural deprivation theories is that the environmental deficits which Negro children bring with them to school make it difficult, if not impossible, for them to be educated either in racially homogeneous or heterogeneous schools. This point of view, intentionally or not, tends to support the pervasive rejection of Negro children and obscures and intensifies the basic problem.

There are more flagrant sources of opposition to any effective desegregation of American public schools. White Citizens' Councils in the South, parents' and taxpayers' groups in the North, and the control of boards of education by whites who identify either overtly or covertly with the more vehement opposition to change are examples of effective resistance. School officials and professional educators have defaulted in their responsibility for providing educational leadership. They have tended, for the most part, to go along with the level of community readiness and the "political realities." They have been accessories to the development and use of various subterfuges and devices for giving the appearance of change without its substance and, in doing so, have failed to present the problem of the necessary school reorganization in educational terms. This seems equally true of teachers and teachers' organizations. In some cases, teachers, textbooks, and other teaching materials have either contributed to or failed to counteract racism.

Within the past two years another formidable and insidious barrier in the way of the movement towards effective, desegregated public schools has emerged in the form of the black power movement and its demands for racial separatism. Some of the more vocal of the black power advocates who have addressed themselves to the problems of education have explicitly and implicitly argued for Negroes' control of "Negro Schools." Some have asserted that there should be separate school districts organized to control the schools in all-Negro residential areas: that there should be Negro Boards of Education, Negro superintendents of schools, Negro faculty, and Negro curricula and materials. These demands are clearly a rejection of the goals of integrated education and a return to the pursuit of the myth of an efficient "separate but equal"—or the pathetic wish for a separate and superior—racially-organized system of education. One may view this current trend whereby some Negroes themselves seem to be asking for a racially segregated system of education as a reflection of the frustration resulting from white resistance to genuine desegregation of the public schools since the *Brown* decision and as a reaction to the reality that the quality of education in the *de facto* segregated Negro schools in the North and the Negro schools in the South has steadily deteriorated under the present system of white control.

In spite of these explanations, the demands for segregated schools can be no more acceptable coming from Negroes than they are coming from white segregationists. There is no reason to believe and certainly there is no evidence to support the contention that all-Negro schools, controlled by Negroes, will be any more efficient in preparing American children to contribute constructively to the realities of the present and future world. The damage inherent in racially isolated schools was persuasively documented by the comprehensive study conducted by the United States Commission on Civil Rights.[1]

Furthermore, the more subtle and insidious educational deprivation for white children who are required to attend all-white schools is furthered by both the black and the white advocates of racially homogeneous schools.

---

[1] U.S. Commission on Civil Rights, *Racial Isolation in the Public Schools* (Washington: U.S. Government Printing Office, 1967).

Attempts at Remedies

In spite of these obstacles in the path of genuine desegregation of American public schools and the attainment of effective, nonracially constrained education for all American children, there have been persistent attempts to compensate for the deficits of racial isolation in the American public schools. A tremendous amount of energy and money has been expended in the attempt to develop special programs designed to improve the academic achievement of Negro children, who are the most obvious victims of inferior, racially segregated public schools.

The United States Commission on Civil Rights report, *Racial Isolation in the Public Schools,* has presented facts which raise questions concerning the long-range effectiveness of these programs. There is some evidence that these special programs do some good and help some children; but they clearly underline the inadequacy of the regular education these children receive. In addition to the fact that they obscure the overriding reality that underprivileged children are being systematically short-changed in their regular segregated and inferior schools, these programs may also be seen as a type of commitment to the continuation of segregated education.

If one accepts the premise which seems supported by all available evidence, and above all by the reasoning of the *Brown* decision, that racially segregated schools are inherently inferior, it would seem to follow that all attempts to improve the quality of education in all-Negro and all-white schools would have necessarily limited positive effects. All programs designed to raise the quality of education in racially homogeneous schools would therefore have to be seen as essentially evasive programs or as the first stage in an inferior approach to a serious plan for effective desegregation of public schools. Given the resistance to an immediate reorganization of the present system of racially organized schools so as to create a more effective system of racially heterogeneous schools, however, one may be required to attempt to increase the efficiency of education in all-Negro schools as a necessary battle in the larger struggle for racially desegregated schools.

The problem of the extent to which it is possible to provide excellent education in a predominantly Negro school should be re-examined thoroughly in spite of the basic premise of the *Brown* decision that racially segregated schools are inherently inferior. Some questions which we must now dare to ask and seek to answer as the basis for a new strategy in the assault against the inhumanity of the American system of racial segregation are:

    (1) Is the present pattern of massive educational inferiority and

inefficiency which is found in predominantly Negro schools inherent and inevitable in racially segregated schools?

(2) Is there anything which can be done within the Negro schools to raise them to a tolerable level of educational efficiency—or to raise them to a level of educational excellence?

If the answer to the first question is *yes* and to the second question is *no,* then the strategy of continued and intensified assault on the system of segregated schools is justified and should continue unabated since there is no hope of raising the quality of education for Negro children as long as they are condemned to segregated schools—there is no hope of salvaging them. If, on the other hand, the answers to the above questions are reversed, it would suggest that a shift in strategy and tactics, without giving up the ultimate goals of eliminating the dehumanizing force of racial segregation from American life, would be indicated. This shift would suggest that given the present strong and persistent resistance to any serious and effective desegregation of our public schools, that the bulk of the available organizational, human, and financial resources and specialized skills be mobilized and directed toward obtaining the highest quality of education for Negro students without regard to the racial composition of the schools which they attend. This attempt would demand a massive, system-wide educational enrichment program designed to obtain educational excellence in the schools attended by Negro children.

Recent experiences in New York City, Boston, Chicago, Philadelphia and other northern cities reveal that this temporary shift in the battleground will not in itself lead to any easier victory. School boards and public school officials seem as resistant to developing or implementing programs designed to improve the quality and efficiency of education provided for Negro children in segregated schools as they are deaf to all requests for effective desegregation plans and programs. The interests and desires of white middle-class parents, and the interests of the increasingly powerful teachers' federations and professional supervisory associations are invariably given priority over the desire of Negro parents for nonsegregated quality education for their children. The interests of the white parents, teachers, and supervisors are often perceived by them as inimical to the desires of the Negro parents. Furthermore, the capture and control of the public schools by the white middle-class parents and teachers provided the climate within which the system of racially segregated and inferior schools could be developed, expanded and reinforced and within which the public schools became instruments for blocking rather than facilitating the upward mobility of Negroes and other lower-status groups. One, therefore, could not expect these individuals and groups to be sympathetic and responsive to the pleas of Negro parents for higher quality education for their children. Negro parents and organizations must accept and plan their strategy in terms of the fact that adversaries in the battle for higher quality education for Negro children will be as numerous and as formidable as the adversaries in the battle for non-segregated schools. Indeed they will be the same individuals, officials, and groups in different disguises and with different excuses for inaction but with the same powerful weapons of evasion, equivocation, inaction, or tokenism.

An effective strategy for the present and the future requires rigorous and honest appraisal of all of the realities, a tough-minded diagnosis of the strengths and weaknesses of the Negro and his allies. We cannot now permit ourselves to be deluded by wishful thinking, sentimental optimism, or rigid and oversimplified ideological postures. We must be tough-mindedly pragmatic and flexible as we seek to free our children from the cruel and dehumanizing, inferior and segregated education inflicted upon them by the insensitive, indifferent, affable, and at times callously rigid custodians of American public education.

In developing an appropriate strategy and the related flexible tactics, it must be clearly understood that the objective of improving the quality of education provided for Negro children is not a substitute for or a retreat from the funda-mental goal of removing the anachronism of racially segregated schools from American life. The objective of excellent education for Negro and other lower-status children is inextricably linked with the continuing struggle to desegre-gate public education. All of the public school, college, and professional school civil-rights litigation instituted by the legal staff of the NAACP arose from recognition of the obvious fact that the segregated schools which Negroes were forced by law to attend were inferior and therefore damaging and vio-lative of the equal protection clause in the 14th amendment of the United States Constitution.

The suggested shift in emphasis from desegregation to quality of education is not a retreat into the blind alley of accepting racial separation as advocated by the Negro nationalist groups, nor is it the acceptance of defeat in the battle for desegregation. It is rather a regrouping of forces, a shift in battle plans and an attempt to determine the most vulnerable flanks of the oppo-sition as the basis for major attack. The resisting educational bureaucracies, their professional staffs, and the segment of the white public which has not yet been infected fatally by the American racist disease are most vulnerable to attack on the issue of the inferior quality of education found in Negro schools and the need to institute a plan immediately to raise the educational level of these schools. The economic, political, military, social-stability, inter-national democratic, humane, and self-interest arguments in favor of an immediate massive program for educational excellence in predominantly

Negro schools are so persuasive as to be irrefutable. The expected resistance should be overcome with intelligently planned and sustained efforts.

The first phase of an all-out attack on the inferior education now found in racially segregated schools should be coordinated with a strategy and program for massive and realistic desegregation of entire school systems. This more complicated phase of the over-all struggle will continue to meet the resistance of the past with increased intensity. It will be necessary, therefore, to break this task down into its significant components and determine the timing and phasing of the attack on each or combinations of the components. For example:

> The evidence and arguments demonstrating the detrimental effects of segregated schools on the personality and effectiveness of white children should be gathered, evaluated, and widely disseminated in ways understandable to the masses of the whites.

> The need to reorganize large public school systems away from the presently inefficient and uneconomic neighborhood schools to more modern and viable systems of organization such as educational parks, campuses, or clusters must be sold to the general public in terms of hard dollars and cents and educational efficiency benefiting all children rather than in terms of public-school desegregation.

> The need to consolidate small, uneconomic, and relative ineffective school districts into larger educational and fiscal systems in order to obtain more efficient education for suburban and exurban children must also be sold in direct practical terms rather than in terms of desegregation of schools.

> The need to involve large metropolitan regional planning in the mobilization, utilization, and distribution of limited educational resources on a more efficient level must also be explored and discussed publicly.

> The movement toward decentralization of large urban school systems must be carefully monitored in order to see that decentralization does not reinforce or concretize urban public school segregation—and to assure that decentralization is consistent with the more economically determined trend toward consolidation and regional planning allocation of resources and cooperation.

A final indication that phase one, the struggle for excellent education for Negro children in ghetto schools, is not inconsistent with phase two, the struggle for nonsegregated education for all children, is to be seen in the fact that if it were possible to raise the quality of education provided for Negro schildren who attend the urban schools to a level of unquestioned excellence, the flight of middle-class whites to the suburbs might be stemmed and some who have left might be attracted back to the city. Hence, phase one activity would increase the chances of obtaining nonsegregated education in our cities. Similarly, some of the program suggestions of phase two such as educational parks and campuses and the possibilities of regional planning and educational cooperation across present municipal boundaries could lead to substantial improvements in the quality of education offered to inner-city children.

The goal of high quality education for Negro and lower-status children and the goal of public school desegregation are inextricable; the attainment of the one will lead to the attainment of the other. It is not likely that there could be effective desegregation of the schools without a marked increase in the academic achievement and personal and social effectiveness of Negro and white children. Neither is it possible to have a marked increase in the educational efficiency of Negro schools and the resulting dramatic increase in the academic performance of Negro children without directly and indirectly facilitating the process of public school desegregation.

Problems of Educational Monopoly

It is possible that all attempts to improve the quality of education in our present racially segregated public schools and all attempts to desegregate these schools will have minimal positive results. The rigidity of present patterns of public school organization and the concomitant stagnation in quality of education and academic performance of children may not be amenable to any attempts at change working through and within the present system.

Until the influx of Negro and Puerto Rican youngsters into urban public schools, the American public school system was justifiably credited with being the chief instrument for making the American dream of upward social, economic, and political mobility a reality. The depressed immigrants from southern and eastern Europe could use American public schools as the ladder toward the goals of assimilation and success. The past successes of American public education seem undebatable. The fact that American public schools were effective mobility vehicles for white American immigrants makes even more stark and intolerable their present ineffectiveness for Negro and Puerto Rican children. Now it appears that the present system of organization and functioning of urban public schools is a chief blockage in the mobility of the masses of Negro and other lower-status minority group children. The inefficiency of their schools and the persistence and acceptance of the explanations for this generalized inefficiency are clear threats to the viability of our cities and national stability. The relationship between long-standing urban problems of poverty, crime and delinquency, broken homes—the total cycle of pathology, powerlessness, and personal and social destructiveness which haunts our urban ghettos—and the breakdown in the efficiency of our public schools is now unavoidably clear. It is not enough that those responsible for our public schools should assert passively that the schools merely reflect the pathologies and injustices of our society. Public schools and their administrators must assert boldly that education must dare to challenge and change society toward social justice as the basis for democratic stability.

There remains the disturbing question—a most relevant question probably too painful for educators themselves to ask—whether the selection process involved in training and promoting educators and administrators for our public schools emphasizes qualities of passivity, conformity, caution, smoothness, and superficial affability rather than boldness, creativity, substance, and the ability to demand and obtain those things which are essential for solid and effective public education for all children. If the former is true and if we are dependent upon the present educational establishment, then all hopes for the imperative reforms which must be made so that city public schools can return to a level of innovation and excellence are reduced to a minimum, if not totally eliminated.

The racial components of the present crisis in urban public education clearly make the possibilities of solution more difficult and may contribute to the passivity and pervading sense of hopelessness of school administrators. Aside from any latent or subtle racism which might infect school personnel themselves, they are hampered by the gnawing awareness that with the continuing flight of middle-class whites from urban public schools and with the increasing competition which education must engage in for a fair share of the tax dollar, it is quite possible that Americans will decide deliberately or by default to sacrifice urban public schools on the altars of its historic and contemporary forms of racism. If this can be done without any real threat to the important segments of economic and political power in the society and with only Negro children as the victims, then there is no realistic basis for hope that our urban public schools will be saved.

The hope for a realistic approach to saving public education in American cities seems to this observer to be found in a formula whereby it can be demonstrated to the public at large that the present level of public school inefficiency has reached an intolerable stage of public calamity. It must be demonstrated that minority group children are not the only victims of the monopolistic inefficiency of the present pattern of organization and functioning of our public schools.

It must be demonstrated that white children—privileged white children whose parents understandably seek to protect them by moving to suburbs or by sending them to private and parochial schools—also suffer both potentially and immediately.

It must be demonstrated that business and industry suffer intolerable financial burdens of double and tripe taxation in seeking to maintain a stable economy in the face of the public school inefficiency which produces human casualties rather than constructive human beings.

It must be demonstrated that the cost in correctional, welfare, and health services are intolerably high in seeking to cope with consequences of educational inefficiency—that it would be more economical, even for an affluent society, to pay the price and meet the demands of efficient public education.

It must be demonstrated that a nation which presents itself to the world as the guardian of democracy and the protector of human values throughout the world cannot itself make a mockery of these significant ethical principles by dooming one-tenth of its own population to a lifetime of inhumane futility because of remediable educational deficiencies in its public schools.

These must be understood and there must be the commitment to make the average American understand them if our public schools and our cities are to be effective. But it does not seem likely that the changes necessary for increased efficiency of our urban public schools will come about because they should. Our urban public school systems seem muscle-bound with tradition. They seem to represent the most rigid forms of bureaucracies which, paradoxically, are most resilient in their ability and use of devices to resist rational or irrational demands for change. What is most important in understanding the ability of the educational establishment to resist change is the fact that public school systems are protected public monopolies with only minimal competition from private and parochial schools. Few critics of the American urban public schools—even severe ones such as myself—dare to question the givens of the present organization of public education in terms of local control of public schools, in terms of existing municipal or political boundaries, or in terms of the rights and prerogatives of boards of education to establish policy and select professional staff—at least nominally or titularly if not actually. Nor dare the critics question the relevance of the criteria and standards for selecting superintendents, principals, and teachers, or the relevance of all of these to the objectives of public education—producing a literate and informed public to carry on the business of democracy—and to the goal of producing human beings with social sensitivity and dignity and creativity and a respect for the humanity of others.

A monopoly need not genuinely concern itself with these matters. As long as local school systems can be assured of state aid and increasing federal aid without the accountability which inevitably comes with aggressive competition, it would be sentimental, wishful thinking to expect any significant increase in the efficiency of our public schools. If there are no alternatives to the present system—short of present private and parochial schools which are approaching their limit of expansion—then the possibilities of improvement in public education are limited.

Alternative Forms of Public Education

Alternatives—realistic, aggressive, and viable competitors—to the present public school systems must be found. The development of such competitive public school systems will be attacked by the defenders of the present system as attempts to weaken the present system and thereby weaken, if not destroy, public education. This type of expected self-serving argument can be briefly and accurately disposed of by asserting and demonstrating that truly effective competition strengthens rather than weakens that which deserves to survive. I would argue further that public education need not be identified with the present system of organization of public schools. Public education can be more broadly and pragmatically defined in terms of that form of organization and functioning of an educational system which is in the public interest. Given this definition, it becomes clear that an inefficient system of public systems is not in the public interest:

—a system of public schools which destroys rather than develops positive human potentialities is not in the public interest;

—a system which consumes funds without demonstrating effective returns is not in the public interest;

—a system which insists that its standards of performance should not or cannot be judged by those who must pay the cost is not in the public interest;

—a system which says that the public has no competence to assert that a patently defective product is a sign of the system's inefficiency and demands radical reforms is not in the public interest;

—a system which blames its human resources and its society while it quietly acquiesces in, and inadvertently perpetuates, the very injustices which it claims limit its efficiency is not in the public interest.

Given these assumptions, therefore, it follows that alternative forms of public education must be developed if the children of our cities are to be educated and made constructive members of our society. In the development of alternatives, all attempts must at the same time be made to strengthen our present urban public schools. Such attempts would involve re-examination, revision, and strengthening of curricula, methods, personnel selection, and evaluation; the development of more rigorous procedures of supervision, reward of superior performance, and the institution of a realistic and tough system of accountability, and the provision of meaningful ways of involving the parents and the community in the activities of the school.

The above measures, however, will not suffice. The following are suggested as possible, realistic, and practical competitors to the present form of urban public school systems:

Regional State Schools. These schools would be financed by the states and would cut across present urban-suburban boundaries.

Federal Regional Schools. These schools would be financed by the Federal Government out of present state aid funds or with additional federal funds. These schools would be able to cut through state boundaries and could make provisions for residential students.

College- and University-Related Open Schools. These schools would be financed by colleges and universities as part of their laboratories in education. They would be open to the public and not restricted to children of faculty and students. Obviously, students would be selected in terms of constitutional criteria and their percentage determined by realistic considerations.

Industrial Demonstration Schools. These schools would be financed by industrial business, and commercial firms for their employees and selected members of the public. These would not be vocational schools—but elementary and comprehensive high schools of quality. They would be sponsored by combinations of business and industrial firms in much the same way as churches and denominations sponsor and support parochial or sectarian schools.

Labor Union Sponsored Schools. These schools would be financed and sponsored by labor unions largely, but not exclusively, for the children of their members.

Army Schools. The Defense Department has been quietly effective in educating some of the casualties of our present public schools. It is hereby suggested that they now go into the business of repairing hundreds of thousands of these human casualties with affirmation rather than apology. Schools for adolescent dropouts or educational rejects could be set up by the Defense Department adjacent to camps—but not necessarily as an integral part of the military. If this is necessary it should not block the attainment of the goal of rescuing as many of these young people as possible. They are not expendable on the altar of anti-militarism rhetoric.

With strong, efficient, and demonstrably excellent parallel systems of public schools, organized and operated on a quasi-private level, and with quality control and professional accountability maintained and determined by Federal and State educational standards and supervision, it would be possible to bring back into public education a vitality and dynamism which are now clearly missing. Even the public discussion of these possibilities might clear away some of the dank stagnation which seems to be suffocating urban education today. American industrial and material wealth was made possible through industrial competition. American educational health may be made possible through educational competition.

If we succeed, we will have returned to the dynamic, affirmative goal of education; namely, to free man of irrational fears, superstitions, and hatreds. Specifically, in America the goal of democratic education must be to free Americans of the blinding and atrophying shackles of racism. A fearful, passive, apologetic, and inefficient educational system cannot help in the attainment of these goals.

If we succeed in finding and developing these and better alternatives to the present educational inefficiency, we will not only save countless Negro children from lives of despair and hopelessness; and thousands and thousands of white children from cynicism, moral emptiness, and social ineptness—but we will also demonstrate the validity of our democratic promises. We also will have saved our civilization through saving our cities.

Dr. Kenneth B. Clark is associated with the Metropolitan Applied Research Center.

THE CASE FOR A FREE MARKET

THEODORE R. SIZER

During the 1960's, the voucher idea received its most thorough exploration and support at Harvard. In "The Case for a Free Market," in January, 1969, Theodore Sizer, Dean of the Harvard Graduate School of Education, explained vouchers with considerable sophistication.

The Alum Rock experiment has deep roots in Sizer's school.

Competition is the newest old panacea for the reform of American schools. The argument for it is simple: The public schools are a monopoly and monopolies offer neither variety nor high quality. As America needs both varied and excellent schools, competitive pressure is clearly required. A marketplace must be created for education, with children and their parents as the choice-making consumers. The consumers, the argument continues, will pick the better schools most of the time and, in so doing, will force the quality of all to improve.

Like all panaceas, this one suffers from oversimplification. Nonetheless, it has considerable merit, particularly if a "competitive" scheme were conceived as a part of a larger, comprehensive effort at school reform. The marketplace should not be the total arbiter of educational quality. Children are, on the whole, poor judges of the "product" they are buying; their parents' judgment is very uneven; and empirical evidence on the quality of schooling is meager and confusing. Still, the "consumer" should have some influence over the school he attends, enough to shape it in appropriate ways, but not enough to terrorize it. In a field where values are paramount—schools are places designed to *influence* children and as such are supremely moral enterprises—no group, students, parents, teachers, or government, should have total control. There should be a balance. Many of today's school systems do not permit sufficient diversity among individual students and individual schools. In doing so, they foster a dull conformity. Competition among schools must be added to the balance.

This article was included in a special issue of *Saturday Review* in cooperation with the Committee for Economic Development. Reprinted with copyright permission of *Saturday Review*, January 11, 1969.

Despite evidence to the contrary particularly that cited in James S. Coleman's report *Equality of Educational Opportunity,* a change in control *can* lead to a change in the quality of children's learning. Some changes in control, such as turning the schools in black communities completely over to black educators, are essentially political maneuvers, provoked by a general dissatisfaction rather than by any specific theory about the means of educational reform. Some possibly inevitable shifts in control may be pedagogically harmful. But changes in control can be significant for children. Many significant things that children learn are untestable, and may be affected by the political structure of a school system. The attitudes of teachers, the pride (or lack of it) that parents have in a school, the extent of accountability of the staff—all may have subtle but important effects on learning. No one yet has documented this, but anyone who has taught in different schools knows that it is true. Those who say that the manner of a school's governance has little effect on pupil achievement and learning are deluded. New forms of control, including those that forward concepts of competition, will touch children.

There are various means to encourage competition, some essentially political and some fiscal. The one most in the public eye at present is decentralization, an effort to give more power over a particular school or school district to those in the immediate community served by that school. The arguments for decentralization usually do not originate in a belief in competition per se, but rather from the conviction that a minority group within a large community has been disregarded by the monopolistic system and will continue to be unless that group can influence the schools it uses. The Ocean Hill-Brownsville community in New York City wants more control over its schools because its leaders believe that their children are getting not only an inferior education but also one dominated primarily by white rather than black values.

Decentralization will create competing schools only in the sense that people unhappy with the schools in one district can move to another, and this possibility is unlikely in many communities due both to the large numbers of people involved and the restriction of lower-class Negroes from most suburban, middle-class white communities. Decentralization will give a small, relatively homogenous community—whether white or black, rich or poor—a school or schools over which it has monopolistic control. It would Balkanize big-city districts and return them, more or less, to the way they were organized seventy-five years ago. The variety in the city would be reflected by the variety in the schools. Each geographical group, more or less, would have its own public school enclave.

For political reasons, drastic and total decentralization may now be essential and inevitable. The black community in particular has been frustrated too long to weigh heavily the debits of such a move. It wants to control what its children learn and it wants to hire and fire the teachers who teach them. It will achieve this goal, but much tension and violence will precede it.

Apart from political realities, total decentralization has little to commend it. The biases of a tiny geographical minority will hold sway over children who, if present patterns continue, will almost certainly not remain in the community where they were schooled. Little village bigotries will get disproportionate attention; teachers will find local pressures difficult to work under (ask anyone who has taught in a small, fundamentalist Protestant town); and pedagogical reform, which rarely arises from the grass roots, will be even more difficult to achieve than it is now.

Nonetheless, the political claims of the black community have become more persuasive than these educational drawbacks. It remains to be seen if a form of decentralization that minimizes pedagogical reaction can be evolved; early reports from the Ocean Hill-Brownsville experiment were hopeful.

While decentralization is primarily a political scheme, a second, more radical plan would employ public money to create separate, private school systems for minorities. This approach would decentralize by persuasion rather than geography. An area with a mixed population could have, cheek by jowl, several public schools—for example, one run by the city (PS 121), one by the Catholic Church (St. Mary's School), and one by the black community (the Martin Luther King Freedom School). Under this scheme, all would receive public financial support in varying measures and in varying ways, perhaps in patterns similar to those used in the United Kingdom or, closer to home, in American private universities. In England, for example, some independent schools receive state aid for each student assigned to that school by a public authority; the school holds places open for such students. Some American private universities receive between 40 and 60 per cent of their annual operating funds from federal sources; they are, in Clark Kerr's term, "federal grant universities." "Public" and "private" are increasingly meaningless terms in U.S. higher education. Perhaps they should be in elementary education, too.

Many who gasp at the prospect of publicly financed black private schools fail to see the extent of the precedent set by Catholics in many large cities. Between a quarter and a third of all school-age children in New York City are educated in Catholic schools, saving the taxpayer (if not the Catholic parents) a very large sum indeed. Their schools were created in the early part of the century to keep Catholic traditions strong and to counteract the implicitly but unmistakably Protestant teaching found in the public schools. They are *segregated* schools—segregated by religion, though open to all.

Catholic schools are facing a financial crisis that can only be solved by some form of public aid to their system. Public aid to their schools may be cheaper in the long run than the costs of absorbing their youngsters into an expanded public system and, if this is true, the pragmatic American will willy-nilly get over his church-state hang-up. Taxes now seem to be a more telling issue than theology.

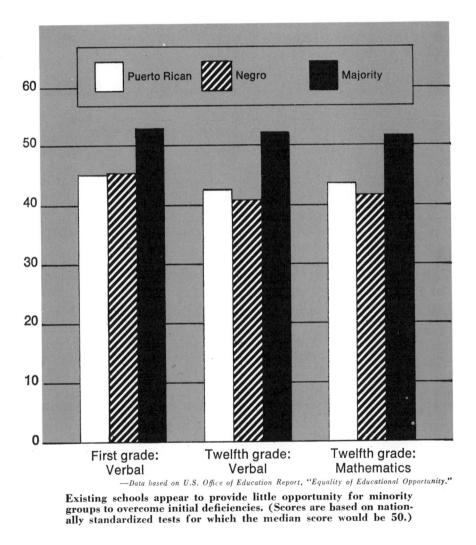

—*Data based on U.S. Office of Education Report, "Equality of Educational Opportunity."*

Existing schools appear to provide little opportunity for minority groups to overcome initial deficiencies. (Scores are based on nationally standardized tests for which the median score would be 50.)

But a black school system? Such a plan would segregate—as did the Catholic schools. Clearly racial, religious, and economic integration must remain a fixed goal, and a central one for the society, but integration in a practical, short-term sense may be in some cities an impossibility now. The best solution, some say, may be a system responsive to and for the black community. This is sad, a measure of the galling failure of integration over the last fifteen years.

Competition in this scheme, then, would be among public systems of special persuasion—white, Protestant-liberal; Jewish; Catholic; black; and others. The competition would be essentially ideological, and children would attend one or another school because of their religion or race or some other persuasion. In many ways such a system would exalt bigotry, separatism, and apartheid. It could be as cloistered and as narrow as geographically decentralized districts. But, as with decentralization, it may be politically inevitable.

Widely differing public and private schools will inevitably have some goals in common. All might agree on some product—the skills of reading for example. Many existing schools, public and private, teach these skills poorly. One way to improve the product would be to create competition, say, among purveyors of reading skills, private companies who would contract for a program within a school, or even of an entire school. The consumer could state the product desired—competence at reading to some definable level—and the contractor would be obliged to reach it. The contractor which did so most cheaply and quickly would prosper—and so would the youngsters being taught.

This third competitive scheme most resembles the industrial sector. Private concerns contract and compete. But the industrial sector requires a *specific,* measurable product, and much of education is unspecific and unmeasurable. Feeling, joy, love, appreciation, candor, and compassion should all be "taught" in school; but how can we measure these in a way suitable for a contract? All must be judged subjectively or taken on faith. Competitive industry has no useful place here. However, it may well have a place in skill training, as the textbook industry has demonstrated. Schools might now contract for more than texts alone, for teams of teachers and pedagogical equipment to come along with the materials. And schools might start insisting that both texts and teachers deliver what they promise. In certain well defined areas, competition among contractors might have considerable merit. Other areas are so ill defined that a contractor could too readily slight them. Such areas need support on faith.

A fourth scheme to increase competition is a classic like those preceding: Give public money *directly* to the children and let them and their parents choose their own school. This idea has deep roots. Its best-known present advocate is economist Milton Friedman.

One version of this scheme gives to poor children a voucher which can be cashed by the particular school that the child and his parents select. The poorer the child the more valuable the voucher: A child from a severely restricted background will require more expensive services than one from a wealthier family.

A major virtue of this plan is that it concentrates resources directly on the particular school, public or private, that a poor youngster attends. No money gets creamed off as it passes through intervening bureaucracies, and a public school with a large number of children from very poor families might obtain through vouchers a sum several times as great as its central budget.

Competition would be forwarded in several ways. The scheme would allow private schools in the slums to survive. If an "open enrollment" policy existed among the schools of a system, it would provoke competition by making a poor child a financial asset: A school with a significant number of poor children—and thus a significantly enlarged budget—could mount a program for *all* youngsters which was notably richer than that found in other schools. Principals of schools might thus compete for poor students. In communities where inter-city pupil transfer plans such as Boston's METCO and Hartford's Project Concern were in effect, wealthy suburban schools might be particularly persuaded to enroll poor inner-city youngsters, thus forwarding class, and perhaps racial, integration. Put boldly, they might be bribed into taking many poor youngsters. Idealism spiced with cash has been a typical American recipe for action.

By giving power to poor parents to choose schools for their youngsters, such a plan provides some of the real freedom of choice enjoyed by the middle class. Some of this freedom will surely be abused, as it was and is under higher education's GI Bill, but it remains a lesser evil than the total monopoly over ghetto education now held by political leaders and professionals. It will distribute power, and give parents some options, some clear leverage on their neighborhood school (the leverage of removing their child and his voucher), and some "desirability" (a poor child brings money with him).

Total free enterprise cannot be tolerated, of course. As with the GI Bill, only accredited schools could cash vouchers, and to be accredited a school would be required to admit students of any race, color, or creed. Public money through vouchers could help schools started with black (or white) initiative, but they could not be used to forward deliberate segregation. Competition, as we have said, may reward bigotry; competition has this risk inherent within it. But bigotry and racism can be held in check if there are adequate civil rights restrictions written into the laws launching and establishing such a program and adequate resources appropriated for policing it. A voucher scheme without such safeguards could undermine the small, but important steps toward integration in places where it is possible. Furthermore, a voucher plan for all children (not just poor children) that replaced some existing sources of public aid would cripple the public schools and would give excessive power to middle-class parents. A voucher scheme must be a supplement to the present system—better yet, a part of a new comprehensive funding plan—and *must discriminate in favor of poor children.*

Such, in admittedly oversimplified outline, are four devices to extend competition among schools. All four will loosen up the present system by changing the power structure. The public monopoly in education would either have within it competing parts or would be pressed to high quality service by publicly financed private schools (in much the same way as our private universities, now heavily supported with public funds, compete with public higher education).

There are, of course, problems with competition as a means to improve the schools. As soon as one gives power of choice to parents, one must provide sound information about the several available options in a community. Accreditation by the state or regional authorities must be strengthened and made relevant, a staggering intellectual and practical task. Evaluation must be extended and improved, on a large scale. The National Assessment Program, launched two years ago, is a small step in this direction. The strengths and weaknesses of schools should not be left wholly to gossip and unsupported assertions.

A problem of equal complexity will come as schools become more varied and hold sharply differing ideologies. The states will have to allow for diversity, but prevent destructive extremism. In a society made increasingly homogeneous by the mass media, education carries a new responsibility for this diversity and for nurturing cultural identities of great variety. The school should no longer be the melting pot, if it ever was. It should be the vehicle for individual and group identity within a broad American system, but not a slave to it. While it is obvious that the state must prevent obvious extremists of any persuasion from dominating any school, it must recognize and honor responsible diversity. The need for the common school has largely passed; television has seen to that. We need more critical, culturally dissenting, and intellectually vigorous people. Today's schools must produce these.

Finally there is the political problem. The public school is Mom and apple pie. The facts that it is a monopoly and that all children with few exceptions are *forced* to submit to *communal* schooling rarely dissuade July Fourth orators. The notion of deliberately creating entities to compete with Mom is jarring indeed, and will be lost on more than a few Washington lobbyists.

However, in context and as part of a large, careful scheme for the reform of American education, one or more schemes to abet competition among schools have considerable promise. Perhaps American educators and politicians are mature enough to see the promise as well as the problems. Curiously these radical notions may be more congenial to the Republican than to the Democratic party.

Policies encouraging competition will only have effect if embedded in a larger plan for educational reform. Decentralization or any other scheme simply added to the present muddle will merely increase the muddle. The system as a whole must be overhauled, and the place of competitive programs carefully arranged within it.

I can do no more here than to sketch an example of what I mean. The following interconnected policies, if adopted together might appreciably improve the education of children:

1) Drastically decentralize certain educational decisions—curricula, the hiring of teachers, the expenditure of funds—to individual schools or small clusters of schools. The principal of the school would be appointed jointly by a parents' council and the central metropolitan authority and would serve at their pleasure. He would have great power and would receive advice from the parents' council and the central authority. Through this policy, most of the decisions directly affecting a youngster will be made by those who know him as an individual and who are accessible to his parents. Such a plan may make his education more relevant than at present, and certainly more flexible.

2) Centralize to metropolitan authorities responsibilities for: raising local taxes and distributing block operating grants to schools; planning, siting, and building school houses; assigning pupils and arranging for a meaningful open enrollment policy; evaluating individual schools and widely publishing for the general public the results of such studies; operating special schools for the blind and other handicapped groups; providing supporting services, such as instructional television and in-service teacher training.

3) Require that the states license teachers and accredit public and private schools; provide grants to equalize and supplement resources for each metropolitan region; provide incentive grants to particularly deserving individual schools; and serve as an agent for mediation between individual schools and their central districts. In addition, states should fund teacher salaries; the unions or teachers' associations should bargain at the state rather than the local level.

These three policies are hardly radical: versions of all have worked successfully in the United Kingdom since 1944.

4) Discriminate in favor of poor children with a federal Poor Children's Bill of Rights. Public and private schools for the poor would thereby be given a major and needed boost.

5) Discriminate in favor of racial minorities and a building program which supports construction *only* of buildings designed to handle diverse student populations within metropolitan authorities.

6) Equalize through federal grants the financial resources available for education in each state.

7) Discriminate in favor of imaginative schools and school districts with federally administered incentive grants, such as those embodied in the original Title III of the Elementary and Secondary Education Act of 1965.

8) Radically increase federal support of research and evaluation in education; and develop and support national, but independent, "consumers' unions" for education to evaluate school materials and industrial contractors' plans, and to publicize widely and in popular form the findings of such evaluations.

Within such a plan, several competitive plans have desirable play, and an improved balance of power is approached. There is decentralization of certain educational functions. Open enrollment within the metropolitan region is possible, and poor children, with their vouchers, are mobile and possibly even sought after by wealthy districts. With vouchers, private schools for the poor are financially possible. Evaluation of individual schools, of school materials, and of private contractors' services are provided for at several levels. The narrowness of total decentralization is guarded against through central evaluation, and the political need for new, mass, private school systems is lessened by significant decentralization.

These suggestions are in many respects drastic. Yet today they may be realistic because school systems are, particularly in many large cities, close to collapse. At such times panaceas may evolve into practical possibilities.

Theodore Sizer is the Dean of the Harvard Graduate School of Education.

THE FREE SCHOOLS OF DENMARK

ESTELLE FUCHS

Advocates of vouchers searched worldwide for similar voucher plans in operation. In Education Vouchers *(see Part II), it says, "A number of foreign countries have also recognized the principle that parents who are dissatisfied with their local public school should be given money to establish alternatives. For a description of the Danish System, see Estelle Fuchs, 'The Free Schools of Denmark.'" Reproduced below, it will be found that the public school system retains no monopoly over the education of the young in Denmark.*

Denmark is a country long acclaimed for its achievements in education. It has had worldwide influence through its extensive programs in vocational and adult education. But more important, Denmark presents for a democratic state a model of public education that is flexible in the use of alternative types of public schools, many of them organized and controlled by parents. It is through their system of Free Schools (*Friskoler*) that the Danes have shown how a modern nation can establish standards of education required for national life and the protection of the young, while at the same time provide for the freedom of parents with special religious, ethnic, economic, or pedagogic interests to oversee and direct the education of their children with minimal interference by the government.

In the United States, a state-controlled education system has come to mean that parents who are dissatisfied with the education provided for their children must either move to areas where school systems are more compatible with their interests, turn to private, non-publicly supported schooling, or exert pressure for internal reform. However, only those in the upper socioeconomic brackets are able to exercise the first two of these options. The very poor and the non-white are limited in their choice of residence, and since the federal and state governments do not subsidize tuition for private elementary education, the costs are prohibitive for those with low incomes.

Although local control over schools is deeply rooted in American tradition, to move in the direction of direct parental control of publicly supported city schools contrasts sharply with present inner-city school organizational patterns.

Reprinted with permission of the author and *Saturday Review,* August 16, 1969. Copyright 1969, Saturday Review, Inc.

It also conflicts with trends toward national assessments and national standards which are imposed on the lower schools by such forces as the universities and nationally standardized examinations, presumably in keeping with the needs of a technologically oriented, mobile, urban nation.

Denmark, however, has a fairly centralized educational system with national standards, but it also makes provision for publicly financed schooling outside the state system. Parents are accorded the right to arrange for the schooling or tutorial instruction of their children, including the right to organize, staff, and supervise the school their children attend. Moreover, the government provides considerable financial and organizational assistance to these private schools. The state's public schools retain no monopoly on the education of the young, although the government retains the right to establish standards in curriculum and sanitation in the independent school.

The roots of this system go back to the beginning of compulsory school attendance in Denmark in 1814. Provision was made then to permit parents to employ alternative education for their children in the form of tutoring in schools separate from the state schools (a principle not firmly established in the United States until 1925 by the Supreme Court decision in *Pierce vs. The Society of Sisters*). In Denmark, two major influences helped establish and maintain the tradition during the nineteenth century. One was that the state religion (Evangelical Lutheran) was taught in the public schools, and those who found such instruction unsatisfactory (because of dissident viewpoints or because they practiced other religions) sought alternative educational forms as a guarantee of their religious liberty.

The other significant factor was the independent school established by Kristen Kold along the lines suggested by N. F. S. Grundtvig. Though deeply religious and a clergyman himself, Grundtvig opposed compulsory education and especially compulsory religious education. In language curiously like that used by the more adamant of present-day critics of American schools, he attacked some of the schools of his time as "schools for death" and "scholastic houses of correction." Extolling folk culture and humanitarianism, he had a deep, lasting influence on all Danish life. The independent school established by Kold, in which the pedagogical emphasis was upon oral presentation, discussions, and singing, and in which rote learning and drill were absent, was soon copied by parents all over Denmark.

The Grundtvig-Kold influence is important because it affirmed the pattern of establishing schools outside the national system. It also helped affirm the deeply rooted resistance to compulsory education so that even today, Denmark, while providing abundant free educational opportunity through the university level, compels school attendance only between the ages of seven and fourteen.

At present, all schools in Denmark, whether state or Free Schools, follow a similar organizational pattern, although there are major differences in matters of religious training, language usage, pedagogical methodology, and educational aims. The system is composed of three departments: the primary school (grades one through seven), the lower secondary school (grades eight through ten), and the higher secondary school (grades eleven through thirteen). More than 500,000 children in both state and Free Schools attend the Primary School Division, the only compulsory division in the system. Upon graduation from the seventh grade or at age fourteen, children may exercise the option of leaving school. Those who choose to remain move in two separate streams, one leading to the academically oriented Real School (*Realskole*), the Higher Secondary School (*Gymnasium*), and eventually the universities, and the other to voluntary classes with a vocational emphasis.

Existing parallel to the regular state system, there are more than 175 Free Schools offering primary schooling. The largest number, 114, are *Grundtvig-Koldske Friskoler,* operating in the direct tradition of the two educators and practicing the pedagogical and religious principles espoused by them. There are nineteen Catholic private schools, one Jewish school, and twenty-eight German schools.

Despite the liberal financing and government cooperation in the formation of independent schools, they are used by only 7 per cent of the children of compulsory school attendance age. The right to educate children at home, outside of any school, is also provided by law, but few parents use this prerogative.

Of the Danish population that does take advantage of the right to use Free Schools, the majority clearly represents those who wish a particular religious education for their children other than that provided in the state schools. Seventh-Day Adventists, Catholics, Jews, and Grundtvigians are among these. The German-speaking ethnic minority also maintains its own schools, and in these the German language is used as a medium of instruction.

Another group chooses the Free Schools for the purpose of insuring a traditional university-oriented education, and at times this group includes upperclass as well as upwardly mobile middle-class people who wish their children to travel in socially prestigious circles. The Zahles Gymnasieskole in Copenhagen is one such school, maintaining high academic standards and attended at times by members of the Danish royal family. Although its doors are now open to children from all segments of the population, the Zahles school retains its prestigious reputation and is characterized by a relaxed yet formal aura of a college preparatory institution.

More recently, those espousing the educational philosophy of John Dewey and influenced by A. S. Neill's Summerhill have founded the Little Schools (*Lille Skole*). Here the educational milieu tends to be fairly permissive and informal, with a heavy emphasis on creativity in the arts and a stress on the development of cooperation and humanitarianism. These schools are based on the principles that pupils must be allowed a great deal of democratic freedom, that the students ought to play as active a role in the educational process and the running of the school as the teacher, that creativity be emphasized, and that parents play an active role in the daily workings of the school.

Laws governing the organization, funding, and regulation of the Free Schools are administered by the Ministry of Education, which must be kept informed concerning location, headmaster, and attendance at each school. Free Schools can be founded by organizations, individuals, or groups of parents, the latter receiving more liberal benefits.

Children are protected because the schools are held accountable for the quality of their instruction and facilities. If, upon inspection, the instruction is found to be not as good as that received by pupils in the ordinary schools, a report is made to the appropriate local school board officials, and if the situation is not corrected within a year, the Ministry of Education decides whether the school should be allowed to continue to function. In general, instruction is required to be at least as good as in the public schools in the basic subjects of Danish and arithmetic. In all other matters the school is free to pursue its particular interests.

Inspectors are chosen by the Ministry of Education. Interestingly enough, however, many schools are given the right to select their own inspector— generally a professional with views sympathetic to the aims of the particular school—who will act in a sense as a citizen notary to certify that the requirements of the state laws governing education are being fulfilled. Permission to choose an inspector is generally granted to schools owned by a circle of parents. That the school may choose its own inspector does not appear strange to the Danes, who argue that his role is to insure that the state requirements are met, not to pass judgment on the school. Since the school meets the religious, pedagogic, or ethnic interests of the parents of the children involved, it ought to be inspected by someone neither antagonistic toward nor unfamiliar with its purposes and style. There are few cases of disapproval of an inspector chosen by groups of parents.

The financial assistance given the Free Schools consists of funds for staff, for children, and for buildings. Schools become eligible for assistance in various ways. A private school, i.e., one owned by an individual or a group such as a church, becomes eligible after it has been in existence three years. In keeping with the more liberal provisions for parents, self-owned institutions and schools run by groups of parents become eligible even sooner, and such a school can receive funds even if it enrolls as few as ten pupils. The Ministry of Education can include in this number children ranging from preschool classes through the tenth grade. The liberality of this provision becomes evident when it is remembered that public education in Denmark becomes available ordinarily only at age seven and is compulsory only through age fourteen, or the seventh grade.

The government provides salaries for the staff members of the Free Schools at a rate equivalent to 85 per cent of the salaries paid public school teachers and headmasters. In many cases, the Free School teachers have smaller pupil loads than those carried by teachers in the public schools, but they are paid on the basis of number of lessons taught rather than on pupil registration. The pupil-teacher ratio is restricted, however, by the fact that the schools must pay the additional 15 per cent of a teacher's salary, and few institutions have enough money to allow for more than one teacher per ten pupils. Usually, as in all Danish schools, the headmaster also teaches.

In addition to funds for salaries, the state provides 50 per cent of the money it would cost the government to keep the child in a regular public school and provides the same services, such as free milk, to the children. Application forms for funds for staff and children are simple, requiring only the names of teachers, lessons taught, names of pupils, attendance records, and certification by an inspector that state requirements are being met.

The Free Schools also receive aid from the government to establish school buildings. State loans are made and paid for at 4 per cent interest, and the state retains mortgage rights to the buildings. There is no time limit set on repayment of the loan, and the loan cannot be recalled as long as conditions under the law are met and the property used as a school. Loans for three-quarters of the costs of additional buildings, improvements, expansion, furniture, capital investment, educational materials, and modernization can also be obtained when schools formerly owned by individuals or organizations other than parents are reorganized into self-owned institutions.

Despite the legal incentives, the actual founding of a Free School requires a great deal of motivation, commitment, organization, and some financial ability. The Lille Skole de Mezasvej in Elsinore illustrates how such a school is founded. Dissatisfied with the public schools for reasons that included large classes, curtailed academic programs for the children, and annoyance that their concern as parents branded them as troublemakers by school authorities, some twenty-nine parents banded together to organize a Little School. They found a building, borrowed money from the banks, and assumed responsibility for the loan. These founding parents then bought wood and paint, and within a few months converted a former hotel to a pleasant, cheerful, sprawling school. The responsibility for paying the loan passes on to each new group of parents. It took four months before government money was forthcoming, but the parents were able to keep the school going until the full financial benefits under the Free School law became available. The founding of the school required an initial investment of about $72 per child.

The vast majority of the Danish population uses the state public schools primarily because they are generally of excellent quality in teaching, physical structure, and opportunity for children. The modest fees associated with Free Schools do not account for their use by only 7 per cent of the population. In this fairly homogeneous nation, with no extremely sharp class differences, the public schools do not present barriers to some children to achievement in the larger society, nor does the teaching within the schools clash markedly with the beliefs and wishes of most parents.

The Free Schools are not without criticism. The Danes are so proud of their modern public school system that many question, for example, the implication of snobbery by those using special preparatory schools. They raise questions of the propriety of the state supporting teachers' salaries at lower pupil-teacher ratios in the Free Schools. Also, they question the propriety of seeking solutions to educational controversy outside of a public school system deemed good for all. The Little Schools particularly are the targets of those who disapprove of permissive education, and who also view the humanistically oriented, protective, and intimate environments provided in these schools as a return to an archaic educational form unrealistic in the preparation of people for modern society.

On the other hand, Danish tradition holds the highest respect for the right of the parent to oversee the education of his child. Essentially a tolerant people, most Danes view the Free Schools with favor, seeing in them a protection of personal religious and political liberty. The Little School advocates see their schools as protection against bureaucratic encroachment by the state through its schools, and as protection against mass fabrication of people without regard to individuality. Like many advocates of American private schooling, some Danes defend the Free Schools because their freedom to innovate and experiment is seen as a stimulus to the public schools. The existence of these schools is regarded as helping to guarantee the quality of public education, because they act as competitors in a situation where the public schools have no monopoly and, therefore, have to maintain excellence.

A significant effect of the existence of the Free Schools is that they remove much conflict from the public schools. Any dissident minority, with minimum expense and with government cooperation, can leave the system and establish its own school. The result of this is that when Danes discuss educational problems, they tend to stress professional, pedagogical concerns or the matter of finance. They rarely discuss the kinds of problems that are considered important in the United States, such as school-community conflict or teacher-administrator difficulties. A striking characteristic of Free Schools is the general coincidence of goals on the part of parents, teachers, and administrators, and the harmonious relations among these groups. Certainly, were a serious disagreement to develop, there would be no point in retaining a child in the school; when serious difficulty arises in public schools, there are alternatives available. Parental control in the Free Schools, through the hiring of a headmaster and the approval of the hiring and firing of teachers, does not appear threatening to school staffs whose pedagogical and philosophical bents coincide with those of the parents.

Since all *Friskoler* are required by law to provide education in Danish, there does not appear at present to be serious concern over the bicultural education received by minority groups. While there are complaints about the *Friskoler* laws, the major ones are that the government does not provide enough financial help, and that it ought to provide 100 per cent of the funds for teachers' salaries, fully equivalent funding for the children, and more money for supplies. Efforts to remove public support for *Friskoler* are likely to be met by serious opposition from conservative traditionalists as well as progressive elements.

Does the Danish experience with Free Schools have relevance to problems facing education in America? There are, of course, basic differences between the two nations that preclude any easy or direct modeling of one system upon the other. One major difference is the fact that in Denmark the Evangelical Lutheran state religion is taught in the public schools. From the very beginning of compulsory education in that country, the existence and support of schools outside the state system was viewed as a guarantee of religious liberty. On the other hand, in the United States, the separation of church and state is seen as essential to religious liberty, and the public support of any educational system that includes religious instruction traditionally has been viewed as a danger to the democratic system. Although this view has been modified by the "child-benefit" theory of aid to education, it remains a strong current in American educational thought.

Another basic difference is that Denmark, despite its German-speaking ethnic minority and several religious minorities, is a fairly homogeneous nation and does not face a race problem. The United States, on the other hand, not only has racial heterogeneity, but includes a multiplicity of ethnic and religious minorities and larger economic class differences. Public, compulsory education was long seen as essential for the accomplishment of the homogenization or Americanization of immigrants whose differences were viewed as threatening to national unity. Although at present the schools are no longer educating many immigrants and the recognition is growing that cultural differences are deeply entrenched in American life and ought to be valued, the traditional belief that the public school somehow acts as unifying force has not disappeared.

Still a third difference is that the Danes, although they may sometimes question the snobbery of certain upper-class schools or the separation of some intellectual groups from the public schools, do not see in the Free Schools a threat to their democratic way of life. In this country, on the other hand, the private school system, where it has been supported occasionally by state governments, has been seen to operate either as an intrusion upon the principle of separation of church and state or, more recently, as an effort to circumvent integration. Thus, state-supported private schools tend to be viewed as potentially anti-democratic.

Yet, the fact remains that affluent Americans have far greater choice concerning the education of their children than do the poor of America's inner cities. Those who are confined to the ghettos either by race or poverty or a combination of both are completely dependent upon a public school system that is compulsory and monopolistic, and which is increasingly viewed as intrusive. Pious talk concerning the democratic nature of the public school system does not change the fact that for many it is unsatisfactory, and that social and economic class has a great deal to do with the educational choices open to a family. Movement to the suburbs or into private schools are not choices readily available to the urban poor. At present a major alternative open to this group, when consciously dissatisfied with the schools, is to engage in social protest, a phenomenon American inner-city school systems have seen develop in recent years.

At first, much of this social protest centered on the eradication of de jure and de facto school segregation. More recent efforts have concentrated on decentralization of school systems and the substitution of local community control. It would appear that even if public school districts were under the direct control of local parent and community groups, this form of organization would not preclude the disaffection of some groups from what would remain essentially a monopolistic, compulsory educational system. As the experience of community control in New York has shown, such programs run the risk of being stillborn, strangled not only by the opposition of conservative forces supporting the traditional system, but also by internal factional dispute.

A publicly supported system that allows for alternative forms of school organization does give the promise of meeting special minority needs, whether they be a desire to rear children via Montessori or Summerhill pedagogy or instruction in Swahili, ballet, or Amish traditions, without disruption of the work of the larger public system. That this would then tend to remove from the school its most militant critics and leaders of needed reform has been observed in Denmark. Yet, there is wide agreement on the difficulty of effecting change within the large bureaucratic systems that our schools have become, and what is often forgotten is that alternatives outside the system are already used by those able to afford them. The provision of alternatives to larger numbers of people opens the possibility of creative use of talent and the implementation of reforms presently inhibited by the organizational needs of schools as they are presently constituted. Should the alternative of publicly funded private schooling be made available, funding short of 100 per cent is likely to facilitate the acceleration of the flight of the upwardly mobile and middle class out of the public system. For alternatives to be truly universal, they must be free and include the provision of supplies, buildings, and funds for staff.

For those who fear the fragmentation of the public education system, the Danish experience supports the view that alternative forms of schooling do not mean the inevitable demise of the state-run public schools. On the contrary, vigorous support for public education and the maintenance of high standards draws the allegiance of the vast majority of the population.

An advantage of a system with publicly supported alternatives is that freedom from the monolithic compulsion by huge bureaucratic organizations may free the public schools of debilitating conflict. But perhaps the most important advantage is that permitting concerned groups of parents and community organizations to set up schools for segments of the population that find the present system unsatisfactory may unleash creative potential and make possible an educational renaissance.

Estelle Fuchs is professor of education at Hunter College in New York.

GIVING PARENTS MONEY FOR SCHOOLING:
EDUCATION VOUCHERS

CHRISTOPHER JENCKS

*The name most associated with vouchers is that of Christopher Jencks,
associate professor at Harvard and President of the Center for the Study
of Public Policy which produced the* Education Vouchers *study (see Part II)
for the Office of Economic Opportunity. Here, Professor Jencks presents
his views and two eminent educators respond to his idea.*

The Office of Economic Opportunity announced last May that it hopes to
fund an experiment which would provide parents with vouchers to cover the
cost of educating their children at the school of their choice. This news has
provoked considerable liberal opposition, including charges that the equipment
is unconstitutional, that it is part of a Nixon plot to perpetuate segregation,
and that it would "destroy the public school system." What, then, does OEO
really have in mind?

If state and local cooperation is forthcoming, the first step will be the establishment of an Educational Voucher Agency (EVA) in some community. This
EVA will resemble a traditional board of education in that it will be locally
controlled and will receive federal, state, and local funds for financing the
education of all local children. But it will differ from a traditional board in
that it will not operate any schools of its own. That responsibility will remain
with existing school boards, both public and private. The EVA will simply
issue vouchers to all parents of elementary school children in its area. The
parents will take these vouchers to a school in which they want to enroll
their child. This may either be an existing public school, a new school opened
by the public school board to attract families who would otherwise withdraw
their children from the public system, an existing private school, or a new
private school opened especially to cater to children with vouchers. If the
school meets the basic eligibility requirements laid down by the EVA, it will
be able to convert its vouchers into cash, which will cover both its operating
expenses and the amortization of capital costs. Such a system would enable
anyone starting a school to get public subsidies, so long as he followed the
basic rules laid down by the EVA and could persuade enough parents to

enroll their children in his school. It would also give low-income parents th same choice about where they sent their children that upper-income parent. now have. This would include all the public and private schools participating in the system.

The effect of these changes on the quality of education would depend on how effectively the EVA regulated the newly created marketplace, and especially on the rules it laid down for determining which schools could cash vouchers and which schools could not. Since the EVA would presumably be controlled by the same political forces that now dominate local school boards, some prophets anticipate that it would soon develop a regulatory system as complex and detailed as that now governing the public schools. If this happened, both publicly and privately managed voucher schools would soon be entangled in the usual bureaucratic and political jungle, in which everything is either required or forbidden. They would probably end up indistinguishable from existing public schools. Nothing would have changed, either for better or for worse.

This vision may, however, be unnecessarily gloomy. Today's public school has a captive clientele. As a result, it in turn becomes the captive of a political process designed to protect the interests of its clientele. The state, the local board, and the school administration establish regulations to ensure that no school will do anything to offend anyone of political consequence. By trying to please everyone, however, the schools often end up pleasing no one. The voucher system seeks to free schools from these managerial constraints by eliminating their monopolistic privileges. Under a voucher system, parents who do not like what a school is doing can simply send their children elsewhere. Schools which attract no applicants go out of business. But those which survive have a much greater claim to run their own affairs in their own way.

Most opponents of the voucher system worry more about the possibility that EVA would establish too few regulations than about the possibility that it would establish too many. They particularly fear the development of a system in which schools would compete with one another in terms of social and/or academic exclusiveness, much as colleges now do. Left to their own devices, many schools would restrict admission to the brightest and most easily educated youngsters, leaving the more difficult children to somebody else. Many would also try to increase their operating budgets by charging supplemental tuition. This would have the not-always-accidental effect of limiting the number of low-income children in the more expensive schools.

An unregulated system of this kind would have all the drawbacks of other unregulated markets. It would produce even more racial and economic segregation than the existing neighborhood school system. It would also widen the expenditure gap between rich and poor children, giving the children of the middle classes an even larger share of the nation's educational resources than they now get, while reducing the relative share going to the children of the poor.

Fortunately, OEO has shown no signs of funding a completely unregulated voucher system. Rather, OEO is contemplating an experiment in which extremely stringent controls are placed on participating schools' admissions policies, and also on their tuition charges. At the same time, it is hoping for an experiment which places minimal restraint on schools' staffing practices and programs.

In order to cash vouchers, a school would have to offer every applicant a roughly equal chance of admission. To ensure this, the school would have to declare each spring how many children it could take the following year. Parents would apply to schools each spring, and unless a school had more applicants than places, it would have to take everyone who had applied. If there were more applicants than places, the school would have to fill at least half its places by a lottery among applicants. It would also have to show that it had accepted at least as high a proportion of minority group students as had applied. Thus no school would be able to cream off the most easily educated children or dump all the problem children elsewhere.

The redemption value of a middle- or upper-income family's voucher would approximate what the local public schools are currently spending on upper-income children. Vouchers for children from low-income families would have a somewhat higher redemption value. This reflects the fact that schools with high concentration of low-income children also tend to have more than their share of educational problems. It should also help discourage schools from trying to attract exclusively middle-class applicants. Participating schools would have to accept every child's voucher as full payment for his education, regardless of its value. Otherwise, parents who could afford to supplement their children's vouchers would inevitably have a better chance of getting their children into high-cost schools than parents who could not supplement the voucher.

These regulations would not result in as much racial or economic integration as massive compulsory busing. But that is hardly a likely alternative. The real alternative is the continuation of the neighborhood school, whose racial and economic composition inevitably and deliberately reflects the racial and economic exclusiveness of the private housing market. Under a voucher system, no child could be excluded from any participating school simply because his family was not rich enough or white enough to buy a house near the school. Furthermore, the EVA would pay transportation costs, so that every family would have genuinely equal access to every participating school. Most families, both black and white, would doubtless continue to prefer schools near their homes. But at least no family would be legally or financially required to choose such a school if they thought it was education-ally inadequate. Those black parents who wanted their children to attend integrated schools would be in an excellent position to ensure that they did so.

If all goes according to plan, the OEO experiment would be far more per-missive with regard to schools' staffing and curricular policies than with regard to admissions. Schools would have to conform to existing state and local regulations governing private schools, but these are relatively lenient in most states. Experience suggests that while such leniency results in some abuses, the results over the long run seem to be better than the results of detailed legal and administrative regulations of the kind that shape the public schools. While these regulations often seem rational on their face (as in the case of teacher certification requirements), they generally create more prob-lems than they solve. Teaching and learning are subtle processes, and they seem to resist all attempts at improvement by formal regulation. Rule books are seldom subtle enough to prevent the bad things that can happen in schools, and are seldom flexible enough to allow the best things.

So instead of telling schools whom to hire, what to teach, or how to teach it, the EVA will confine itself to collecting and disseminating information about what each school is doing. Every family will be given extensive informa-tion about every participating school. This should ensure that families are aware of all the choices open to them. It should also help discourage mis-leading advertising, or at least partially offset the effects of such advertising.

One common objection to a voucher system of this kind is that many parents are too ignorant to make intelligent choices among schools. Giving parents a choice will, according to this argument, simply set in motion an educational equivalent of Gresham's Law, in which hucksterism and mediocre schooling drive out high quality institutions. This argument seems especially plausible to those who envisage the entry of large numbers of profit-oriented firms into the educational marketplace. The argument is not, however, supported by much evidence. Existing private schools are sometimes mere diploma mills, but on the average their claims about themselves seem no more misleading, and the quality of the services they offer no lower, than in the public schools. And while some private schools are run for little but profit, this is the excep-tion rather than the rule. There is no obvious reason to suppose that vouchers would change all this.

A second common objection to vouchers is that they would "destroy the public schools." Again, this seems farfetched. If you look at the educational choices made by wealthy parents who can already afford whatever schooling they want for their children, you find that many still prefer their local public schools if these are at all adequate. Furthermore, most of those who now leave the public system do so in order to attend high-cost, exclusive private schools. While some parents would doubtless continue to patronize such schools, they would receive no subsidy under the proposed OEO system.

Nonetheless, if you are willing to call every school "public" that is ultimately responsible to a public board of education, then there is little doubt that a voucher system would result in some shrinkage of the "public" sector and some growth of the "private" sector. If, on the other hand, you confine the label "public" to schools which are really equally open to everyone within commuting distance, you discover that the so-called public sector includes relatively few public schools. Instead, racially exclusive suburbs and economically exclusive neighborhoods serve to ration access to good "public" schools in precisely the same way that admissions committees and tuition charges ration access to good "private" schools. If you begin to look at the distinction between public and private schooling in these terms, emphasizing accessibility rather than control, you are likely to conclude that a voucher system, far from destroying the public sector, would greatly expand it, since it would force large numbers of schools, public and private, to open their doors to outsiders.

A third objection to vouchers is that they would be available to children attending Catholic schools. This is not, of course, a necessary feature of a voucher system. An EVA could perfectly easily restrict participation to non-sectarian schools. Indeed, some state constitutions clearly require that this be done. The federal Constitution may also require such a restriction, but neither the language of the First Amendment nor the legal precedents are clear on this issue. The First Amendment's prohibition against an "establishment of religion" can be construed as barring payments to church schools, but the "free exercise of religion" clause can also be construed as requiring the state to treat church schools in precisely the same way as other private schools. The Supreme Court has never ruled on a case of this type (e.g., GI Bill payments to Catholic colleges or Medicare payments to Catholic hospitals). Until it does, the issue ought to be resolved on policy grounds. And since the available evidence indicates that Catholic schools have served their children no worse than public schools, and perhaps slightly better, there seems no compelling reason to deny them the same financial support as other schools.

The most common and most worrisome objection to a voucher system, in my view, is that its results depend on the EVA's willingness to regulate the marketplace vigorously. If vouchers were used on a large scale, state and local regulatory efforts might be uneven or even nonexistent. The regulations designed to prevent racial and economic segregation seem especially likely to get watered down at the state and local level, or else to remain unenforced. This argument applies, however, to *any* educational reform, and it also applies to the existing system. If you assume that any given EVA will be controlled by overt or covert segregationists, you must also assume that this will be true of the local board of education. A board of education that wants to keep racist parents happy hardly needs vouchers to do so. It only needs to maintain the neighborhood school system. White parents who want their children to attend white schools will then find it quite simple to move to a white neighborhood where their children will be suitably segregated. Except perhaps in the South, neither the federal government, the state government, nor the judiciary is likely to prevent this traditional practice.

If, on the other hand, you assume a board which is anxious to eliminate segregation, either for legal, financial, or political reasons, you must also assume that the EVA would be subject to the same pressures. And if an EVA is anxious to eliminate segregation, it will have no difficulty devising regulations to achieve this end. Furthermore, the legal precedents to date suggest that the federal courts will be more stringent in applying the Fourteenth Amendment to voucher systems than to neighborhood school systems. The courts have repeatedly thrown out voucher systems designed to maintain segregation, whereas they have shown no such general willingness to ban the neighborhood school. Outside the South, then, those who believe in integration may actually have an easier time achieving this goal than they will with the existing public school system.

Christopher Jencks is an associate professor at the Harvard School of Education and co-author, with David Reisman, of *The Academic Revolution.* He is also a contributing editor of *The New Republic.*

THE UNKNOWN GOOD:
EDUCATION VOUCHERS

ROBERT J. HAVIGHURST

> Now all the Athenians and the strangers sojourning there spent
> their time in nothing else, but either to tell or to hear some
> new thing.
>
> And Paul stood in the midst of the Areopagus and said, "Ye
> men of Athens, in all things I perceive ye are very religious.
> For as I passed along, and observed the objects of your
> worship, I found also an altar with this inscription: *TO AN
> UNKNOWN GOD.* What therefore ye worship in ignorance, this
> I set forth unto you." *Acts 17:21-23.*

The similarities of contemporary America and the Athens of St. Paul's day
have been remarked before. One of the more engaging characteristics of both
societies is their openness to new ideas. In the U. S., we like to "tell or to
hear some new thing," and we also have the money to go a step further — to
try out new things.

In our present state of urban malaise, we find ourselves discontented with
most of our social institutions, including our schools. Some people are concerned about the poor reading and arithmetic and speaking of the children of
our urban slums. Others complain about the schools in the middle-class sections of metropolitan areas, charging that the boys and girls are being regi-
mented into a faceless conformity to materialistic values.

With the ranks of the discontented being recruited from such diverse quarters,
the educational Establishment finds itself caught in the middle, pushed from
different directions to make basic school reforms. Furthermore, the Establishment cannot weaken its already difficult position by saying that the public
expects too much of the schools — at least half of what the child learns and
more than half of his attitude toward learning come from the home. However
true this may be, the educators *have to* claim that the school system is *very*
important, and they *have to* claim that the schools can do *much more* than
they are now doing for disadvantaged children.

While the educational Establishment slogs along, trying to do things a little better here and a little better there, the critics and the discontented demand drastic reforms. This is fertile soil for the idea of giving parents public money to find better schools for their children. Thus the current discussion of voucher schemes gets a start; it is amplified by the readiness of the American public to listen to new ideas.

Within a very short space of time, the voucher idea has proliferated into several quite different proposals for practice. Carr and Hayward* have described and criticized five different voucher schemes — those of Milton Friedman, Theodore Sizer and Phillip Whitten, Henry Levin, James S. Coleman, and Christopher Jencks.

The "free-market" proposal of Friedman would provide every child with a flat grant or tax credit which his family could use to pay tuition at the school of its choice. The public schools would continue to exist and would charge tuition equal to the amount of the grant. But private schools would be in a good position to compete with public schools, since they would get the same amount of public money per pupil as the public schools. Thus, it is argued by Friedman and others, the quality of education would be improved by removing it from its present status as a near-monopoly of the public schools and subjecting it to the competition of the free market.

But a critical look at this unregulated free-market proposal has led to something like the following judgment:**

> . . . an unregulated market would redistribute resources away from
> the poor and toward the rich, would increase economic segregation
> in the schools, and would exacerbate the problems of existing
> public schools without offering them any offsetting advantages.
> For these reasons we think it would be worse than the present
> system of public schools.

This quotation comes from the report of a team headed by Christopher Jencks which was supported by a grant from the U.S. Office of Economic Opportunity. This report is a model of careful and critical analysis of a variety of voucher proposals. It starts with the proposition that public money might well be used to support a *variety* of schools, but this has not been done in the United States. "As a result, we have almost no evidence on which to judge the merit of Adam Smith's basic principle — namely, that if all parents are given the chance, they will look after their children's interests more effectively than will the state." It concludes with a proposal for a voucher system that, they contend, "would make it possible for parents to translate their concern for their children's education into action. If they did not like the education their child was getting in one school (or if the child did not like it), he could go to another. By fostering both active parental interest and educational variety, a voucher system should improve all participating schools, both public and private."

The Jencks report proceeds with an exhaustive analysis of "seven alternative economic models," which include the five analyzed by Carr and Hayward. It comes out in favor of the "regulated compensatory model" summarized by Jencks in the *New Republic* article reprinted in this *Kappan.*

This would require a school that participates in the program to accept at least as high a proportion of black or other minority group students as had applied, and to fill at least half of its places by a lottery among applicants. It would also give a higher-value voucher to low-income children than to middle- and higher-income children.

The program would be sponsored and supervised by an Educational Voucher Agency (EVA), which would act like a school board in some respects and might conceivably be an arm of a local public school board.

Now, with this proposal before it, the Office of Economic Opportunity will presumably try to locate several communities that will set up EVAs to organize voucher plans supported by public funds for a major experiment, which should continue for a minimum of five years, and preferably for eight years.

The proposal assumes that about one-sixth of the families would choose privately controlled voucher schools under the ground rules that are proposed. This 16% compares with the estimate this writer has frequently made, that no more than 20% of American parents would bypass the nearest school in sending their children to school, given some freedom of choice. An experiment that included as many as 15% of children from a socioeconomic and racial cross-section of society would be impressive. This writer hopes it will come about.

Thus the *unknown good* about which there has been so much interesting discussion would be explored and would become known. Is there in America a modern Athens to take this challenge seriously?

Robert J. Havighurst is professor of education, University of Chicago. His special interests in recent years include studies of urban education and the "new criticism" of education.

*Ray A. Carr and Gerald C. Hayward, "Education by Chit: An Examination of Voucher Proposals," *Education and Urban Society,* February, 1970, pp. 179-91.

**Center for the Study of Public Policy, *Financing Education by Grants to Parents, A Preliminary Report.* Cambridge, Mass.: The Center, 56 Boylston St., March, 1970.

VITAL QUESTIONS, MINIMAL RESPONSES: EDUCATION VOUCHERS

A. STAFFORD CLAYTON

The experiment which the OEO hopes to fund would presumably provide some evidence that granting vouchers in support of the school of parental choice would lead to certain educational innovations. Professor Jencks tells us that these innovations are presently restricted by the bureaucratic and political constraints of a monopolistic public school system. An experiment in this instance means trial of a voucher system in some community as yet unidentified. We are not told how the experiment will be designed, what controls will be exercised, and what criteria will be used in assessing its results. Without these, there is little hope of determining whether the prescription helps to treat the disease without creating more complications than the patient can withstand.

What Jencks offers is more an argument than a description of an adequately planned experiment. The source and character of the Educational Voucher Agency to be established in each community is not described beyond saying that it is locally controlled. It is not clear how the EVA will be funded so that the redemption value of vouchers will "approximate what the local schools are currently spending on upper-income children" and be worth something more for children of low-income families. More important, what criteria are to be used in appraising results as indicators of desirable national policy is not only unclear but the argument itself is disturbing and unsatisfactory.

The Educational Voucher Agency "will not operate schools of its own," will not restrain schools' staffing practices, programs, and curricular policies. It will inform parents about what each school is doing. It will decide which of all schools, both public and private, can cash the vouchers issued by the EVA. It will lay down the basic requirements that schools will have to meet in order to insure that they are "really equally open to everyone within commuting distance." It will pay transportation costs, establish the monetary value of vouchers so that the poor will benefit from them more than the affluent, and enforce the rule that participating schools "accept every child's voucher as full payment for his education."

How these various responsibilities are feasible of execution under a locally controlled EVA surpasses understanding. But perhaps we are not to take local control too seriously. Each EVA will receive federal, state, and local funds, presumably in the amount of those currently used in support of public schools. It will distribute these according to stringent basic rules. Nothing is said about the establishment of a super-EVA, a kind of Educational Voucher Authority, to ride herd on locally controlled Educational Voucher Agencies. However, what is said about the stringent controls to be placed on participating schools' admissions and tuition charges suggests a policing as well as a policy function to be performed by somebody, presumably the OEO. Without such an arm of federal control it is difficult to see how local EVAs are going to regulate the education marketplace. In the light of the current politics of education, including the policies of the White Citizens Councils, the pressures from organizations on the radical right, and the increasing effectiveness of teacher organizations, Professor Jencks has good reason to be concerned with the vigor with which local EVAs will regulate the marketplace.

However, other fundamental questions "to be resolved on policy grounds" plague the voucher system. These questions pertain to the four areas of common objection to which Jencks offers rather minimal and superficial responses.

His consideration that "parents may be too ignorant to make intelligent choices" misses the heart of the matter. Many of us, I should think, would like to see parents make intelligent choices among schools for their children, based on ingredients of the schools' programs. But we must remember that participation of the total range of parents in these matters, especially under the conditions of modern life, is a slender reed to lean upon. Jencks would have parents apply to schools each spring to elect the school in which their vouchers would be cashed. Considering what we know about family living conditions in urban areas, in the South, and in many towns and villages, is the proposed voucher policy not highly preferential to white middle-class suburban Americans?

Jencks' consideration of the question of "destroying the public schools" and supporting denominational schools does not come off any better. The case is made that a voucher system could be limited to nonsectarian schools but that until the Supreme Court rules on this kind of equal support for private as well as public schools there is no "compelling reason" to deny support to all schools.

The policy of providing subsidies from public funds to pay for all schooling, public and denominational, is not without a history in other countries as well as in our own. In France general subsidies to pay for schooling have been in effect since 1951. The question of aid to private schools has been one of the most controversial questions in French politics, and some have found that the continuing conflict and divisiveness over the question contributes to the paralysis of French educational reform. In the Netherlands complete equal support of public and denominational schools since 1920 has led to a reversal of the ratio of enrollments in public and private schools. The denominational school is now the rule, the "neutral" school the exception. Not only this, but the pervasive columnization of Dutch society into Roman Catholic, Protestant Christian, and "neutral" ways of life — it has been said that the Dutch live separately as three peoples — is traceable in large part to decisions by parents to send their children to schools of their choice. In England subsidy of the parents' choice has led to Anglican and Free Church efforts to reestablish in their schools their own forms of denominational Christianity, largely in response to the effectiveness of the Catholic hierarchy in obtaining support for its schools.

This is not to suggest that we should make overly simplistic intercultural comparisons in attempting to assess the consequences of a voucher system. However, in the absence of an inclusive consideration of criteria by which a proposal is to be evaluated, are we justified in dismissing the dangers with the offhand suggestion that there may be "some shrinkage in the public sector"? Will denominational as well as racist interests see a voucher system, even under the benign scrutiny of the OEO and the federal courts, as an opportunity to extend equal access to schooling, including innovative educational programs? Or will a voucher system encourage those attitudes of exclusiveness which reduce community among us?

It may be that the OEO has in mind an experiment in education vouchers which will protect the interests of freedom and equality in the sense in which I have tried to point to them. It may be that criteria for the appraisal of the experiment will reveal that these values are operative as we search for a new educational policy. We cannot tell from what Professor Jencks has written here.

A. Stafford Clayton is professor of history and philosophy of education, Indiana University. He is author of *Religion and Schooling: A Comparative Study* (Blaisdell, 1969).

FOUR OPINION POLLS

According to the first three polls, teachers, administrators, and school board members oppose education vouchers. But the fourth poll reported indicates that parents feel otherwise. It is interesting to compare the figures of these four polls with those reported in the Alum Rock Feasibility Study in Part III.

Reactions to vouchers: hostility, scepticism

"A method to circumvent the principle of separation of church and state."—
" . . . can only mean the deterioration of the public school system." —
" . . . a move to promote segregation and deepen the class and racial divisions in our society."

Comments like these and the voting on this month's Opinion Poll show that most school administrators are deeply sceptical about voucher plans — with a full 80 per cent expressing strong opposition to the Office of Economic Opportunity's proposed voucher experiment.

What's more, schoolmen's hostility to vouchers seems to have increased dramatically in the past year. A *Nation's Schools* poll last March showed a 43 per cent approval of the voucher concept. This month, only 20 per cent favored trying out the OEO's voucher proposal. Even fewer — 18 per cent — indicated that they would be willing to experiment with a voucher plan in their own district.

Asked in a separate question (not shown in box) to explain their principal objections to the use of vouchers, administrators offered a variety of reasons, many of which have already been publicized by the coalition of educator groups (including the AASA and the NEA) currently pushing for a Congressional investigation of OEO's voucher proposal. Among the most frequently occurring objections were the following:

1) That the Constitutional guarantee of separation of church and state would be violated if parents were to put the voucher toward payments for a parochial or private school education for their children. Comments indicated

Reprinted with the copyright permission of the *Nation's Schools,* January, 1971.

that many schoolmen would agree with a New York administrator who labeled the plan "a subterfuge for subsidizing private schools."

2) That voucher plans would encourage segregation and, as a California superintendent put it, "work to deepen the class and racial divisions in our society." A frequently repeated objection was that parents would use their voucher tickets to create schools segregated by race or wealth. A Pennsylvania superintendent predicted that "the plan would tend to foster elite schools for the well-to-do with the public schools ending up as places for minorities and misfits. Public education would die in communities where there are private schools because of racial issues," he said.

3) That vouchers will result in an experiment in hucksterism by profit-making firms that would use high-powered advertising to recruit students. Several schoolmen expressed fears that the voucher system would lead to the proliferation of inefficient, fly-by-night private schools.

4) That vouchers would create insurmountable administrative problems in the areas of planning, scheduling, budgeting and staff retention.

"The chief obstacle," according to one administrator, "is not knowing how many you could plan for in next year's enrollment. This would make staffing and educational costs almost impossible to predict and control and completely disrupt planning in most schools."

Many schoolmen questioned the wisdom of making parents and/or children the arbiters of educational standards. "I don't think that parents are qualified to judge their children's needs, since they cannot view them objectively. This is an educator's job," said a New Jersey superintendent. A colleague from Colorado added that he felt "parents would move their children from school to school on the basis of opinions and hearsay rather than facts about educational programs and the sudden shifting would cause more problems than it would cure."

How administrators voted

1. The Office of Economic Opportunity has announced that it hopes to fund an experiment involving a voucher tuition plan which would provide parents with the money to pay for the cost of educating their children at the school of their choice. Are you in favor of trying out such a plan?

   80% No   **20% Yes**

2. Would you be willing to see some kind of voucher plan inaugurated on an experimental basis in your district?

   82% No   **18% Yes**

The opinion poll survey, conducted monthly by the editorial staff of Nation's Schools, *is based on a five per cent proportional sampling of 14,000 school administrators in 50 states. This month's poll brought a 32 per cent response.*

The things that school leaders like best — and least

The things boardmen like best

	I like	I dislike	I can take or leave	No opinion
Accountability	87%	4%	6%	3%
The American School Board *Journal*	76%	3%	15%	6%
Conventions	70%	6%	20%	4%
Sesame Street	68%	7%	19%	6%
Year-round school	57%	17%	21%	5%
Federal revenue-sharing	55%	24%	16%	5%
Sex education	54%	15%	27%	4%
Performance contracting	52%	17%	13%	18%
Spiro T. Agnew	52%	28%	17%	3%
Richard Nixon	51%	24%	20%	5%

The things boardmen DON'T like

	I like	I dislike	I can take or leave	No opinion
Busing to achieve integration	8%	76%	12%	4%
Teacher tenure	13%	70%	12%	5%
The new permissiveness in movies	9%	66%	21%	4%
Parochiaid	16%	64%	12%	8%
Collective bargaining with teachers	23%	54%	19%	4%
Teacher unions/associations	14%	51%	24%	11%
Long-haired men and boys	10%	51%	36%	3%
Senator Kennedy	21%	51%	23%	5%
The midi	21%	51%	12%	16%

The things boardmen are so-so about

	I like	I dislike	I can take or leave	No opinion
Senator Muskie	35%	33%	24%	8%
Higher pay for teachers	40%	26%	27%	7%
Mayor Daley	20%	30%	33%	17%
Voucher plans	25%	31%	24%	20%
Ralph Nader	48%	20%	27%	5%
Women's Lib	12%	48%	35%	5%
The vote for 18 year olds	49%	35%	13%	3%
Senator McGovern	20%	46%	27%	7%

On voucher plans, boardmen and administrators part company

The things administrators like best

	I like	I dislike	I can take or leave	No opinion
The American School Board *Journal*	92%	0%	8%	0%
Accountability	84%	6%	10%	0%
Sesame Street	80%	5%	11%	4%
Conventions	70%	1%	29%	0%
Higher pay for teachers	62%	12%	25%	1%
Sex education	58%	6%	32%	4%
Spiro T. Agnew	56%	18%	21%	5%
Year-round schools	56%	14%	30%	0%
Vote for 18 year olds	52%	30%	18%	0%
Ralph Nader	52%	10%	33%	5%

The things administrators DON'T like

	I like	I dislike	I can take or leave	No opinion
Busing to achieve integration	7%	81%	10%	0%
Parochiaid	8%	79%	13%	0%
Voucher plans	8%	71%	15%	6%
The new permissiveness in movies	7%	65%	28%	0%
Teacher tenure	15%	58%	27%	0%
Long-haired men and boys	2%	55%	39%	4%
Collective bargaining with teachers	18%	52%	30%	0%
Teacher unions/associations	5%	51%	43%	1%

The things administrators are so-so about

	I like	I dislike	I can take or leave	No opinion
Performance contracting	33%	33%	32%	2%
Senator Muskie	39%	21%	39%	1%
Richard Nixon	49%	15%	33%	3%
The midi	32%	44%	24%	0%
Federal revenue-sharing	49%	21%	24%	6%
Mayor Daley	24%	32%	39%	5%
Senator McGovern	18%	39%	33%	10%
Women's Lib	7%	39%	52%	2%
Senator Kennedy	24%	44%	30%	2%

1000 school board members and 300 superintendents responded to the poll.

Teacher Opinion Poll:
Accountability, Vouchers, and Performance Contracting

Public concern for improving the quality of education has recently given rise to a variety of novel proposals. Among these are a system of teacher accountability, whereby teachers would be paid on the basis of their pupils' achievement; a voucher plan, under which parents would receive vouchers of a specified value which they might use to pay for their children's education in the school of their choice, public or private; and performance contracting, in which an outside agency contracts with a school system to raise the achievement of pupils a specified amount within a specified time as a precondition for receiving payment.

Some persons argue that such methods of introducing competition for material rewards into education would motivate schools and teachers to superior performance. Others believe that the methods of business competition are not appropriate to education and that their introduction would impair the education process, undermine the public school system, and result in injustice to teachers and students. [See "Accountability and the Classroom Teacher" by Joseph Stocker and Donald F. Wilson in the March 1971 issue of *Today's Education.*]

What do public school classroom teachers themselves think of such proposals?

A recent Teacher Opinion Poll shows that the nation's public school teachers as a whole are opposed to accountability payment, a voucher plan, or performance contracting. More teachers oppose accountability payment (88 percent) than oppose a voucher plan (71 percent), and more oppose a voucher plan than oppose performance contracting (48 percent). Teachers with negative views on accountability outnumber those with positive views by 11 to 1, while about 3½ times as many oppose as favor a voucher plan. On performance contracting, opinions are more evenly divided with about 1¼ as many opposed as in favor.

On accountability, the survey addressed the following question to a nationwide sample of public school classroom teachers:

"Do you think public school teachers should be paid according to the achievement of their pupils (accountability)?"

Reprinted with December, 1971 copyright permission of *Today's Education.*

Responses, indicated separately for classroom teachers in elementary and in secondary schools, were as follows:

	Yes	*No*	*No opinion*
In the elementary school	7.9%	88.0%	4.1%
In the secondary school	7.5	87.6	4.8

In the same survey, a question on the voucher plan read thus:

"It has been proposed that parents be paid an amount equivalent to the local school system per pupil cost of educating their children and they then may use this amount to send their children to any school they wish, public or private (voucher plan). Do you favor or oppose this proposal?"

Seventy-one percent of respondents either *strongly* opposed or *tended* to oppose such a plan. Forty-five percent were *strongly* opposed, more than 7 times as many as were *strongly* in favor. A total of 21 percent either *strongly* favored or *tended* to favor a voucher plan.

Strongly favor	6.1%
Tend to favor	14.7
Tend to oppose	26.3
Strongly oppose	44.7
No opinion	8.2

A similar type of question asked teachers in the survey their opinions on performance contracting:

"Some school systems are contracting with private businesses which guarantee improvement in reading and other subjects by pupils in the school system (performance contracting). Do you favor or oppose this practice?"

Nearly one-half the respondents indicated some degree of opposition to performance contracting, but these were almost evenly divided between those who *tended* to oppose and those who *strongly* opposed the practice. A substantial proportion, about 3 teachers in 10, said they *tended* to favor it, but very few, less than 1 in 10, were *strongly* in favor.

Strongly favor	7.5%
Tend to favor	30.5
Tend to oppose	25.7
Strongly oppose	22.0
No opinion	14.4

In follow-up of this question on performance contracting, another question asked:

"Do you think local education associations should contract with school systems for this purpose?"

Many teachers, nearly 2 in 5, did not have an opinion on this question, but among those who did, negative views were more prevalent than positive ones.

Yes	24.0%
No	38.4%
No opinion	37.6

Analysis of responses to these questions on the basis of grade level taught, sex of respondent, size of school system, geographical region, and type of community where teaching did not reveal any consistent patterns of major differences in the distribution of opinions.

Taken together, the results of this survey strongly suggest that public school teachers in general do not believe that the type of competition for money customary in the business world should be applied to education.

Although attitudes toward performance contracting are less unfavorable than toward a voucher plan or accountability, there appears at present to be little enthusiasm on the part of teachers to have their local professional organizations become involved in such contracts.

—NEA Research Division.

Parents favor education vouchers in Seattle.

Third Seattle Survey
A Summary of Major Findings
Concerning Citizen Opinions Toward the Voucher Plan

Prepared by

Bureau of School Service and Research
University of Washington

March 31, 1972

Summary

This survey effort, conducted in February, 1972, by the Bureau of School
Service and Research (BSSR) was designed to provide the Seattle School
Board with comprehensive, current information and a detailed analysis of
opinions of citizens living in the proposed voucher demonstration area.
Included in the survey instrument were thirty-nine questions that provided
data on opinions of citizens: (1) toward some specific aspects of the voucher
model, (2) toward information received on the voucher plan, and (3) citizens'
recommendations to the School Board concerning implementation of a
voucher plan.

Trained interviewers asked the respondent six of the thirty-nine questions.
After recording the replies, the interviewers left with respondents a packet of
information about the voucher plan along with the remaining part of the
survey instrument (to be completed and mailed to the BSSR by the respondent after reading the information).

Of the 2,584 citizens interviewed, 1,425 mailed back the survey instrument,
representing a 55.1 percent return. This high rate of response is noteworthy,
considering the length and complexity of the survey.

Overall Voucher Plan: Opinions and Recommendations

The analyses presented in this report suggest that when citizens were given
the option of expressing an "undecided" position as well as a favorable or
unfavorable opinion about the *general idea* of a voucher plan, approximately
the same number of people favor (39.2 percent) as oppose (37.3 percent) a
voucher plan, with the remaining people (23.5 percent) undecided. However,

when these same people were asked to give a definite recommendation to the School Board regarding the *specific voucher plan proposed for Seattle,* there was a considerable shift among those in the undecided category. Approximately 56.5 percent recommended action toward the implementation of the proposed voucher plan by 1973.

Major Conclusions

Analysis of the data gathered in this survey suggest the following major conclusions:

1. A majority of citizens in the potential demonstration area recommend the implementation of a voucher plan in Seattle by 1973.

2. Ethnic minority groups and lower income groups had the most favorable opinions toward the voucher plan.

3. Citizens tended to support all but one of the components of the proposed voucher model (including upper limits for minority enrollment and protection against racial discrimination; choice of neighborhood school guaranteed; OEO support for all extra costs; lottery to be used in over-applied schools). The one component exception was the compensatory voucher for economically disadvantaged children.

4. Citizens tended to support the purposes of a voucher plan, particularly those concerning choice, control, responsiveness, and aid to private and parochial schools. Citizens did not favor providing parents with funds to start their own schools.

5. Nearly equal numbers of individuals indicated agreement, disagreement, or indecision concerning the possible outcomes of a voucher demonstration (racial and economic segregation; unhealthy competition among schools; quality of education, higher state and local taxes). On the other hand, a susbstantial number of citizens favored increased federal aid.

6. Most individuals were of the opinion that the information they had received was adequate.

APPENDIX D: SUMMARY DATA TABLES

Table D-2
Opinions by Subgroups About Voucher Components and Issues

Statement	Parent Status (K-6) of Respondent Group	Percent of Respondent Group		
		Agree	*Undecided*	*Disagree*
The voucher plan would increase	Total	51.4	23.7	24.9
chances for parents to be involved	Public School	46.8	23.0	30.2
in school affairs.	Non-public School	50.9	21.8	27.3
	Non-parents	54.0	24.3	21.7
Private and church schools	Total	45.4	20.4	34.2
should receive tax money for	Public School	45.6	19.4	35.0
education except for religious	Non-public School	69.1	10.9	20.0
instruction.	Non-parents	43.2	21.1	35.7
The voucher plan would make	Total	29.3	34.2	36.5
schools more racially and	Public School	28.7	32.3	39.0
economically segregated.	Non-public School	36.4	18.1	45.5
	Non-parents	29.2	36.7	34.1
The voucher plan would create	Total	32.1	30.0	37.9
unhealthy competition among	Public School	34.0	28.8	37.2
schools.	Non-public School	25.5	23.6	50.9
	Non-parents	31.5	21.0	37.5
The proposed voucher system	Total	33.2	31.5	35.3
would improve the quality of	Public School	33.1	26.4	40.5
education in the Seattle Public	Non-public School	45.5	20.0	34.5
Schools.	Non-parents	32.5	34.9	32.6
Parents should be able to choose	Total	75.1	13.6	11.3
schools for their children.	Public School	77.9	11.3	10.8
	Non-public School	85.5	5.5	9.0
	Non-parents	72.9	14.9	12.2
There should be no more than 40	Total	42.7	31.8	25.5
percent of any one minority group	Public School	41.8	32.5	25.7
in a voucher school	Non-public School	41.8	25.5	32.7
	Non-parents	43.2	32.2	24.6
The federal government should pay	Total	55.5	21.5	23.0
for extra costs needed to test a	Public School	56.4	18.3	25.3
voucher plan.	Non-public School	65.5	14.5	20.0
	Non-parents	54.7	23.6	21.7
Children entering K-1 should be	Total	83.5	10.4	6.1
able to go to a school where a	Public School	87.3	7.7	5.0
brother or sister is already	Non-public School	89.1	7.3	3.6
enrolled.	Non-parents	81.2	11.9	6.9
A school should run the risk of	Total	45.6	23.5	30.9
being closed if it does not	Public School	49.4	21.1	29.5
respond to parents' needs.	Non-public School	45.5	21.8	32.7
	Non-parents	43.5	24.5	32.0

Table D-2—*Continued*

Statement	Parent Status (K-6) of Respondent Group	Percent of Respondent Group		
		Agree	Undecided	Disagree
Schools should be more responsive to the needs of children from poor families.	Total	59.5	22.0	18.5
	Public School	58.7	19.1	22.2
	Non-public School	56.4	25.4	18.2
	Non-parents	61.3	22.0	16.7
Under a voucher plan, principals and teachers would listen more to parents' wishes since parents would choose their children's schools.	Total	49.5	26.0	24.5
	Public School	48.7	22.9	28.4
	Non-public School	52.7	21.8	25.5
	Non-parents	49.9	27.6	22.5
Students now enrolled in a school should be allowed to stay there if the voucher plan is tried.	Total	83.5	13.1	3.4
	Public School	85.1	11.3	3.6
	Non-public School	81.8	12.7	5.5
	Non-parents	82.4	14.4	3.2
Parents should be able to choose the teacher as well as the school for their children.	Total	22.7	23.0	54.3
	Public School	27.3	24.3	48.4
	Non-public School	18.2	10.9	70.9
	Non-parents	20.7	23.1	56.2
The school district should give principals more freedom to run their own school.	Total	52.8	31.3	15.9
	Public School	50.5	33.4	16.1
	Non-public School	47.3	25.4	27.3
	Non-parents	54.2	30.9	14.9
In order to create better programs for the poor, vouchers for children from poor families should be worth more than vouchers for other children.	Total	32.0	25.0	43.0
	Public School	33.4	21.2	45.4
	Non-public School	27.3	29.1	43.6
	Non-parents	31.5	26.8	41.7
Parents are well enough informed to choose their children's schools.	Total	24.7	26.2	49.1
	Public School	25.3	21.7	53.0
	Non-public School	25.5	25.4	49.1
	Non-parents	24.1	28.4	47.5
Higher state and local taxes would result from a voucher plan.	Total	41.0	38.8	20.2
	Public School	43.5	36.1	20.4
	Non-public School	41.8	29.1	29.1
	Non-parents	39.4	41.5	19.1
Minimum controls preventing schools from denying admission to children because of race are necessary.	Total	54.6	21.8	23.6
	Public School	57.1	20.2	22.7
	Non-public School	60.0	16.4	23.6
	Non-parents	53.5	22.5	24.0
Where more children apply than a school has spaces for, there should be a lottery system so that each child not currently enrolled has the same chance to go to that school.	Total	55.1	24.7	20.2
	Public School	50.5	25.9	23.6
	Non-public School	56.4	21.8	21.8
	Non-parents	57.2	24.1	18.7

Table D-2—*Continued*

Statement	Parent Status (K-6) of Respondent Group	Percent of Respondent Group		
		Agree	*Undecided*	*Disagree*
Parents not happy with their public schools should be given funds to start their own schools.	Total	11.5	22.2	66.3
	Public School	14.9	19.7	65.4
	Non-public School	12.7	29.1	58.2
	Non-parents	8.9	22.6	68.5
Increased federal aid in the Seattle Public Schools would be good for our schools.	Total	49.2	29.8	21.0
	Public School	51.8	26.4	21.8
	Non-public School	40.0	29.1	30.9
	Non-parents	48.6	31.4	20.0
I would like to see Seattle test the voucher plan at the high school level.	Total	40.0	28.1	31.9
	Public School	42.0	23.4	34.6
	Non-public School	45.5	23.6	30.9
	Non-parents	38.7	30.5	30.8

VIEWPOINTS:

Most spokesmen for educational groups quickly and vehemently attacked the voucher idea. Here are some sample statements:

NATIONAL ASSOCIATION OF STATE BOARDS OF EDUCATION

The National Association of State Boards of Education as an organization has not taken a stand on any voucher system of financing a student's education, although the topic will undoubtedly be discussed at our next national convention. NASBE has adopted a resolution on aid to nonpublic schools which may serve as a guideline to the discussions. This resolution is as follows:

> The National Association of State Boards of Education believes that the foundation of our American system of education is free public education. The Association, therefore, opposes the use of public funds for nonpublic education under any circumstances which would jeopardize the welfare, stability or support of the system of public education.

Reprinted from *Compact*, February 1971

My remarks on voucher systems, therefore, represent only my personal opinions and should not be construed as related to any past or future NASBE resolution.

I regard all of the various plans to award educational vouchers to parents as menaces to public education. I am totally opposed to all the voucher schemes which have come to my attention. I have read the proposals of several governors, the proposals of proponents of aid to parochial schools, the proposals of militants on the right and the left, and the proposals of the U. S. Office of Economic Opportunity. The idea has certainly spread like a prairie brush fire.

Vouchers have been proposed for several reasons including:

1) The inner-city schools have failed their constituents; 2) parents should have the economic freedom to determine their children's schools; 3) parents should not have "double" taxation for education; 4) the schools which certain children must attend are not relevant to their cultural needs and expectations; 5) the public schools need strong competition in order to improve.

Certainly some logic is inherent in these and other related arguments, but the arguments against voucher systems are much stronger.

The public schools are far from perfect. Much reform is needed. However, much of the inappropriateness of public education is technological and traditional and can be corrected by improved technology. We know a great deal about what to do to improve curricula. To translate this knowledge into better educational systems we need more funds for equipment, facilities and the retraining of teachers. Dissipation of resources now would hardly prove helpful.

The O.E.O. proposals for experimentation with vouchers were submitted in good faith by an organization desiring to rectify poverty. Their plan has many built-in controls and is limited to areas of poverty. However, the implementation of voucher systems would not stay in such areas nor with such controls. The plan would spread where it could have a devastating effect on our democratic society—perhaps even becoming an easy means to re-establishing a class-conscious educational thrust.

If parents were given money which must be spent on education, overnight all kinds of hucksters would suddenly be in the education business, promoting special interest schools. We would not only have growth in religious schools but also growth in schools of questionable democratic motives. Furthermore, if vouchers for elementary and secondary schools become accepted, then why not vouchers for higher education? The administrators of sorely pressed private colleges could not be expected to refrain from a voucher bonanza.

Administering the public elementary and secondary schools would be a chaotic task. Administrators would never know how long their student bodies would be stable or what education fads the parents might find stylish. All other schools public and private would find it difficult to serve a large rather capricious element of the public.

Public school administrators who now see salvation in vouchers surely must realize that a massive infusion of public monies into their schools will bring with them a myriad of regulations, overseers and restrictions. The uniqueness of private schools—that which justifies their existence—will surely be lost. Private schools will become de-facto public schools. If this occurs without better curricula and better teachers, nothing will be gained but much will be lost.

I would prefer to see new educational monies spent on improving the technology of education, increasing relevance and parent participation, and not spent in devising a new delivery system.

NCEA

In their present forms and under present circumstances, neither the Educational Voucher Plan nor Educational Performance Contracting can be considered, either singly or as a combination, the best or only solution to current educational ills. But because they represent the studied efforts of highly regarded individuals in education, government, and industry, it obviously is in the national interest to provide every opportunity to determine the impact—for good or for bad—that these devices generate, with a view toward subsequent expansion, alteration, or abandonment, as their tested merits indicate. It is understood, of course, that prudent and proper supervision and safeguards are to be exercised in all such experimentation and in all such new and innovative programs.

It is distressing to note, therefore, particularly in the case of the Voucher Plan, the powerful and obviously well-organized opposition, even to plans for experimentation. Perhaps it is necessary and pertinent to point out that the Voucher Plan cannot be viewed as the solution to the much publicized fiscal problems of Catholic schools. Even if implemented immediately on a national scale, the Voucher Plan could not possibly insure the continued operation of parochial schools now on the verge of closing for financial reasons.

AMERICAN JEWISH CONGRESS

The American Jewish Congress opposes institution of voucher plans because we believe that any such plan would impair two vital aspects of our system of democracy—publicly financed and publicly controlled schools and the separation of church and state.

The voucher plan is designed to deal with serious problems facing the public schools, the foremost being their failure to meet the educational needs of the disadvantaged. However, we do not believe that the voucher plan, in any form, would deal effectively with that problem. In practice and effect, the only nonpublic schools receiving voucher funds would be those already in existence (predominantly church affiliated) and those that would be established to cater to the upper classes.

It is illusory to hope that vouchers would induce independent entrepreneurs to build any significant number of schools for disadvantaged children. Neither could they be compelled or induced to do so either by statutory safeguards against discrimination—racial, economic or educational—or incentive payments to encourage acceptance of underprivileged children. True, a few militant minority organizations and parent groups might undertake establishing independent schools. Such a movement, however, would not make more than a small dent in the massive educational deficit in deprived areas. Meanwhile, the bulk of the private schools brought into existence by the voucher program, at least aside from church-affiliated schools, would be selective and, in effect, discriminatory. Their existence would accelerate the flight from the public schools of favorably placed families.

Finally, acceptance of the voucher plan, even on an experimental basis, would deflect the attention of the public and of public officials from what should be their primary concern in education, overhauling the public school system so that public schools work for all students.

The threat to separation of church and state is no less grave. While it is doubtful that the voucher plan would significantly increase the number of non-sectarian nonpublic schools, there is no question that it would give massive aid to the existing systems of sectarian schools. Regardless of technical formulas designed to evade constitutional problems, the simple fact is that voucher plans would make possible the creation and continuance of religious schools—that is schools established for the purpose of fostering specific religious tenets. That would be a plain violation of the principle of separation of church and state, under which religion has prospered in this country.

COUNCIL OF CHIEF STATE SCHOOL OFFICERS

Voucher System

The Council of Chief State School Officers believes that the voucher system could increase racial segregation, provide public financial support to non-public schools, encourage exploitation of children for profit, and increase operational costs for schools and, therefore, it should not be supported at this time.

The Council understands that the President's Committee on Educational Finance will include a thorough study of the voucher system. The Council will re-examine its position on this matter when this study is completed. In the meantime experimentation in the development of procedures geared to providing increased flexibility in the interest of individual students should be developed by state and local education agencies.

AASA

Vouchers for Education

We view with grave alarm the voucher system for education developed by the Center for the Study of Public Policy. Some possible implications of a voucher system are—

> The schools, traditionally operated in the public interest, would be removed from public to private control — control by each parent, which carries decentralization to absurdity.

> Noneducational issues, such as race, background, or ideology of students or staff, could determine a school's income, hence its size, its ability to function effectively, and its survival.

> A massive bureaucracy would be necessary to enforce safeguards and regulations.

> The voucher proposal could be misused and foster further segregation or separation within our society.

> The OEO proposal would provide support for those students in private schools who should not be supported by public, state and local funds.

AASA vigorously opposes any implementation of a voucher system in education.

PTA

The PTA is well aware that changes must be made within the public schools to provide equal and excellent educational opportunity for all children, but we cannot support a voucher system of tuition credits as a means of bringing about improvement. Rather, we believe that such a system could well bring about the disintegration of the public school system, and would create division and separation in the community. The PTA therefore expresses its strong opposition to the voucher system and reaffirms the necessity of working vigorously for the best in education within the public school system.

EDUCATION COMMISSION OF THE STATES

RESOLUTION NUMBER VII
Educational Innovation

WHEREAS a major strength of the public school system lies in its capacity to develop and assess differing approaches to the education of children,

NOW, THEREFORE, BE IT RESOLVED that the Education Commission of the States urges local school systems, assisted by state and federal resources, to experiment with demonstration projects for such educational innovations as performance contracting and educational vouchers, provided that such projects contain appropriate involvement of parent and professional educators in their development and provide safeguards against racial and economic discrimination and provisions for evaluation.

Approved: July 8, 1971

FINAL DISPOSITION: Adopted as Amended
July 9, 1971

BOARDMEN CAN'T THINK OF ONE GOOD THING
TO SAY ABOUT VOUCHER PLANS

On the issue of vouchers, school boards seem to agree with teachers. The National School Boards Association, in its 1972 convention, urged all citizens to "oppose the use of the voucher system as a method of school financing," because NSBA does not believe the voucher system can fulfill its stated purposes to both provide alternatives to the public schools and to improve public schools. The emotional vehemence of anti-voucher feeling is well revealed in the statements of these eight school board members.

If you want to siphon school funds that already are in dangerously short supply, dilute educational opportunities for youngsters, encourage racism and make a farce of the constitutional separation of church and state, then go along with the "educational voucher system" being tried out by the federal government this fall in a few school districts.

That acid assessment, sprinkled over these pages, is supplied by every one of the eight school board members who were invited by the *Journal*, on a random basis, to discuss their views of the Office of Economic Opportunity's piloted educational voucher plan (which works like this: parents are given a voucher equal or better in dollar value to their child's per-pupil share of the public school expenditure and allowed to "buy" a year of education for him at any school, public or nonpublic, they choose).

The idea is a nightmare, says Sam Joyner Jr., a 19-year veteran board member from Lawton, Okla. Joyner is, in fact, alone among the eight participating boardmen from districts of varying sizes to cite an advantage of the voucher plan: "The *only* advantage is that the threat of such a monstrosity should spur us all to redouble our efforts to improve our present public schooling in the United States, and to continue our efforts to make it more responsive to the needs of our children."

And that troublesome Constitution — it keeps popping up with the boardmen on these pages even though they were asked to pretend, for purposes of discussing the question, that it isn't there. Constitutional considerations are grave and can't be ignored, insists William S. Warfield, board member from tiny Livingston, Mt. "Whatever its intention," Warfield warns, "the voucher plan amounts to public aid to nonpublic schools," a contention that does not seem unreasonable in view of the apparent lack of any provision in the proposed voucher plan to prohibit, for example, the entire student body of a parochial school from obtaining vouchers from the federal government, turning them over to the religious authority in charge of the school, and, in effect, transferring financial support of the parochial school from private to public sources.

An educational voucher plan might also serve to finance racist groups that might be encouraged to start their own segregated private schools, offers Chicago suburbanite Roy C. Jones who put in 14 years as an elementary school board member to be followed by the past six on a junior college board.

When you ask boardmen their views on the voucher plan you're really asking, in Jones' view, whether "we're in favor of allowing a multitude of new schools to be formed, in addition to the ones we now have, and, in effect, of having all schools operate at public expense."

We emphatically are not in favor of that, says W. Casper Holroyd Jr., chairman of the school board in Raleigh, N.C., offering "as an alternative solution a plan whereby the federal government could return income tax dollars to the local school districts to permit us more flexibility on a local level."

Adds Joyner: "I am sure [a voucher] plan would be welcomed by many parochial schools and the many private academies that have sprung up during the past few years, but it would certainly cut the throat of our public schools and make intelligent community educational planning a nightmare."

Here is how the eight boardmen from as many states expressed their opposition:

DON'T VOUCHER PLANS CATER TO RELIGIOUS OR RACIAL PREJUDICE?

ROY C. JONES

The question seems to be asking if we're in favor of allowing a multitude of new schools to be formed, in addition to the ones we now have, and, in effect, of having all schools operate at public expense under an educational voucher system.

No discussion of this question can ignore the public school system as it has been developed in the United States. Can this system be spread out among the many religious and racial schools now existing and the new ones likely to be formed, and still give each child the educational opportunities he needs?

In all our thinking, the child must come first. Do we want to foist our religious or racial prejudices upon him to the extent of shorting him in his educational opportunities? James B. Conant, in his studies of public schools, has pointed out the advantages of having school systems large enough to give all students an opportunity to choose their course in educational development. If we change to a system of widespread personal choice schools, it seems to me that many students would be placed according to the prejudices of their parents. That would not only weaken the public school system, but too often our youngsters wouldn't receive the training they need to prepare them for life in this ever shrinking world.

Certainly we should not let ourselves be forced into a "voucher school system" by religious and racist groups.

The public schools give and — if we take our responsibilities as boardmen seriously — will continue to give our students the educational opportunities they need to be able to meet on common grounds with people from all walks of life, to further the scientific and social developments necessary to the continuance of life in this world.

Roy C. Jones is a member of the Triton community college board, River Grove, Ill. Mr. Jones, a utility company division supervisor, served for 14 years as an elementary school board member and for the past six years has served on the board of Triton College, a public institution with an enrollment of 6,000 in grades 13 and 14.

IT MEANS PLACING EDUCATION
IN THE HANDS OF BIG BUSINESS

LAURA T. DOING

It would be impossible, I feel, for a voucher plan to improve public education in this country. Since school boards and administrators could never project in any accurate manner enrollments and, therefore, the need for facilities, teachers, textbooks, instructional materials, equipment, and so forth, a voucher system could only result in pandemonium.

The only manner in which a voucher system could work would be to remove all local units of government from educational service and place education in the domain of big competitive business. I cannot see how that could possibly solve any of education's problems.

———————

Laura T. Doing is a member of the Wichita Falls, Tex., school board (6-2-4, enrollment 21,000). Mrs. Doing, a journalist, has served on the Wichita Falls board for 14 years.

RESULT: FRAGMENTATION OF PUBLIC EFFORT
TO EDUCATE ALL OUR YOUNG

WILLIAM S. WARFIELD

Only because the rules ask it do I put aside the constitutional aspects of this question — I think they are grave and, I hope, they will be clarified once the U.S. Supreme Court rules directly on the question of aid to nonpublic schools for furnishing secular services (perhaps soon, on the Pennsylvania appeal).

I do not think educational progress would be served best by adopting an educational voucher plan.

Historically we have maintained the right of people to send their children to qualifying schools of their own choice. At the same time, one of the great strengths of our country has been the establishment and maintenance of a strong, free public school system supported by *all* the people. Whatever its intentions, the voucher system amounts to public aid to nonpublic schools. Any substantial public aid, direct or indirect, to nonpublic schools would be a significant departure from the philosophy of a free, universally supported public school system and would, in my opinion, result in a fragmentation of our public effort to educate the nation's young.

Public schools in many if not most areas are suffering from inadequate funding in their efforts to maintain high quality education in this fast moving age. To put further strain on the public coffers by providing aid to nonpublic schools would, I am afraid, result in making it even more difficult for the public schools to obtain sufficient funds.

If money were no problem, would a "voucher plan" improve schooling in the U.S. and would it perhaps equalize educational opportunity? One can only speculate as to the possible good effects of a competitive education setup, but I am still inclined to think that, while our public school system admittedly is not perfect, our future lies in preserving and strengthening it. Of course, there needs to be some equalizing of educational opportunity, but I would prefer to increase the state level equalizing efforts, thereby relieving local property of having to carry the lion's share of the funding and thus helping to close the gap between poorer and richer school districts.

William S. Warfield IV is a member of the Rosedale district school board, Livingston, Mt. (1-8, enrollment under 100). Mr. Warfield, a rancher, has served on the Rosedale board for 16 years.

VOUCHER MAY BRING A WORSE IMBALANCE THAN WE HAVE NOW

HILDA L. JAFFE

Why, oh why, would the federal government want to aim another blow at the poor (literally and figuratively) public schools? What has become of public commitment to public education? Why turn over ransom money to child buyers?

I firmly believe that public funds must be concentrated in public schools. Any plan that would permit money to be diverted to private schools would serve only to weaken public education further.

In today's society, the public school is probably the only place where the broad spectrum of children from different economic, religious and ethnic backgrounds can meet as equals. Doesn't federal officialdom really want to work toward a healthy society?

Certainly there is need for educational competition. Parallel systems serving an area can and should offer alternatives to parents. Private schools, however, are not subject to the stringent state standards for staff, building and fiscal procedures that aggravate public school costs. If large quantities of tax money are permitted to flow into private schools, the financial injury is further aggravated.

Poorer school districts already have lost the confidence of many constituents who now would be lured away by the golden promises of private schools eager to receive federal money in addition to other resources. But where does that leave the poor schools as they lose both students and money from local per capita tax support? Surely they will not be capable of equalizing educational opportunities with private schools within their own area, let alone with richer school districts.

The result of this free enterprise? Greater educational imbalance than before. And further "proof" that public schools fail the youngsters. And around goes the vicious cycle.

Vouchers? Perhaps. But as public *IOUs* for public schools to educate the public's children.

—————

Hilda L. Jaffe is a member of the Verona, N.J., school board (K-12, enrollment 3,000). Mrs. Jaffe, a housewife and civic leader, has served on the Verona school board for eight years.

THE THREAT OF THIS NIGHTMARE
SHOULD PROMPT US TO IMPROVE

SAM JOYNER JR.

My reaction to the "educational voucher plan" is negative. The only advantage that comes to mind is that the threat of such a monstrosity should spur us all to redouble our efforts to improve our present public schooling in the United States, and to continue our efforts to make it more responsive to the needs of our children.

I am sure such a plan would be welcomed by many parochial schools and the many private academies that have sprung up during the past few years, but it would certainly cut the throat of our public schools and make intelligent community educational planning a nightmare.

Implementation of a voucher plan would also be a nightmare. Someone, not me, would have to evaluate all participating schools, advise all parents of the various qualifications of those schools, then motivate the parents to make a choice, making sure some school did not "sell" itself to a particular group. Some agency would have to decide which lucky students would go to a so-called "best school" of a competing group, and have to explain to the rest why they could not.

I am grateful that, although we have some low income or disadvantaged areas in our district, we do not have inferior schools in those areas. And this very thing, in my opinion, can be the salvation of all public schools. Our public schools are the finest vehicle I know for educating *all* our children. Certainly, they need changing – constantly – if only for the reason that progress means change, but I think we've awakened albeit slowly to the point where progress is being made, not only in our schools but in motivating home influence. I would suggest deep study indeed before any voucher plan is adopted. Better still, spend that time and money in an effort to strengthen our public schools.

Sam Joyner Jr. is a member of the Lawton, Okla., school board (6-3-3, enrollment 20,000). Mr. Joyner, a merchant, has served on the Lawton board for 19 years.

ONE DANGER IS THE CONTROL THE FEDERAL GOVERNMENT WOULD GAIN

FRED M. HEDDINGER

This theory of a "voucher plan" was first advanced, to my knowledge, several years ago. At that time, it was being suggested as a way of achieving integration and racial balance. Since then, various special interest groups have jumped on the bandwagon, including the U.S. Chamber of Commerce, which called such a plan a chance for competition.

Such voucher plans, it would seem, will ultimately make a shambles of public education. Unfortunately, little is being done to present the positive accomplishment of the present system of American education while all manner of critics and would-be reformers are given encouragement and accommodation for destructive criticisms.

One of the inherent dangers of such a plan – a voucher plan, with the federal government setting forth the eligibility criteria – is the control that this would ultimately give federal agencies over programs and subject matter. It is inconceivable that any such plan will allow people generally to spend these funds as they personally see fit, even though this argument may now be advanced as a selling tool.

Fred M. Heddinger is a member of the Wilkinsburg, Pa., school board (K-12), enrollment 5,300). Mr. Heddinger, executive director of the Pennsylvania School Boards Association, has served on the Wilkinsburg board for 19 years.

FINANCES WOULD BE DILUTED AND
SCHOOLS WOULD BE DOWNGRADED

ROBERT G. SIMMONS JR.

I am opposed to the plan of issuing vouchers for education of each child to be redeemed at any school, public or private, and my objections are, as the *Journal* requested, listed in addition to those constitutional and legal problems which obviously develop.

In my opinion, most communities in the United States cannot support two good school systems. This method might even permit three. The obvious result would be to dilute the financial resources of the community and downgrade the schools rather than improving them. Likewise, it would create divisions — both economic as well as making possible racial divisions — which are not good for any community and would permit the persons who could afford to send their children to private schools to benefit thereby, and they would lose their interest in voting bonds and mill levies in support of the public schools.

Public schools would be relegated to a poorer system, and the poorer people would be unable to pay the additional expenses of going to other schools; thence, we would have public schools damaged and the education of the poor people, who need it the most, downgraded.

Robert G. Simmons Jr. is a member of the Nebraska state board of education, Lincoln. Mr. Simmons, an attorney, has served on the Nebraska state board for five years.

EDUCATIONAL OPPORTUNITIES WILL
BE LESSENED, NOT BROADENED

W. CASPER HOLROYD JR.

I am a strong believer in public education as I recently heard it described by the dean of education of North Carolina State University: "In public education, the United States has accomplished the Impossible Dream." Given an opportunity to buy their education, a lot of parents will make a decision to move their children from public schools to the private ones without realizing that their educational opportunities in these schools will be less than those offered in the public school systems.

While serving as a school board member, I have become convinced that through public education as we now have it — and hope to improve it — we still can resolve many of this country's problems.

I do not see where a voucher plan would improve schooling in the United States; nor would it close any gaps between the poor and the richest school districts. I can offer as an alternative solution a plan whereby the federal government could return income tax dollars to the local school districts to permit us more flexibility on a local level.

W. Casper Holroyd Jr. is chairman of the Raleigh, N.C., school board (6-3-3, enrollment 25,000). Mr. Holroyd, an insurance salesman, has served on the Raleigh board for five years.

SLATES AND HAMSTERS

JOHN R. COYNE JR.

Voucher plans have found many friends among political conservatives, perhaps because the idea stresses the classic arguments of the value of individual choice and open competition. Here is a forceful conservative statement from The National Review.

American education is, we all agree, in rotten shape.

We spend about $40 billion per year on education — more, writes Peter Drucker in *The Age of Discontinuity,* "than on all other nondefense community services together — health care, welfare, farm subsidies . . ."

What do we get for this massive investment? No one really knows. There is no comprehensive published information on how school children are faring nationwide. Why not? Because, some critics contend, the educationist establishment doesn't dare release available figures. The nearest thing to a national report yet issued, compiled in 1966 for the Defense Department, shows that one out of every four American men fails the Armed Forces Qualifying Tests because he can't read an elementary passage, write a simple sentence or add a basic sum. One-quarter of our population, in other words, after at least ten years of spending five hours or more per day in American classrooms, is functionally illiterate. The percentage in the ghettos is much worse: There, two out of three flunk the qualifying tests.

We all know the schools are doing a dismal job. The question is: How do we make them better? Restructure the classroom itself, runs one of the hoariest reformist recipes. But how? Liberals argue that classrooms are structured too rigidly. Charles E. Silberman, for instance, author of *Crisis in American Education,* says that schools stifle children by tending "to confuse day-to-day routine with purpose and to transform the means into the end itself." If the emphasis were on "creative" learning rather than on order, children would *want* to learn and therefore would do so.

But such ideas offend conservative parents who believe that the schools aren't structured tightly enough. Imagine for instance the reaction of Max Rafferty were he to wander into that North Dakota school celebrated by Silberman, where rabbits, chickens, hamsters, children and white rats all learn together in cardboard boxes. Most conservative parents would probably react similarly, insisting that if schools just forgot about such fripperies and returned to the three Rs, fifth graders would once again be conjugating irregular Latin verbs, just as they did back in 1906 when things were good.

Now it well may be that there is nothing wrong with either approach. Perhaps your little Gwendolyn will one day win a Nobel Prize in zoology because of those hours spent in a cardboard box with a hamster. And perhaps Waldo will eventually hold a chair in classics at Harvard because he learned to conjugate Latin verbs on his slate in the fifth grade at East Overshoe grammar school. But the problem is this: If Waldo lives in Minot, North Dakota, he will not be conjugating, for, unless his parents have a good deal of money, they will send him to the public school to which he is assigned. And if Gwendolyn's parents live in East Overshoe, the same will be true for her. Thus Waldo will be paired with the hamster, Gwendolyn will scribble unhappily on her slate. And the parents will be able to do nothing whatsoever about it, even though East Overshoe may lie only five miles from Minot.

Everyone Revolting

And yet Waldo and Gwendolyn are lucky. Imagine the plight of destitute black parents in places such as New York or Newark, where ghetto schools are daily torn by violence, where white unionized teachers, quite obviously more concerned with paychecks than teaching, strike at will, where children seldom reach the eighth grade able to read. Such schools have given up even the pretense of attempting to educate. Yet when frustrated parents try to act, as they did in New York in Ocean Hill-Brownsville, for instance, they are crushed by the self-serving educationist bureaucracy. And so ghetto-school parents have no options. They are denied a voice in running their schools and because they are poor they are unable to vote with their feet. The result? A generation of sub-literate black children. And violence. The brutal beating of a striking group of white Newark teachers by a crew of blacks should surprise no one familiar with the frustrations of ghetto parents.

And it is not only black parents who are in revolt against the educationist structure. Middle- and upper-middle-class parents are also rebelling by firmly closing their pocketbooks. In the *Phi Delta Kappan,* George Gallup writes: "Budgets and bond issues are being voted down in increasing number . . . in the last year (fiscal 1969) school bond issues were voted down by voters at a record rate. By dollar value, voters approved less than 44 per cent of the $3.9 billion in bond issues put to the electorate. The $1.7 billion that passed comprise the lowest total since 1962. A decade ago 80 per cent of such bond issues were approved." And this before the recession. If the trend persists, we will see widespread closings of public schools.

Educationists Lobby

It becomes increasingly clear that the American public has lost faith in its system of public education. To borrow a phrase currently in vogue, the system is unresponsive to the needs of the people. "The same thing is wrong with the school system that is wrong with the Post Office," says Milton Friedman. "The government monopoly tends to be inefficient and costly, and most important of all, it is not responsive to the wishes of its customers." And how to make the system responsive? According to psychologist Kenneth Clark, the key is "aggressive competition." Let schools compete for students by promising to educate them better than other schools. And if they fail to keep their promise, let them close down. "We need a spectrum of educational institutions giving families a variety of schools," writes Dean Theodore Sizer of the Harvard education school. A responsive system, said OEO Director Donald Rumsfeld, must be one in which "poor parents would be able to exercise some opportunity to choose similar to that now enjoyed by wealthier parents who can move to a better public-school district or send their children to private schools." Responsiveness, competitiveness, flexibility, mobility, free choice, variety. Slates and hamsters. Almost all critics believe that these are the necessary ingredients of a successfully restructured school system. And an increasing number of them, no matter what their ideological or political hue, agree that this restructuring can best be accomplished by adopting the voucher system.

Although the basic idea can be traced back to Adam Smith, the voucher plan was first proposed in contemporary form by E. C. West in 1965 in *Education and the State*. West, an English economist, believed that education should be removed from the direct control of the state and that the poor as well as the rich should be able to exercise some measure of control over the education of their children. In America the plan is lauded by conservatives such as Milton Friedman, left-radicals such as Christopher Jencks, and numerous Administration officials.

There has been an unusual amount of academic haggling over the details of the plan's administration, so that many have come to view it as hairily complex. But actually it's a simple scheme. An issuing agency—state, city, town, school board—gives to the parents of a school-age schild a chit approximately equal to the amount it takes to educate that child during the school year, say about $800. The parents then hand over this voucher to the school—public or private—in which they want to enroll their child. The school turns the voucher in to the issuing agency, and the agency reimburses the school. Advocates of the system believe that it would encourage competition among public schools and would also encourage the growth of a network of private innovative schools competing with the public schools for students, such competition providing an incentive for both public and private schools to maintain high standards. Gwendolyn's parents, in other words, wouldn't have to move from East Overshoe to give her her hamster.

Despite the attractiveness of the voucher plan, it has so far been given little chance to prove itself. Virginia put it into effect statewide in 1958, but it never really worked out, operating as it did in the shadow of the Supreme Court desegregation decision. And in addition to racial complications, the stipends were never quite large enough, so that by 1967 the experiment was largely deemed a failure. In Maine and New Hampshire, about two thousand children are involved in plans roughly similar to proposed voucher plans, but their situation is the result of demographic expediency (they live outside organized school districts). New York legislators have proposed a modified voucher plan for parochial school students in New York, a governor's commission has come out for vouchers in Maryland, and voucher bills have been introduced in the California legislature.

The voucher system has trouble getting a trial, primarily because it is vehemently opposed by the educationist establishment. It is no coincidence that on the day the OEO expressed interest in trying it out in Kansas City, an educationist coalition, led by the American Federation of Teachers, was formed in Washington "to work against the implementation of the education voucher plan anywhere in the United States."

Anyone can figure out why the educationists fear the voucher system. It would force them to produce or lose their cushy benefits. Still, several of their objections to vouchers merit consideration, for some of them are also shared by people with honest doubts. There are four general arguments against vouchers: 1) the voucher plan would turn public schools into "dumping grounds," serving only children rejected by all other schools; 2) the plan would encourage racial segregation; 3) the plan would make "hucksterism" the order of the day: private schools would dazzle parents with fads and gimmicks and parents would be too bewildered to choose schools wisely; 4) vouchers would encourage the growth of parochial schools at the expense of others, and vouchers cashed in by church schools would violate the constitutional principle of separation of church and state.

Jencks' Plan

Dr. Jencks, architect of the voucher plan favored by OEO, addresses himself to the first two arguments. "Dumping grounds" is obviously code for all-black schools: Blacks would stay in public schools, everyone else would flee to private schools, and the result would be, objection 2), segregation. To prevent this Jencks has worked out an involved system. His voucher agency, which would disperse all local, state and federal funds for the sole purpose of redeeming vouchers, would include a certain number of blacks. Schools would be required to accept vouchers as full payment and would not be allowed to raise tuition above voucher level, thereby insuring that the poor would not be penalized for poverty. Schools would choose students partly by processing applications and partly by lottery, and financial supplements would be offered to those schools choosing low-income children, thereby making it profitable to take poor blacks.

Milton Friedman, who finds the Jencks plan unnecessarily complex and fears that it will result in a bureaucracy just as complex as the present one, gives the first two objections short shrift. In the first place, he says, the city schools are *already* dumping grounds, and there is nothing on the horizon, given the present system, that promises to change this. New York City schools are among the most segregated in the world, and the flight to the suburbs simply strengthens the pattern. Conceivably, says Friedman, as a variety of schools develops catering to special talents and needs, the voucher system could lessen the white exodus from the cities and might even bring some people back. Things could certainly get no worse.

No matter what angle you examine it from, the "dumping ground" argument seems a curious one, almost as if the educationists hadn't quite thought their argument through. For what they are saying is that public schools are so wretched that no one with any ability at all would stay in them if there were alternatives.

An Alternative

The "hucksterism" charge, leveled most frequently by AFT President David Selden, seems anchored in the notion that parents are incapable of choosing wisely for their children, that they must be led by the hand by those wiser than they, in this case, presumably, the AFT. Parents surely know at least as much about education as they do about, say, medicine. Yet no one seriously champions the creation of some elite body that would dictate to Mrs. Garkle which doctor should remove Gwendolyn's tonsils.

The church-state argument is the most complex. Voucher defenders claim that there is no constitutional problem involved, since if parents sent their children to parochial schools the government would not be making payment to the schools but to the parents. This, of course, is an argument that will have to be resolved by the courts. But to those critics who believe that the voucher system would benefit church schools at the expense of the public, Milton Friedman offers an ingenious answer. At present, says Friedman, in most parts of the country, parents send their children to parochial schools not because they're religious but because they're *private*. Parochial schools, in other words, offer the only alternative to public schools that middle- and working-class parents can afford. The voucher system, Friedman argues, would create a new kind of public school that every middle-class family could afford.

Closely related to this argument is the contention that the price of land and construction would prevent private secular schools from coming into existence in sufficient number to compete with the parochial. Tuition in the form of vouchers can keep a school running, but before you collect tuition, you have to build the school. This objection is one of the most telling, but it touches upon things we as yet have no way of evaluating, and it is invalid insofar as it rests on the false assumption that the quality of education is somehow directly related to the cost and effectiveness of the physical plant. Why couldn't a small experimental school in a tenement, renovated by teachers, parents and students, provide just as rewarding an education as some $5-million concrete-and-glass complex? Or why couldn't a remodeled Victorian house in Westport do the same? The quality of education can't be measured by the number of feet of carpeting in the library.

It remains doubtful whether the voucher system will get a chance to prove itself. The word out of Washington until very recently was that it is dead as an OEO project. But on January 20, in a speech in Wilkes-Barre, Pennsylvania, Frank Carlucci, new OEO acting director, announced that his agency would award preliminary planning grants to school districts in Indiana and California interested in setting up experimental voucher programs. And San Francisco, San Diego and Seattle have also expressed strong interest in similar grants.

Crusade To Stifle

But there's tough going ahead, for the educationist lobby is digging in. "The critics," said Rumsfeld, "are certain, or so they say, of their own concern for education and they deny that anyone else is concerned or can have any reason to be dissatisfied. They fear experimentation because it may call into question their own dogmas and orthodoxies. They seem to be embarked on a crusade to stifle efforts . . . to improve." Some of these critics, theorized Rumsfeld, "think their profession must be insulated from change. They fear the consequences of new techniques because, I suspect, they doubt their ability to adapt to them. They conceal their fear in the fog of educational jargon and claim that only they can evaluate themselves. They reject the idea of accountability and want to ensure that their paychecks and perquisites are maintained regardless of what is achieved in the classroom."

The hard truth, of course, is that education is under the control of a monopoly which, although perhaps the single most powerful lobbying group in Washington, is much less adept at educating than lobbying. When the teachers' groups become just one more special-interest group with a vested interest in protecting themselves at the expense of the people they supposedly serve, then we must view with suspicion the misgivings they express over experimentation. When they call the idea of a voucher system "a tragic mistake," as does the AFT, then we must wonder whether they mean a tragic mistake for the country or for the AFT. Says Harvard's Dean Sizer: "Given the condition of the schools that serve poor youngsters, it takes a depressing amount of paranoia to suggest that we should not even give the voucher plan a reasonable trial."

John R. Coyne Jr. is a Special Assistant to Vice President Agnew.

VOUCHERS — SOLUTION OR SOP?

DAVID SELDEN

*The American Federation of Teachers has been among the most vehement
and frequent critics of voucher plans. The AFT has consistently opposed
what it calls "gimmicks" which detract from what it considers the best
path, that of putting more money and effort into improving the present
system of schooling. AFT's president, David Selden, is a phrase-maker of
considerable wit: "Like a bright, shiny, quick-moving lizard running over
a rotting log, the voucher scheme diverts our attention from the decay
underneath. But what will we do if Mr. Jencks' entertaining little lizard
grows up to be a fire-breathing dragon?" (See AFT's response to the
Alum Rock experiment in Part IV.)*

One of today's most controversial educational issues is the voucher plan—a
scheme designed to give students choice of school rather than requiring them
to attend schools to which they are assigned. Parents would be given certificates equal to the cost of educating their children and could then spend these
certificates in any public or private school with room to accommodate their
children.

Opponents of the voucher plan are divided into two camps: those who believe
that it will not work and those who believe it will. Those who oppose the
voucher plan on grounds of impracticality have found themselves at a serious
disadvantage because, as each new detailed objection has been registered, proponents of the plan have added new qualifications and safeguards designed to
eliminate the objection. Those who oppose the plan as a matter of principle
are raising more fundamental objections. They hold that the voucher plan is a
dangerous and divisive proposal which could even destroy the public school
system.

Innocence Abroad

Actually, there is no single voucher plan. One of the first to use the term was
conservative economist Milton Friedman who was trying to find a way to turn

Reprinted with permission of the American Federation of Teachers, 1972. (1012
14th Street, N.W., Washington, D.C. 20005.) The article originally appeared in the
Teachers' College Record, February, 1971.

the schools over to private enterprise. Later, Christopher Jencks and his associates at the Harvard Graduate School of Education saw vouchers as a way to bring about educational changes. They were and still are deeply concerned about the failure of American schools to educate underclass students, particularly those who live in the black slums and ghettos of our big cities. Jencks and others observed that while schools in nearby Boston and in other cities are overcrowded and run-down, many middle-class suburbs of those cities have underutilized school facilities.

Furthermore, the voucher advocates took heed of the central finding of the Coleman Report to the effect that the most influential element in a child's education is his social milieu. If such children could be helped to leapfrog out of the city and into suburban schools, they would thus be receiving intrinsically better educational service on the one hand and a more learning-supporting environment on the other.

Jencks and his associates further observed that throughout the nation there are a number of small, highly innovative private schools which are apparently achieving spectacular results. Yet many of these experimental schools live a hand-to-mouth existence. If a way could be found to give such schools financial security, the probability of developing useful, new educational techniques would be increased.

Hence, vouchers. What has happened to the original pure-hearted voucher concept, however, is a classic example of good intentions gone bad.

Mechanical Problems

One of the early problems encountered in making the voucher scheme viable was the obvious fact that putting an urban educational price tag on a poor kid would still leave him unable to afford a suburban school. Therefore, one of the first elements that was added to the concept was that children from poverty slum families would be given added educational green stamps, so that they could afford a more expensive education than they would get if they stayed in their urban attendance districts. This voucher override caveat introduces a vital cop-out right at the outset.

Although educational arguers concede that suburban education is better and that it costs more, they do not concede that *urban* education could be improved if more money were to be spent in the cities. The more vociferous critics of our public schools proceed from the premise that we could educate children if we, (1) really wanted to do a job, and (2) had the right idea about how to teach. They vigorously dispute assertions by teachers and their organizations that well-qualified and well-paid teachers with small classes, reasonable classroom-hour loads, ample remedial assistance, and good physical surroundings have much to do with the quality of instruction. Yet many of these same critics support the voucher plan, despite its initial concession that good education will cost more than we are now spending in slum schools.

Money alone is not an absolute determinant of educational quality. A study by the NAACP in 1969 showed that a large proportion—although not the majority by any means—of so-called compensatory education programs financed under Title I of the Elementary and Secondary Education Act proved to be educationally worthless. On the other hand, it is impossible to effect any large-scale improvement in education without having more money to hire teachers and other personnel and to invest in new schools and equipment. And if more money can be made available for education, it should be spent to improve the public schools in the areas of greatest need.

The voucher bounty idea would introduce incentives for operators of private schools and, of course, for suburban school boards. Supporters of the plan pooh-pooh the possibility that the profit motive would stimulate added hucksterism in education. However, unless safeguards against profiteering were carefully drawn and enforced, voucher money would most certainly tempt unscrupulous educational entrepreneurs in the same way that the GI Bill stimulated the growth of all those electronics, watchmaking, and key punch "schools." Most of the victims of those enterprises were ex-servicemen from the underclass who were looking for educational shortcuts. The greater educational need of underclass children and their parents makes them more vulnerable to the blandishments of fly-by-night school operators.

Open Enrollment

The term voucher plan is so catchy that one almost takes for granted that this is something new, but it is not. In the early, liberal, integrationist days following the U.S. Supreme Court's 1954 school desegregation decision, many school districts adopted so-called open enrollment plans. Black children who otherwise would have been attending all-black slum schools were permitted to transfer to other schools if those schools had space to receive them. Many of these plans also provided free busing, again on a voluntary basis. While most of the open enrollment plans were theoretically "two way," it was inevitably black children who rode the bus—a segregating activity in itself.

Most open enrollment plans have been abandoned or have dwindled to insignificance. As a matter of fact, they never did enlist masses of students, and for the most part, the children who rode the bus were those with strong parental support and high motivation. These were the very children who were more likely to succeed regardless of the school they attended. They were also the very children whose presence could have provided stimulation for less striving children in their ghetto schools.

Most observers of the open enrollment plans quickly came to the conclusion that the programs were ineffective in combatting racial segregation and that very little, if any, educational gain resulted.

As an aside, the open enrollment plans, confined mostly to Northern cities, simply proved that a *little* busing would accomplish nothing; the much more extensive busing program now being followed in many Southern cities bears educational promise through its significant effect upon the social mix in schools.

Racism and Politics

Another scheme very close to the voucher idea is "freedom-of-choice," now outlawed by many court decisions. The freedom-of-choice plans were designed to *promote* racial segregation. They were based upon outright subsidies, very similar to vouchers, given to parents to trade in at the "school of their choice." Of course, black parents were not permitted to use their vouchers at white schools.

The original proponents of vouchers abhor racial discrimination, and they have again proposed mechanical regulations which would supposedly guard against use of the vouchers to promote freedom-of-choice academies. For instance, they would require that at least 25 percent of the student population be of a minority ethnic group before a school would be eligible to receive voucher students.

The proposed 25 percent safeguard illustrates another basic problem of the voucher idea. Since the plan's success seems to depend, in part at least, on federal aid, one can readily see the shape of the future. The percentage figure would loom as a major proving ground over which pro and con lobbyists would clash, just as they now struggle to influence percentages in taxes, tariffs, and oil depletion allowances.

Even if Congress passed a proper percentage, however, it still would have to be enforced. Ironically, some of those who purport to fear the specter of federal intervention in local affairs are also advocating the use of vouchers, not recognizing, presumably, the massive federal regulatory apparatus which would be necessary to prevent abuse.

European Experience

School finance systems very similar to vouchers have been in use in a number of European countries for many decades. In Belgium, Holland, and Denmark, for instance, children receive equal subsidies, regardless of the sponsorship of the school they attend—public, private, nonsectarian, or religious. Contrary to the objections usually raised, the effects of government subsidies have been far from catastrophic. While the percentage of students at religious-sponsored schools has increased somewhat, the proportion now seems to be stabilized. Furthermore, apparently the religious schools are becoming less and less sectarian and more and more like the public schools. It is predicted that there will be very little difference between the two types of schools in five to ten years.

The European system, however, couples close supervision by the state with certain standard requirements—in staffing and equipment, for instance—which all schools must meet. Of course, all schools must teach a standard curriculum prescribed by the state, and there are single national teacher-salary schedules and pension systems.

It cannot be said that public subsidy of private schools creates illiberal, divided, and strife-torn societies, since the three countries under discussion are among the most liberal and peaceful in the world. But it must be noted that economic and social conditions in those countries differ greatly from those in the United States. First, there is no large economically deprived underclass in Belgium, Holland, or Denmark. Second, there is no large racially isolated group. Third, government is much simpler and more centralized. What seems to have become acceptable in small, middle-class, ethnically homogeneous countries under strong centralized control or supervision would not necessarily be applicable to the United States with its huge problems and deep unresolved racial, sectional, and religious antagonisms.

Incidentally, France does *not* subsidize private schools.

Religious Warfare

The dynamite which lies ready for detonation just below the surface of the voucher controversy is the growing issue of public support for religious-related schools. At several meetings called by the sponsors of the voucher plan in an effort to "clarify" the situation, the line-up of religious teams was as apparent as if they had worn colored jerseys. On the one side were those Jewish and Protestant organizations traditionally zealous in maintaining the principle of separation of church and state. On the other side were the Catholic organizations and a scattering of other denominations trying desperately to save their church-related school systems. Even though Jencks and company say that vouchers would not be used to any great extent to solve the financial plight of the church schools, spokesmen for those institutions quite obviously think otherwise.

Jencks thinks that the church schools would have a hard time meeting his 25 percent minority race qualification. Church spokesmen, however, feel that with federal support tuition for such schools could be reduced and the number of "free" students could be greatly increased, thus helping to improve racial integration in such schools and at the same time preventing their possible collapse. The religious advocates of vouchers point out that church-related schools now enroll hundreds of thousands of children who otherwise would be the responsibility of the public system. Unless these schools receive financial aid, they will be forced to curtail operations and send students flooding into already overcrowded public facilities. Vouchers seem to offer a way out.

The tuition subsidy plan now in use in New York state, which provides state funds for college students to attend institutions of their choice, whether public or private, seems to be in conformity with constitutional requirements. Other scholarship plans using federal funds have also been in existence for many years without arousing successful legal objection. Even so, introduction of the voucher plan is almost certain to result in speedy legal challenge by its opponents on grounds of separation of church and state.

Several cases now in the judicial works will have a bearing on the legal status of vouchers. One of these is *Flask v. Gardner,* which challenges the use of federal funds to pay for educational services conducted in religious-sponsored schools under Title I of ESEA. If the courts should decide that the use of funds in this way is unconstitutional, the legality of the voucher concept so far as the religious-related schools are concerned would be dubious indeed.

The other test case is *Lemon v. Kurtzman.* Pennsylvania now provides state aid directly to private schools—most of them church-connected. A number of organizations have filed amicus briefs in opposition to the use of funds for such a purpose, but U.S. Attorney General John Mitchell announced in September, 1970, that his department would file an amicus brief on the side of the state, thus declaring in favor of such subsidies.

Polarizer

The Nixon Administration has not been slow to realize the political potentialities in the voucher controversy. Donald Rumsfeld, who was appointed by the President to become Director of the Office of Economic Opportunity (presumably on the basis that since he voted against every bill which created OEO he could not be accused of favoritism), started down the Spiro Agnew polarization trail in 1970. Rumsfeld was seeking quite obviously to exploit another of those neat splitters which have become the hallmark of the current administration's political style.

By pushing the voucher plan, Rumsfeld attacked teachers, who are almost universally opposed, and the "liberal elements" who favor strict separation of church and state. At the same time, he declared himself in support of people who, according to cynical political analysis, are thought to be in the hard-hat category. He also gave aid and comfort to people who secretly hope vouchers will lead to a revival of the Southern freedom-of-choice plans.

In promoting the voucher plan, Rumsfeld displayed a flair for half-truths. In a speech given September 23, 1970, before the San Francisco Chamber of Commerce "Urban Roundtable," he first detailed the all too obvious defects and shortcomings of our current system of education. Then he totaled up all the money spent by all levels of government on education. In the same paragraph he threw in an observation—unsupported—that "the pupil-teacher ratio is lower today than ever in the nation's history."

What Rumsfeld left out was that the percentage of gross national product for education remained practically constant for decades and that "pupil-teacher ratio" is an almost meaningless figure. Furthermore, if the ratio has gone down, how much has it decreased? A page later in the same speech, he rejected the idea that the amount of money spent on education has much to do with the quality of education. What we need, he said, are new ideas, and he charged that the American Federation of Teachers and other teacher organizations don't want any new ideas, since they are against the voucher plan and have been against other "experiments" launched under the aegis of the OEO.

Quoting directly from the Rumsfeld remarks, he stated: "They [teacher interest groups] charge that money, not new approaches, is the answer to improving educational skills." He then went on to quote President Nixon, "When we get more education for the dollar, we'll start asking for more dollars for education."

As a matter of fact, the voucher plan does not add a single new educational technique, nor can it guarantee that giving pupils more mobility will result in the development of new techniques.

Lizard or Dragon?

One of the chief objections which can be leveled fairly at the voucher idea is that it, like so many catchy educational schemes, tends to divert attention from the real and basic needs of children and the schools. Whether education is carried on by people—teachers and paraprofessionals—or by machines watched over by people, there *is* a relationship between cost and educational effort.

No one would deny that it is possible to waste school money, but all other things being equal—the educability of students, the intelligence of teachers and administrators, the social milieu in which the school must operate—the more money you spend on education, the more education is produced. It is silly, if not malicious, to suggest that money-starved school systems will have "to do better" before the great white fathers in Washington will give them more support.

Like a bright, shiny, quick-moving lizard running over a rotting log, the voucher scheme diverts our attention from the decay underneath. But what will we do if Mr. Jencks' entertaining little lizard grows up to be a fire-breathing dragon?

David Selden is President of the American Federation of Teachers.

ANTI VOUCHER HOUSE TESTIMONY (Excerpted)

COMMITTEE ON EDUCATION AND LABOR
Washington, D.C.
April 2, 1971

We fear deeply that the hidden agenda of the voucher planners is to create a market for the invasion of profitmaking agents . . .

The Chairman. A quorum is present.

Our first witness is the representative of the National Education Association.

Mr. McFarland. I have with me David Selden, president of the American

Federation of Teachers. The American Federation of Teachers and NEA co-chair a coalition on the voucher system.

Mr. Chairman and members of this committee, we appear today as supporters of the original goals of OEO as those goals were intended by the Congress.

We are speaking for 11 organizations, with an aggregate membership of millions of Americans. These organizations are:

> American Association of School Administrators
> American Association of University Women
> American Ethical Union
> American Federation of Teachers
> American Humanist Association
> American Jewish Congress
> American Parents Committee
> Americans United for Separation of Church and State
> National Association of Elementary School Principals
> National Education Association
> Unitarian Universalist Association

Several of the above listed organizations will testify today as to their specific objections to the voucher program. The coalition of organizations endorsing this statement is urging the committee to order the Office of Economic Opportunity to discontinue all grants for feasibility studies and funding of voucher programs at least until the Education and Labor Committee has held thorough hearings and assessed the impact of such proposals—not only on the public school system, but also on other institutions and values of American society.

It is well known by the chairman and this committee that these organizations were supporters of the original goal of the OEO—ending poverty. That is why it has been so painful for us to witness the attempt to change OEO by prematurely removing from its responsibility programs that work, eliminating programs before they have a chance to work, and becoming involved in programs that can never work—all in the name of ending poverty.

We believe that a larger issue than the voucher system is involved. The attempt of executive offices to distort, bypass, or thwart the will of Congress, not only in the withholding of appropriated funds, but also in the initiation of programs which Congress has not authorized, is becoming increasingly a matter of concern. Under the guise of research and development, such congressional mandates as the poverty program are being ignored. The original purpose of OEO—assistance to the poor—has been redirected into an ill-conceived attempt to reprivatize our social services.

We believe that programs approved by Congress should be carried out. We believe that no so-called experiments which are directly or indirectly aimed at altering or possibly destroying basic American institutions such as the public schools should be undertaken without clear direction from the Congress as representatives of the American people. . . .

Mr. Selden. Mr. Chairman, I just want to personally reinforce what Mr. Mc-Farland has said in behalf of our coalition. We fully support the statement. Furthermore, although I don't speak for the AFL-CIO, I have been assured by representatives of the AFL-CIO that they stand in the same position.

We find particularly objectionable the use of OEO funds, which are really supposed to be used to develop economic opportunities for the poor, to promote educational experiments which have been rejected or will not be promoted by the regular educational arm of the Government. I am referring, of course, to the Office of Education. If an experiment of this kind had educational merit it certainly could have been promoted through the use of title III funds.

There is no need to go around to the backdoor and, under the guise of combating poverty, embark on an educational program which could have very far-reaching bad effects. Cancer starts with a small virus, I believe; and, while the programs that OEO is promoting in the so-called voucher system are rather small, compared to the total educational enterprise, nevertheless we fear the spread of this virus once it is allowed to take hold. . . .

Mr. McFarland. When Dr. Adron Doran, as the spokesman for NEA, appeared before this committee on April 21, 1964, we pledged the Association's support for the efforts of the Congress to eradicate poverty in this land. That pledge is still valid. We were pleased when this committee agreed with us that the Office of Economic Opportunity should not become involved in the ongoing education program of the schools, but rather should confine its activities to direct community services to the poor and to programs designed to equip poor adults to enter the world of work. Clearly, OEO was not designed to compete with the Office of Education or the established public school system.

We have watched with grave concern the destruction of the Job Corps, the downgrading of VISTA, the attempts to cut back funds for Headstart, and other similar actions. We fear that the original intent of the poverty program is being subverted from one of attack on the root causes of poverty to one which would serve as a free-wheeling research and development agency—related only very tenuously to the war on poverty.

The latest venture of this so-called research and development function of OEO is the promotion of educational voucher plans. The theory seems to be that the public school system, under the control of school boards elected by the communities they serve, is not competent to design educational programs to meet the needs of all children.

We fear that vouchers are an unconstitutional support for nonpublic schools, that they will lead to social and racial resegregation, and that they will lead to the enrichment of private sector hucksters who see this system as a bonanza.

Delegates to the 1970 NEA convention adopted the following resolution:

> The National Education Association believes that the so-called voucher plan under which education is financed by Federal or State grants to parents could lead to racial, economic, and social isolation of children and weaken or destroy the public school system.
>
> The association urges the enactment of Federal and State legislation prohibiting the establishment of such plans and calls upon its affiliates to seek from Members of Congress and State legislatures support for this legislation.

OEO has announced its intent to sink $6 to $8 million per year for the next 5 to 8 years into a so-called "voucher plan" for education. The objective is to induce local public schools to pay sums of money, equal to the school district's per-pupil cost, to parents, with the provision that the parent would select the school—public or private—which his child is to attend. The OEO planners expect the money, except for administration and transportation costs, to be contributed from local and State public school funds. The OEO planners expect the voucher stipends to be deducted from the local school district's funds. According to OEO, . . . OEO "would pay the additional costs of educating students not now in the public schools." Thus, the proposal constitutes Federal aid to private schools, but not to public schools. In fact, it will reduce funds available for public education.

While the OEO plan includes what the planners consider to be adequate safeguards to prohibit racial segregation or support for religious instruction, we are fearful that such safeguards will not be characteristic of other voucher plans which will be devised in the wake of the OEO experiment. We also have strong reservations about the element of selling which nonpublic schools, especially those operated for profit, may pursue to induce parents to patronize their schools.

We are not opposed to innovation and experimentation designed to improve the quality of American education. Indeed, a major program of NEA, under its Center for the Study of Instruction, is to promote and evaluate innovative programs and to disseminate the findings of experimental research to the school systems throughout the land. But we are opposed to ventures in the guise of experimentation which are designed, despite disclaimers to the contrary, to destroy the system of public education.

We also fear that the promoters of the voucher plans in OEO have designed this as a straw to break the backs of those of us who, with the committee, hope that if we keep OEO alive long enough it would, with proper management, come again to serve its true constituency, the poor. OEO was never intended to become a sort of inhouse Rand Corp. for the systems-happy bureaucrats of any administration. We are not opposed to OEO or to continuing authorization for OEO if it is to once again be made the servant of the poor.

Mr. Mazzoli. . . . You mentioned in your statement, . . . Mr. Selden, that cancer starts, in your opinion, with a virus. . . . I am not a doctor, but I must accept that hypothesis. You more or less characterized the fact that probably the OEO venture in the voucher plan might lead to an erosion in the body, an erosion of public education in this country?

Mr. Selden. That is right.

Mr. Mazzoli. Do you feel this is a fair characterization of an effort to try to find a better way to try to teach our students?

Mr. Selden. The voucher plan proposes no better way or no different way to teach students. There is nothing in the plan that has any suggestion at all about methods or even goals of education. It is simply a way to channel public funds into private schools.

Mr. Mazzoli. Do you think that the Headstart program which was originally started under OEO is a good program?

Mr. Selden. Yes; and it ought to be supported. It is an example of what can be done with categorical aid. What the OEO is attempting to do in the voucher program is just the opposite. It is giving free money to anyone who can come along and grab it.

Mr. Mazzoli. Let me ask the question in this fashion. Headstart was an innovative approach in U.S. education?

Mr. Selden. Right.

Mr. Mazzoli. Headstart was the product of apparently research and development, the impetus of which was supplied by OEO. This has now been found to be a good program. Is there any possibility that a plan like vouchers could be found in the years to come to be in the very same category?

Mr. Selden. No. The chances of vouchers doing anything for education are very remote. On the other hand, the chances of vouchers doing something that could be quite harmful to education are very immediate. It is a clear and present danger. The two things are not at all comparable. . . .

Mr. Mazzoli. May I suggest this, though? Is not the voucher plan and is not performance contracting the result of citizen discontent to some extent with public education, and therefore there is an innovative approach taken, in this case, through the agency of OEO, to find out if there is a better way to train and educate our children?

Mr. McFarland. May I answer that?

This is true in performance contracting, but not in the case of the voucher plan. Mr. Glennan of the research staff of OEO indicated to us that the basic premise for the experimental so-called voucher plan was to determine whether or not poor parents could make good choices concerning where their children should go to school. Underneath it all—and I don't think this is understood by the general public—the funding that OEO proposes to contribute for the voucher plan would not go for the education of the children per se. The major funding would still come from local, State, and possibly Federal sources from the various categorical programs.

Mr. Mazzoli. Is not the voucher plan a direct result of what at least OEO people have seen in the community, a need they feel to spur on some competition maybe, to provide in competition a better kind of education for the kids who are tough to teach anyway? Is this not part of the thinking process?

Mr. Selden. Mr. Mazzoli, you ask if voucher schemes and performance contracting are not a response to public dissatisfaction with the schools. I would have to say that there is widespread dissatisfaction. We are dissatisfied with the schools, and I think Chairman Perkins is dissatisfied with the schools. I have heard him say on many occasions that we need better schools, need more money so that we can get those schools. . . .

. . . It is true; your fundamental observations are correct, that the inadequacies of our public schools today leave us open to the quacks and the people who come in with false cures.

Mr. Mazzoli. Could we characterize your testimony by saying that performance contracting plans are false cures and are quackery?

Mr. Selden. Yes, sir.

Mr. Mazzoli. In the testimony this morning, basically the indication, I gather, is that performance contracting and voucher theories are not the proper province of OEO because they are designed to cure poverty and this is not their particular area. Now let me ask you, Mr. McFarland, do you think that the lack of school education is a root cause of poverty?

Mr. McFarland. Yes, I would agree with that.

Mr. Mazzoli. Is not the OEO's purpose and function to innovate, experiment, and perhaps engage in plans and programs which are designed to cure poverty?

Mr. McFarland. Yes. . . .

Mr. Mazzoli. Let me ask the following. Why should not, then, OEO get into education, if, in fact, you have stated that lack of education is a part of the root causes of poverty?

Mr. McFarland. We do not believe that the voucher system's intent or expressed purpose would achieve this at all.

Mr. Selden. Let me respond specifically. On the question of whether OEO should be in the business of educational experimentation at all, I don't think they should, because there is another branch of the Government which has that as its responsibility. So, you have OEO coming in with a program which, if it were to be carried on at all—we don't like the program in the first place— should not overlap in its intent and function the Office of Education.

We believe in strengthening the Office of Education, not diluting its function by parceling out educational projects among other governmental agencies.

Mr. McFarland. May I add something here? Really there is no voucher plan. You have the Jencks study at Harvard, you have the Friedman plan, and three or four others. It is our understanding that OEO has let several planning grants to several school systems to determine the feasibility of the voucher plan.

Mr. Mazzoli. Let me add this point. Am I correct in saying that you are as much or more opposed to voucher plans and performance contracting on the basis that they intrude upon what you believe to be the province of the

Office of Education than the fact that they are quackery, as they have been characterized today?

Mr. McFarland. I would modify that slightly to say that there are many possible insidious outgrowths of the voucher plan that would be harmful to the public school system. In travels around the country and in speaking to school people who have been involved in meetings handled by OEO on education turnkey, it's evident that they were left with the impression that Federal funds would be available for the education of the children. In other words, they were led to believe that Federal research money from OEO would be available to educate the children who would be coming into the school system in addition to local and State funds. Now, I don't think this is true. I don't think this is possible.

We are raising the whole question here of whether or not, by an experimental program, an agency of the Federal Government is going to completely change the public school system. I think this is such a major question that it should be considered by itself, by this authorizing committee.

Mr. Mazzoli. Now I want to summarize, because we have other members and the Chair has been very kind to me, but I think we can summarize by saying that your objection to these two plans is much more on the basis of the theory or psychology or philosophy of this type of education than the fact that the powers and authority of Congress are eroded by the executive branch of government?

Mr. McFarland. Both, and I would make a slight distinction. My distinction is in reference to performance contracting. This is being done presently by the Office of Education.

The Chairman. Mr. Steiger?

Mr. Steiger. Thank you, Mr. Chairman.

Is Christopher Jencks a quack?

Mr. Selden. I used the term "quackery." Christopher Jencks has a lot of very strong opinions I think are nonsense. It is possible that he also has some opinions that I think are very good.

Mr. Steiger. Is Dean Sizer of Harvard a quack?

Mr. Selden. Harvard did have a conference last fall. I participated in it. There were a number of people who did. You ought to get the results of that symposium. All the various proponents of the plan were there. I think you will find that those present were quite strongly—maybe 2 to 1 is a fair estimate—opposed to the voucher scheme.

Mr. Steiger. Apparently the point that Mr. McFarland has made is that there is not yet a voucher plan. Is that correct, Stan?

Mr. McFarland. Yes. We have met several times with the OEO people, including Mr. Rumsfeld when he was Director of OEO. They made it very clear that there is not a voucher plan per se. It is a very nebulous thing. When we ask specific questions about what is the intention of OEO and so forth, the response is that OEO is not promoting a voucher plan per se. They are promoting the concept. As I have indicated——

Mr. Steiger. It is very difficult for me to fully comprehend how the National Education Association can arrive at the point where it is asking Congress to prevent OEO from going ahead with something. What are you attacking, if it is not there yet, if it has not been tried yet? You are apparently saying that no matter what it is, or what form it is in, you don't want it.

Mr. McFarland. I am saying, because of the thrust of what we understand from OEO——

Mr. Steiger. But you are attacking something that has not even been put in a city, aren't you?

Mr. McFarland. Well, we are attacking the concept, Mr. Steiger, because we feel that it is not going to be good for the public schools.

Mr. Steiger. But you don't know that now, do you? On what basis? What proof do you have? What kind of statistics? What kind of information can you give the committee that indicates——

Mr. McFarland. I would like to turn this around and ask the question the other way. What proof does OEO have that the voucher plan might work? As I indicated earlier, the basic premise of the experimental program was not to improve education per se but to determine whether or not parents of the poor could make adequate decisions concerning where their children should go to school.

Mr. Steiger. In the hope that they might receive better education than they are receiving now. I trust the chairman will allow OEO to come here to explain the voucher plan, which at this point he has not been able to do. You are here in an advocacy position telling the Congress that it does not make any difference what it is, you don't like it, period. You don't want OEO to be able, under the law, to undertake this experiment, if I understand your statement correctly.

Mr. McFarland. Mr. Steiger, if you will refer to the latter part of the statement, we are asking this committee or the Congress to take a very hard look at this before the experimentation continues.

Mr. Steiger. I see. You want to prejudge the experiment? Your posture is one of saying that you don't want to see the results of the experiment. You just don't want the experiment to go on?

Mr. McFarland. We are suggesting that OEO should present their experiment to this committee for their consideration.

Mr. Steiger. But you are asking us not to judge it; you are asking us to cut it off.

Mr. McFarland. That is right. We are expressing our concerns. That is our input to you. I am sure OEO will come in when they have an opportunity to testify and take the other position.

Mr. Steiger. I am trying to find out why you want us to cut it off. Frankly, you have not answered that.

Mr. McFarland. To me, basically the voucher plan is an alternate way of financing nonpublic schools. The funding situation at the local and State level is critical. Federal support of public education has proportionately decreased in the last several years. For the life of me, I do not understand how a public school district can split up the pie, the present financial pie, to educate these additional children on the basis of an experiment designed to determine whether or not poor parents can make an adequate judgment as to where their children should go to school.

The Chairman. Why don't we give it to the poor in the area of preschool where we don't get in a religious controversy? That is where we should be giving these funds in preschool. Instead of getting something out here and getting a controversy started, where to say the least there is no proof of success anywhere along the line.

Mr. Steiger. Let me return to what I began to say before the chairman made this comment.

On page 3, you say:

There is a hidden agenda of voucher planners. One is to destroy OEO by costing it its friends, such as NEA and other groups here today, and then secondly to create a market for the invasion of profitmaking agents who, by their own admission, seek to invade the social service area not only of education, but also of health.

Would you expand on that? What are you talking about? . . .

Mr. McFarland. We have serious questions about its relationship to the elected school boards. The Jencks plan, for example, talks about setting up a voucher agency that would train and give information to parents to assist them in making adequate decisions as to what schools their children should attend. It is unclear in any proposal as to really what the relationship would be between these ad hoc groups and the elected representatives, the school boards in this case.

Mr. Steiger. Let me go back to the point I have tried to make. No one can argue with raising questions, but the questions you raise, it seems to me, none of us can answer now, rightly or wrongly.

Mr. McFarland. We have raised them with OEO and we have not been able to get any satisfactory answers. I was hoping you might be able to get some answers by raising the questions here. . . .

Mr. Steiger. Could either of you comment on one suggestion which has been raised about vouchers, that is, de facto residential segregation is an important problem with which we have to come to grips, and one of the underlying concepts of voucherism is to make possible the transferability of pupils between schools; is that a better idea, let us say, than busing as it is now done?

Mr. Selden. I personally feel that our school systems, our school districts as set up, are probably unconstitutional because they do foster racial segregation. But I want to point out that we have a great deal of experience with voluntary busing. I am not criticizing what is being done in the South. We are supportive of this and think it should be extended to northern cities.

But in the early days of integration, after the 1954 Supreme Court decision, there were many northern school systems that put voluntary open enrollment plans into effect. That is, children would be bused free of charge out of their slum ghetto environments and allowed to attend schools on a space-available basis in the middle-class areas of the school district involved. Almost none of those open-enrollment programs are still in operation.

In the first place, there wasn't space available for many of the children who wanted to transfer out, and I think you will find that there wouldn't be spaces available in the suburbs, either, for slum children that have vouchers in their hands.

The other reason is, that the busing was all one way and it was not compulsory. It was a great deal of effort for young children to ride that bus a long distance to another school. It was an effort for the parents of the child to confer with the teachers about how the child was doing. The open enrollment plans have failed.

Mr. McFarland. Mr. Steiger, I am glad you raised that question, because that is one of our questions. This could work in reverse. In other words, the voucher plan would not assist in integration. . . .

Mr. Steiger. I might just say, Mr. Chairman, that I have listened today and have read the testimony in an effort to better understand this strange kind of opposition that exists to that experimentation being undertaken by OEO. I make no bones about whether a good result or bad result will come from the concept or the specific plan for vouchers or performance contracting.

None of us know that. You don't know and we don't know it. To raise question is fine, but I simply say to you in all honesty that to come out, as you have done, in opposition to even undertaking it leaves me absolutely cold.

Mr. Mazzoli. I must say, Mr. Chairman, that I have to agree with him. That was my major problem this morning, the very fact that such clear lines of total opposition were drawn by the two gentlemen without really having any knowledge on their part as to whether or not these two plans will work.

Likewise, OEO has no experimental results to show whether the plans will work. They are simply proposing this, and we are trying to find out should they continue in their experimental efforts.

I share the gentleman from Wisconsin's concern and puzzlement over the fact that there is fairly such strong opposition without having the things followed through. . . .

The Chairman. Mr. Hawkins.

Mr. Hawkins. Mr. Chairman, I disagree with the gentleman. It seems to me that the witnesses are really not opposing experimentation, but they are really opposing experimentation with the poor. It seems to me that this is the worst possible abuse of money. If you are going to experiment, don't take it away from the poor people. . . .

Mr. Mazzoli. I believe the gentleman said one of their main objections to this was that the programs would remain in OEO, interestingly enough. If it is going to be done, they want to shift it to the Office of Education and not stay in OEO.

Mr. Selden. You are misrepresenting my position on this.

Mr. Mazzoli. I thought one of the main objections here was the fact that experimental education programs should be done under OE and not OEO.

Mr. McFarland. Conducted in the regular public school systems, K through 12.

Mr. Selden. In the first place, I am opposed, my organization is opposed to vouchers and performance contracting as a matter of principle. We don't want them transferred any place except out.

Just a minute! I have a right—maybe I don't have any right here, I don't know—anyway, we think that OEO got into the education business by the back door and is promoting educational experiments which really, if they were to be done at all, ought to be done through the regular educational arm of the Government, the Office of Education.

But we do have specific objections to both of these proposals and we think that this is what happens when you have people who really don't understand anything about education coming along and putting some money into it.

Mr. Mazzoli. In other words, if the money is going to be used, OEO should not use it; it should be done by the Office of Education?

Mr. Selden. I feel that clarifies my statement.

Mr. Mazzoli. I yield back to Mr. Hawkins.

Mr. Hawkins. I don't think that there is anything new to this idea of the private system operating schools. It preceded the public school system, itself. It was largely confined to the elite. There is nothing strange about companies operating programs of this nature. I would doubt so some extent whether experimentation is needed, but I am willing to stipulate that if we are going to have experimentation, then, give somebody else the money to play around with and don't take it out of the mouths of the poor.

The Chairman. Thank you very much, gentlemen. I think it is very appropriate that these questions be raised at this time. It will be most helpful in the consideration of the various programs and evaluating the various programs by the committee, that these questions be raised so that we can consider them fairly.

PRO VOUCHER SENATE TESTIMONY (Excerpted)

U.S. SENATE
SELECT COMMITTEE ON
EQUAL EDUCATIONAL OPPORTUNITY
Washington, D.C.
December 2, 1971

There is a strong feeling among a lot of public school people that the profit motive is a bad motive and that schools run for profit will be bad schools, and that a voucher system will produce a lot of Pappy Parker's Fried Children.

STATEMENT OF DR. CHRISTOPHER JENCKS

Dr. Jencks. I am Christopher Jencks, Associate Professor of Education and former President of the Center for the Study of Public Policy, a nonprofit educational research corporation located in Cambridge, Mass.

In December of 1969 the Center received a grant from the Office of Economic Opportunity to study the feasibility of using vouchers or grants to parents to finance elementary education. I would like today to summarize briefly for your committee the results of our study.

Basis of Voucher Plans

The basic idea behind all so-called voucher plans is that parents should have more choice about the schools their children attend. Advocates of voucher systems propose that instead of appropriating money directly to schools and then assigning students to these schools, the government should give money directly to parents. Parents would then use the money to pay for the cost of educating their children at the school of their choice.

Beyond this simple idea, however, there is no consensus among voucher advocates. There are dozens of different voucher proposals, and they have very little in common. Anyone who studies the different plans with care will find that they would have drastically different effects. Some, for example would increase racial segregation in the schools, while others would decrease it.

Some would keep parochial schools alive financially, while others would probably kill them. Some would encourage educational innovation, while others would help perpetuate traditional arrangements. This makes it silly either to favor or to oppose vouchers in general. One must favor or oppose a particular voucher plan. The merits of a plan depend on the details, not on the general slogan.

Vouchers To Maintain Segregation

There are three general kinds of voucher plans. The first variety is designed to maintain racial segregation by giving parents money to send their children to segregated private schools. This is the kind of voucher plan that was developed in the South during the 1950's.

Voucher plans of this kind have repeatedly been declared unconstitutional by the Supreme Court and by lower Federal courts. I can see no reason to anticipate any change in the Court's attitude on this matter, even in light of its changing composition. Nor do I know of any serious effort to launch such a voucher program at the present time.

Senator Mondale. Were those State-supported systems, the school systems in the South which would give a per capita grant to a student which could be applied to a private segregated academy?

Dr. Jencks. That is the basic idea. There are five States that adopted proposals of that kind and in all cases they were thrown out by the courts. The most recent Supreme Court decision on this made it clear that they would throw out any other program of this kind which didn't have some kind of safeguards built in to preclude a segregated academy receiving public money.

At the present time, I don't know of any serious effort to launch a voucher effort of this type, the kind that support segregated academies. That isn't to say there aren't a lot of people that would like to; but, as far as I know, that is not a live issue in the South—nor, as far as I know, in the North.

Nonetheless, civil rights groups have repeatedly opposed experimentation with vouchers on the grounds that once the idea of a voucher system becomes respectable, segregationists will find a way to turn it to their own ends.

Vouchers for Parochial Schools

The second variety of voucher system is designed to support parochial schools. These are systems which have been introduced in a number of State legislatures in the South in the last couple of years. Voucher systems of this kind have never been reviewed by the Supreme Court. A good argument can be made for the view that vouchers which provide a completely free choice between religious and nonreligious schools do not violate the first amendment. Nonetheless, the Supreme Court's recent decision regarding aid to parochial schools suggests that the majority of the Court would probably reject this argument. Those who hope to keep the parochial schools alive by using vouchers are therefore likely to be disappointed.

Vouchers To Promote Innovation

The third variety of voucher system is designed not to maintain segregated schools or parochial schools but to promote educational innovation. The voucher system designed by the Center for the Study of Public Policy is of this type. This is also the system that has been under discussion between the Office of Economic Opportunity and public school systems around the country. It has very little in common with systems whose primary purpose is to maintain segregation or to maintain the parochial schools.

The reasons for the differences which I will outline in a moment have to do with the regulations that are imposed on schools that want to cash vouchers. Those regulations make it essentially impossible to maintain a segregated school and they are in many ways incompatible with the notions that the parochial schools have about how they would like to operate.

The Center has proposed an education voucher system for elementary education. The system would work in the following manner:

> 1. An Educational Voucher Agency (EVA) would be established to administer the vouchers. Its governing board might be elected or appointed but in either case it should be structured so as to represent

the community it served. The EVA might be an existing local board of education, or it might be an agency with a larger or small geographic jurisdiction if the voucher experiment were conducted in a part of a school district or if the voucher experiment were conducted in several school districts. The EVA would receive all Federal, State, and local education funds for which children in its area were eligible. It would pay this money to schools only in return for vouchers. In addition, it would pay parents for children's transportation costs to the school of their choice.

Per Capita Payments

The effect of this is that every school's budget is a function of the number of students that it enrolls in a straightforward way. An eligible school, regardless of its character, gets so much a child. This, incidentally, is one way to bring a State's educational finance scheme into conformity with the kinds of requirements that the *Serrano* decision sets up for financing. Every school gets the same budget both between districts and within districts on a per capita basis.

  2. The EVA would issue a voucher to every family in its district with children of elementary school age. The value of the basic voucher would initially equal the per-pupil expenditure of the public schools in the area. Schools which took children from families with below-average incomes would receive additional incentive payments. These "compensatory payments" might, for example, make the maximum payment for the poorest child worth double the basic voucher. In effect the vouchers of low-income children would be somewhat lower than the average public school expenditure now.

Senator Mondale. Have you worked out a figure—for example, in Massachusetts—of what the basic voucher need is?

Dr. Jencks. I haven't done it for Massachusetts, but in California in the districts that we have been working in, it varies quite dramatically from district to district, which, of course, is the basis for the *Serrano* decision. In San Francisco, if I recall, the numbers we came up with were around $1,200 a child; 60 miles away in Alum Rock, where we have been working, it was only $900 a child.

Senator Mondale. What would you add for compensatory payment?

Dr. Jencks. That is a matter which OEO has been negotiating with local districts, and therefore what I say is my opinion and not OEO's opinion, but in general they have been talking about a figure which would be half to a third of the basic voucher increment for compensatory funds for those people who are eligible. When we proposed this we had a notion of a sliding scale which could run up to double the value of the basic voucher for a child who was absolutely at rock bottom, but the average compensatory payment would be still something like one-third of the basic voucher. The sliding scale means that instead of being just in or out, you get an amount more or less proportional to your income.

Senator Mondale. Fine.

Requirements for Participating Schools

Dr. Jencks. Going on with my prepared statement.

3. Now to become an "approved voucher school," which means in order to cash the vouchers that you receive, a school has to meet a set of requirements, and these requirements are crucial to the voucher system we have developed, and make it quite different from the voucher systems that have been discussed in most State legislatures up to now. The requirements are as follows:

a. A school would have to accept each voucher as full payment for a child's education and charge no additional tuition. That means from the parents' point of view all schools in the system are free, just as public schools are now.

b. A school would have to accept any applicant so long as it had vacant places.

c. If it had more applicants than places, a school would have to fill at least half of its places by picking applicants randomly and fill the other half in such a way as not to discriminate against ethnic minorities. The net effect is that, for instance, a school with 25-percent black applicants will end up with 25-percent black students.

d. The school would have to accept some uniform standards established by the EVA regarding suspension and expulsion of students. That means you can't get around the requirement that you admit a cross section of the applicants by letting in students who aren't very smart and then throwing them out the morning after the applications procedure is over. Exactly what those procedures would be is a very difficult question. Our general rule has been that procedures for expulsion would have to be the same as those of the public schools, but the question as to just whom the public schools can expel and whom they can't is in itself very troublesome. I don't want to make any commitment on that, except all the schools in the system would have to have the same rules.

e. That participating schools must agree to make a wide variety of information about its facilities, teachers, program, and students available to the EVA and to the public.

f. Participating schools would have to maintain accounts of money received and disbursed in a form that would allow both parents and the EVA to determine where the money was going. Thus a school operated by the local school board of education—a "public" school—would have to show how much of the voucher money was actually spent in that school and how much was going to support the central administration or to a school down the street. Similarly if there were a school operated by a profitmaking corporation, it would have to show how much of its income was going to the stockholders and how much was actually being spent on education in the school where the vouchers were being cashed.

g. All schools in the system would have to meet existing State requirements for private schools regarding curriculum, staffing, and the like. Those vary enormously from State to State, so that the meaning of that requirement is quite important in New York State where there are many requirements for private schools, but is much less important in a State like California where there are virtually no requirements for private schools.

The basic assumption is that whatever rules a State has established as the minimum requirements under which a school meets the compulsory attendance laws would apply to the schools of this system.

4. The EVA could also set other requirements for schools wishing to cash vouchers. The aim of the voucher system is, however, to keep these requirements to a minimum. This is usually the case with respect to existing State requirements for private schools. If the EVA begins to establish elaborate rules regarding the structure of governing boards, the subjects taught, the qualifications of the teachers, and so forth, the net result could be to stifle innovation and narrow choice rather than to improve the situation.

5. Just as at present, the local board of education—which might or might not be the EVA—would be responsible for insuring that there were enough places in publicly managed schools to accommodate every elementary school-age child who did not want to attend a privately managed school. No child would have to go to a privately operated school. If a shortage of places developed for some reason, the board of education would have to open new schools or create more places in existing schools. Alternatively, it might find ways to encourage privately managed schools to expand, presumably by getting the EVA to raise the value of the voucher.

Enrollment Procedures in Voucher Schools

6. Every spring, each family would submit to the EVA the name of the school to which it wanted to send each of its elementary school-age children the following fall. Any child already enrolled in a voucher school would be guaranteed a place, as would any sibling of a child enrolled in a voucher school. So long as it had room, a voucher school would be required to admit all students who listed it as a first choice. If it had more applicants than places, a school could select among applicants for up to one-half of its places. It could not, however, select these applicants in such a way as to discriminate against racial minorities. It would then have to fill its remaining places by a lottery among the remaining applicants. All schools with unfilled places would report these to the EVA. All families whose children had not been admitted to their first-choice school would then choose an alternative school which still had vacancies. Vacancies would then be filled in the same manner as in the first round. This procedure would continue until every child had been admitted to a school.

7. Having enrolled their children in a school, parents would give their vouchers to the school. The school would send the vouchers to the EVA, and if the school met the requirements established by the EVA, it would receive a check for the value of the vouchers.

Fallacy of Public/Private Distinction

If established, a system of this kind would blur the traditional distinction between "public" and "private schools. In my view, this would probably be a good thing, since the traditional distinction is in some ways misleading.

Indeed, a lot of our thinking about the voucher system is based on an attempt to rethink the question of where the line between public and private should be drawn, and what it makes sense to think about as public schools or private schools.

Since the 19th century, we have classified schools and colleges as "public" if they were owned and operated by a governmental body. We go right on calling colleges "public," even when they charge tuition that many people cannot afford. We also call academically exclusive high schools "public," even if they have admissions requirements that only a handful of students can meet. We call neighborhood elementary schools "public," despite the fact that people from outside the neighborhood cannot attend them, and cannot move into the neighborhood unless they have a white skin and a down payment for a $30,000 home, or both. And we call whole school systems "public," even though they refuse to give anyone information about what they are doing, how well they are doing it, and whether children are getting the education their parents want. Conversely, we have always called schools "private" if they were owned and operated by private organizations. We have gone on calling these schools "private," even when, as sometimes happens, they are open to every applicant on a nondiscriminatory basis, charge no tuition, and make whatever information they have about themselves available to anyone who asks.

Definitions of this kind conceal as much as they reveal. They classify schools entirely in terms of who runs them, not how they are run. If we want to describe what is really going on in education, there is much to be said for reversing this emphasis. We would then call a school "public" if it were open to everyone on a nondiscriminatory basis, if it charged no tuition, and if it provided full information about itself to anyone interested. Conversely, we would call any school "private" if it excluded applicants in a discriminatory way, charged tuition, or withheld information about itself. Admittedly, the question of who governs a school cannot be ignored entirely when categorizing the school, but it seems considerably less important than the question of how the school is governed.

Regulatory System Principles

Adopting this revised vocabulary, the Center proposed a regulatory system with two underlying principles:

    1. No public money should be used to support "private" schools, in our sense of the word private.

2. Any group that operates a "public" school should be eligible for public subsidies.

What benefits might result from such a system of educational finance? I have spent several years sorting through the welter of claims made for vouchers. My main conclusion is most of the claims are silly.

There are two things which I think a voucher system should be expected to do.

1. New kinds of schools could be established, new kinds of people could be drawn into teaching, and new ideas could be tried out, with far less difficulty than under the existing system of educational finance. If a group of public school teachers wanted to do things differently, for example, and if the school administration were unwilling or unable to support their efforts, they could establish their own school—subject only to the requirement that they persuade some parents that their school made sense and that they enroll enough students to balance their books. This possibility has, of course, always existed for teachers who were willing and able to cater entirely to children whose parents could afford to pay tuition. But, under a voucher system, innovators could recruit students from all economic groups instead of just the children of the rich. While we expect that teachers would be the primary instigators of new schools, we also anticipate some schools sponsored by parents, community groups, business corporations, and perhaps even local public school systems.

2. This last possibility highlights the second potential benefit of a voucher system. A voucher system is not just a device for supporting innovative schools "outside" the public system. It is also a device for supporting new kinds of schools "inside" the public system.

Traditionally, public schools have had a very hard time developing unusual programs, because attendance at the neighborhood public school was virtually compulsory for everyone living in a neighborhood. Here I am talking about elementary schools. This meant that public schools could not do anything that would be really unpopular with large numbers of parents. Almost everything new falls into that category, so public schools have tended to avoid trouble by offering children mostly the same kind of schooling their parents had. This is inevitable in institutions which must serve a very diverse clientele on an involuntary basis. But there is no reason why public school systems should not be able to establish innovative and experimental programs on a voluntary basis for those who want them. If some people want a Montessorri school, and others do not, a public school system should be able to satisfy both groups by establishing both kinds of schools, instead of having to engage in a protracted squabble about whether to have only one or the other. The same thing applies to open classrooms and to many other potentially controversial programs. Once parents have a choice about where they send their children, the public schools can set up all kinds of alternatives on a take-it-or-leave-it basis.

Objections to Voucher System

There are some problems, nonetheless. One common objection to a voucher system of this kind is that many parents are too ignorant to make intelligent choices among schools. Giving parents a choice will, according to this argument, simply set in motion an educational equivalent of Gresham's Law, in which hucksterism and mediocre schooling will drive out high quality institutions. This argument seems especially plausible to those who envisage the entry of large numbers of profit-oriented firms into the educational marketplace. The argument is not, however, supported by much evidence. Existing private schools are sometimes mere diploma mills, but on the average their claims about themselves seem no more misleading, and the quality of the services they offer no lower, than in the public schools. And while some private schools are run by hucksters interested only in profit, this is the exception rather than the rule. There is no obvious reason to suppose that vouchers would change all this.

A second common objection to vouchers is that they would "destroy the public schools." Again, this seems far-fetched. If you look at the educational choices made by wealthy parents who can already afford whatever schooling they want for their children, you find that most still prefer their local public schools if these are at all adequate. Furthermore most of those who now leave the public system do so in order to attend high-cost, exclusive private schools.

While some wealthy parents would doubtless continue to patronize such schools, they would receive no subsidy under the proposed system, because—and this point should be emphasized—most of these private schools either spend far more money than the public schools or have an admission system which is in no sense nondiscriminatory. In our conversations, these schools show very little interest in participating in a voucher system that would require them to change. So a voucher system really is completely irrelevant as far as this tiny handful of exclusive private schools is concerned.

Nonetheless, if you call every school "public" that is ultimately responsible to a public board of education, then there is little doubt that a voucher system would result in some shrinkage of the "public" sector and some growth of the "private" sector. If, on the other hand, you confine the label "public" to schools which are equally open to everyone within commuting distance, you discover that the so-called public sector includes relatively few genuinely public schools. Instead, racially exclusive suburbs and economically exclusive neighborhoods serve to ration access to good "public" schools in precisely the same way that admissions committees and tuition charges ration access to good "private" schools.

If you begin to look at the distinction between public and private schooling in these terms, emphasizing accessibility rather than control, you are likely to conclude that a voucher system, far from destroying the public sector, would greatly expand it, since it would force large numbers of schools, public and private, to open their doors to outsiders if they wanted to get public funds.

A third objection to vouchers is that they would be available to children attending Catholic schools. This is not, of course, a necessary feature of a voucher system. The courts, a State legislature, or a local EVA could easily restrict participation to nonsectarian schools. Indeed, some State constitutions clearly require that this be done.

OEO in its negotiations with a number of States and school districts has indicated its willingness to go along with whatever arrangements with Catholic schools the State wanted to make. In some States the constitution is quite explicit that no State and local funds may go to Catholic schools. OEO has taken the position that the Federal Government would abide by the State law.

The Federal constitution may also require such a restriction, but neither the language of the first amendment nor the legal precedent is clear on this issue. Until the Supreme Court rules, this issue must be resolved on political grounds.

If I may make a small addendum, it is my personal conviction that Catholic schools should be allowed to participate in this kind of a system, but it is not an integral feature of the kind of program we have been discussing. Neither OEO nor the Center has any firm position on the matter.

Effect of Vouchers on Segregation

A fourth objection to vouchers—and I think this is the one which this committee and other people are probably the most concerned about—is that they would promote, or at least maintain, segregation. This fear may seem surprising in light of the rules described above. The rules insure that any student has the same chance as any other of attending any school in his district that appeals to his parents. No longer would blacks be forced to attend all-black schools simply because they lived in all-black neighborhoods. If blacks apply to good schools outside their neighborhoods, they must be admitted in exact proportion to the percentage that apply. On the other hand, the regulations do not force students to attend a school simply because some judge, legislator, or school administrator has decided that that is the right kind of school for the child. Blacks would not be required to apply to predominantly white schools. They would simply be guaranteed the right to attend them if they wanted to do so.

If you believe that blacks would not want to attend predominantly white schools, and if you also believe that they should be made to attend such schools whether they want to or not, then you should oppose this experiment. This is not a compulsory busing scheme, and it will not produce those results.

Some opponents of vouchers agree that a system with the regulations described above would not create more segregation and might in fact create less than the present system. But they fear that the regulations would be altered or ignored by State and local authorities. This is a reasonable fear. Certainly all our experience with Federal regulations suggests this is something to worry about. But we can see no more reason to suppose that a regulated voucher system would be perverted to racist ends than that the existing system of neighborhood public schools will be used for racist ends. If a local school board or EVA wants to maintain segregation, and if the Federal Government is not prepared to blow the whistle, segregation can be maintained without vouchers as easily as with them. If either the local school board or the Federal Government is committed to preventing discrimination, they can do so at least as easily in a regulated voucher system as in a traditional public school system.

My conclusion is that the issue with respect to segregation is a matter of political will, and if the will exists you can deal with the segregation problem with a voucher system or without a voucher system. If the will doesn't exist you are out of luck.

Demonstration Projects

Finally, I should say that I am not here to offer an endorsement of the voucher system I have described. I helped develop the proposal, but for that very reason I am acutely conscious of the many uncertainties involved. I would be appalled if Congress or a State legislature were to consider imposing a voucher system across the board. What I would like to see, and what OEO has been considering, is a limited number of demonstration projects in communities that are interested in trying out the idea. If such demonstrations take place, they will allow everyone to judge for themselves whether a voucher system is as good as its advocates claim, as bad as its critics claim, or simply another in the long series of proposals that turned out not to make any difference one way or the other. Without a demonstration, discussions of vouchers will continue to be mostly rhetoric.

Senator Mondale. Thank you very much, Dr. Jencks. What is the state of the OEO effort; how much money is involved; how many communities are experimenting with voucher systems; and, what magnitude of financial or community involvement is hoped for?

Dr. Jencks. Money committed so far has been a series of grants to the Center for the Study of Public Policy which have totaled about $0.5 million, first to develop the plan, then to get a lot of people involved who were interested in providing technical assistance to communities, advice to interested State legislators, and so on, plus a series of planning grants to specific school districts. There are presently three such planning grants, and there are several more under negotiation.

In addition there was a planning grant made to Gary, Ind., which conducted a preliminary study of the subject and then decided not to participate in a voucher demonstration project at this time. This was largely because the superintendent felt that the political situation in Gary was too delicate, and that there were too many other problems to take on something so controversial at this time.

The three planning grants which have gone a step further are in Alum Rock elementary school district, which is part of San Jose, in San Francisco, and in Seattle. OEO is now considering several other planning grant applications from other districts.

Those planning grants have a two stage process. The initial grant is usually for some sum between about $20,000 and $50,000 for a preliminary feasibility study in the district, and then more substantial sums, on the order of $100,000, to develop a full scale scheme for what the city might do if it wanted a voucher demonstration project.

I don't know the exact amount of money that has been committed overall by OEO but as a rough guess I would say it is between three quarters of a million and a million dollars over the last 2½ years.

If the thing goes forward—and it is not at the moment clear that any school district has met all the requirements for going forward, including the requirement that it wants to go forward—the order of magnitude of money would be a couple of million dollars a year of OEO money, plus anywhere from five to 10 times that amount from State and local funds already available in the district. That is, a couple of million dollars of OEO money would go to education, and probably another million dollars of OEO money would go for evaluation, research and technical assistance that goes with a demonstration project.

The total OEO commitment depends, of course, on the number of sites which are actually involved. If we are talking about, let's say, $2 or $3 million a year a site for two sites you get a number on the order of $5 million a year. If you get many more sites, which would be much more desirable in terms of learning something, the sum of money would be larger.

State Legislation

At the moment, however, there is no school district that is firmly committed to going ahead with the demonstration project. Now that is a long and complicated story. A demonstration project requires that a whole series of things be done. In most States it requires that there be enabling legislation passed by the State legislature. At this point, no State legislature has passed such legislation.

Senator Mondale. Has it been tried?

Dr. Jencks. The only State where there has been a serious effort to pass such legislation is California. The bill in California was defeated by a one-vote margin in the Senate Finance Committee. It was passed by the assembly and passed out by the Education Committee, and then defeated in the Finance Committee by one vote about 2 weeks ago. Presumably if the two districts that are interested in participating, Alum Rock and San Francisco, decide they do want to go forward, there will be another attempt to pass enabling legislation next year, but that is dead for this year in California.

No other State legislature has given serious consideration to the matter. There have been discussions with the legislative leaders in some States, and some of them have indicated that they thought such a piece of enabling legislation could be passed without great difficulty. Others have indicated they thought it would be difficult to pass.

There are a few States which have either existing legislation under which a voucher demonstration could be done or a provision by which the State Board of Education can waive the provisions of it being done.

So it is not the case that every State requires enabling legislation.

There is also at this point no school board which has firmly committed itself to going forward. All three boards that are actively involved in this, Seattle, San Francisco, and Alum Rock, have decided to take the next step at each point of choice, but they have not gone to the point of saying, "Yes, we want to do it."

Senator Mondale. Would a city the size of San Francisco have to agree to make it citywide?

Dr. Jencks. No; I should have clarified. The kind of demonstration we are discussing is a demonstration that would involve something on the order of 10,000 elementary schoolchildren. In a city the size of San Francisco this means that the San Francisco School Board would designate an area of the city as the target area for the voucher project. They could designate whatever area seemed to be appropriate and establish an EVA which was specific for that area of the city. The voucher experiment would just cover that part of the city.

Senator Mondale. Well, how would you avoid excluding the lower income groups of the area?

Dr. Jencks. I think OEO would require that, in order to be acceptable, a demonstration area would have to be mixed so that you would get many ethnically and racially mixed schools in it.

In the case of San Francisco I think this is not a problem. I don't think there is a chance in the world that Judge Wygal would approve such an experiment unless it had this characteristic. I am not sure he would approve the experiment no matter what characteristics it has, which is another complication in San Francisco.

Another problem arises in Seattle, which is engaged in rather complicated litigation with respect to racial balance in the public schools. All of our negotiations with Seattle are under the additional constraint that they will have to satisfy whatever court orders finally come down on the integration of the public schools.

OEO Funds

Senator Mondale. Take the existing per capita public contribution and then you add something from the Federal Government into the voucher—how much money would OEO be contributing to sort of sweeten the pot? About how much is sweet enough?

Dr. Jencks. Well, one of the problems with interesting local districts in this experiment, I would say, is that OEO has been very reluctant to engage in what, without prejudice, I would call bribery. The Federal contribution has been designed to meet all the additional costs of the experiment, which means some direct educational costs. That is, for instance, a city in which parochial schools were to participate, there would be public money going to support costs which had previously been borne entirely privately. Similarly they would pick up any other direct costs.

But the only additional money which would flow to the public school system is the extra payments for compensatory vouchers. Therefore, the magnitude of the compensatory payments that are attached to the vouchers of low-income children has become crucial with respect to how much money the local school district is actually going to get out of this.

I think it is fair to say, for better or worse, that OEO has not been very openhanded in its negotiations on this point. They have agreed to the principle and they believe in the principle, but they have not been conducting these negotiations in such a way as to make a school district want to participate simply because of the money they would get out of it. And I think this helps account for the fact that there isn't a long queue of applicants at OEO waiting to get on this gravy train.

My guess is that something on the order of $1 million in compensatory payments might flow to a local district, and if you spread that over 10,000 children, you are talking about something like $100 a child. The compensatory payments, of course, would be more than $100 a child. That is, compensatory payments might be $300 a child for a third of the students. But the net increment to the district prorated over the whole population would be on the order of 10 percent. In some districts it could be less than 10 percent, in some districts it would be more. But it is not enough to make a district go in for this.

Senator Mondale. OEO just pays for the additional cost—no dividends to the taxpayer?

Dr. Jencks. Right. And that is one of the things that OEO has always been committed to; they were absolutely committed to the principle this should not be used to substitute Federal money for local tax efforts.

Senator Mondale. But, it is not big enough for them to say, "Well, we are going to get a lot of new money to really give these poor children a chance." The $100 a head doesn't make enough difference.

Dr. Jencks. No, OEO has not been at all oriented that way. From the point of view of a demonstration project, you can say that is good because it means you are treating vouchers as an issue independent from extra money, or you can say it is bad because it makes the experiment suffer under the same financial constraints as public schools.

Senator Mondale. So it would be fair, at this point, to say no school district has committed itself solidly toward the project?

Dr. Jencks. I think that is correct.

Senator Mondale. Three of them are actively looking at it?

Dr. Jencks. Right. In addition, several are looking at it that have not at this point had OEO grants.

Senator Mondale. We have no experience with the voucher system in being—

Dr. Jencks. That is correct.

Senator Mondale. Of the kind that you have designed.

Examples of Voucher-Type Systems

Dr. Jencks. That is correct. We have no real experience with any sort of voucher system if the truth were told. We have brief experience with the systems that were set up in the South, but in every case that I know of they were liquidated by the courts within a year or so of the time they were set up.

Senator Mondale. There might be examples of impacted aid given to the voucher system.

Dr. Jencks. There are examples which I haven't discussed but which might be of some interest. There are a number of school districts in northern New England which do not maintain public high schools but instead provide payments to parents to send their children to either a neighboring high school or private academies, depending on the parents' choice. Those arrangements are essentially very ad hoc. That is, they exist under regulations which are developed by the local school board. They don't have any very elaborate theory behind them. They are simply an example of a poor district saying that children should go to high school, that we can't run a high school, so we pay out money for high school directly to parents.

Senator Mondale. You know, the Federal impact aid has done very significant things in some States with Indian reservations. We were working with the new Indian Education Act in my State which would get rid of that impact aid and set up a new category of independent student assistance. Some of the Indian educators said this is the worst thing you could do because, right now, there's $800 or $900 a head on these Indian students at or near reservations. Now that the impact aid money has risen that high, we find that all those public schools—that used to resent an Indian getting close—are often competing for these children. They go to see their parents, do everything they can to encourage the children—to make the children want to come there—and, for the first time, the Indians are wanted. Of course, it is the money riding on their head that helps a little there. I wonder if there aren't some sort of ad hoc voucher systems, of that kind, that might be looked at.

Dr. Jencks. There are a number, and we have actually been interested in the Indian situation for just that reason. And although I haven't done a detailed study of it, there is some interesting experience from Denmark where they set up a system of this kind. It is interesting particularly in light of the question of how many people will want to pull out of the local public schools. The Danish experience, as I understand it, has been that about 10 percent of the population did not want to attend the regular public school, but instead set up one or another kind of experimental school.

Now, of course, there are drastic differences between Denmark and the United States; there are no big ethnic, linguistic or religious minorities.

Educators' Attitudes About Vouchers

Senator Mondale. It is my impression that most of the professional education groups would like to see this whole idea dropped. If so, how do you evaluate their motivations and reasons?

Dr. Jencks. Well, there are several factors. First, I would say that I think your impression is accurate.

Next I would say that our experience in dealing with the professional groups has been rather as follows. The conversation tends to go "we are against vouchers, now can you tell us what they are." And the opposition has been linked to a series of ideas about the proposal which made people think they were against it because they thought the proposal was something other than what it was. However, many were against it even after they understood what it was about.

The initial response has been on two bases. First, when somebody says vouchers, some people think of segregated systems; and if they are against segregation they are against vouchers. Second, the NEA and the education groups in general have been opposed to any money going to the private sector. In their mind that basically means Catholic schools, and as you know, there have been resolutions passed at NEA meetings, and so forth, opposing any form of aid to private schools on any terms whatever, and asking for repeal of whatever aid there is. I think that kind of orientation has played a big part in their opposition.

Now beyond that I think there is a very strong feeling on the part of a lot of people in the education establishment that they have built up a set of working relationships with the existing public authorities and local school boards, and so forth, and that they therefore have some voice in how things go at the local level and at the State level.

They don't know what would happen if you were to have a system of this kind, and therefore it involves a big risk. In effect they would rather live with the devil they know that the devil they don't. That seems to me entirely understandable. But it is exactly the state of mind which makes it very difficult to do anything new.

The last thing, I suppose, is that there's a very strong feeling among a lot of people that this is a device for getting business into education and that that is a bad idea. There is a strong feeling among a lot of public school people that the profit motive is a bad motive and that schools run for profit will be bad schools, and that a voucher system will produce a lot of Pappy Parker's Fried Children. I don't think there is much basis for this kind of anxiety, because I don't think it will turn out that you can make very much money running schools. People who have run private schools for the rich have generally found that proprietary schools were not get-rich schemes. Very few of those schools are run on a profit-making basis.

The private corporations that have gone into performance contracting have found this is not as profitable or easy to do as they had imagined. And frankly, I think the whole argument that business is going to be able to run schools more efficiently than those "socialists" known as public educators is a lot of nonsense. I think it will turn out that the public school system, in terms of simply keeping costs down and operating within a tight budget, is run as efficiently as it would be on almost any basis. . . .

OEO EXPERIMENTS IN EDUCATION

THOMAS K. GLENNAN

Often quoted and misquoted by both advocates and critics of vouchers,
Thomas Glennan has often been the spokesman for the Office of Economic
Opportunity. The reader may wish to compare these remarks (circa November,
1970), with the April 1972 announcement of its Alum Rock experiment (see
Part III.).

Let me address the reasons why the Office of Economic Opportunity is involved in education and suggest why these activities are being carried out by
the Office of Economic Opportunity rather than by the Office of Education.
President Nixon, in his August 11, 1969 message on the reorganization of
OEO stated: "It is in the Office of Economic Opportunity that social pioneer-
ing should be a specialty. It is the OEO that should act as the 'R&D' arm for
the government's social programs." He went on to say: "It should be free to
take creative risks. It should set up a variety of demonstration projects, carefully test their effectiveness and systematically assess their results."

This is a broad charter indeed from the President; one which is extraordinarily
difficult to carry out. But, why has the Office of Economic Opportunity emphasized education? I suppose that no one would deny the need for reforms
and change in education. Even so, most of us would agree that taken as a
whole the educational system performs better today than it has at any time
in its past. More people have more skills and more knowledge than at any
time in our history. At the same time, however, there is more public dissatisfaction with the educational system today than there has been at any time in
its history in this country.

The nation's school system, public, private and parochial faces rising expectations on the part of many segments of the population concerning the performance of the schools. And, for no part of the population is this more true
than for the poor and the disadvantaged who see the nation's school system
as an essential contributor—perhaps the main contributor—to success of their
children and an essential means of equalizing opportunity. But, in many instances, it appears that the school system is failing to meet these expectations.

Reprinted from *Compact,* February 1971

In school system after school system we have found enormous numbers of poor children who are far behind the skill levels that we would judge to be appropriate and indicative of future competence in our society.

OEO Experiments with Contracts

What is the Office of Economic Opportunity doing? We are fielding a major experiment with performance contracting. The intent is to make information available to the nation's school system both on the performance of the contractors and on the administrative problems associated with performance contracting. It is not out intent to support a national program of performance contracting. Nor do we at this time advocate large scale adoption of performance contracting.

And with Vouchers

We are also exploring the possibility of mounting a demonstration or experiment with education vouchers. The basic idea of a voucher system is relatively simple. A local public agency issues a voucher to parents. The parents take the voucher to the school of their choice. The school returns the vouchers to the agency. The agency then sends the school a check equal to the value of the voucher. As a result, public subsidies for education go only to schools in which parents choose to enroll their children. Schools which cannot attract applicants presumably do not remain in business.

Advocates of a voucher program claim a number of potentially significant benefits. They suggest:

(1) Individuals would have a greater freedom within the public education system because they would not be required to accept standardized programs offered in assigned public schools. Middle income and poor parents will have the same freedom to choose schools that wealthy parents can exercise. (2) Parents would be able to assume a more significant role in shaping their child's education, thus renewing the family's role in education. (3) A range of choices in schools would become available. Small new schools of all types will come into operation—Montessorri, Summerhill, open classroom and traditional style schools. (4) School administrators and teachers could arrange their curriculum to appeal to a particular group or to reflect a particular group or to reflect a particular school of thought on educational methods. Schools could emphasize music, arts, science, discipline or basic skills. Parents not pleased with the emphasis of one school could choose another. (5) Resources could be more accurately channeled directly to a target group—the poor—

since funds would follow the child holding the voucher. (6) a form of accountability to parents would be introduced since parents would be free to withdraw their children if the school did not perform in accordance with their desires.

On the other hand, there are numberous problems that a voucher system is alleged to have. It is said that a voucher system will promote and encourage economic segregation within the school system because well-to-do parents will add money to the vouchers and thus be able to choose schools that charge additional fees. A second alleged shortcoming is that vouchers could lead to and be a vehicle for racial segregation within the schools. Indeed, where vouchers have been tried in the South, courts have found that they were unconstitutional because of this. A third major issue is the concern that the system would lead to the support of religiously sponsored education and therefore violate the prohibitions of the Constitution. A fourth concern is that the use of a more nearly free market in education would lead to false claims by providers of educational services that would mislead and misinform an unsophisticated public. In short, hucksterism would enter the educational market.

A fifth concern is that parents, particularly low income parents, may not be competent to choose sources of education for their children or, if competent, may not make the effort necessary to do so. On the part of the administrators within the public education system there is grave concern as to the feasibility of administering an education vouchers program. Critics have questioned whether alternative sources of education would be forthcoming, how they would be financed and whether their cost would be reasonable. Finally, there is considerable concern that a voucher system would jeopardize the existence of the entire public education system in the country and that the public schools would become schools of last resort.

These are very legitimate concerns. On the other hand, the suggested benefits are very attractive. A year ago OEO made the assessment that the attractions were significant enough to merit giving the proposal further examination. As a consequence, we commissioned a planning study that was intended to look at the desirability and feasibility of an educational voucher system and to consider possible designs for an experiment with such a system. To do this we gave a grant to the Center for the Study of Public Policy in Cambridge, which has been studying the program for nearly a year.

Perhaps the most significant conclusion we have reached is that a simple unregulated voucher system of the sort most frequently envisioned would be a disaster for the nation's school system. It would be likely to have most of the problems that critics of the voucher system have claimed.

On the other hand, the Center indicated that there was no need to view the educational marketplace as free of regulation. As a consequence, the major part of the report they submitted to us last spring delineated the features of regulation that would be required in this market to meet many of the problems. These regulations focus on three areas: The admissions policy of the voucher schools; the type and quality of data that must be provided by the schools; and the services for which public monies can be used.

Specifically these basic rules have been recommended by the Center:

(1) No school may discriminate against pupils or teachers on account of race or economic status, and all schools must demonstrate that the proportion of minority pupils enrolled is at least as large as the proportion of minority applicants.

(2) Schools must be open to all applicants. Where a school is over-applied, some portion of the students may be selected by any criteria the school wishes except race. Some schools may want to give preference to siblings of children already enrolled, to children of a particular neighborhood, to children with particular capabilities and interests, or to children of particular religious faith, etc. For the remaining positions the choice from among applicants should be on a fair and impartial basis. The Center suggested the choice might be made by lottery among the remaining applicants.

(3) The school must accept the voucher as payment in full for all educational services at the school. In other words, no school may require parents to make additional payments out of pocket. Schools may seek additional sources of funds from the government, from foundations, or from interested citizens and parents; but in no case can the admission of a child to a school be conditioned upon such contributions in the child's behalf.

(4) No school may use money to support religious instruction. Parochial schools may participate, however, providing they raise money for religious activity from other sources and keep separate accounting systems, and providing this support is consistent with the state constitution. Of course, they must also comply with all other rules including the requirement of open enrollment.

(5) All schools must make information available to parents concerning the school's basic philosophy of education, the number

of teachers, teacher qualifications, facilities, financial status and pupil progress. In short, schools must provide sufficient information to enable parents to make wise decisions when they select the schools.

These elements of regulation can be viewed as leading to a very significant change in one's point of view about the nature of the voucher system. In most people's minds the voucher system is considered to be, in part, a means of supporting private education. It might better be viewed as making education in private schools more public. In order to participate, private schools (as well as current public schools) would have to submit to regulation of their admissions policy, publication of their curricular objectives and capacities and regular audits of their books. In a real sense, they become "public" schools. The voucher system can be said to lead to a system of public schools that are open to the public and responsive to the public but not necessarily managed by the public.

The Center also strongly recommended that in a voucher system focused on the disadvantaged, compensatory payments must be given to schools enrolling disadvantaged youngsters. There are two reasons for this. One is to ensure that additional resources be focused on the disadvantaged child. The other is to provide an incentive to schools to enroll some proportion of disadvantaged youngsters. The Center also concluded that there is a need for excess capacity within community's school systems in order to ensure that free choice in fact exists for all students. If the capacity of the total school system, public and private, is just equal to the number of students, there will be a substantial proportion of students who get into only the schools of their last choice.

Many questions remain to be answered, questions that can only be answered by actual operations. Currently, we are working with a number of communities to examine the implications of initiating such an experiment.

The most obvious questions are: Will the education of the children be improved? Will the community consider that the type of education provided by such a system meets the public needs of public education? Is a regulated voucher system administratively feasible?

The final questions concern such things as: Can an admissions policy such as that outlined by the Center work? What is to be done about late comers, transferrers, dropouts, etc.? How can the job security of tenured teachers be protected? What kinds of changes and administrative procedures within the current public schools will be required to allow principals to respond to the interest of the community? What sorts of counseling should be provided to parents on educational alternatives and who should provide it? How will capital for the startup cost of new schools be provided?

The Voucher Experiment

To investigate these questions we are proposing an experiment at the elementary school level. We have chosen the elementary level for several reasons. This level covers a period that is crucial in the development of children's basic skills and learning motivation. It is a time at which the parents are particularly concerned with their children's education. In addition, since it is hoped that additional sources of education will be developed within a community, the elementary school level is desirable because it reduces the required capital necessary to start new schools.

The voucher plan would be administered by a locally selected Educational Voucher Authority (EVA). This would be a public body, which might be the current board of education augmented by members of the community and representatives of alternative sources of education. Alternatively, it might be a new board empowered to receive funds from the local school system and disburse them to the parents.

All students of appropriate age within the experiment area would be eligible to receive vouchers which could be used at schools meeting requirements established by the community. The Education Voucher Authority would pay particular attention to facilitating parents' choices of schools by providing information and counseling and technical assistance.

The experiment would continue for about five years to allow development of new schools. The educational results of such an activity would not be clearly apparent for three to five years. While the Office of Economic Opportunity is unable to commit funds for this length of time, it would do everything possible to insure continuity in the program.

A lengthy planning period, in addition to the planning already done, would precede the experiment to enable the establishment of political machinery reponsive to parents, development of administrative procedures, and modification of the existing public school system's operations to fit into the voucher plan.

It is expected that the experiment would be mounted in a large urban area with a fairly heterogeneous population. A variety of economic, social, and racial groups is necessary so that the effect of the voucher system upon integration of race and class can be tested.

The value of the voucher would be approximately equal to the total per-capita expenditures currently being made in the local public school system. It is not the intent of this agency to reduce the tax burden of the local taxpayer or to substitute federal funds for local and state funds. As a consequence, the Office of Economic Opportunity intends to provide for expenses of administration and evaluation of the project, expenses for additional transportation necessary to allow students a real choice of schools and expenses associated with the transition of the public school system to a voucher school system. The latter might include the maintenance of unused facilities or the fulfillment of obligations to teachers who would not be required if the system lost some portion of its students. OEO also would provide support for those students in nonpublic schools who are not currently being supported by state and local funds. In addition, the Agency would help support special compensatory programs if the community wishes to include them in their program.

We would like to initiate such an experiment in September, 1971. We will not do so unless both the school system and we are convinced that a successful experiment can be mounted. Because of the fact that state and local funds are required in this experiment, the approval of a large number of people is required before any program can move forward. Special enabling legislation would be required in virtually any state to permit such an experiment to take place. We will require the active and enthusiastic support of both the local superintendents of education and boards of education. The Economic Opportunity Act requires us to seek the approval of the governor and of the local community action agency.

The Office of Economic Opportunity is not advocating the voucher system. We are not advocating the widespread use of performance contracting. We find both of the ideas attractive but unproven. We think both of them merit examination and careful study. We have tried to subject both to wide public debate and scrutiny. The final test in both instances will be the experiment.

Dr. Glennan is director of the office of research and evaluation for the Office of Economic Opportunity. This article is based on a talk he made to the Council of Chief State School Officers in Miami in November, 1970.

VOUCHERS AND THE CITIZEN
SOME LEGAL QUESTIONS

WALTER MC CANN AND JUDITH AREEN

Sound educational planning should ultimately control the shape of educational change, whether it be voucher plans or something else, not quick acquiescence to supposed legal barriers which might be removed by appropriate legislation.

Displaying unusual humility for a member of the legal profession, Mr. Justice Jackson once warned the Supreme Court that it must avoid becoming the "super board of education for every school district in the nation."[1] Thoughtful lawyers and judges are justifiably reluctant to intervene in school matters, but they are continually called upon to deal with legal matters which inevitably influence the education of children. Probably no single event has had more impact on the shape of American education in the last fifteen years than the Supreme Court's decision in *Brown v. The Board of Education.*[2] There is little evidence that courts and lawyers, or professors for that matter, are overwhelmingly qualified to make educational policy. Yet they will continue to wind up in that position as long as educators, students, and parents ask, as they must, "what the law is" on particular issues.

This discussion of the "law" on education vouchers should be read, therefore, with some skepticism. The ability of lawyers to predict what the courts might do with such a radically new approach to public education is unavoidably limited. More importantly, educators must be wary lest important educational decisions needlessly become the captive of tentative legal predictions. Sound educational planning should ultimately control the shape of educational change, whether it be voucher plans or something else, not quick acquiescence to supposed legal barriers which might be removed by appropriate legislation.

Here we will focus on three of the legal issues most often raised in discussion of voucher systems: race, religion, and maintaining quality in schools. State constitutions and laws vary widely in their treatment of these issues, particularly of religion. Because exhaustive treatment is beyond the scope of this article, and probably the patience of its readers, most of the discussion,

Reprinted with the permission of the Authors, *Teachers College Record,* February, 1971.

therefore, will focus on federal standards and cases, although representative state laws will be discussed where appropriate.

Complicating the analysis are the many quite different programs which huddle under the rubric education vouchers. Furthermore, legal questions cannot easily be answered in the abstract. Is aid to religious schools constitutional? Are voucher systems legally permissible? Is racial balance required? Ask a lawyer these questions and the unsatisfying response is predictable: "It depends." It depends on the particular facts, plans, and programs under scrutiny. It depends on how things would work. We will try to reduce the tangle of dependency in our legal analysis by dealing generally with the regulated model proposed by the Center for the Study of Public Policy to the Office of Economic Opportunity, both because we are most familiar with that plan and because it embodies the education safeguards most consistent with the Constitution. We begin, then, with a brief outline of the proposed voucher plan.

Brief Description

The Center has proposed that vouchers or tuition grants be made available on a demonstration basis to parents of elementary school children. The vouchers would be roughly equal to the present per pupil expenditure level in the public schools, with suitable adjustments for rental and renovation costs over the duration of the experiment. Parents could use a voucher to pay the education costs of their child at the school of their choice as long as the school agreed to three conditions: 1. to charge parents no tuition in excess of the voucher level; 2. to admit students without regard to race and to allocate at least one half of the open places randomly among the applicants to the school (as long as there were fewer applicants than places, random allocation would be unnecessary); and 3. to provide to parents all information about the school requested by the local group running the voucher demonstration. In addition, the Center has recommended that compensatory funds be provided to supplement the vouchers of educationally disadvantaged students. This would provide funds for the additional costs of their education and an incentive to schools to admit these students.[3]

Many existing private schools presently charge tuition far in excess of the public school expenditures. They would undoubtedly find the limitation unacceptable. Under the proposed voucher system, they would probably continue to operate as they do now, without public funds. But a new market would be created. Some schools would undoubtedly believe that they could offer strong educational opportunities for the same cost as public schools, and with the required open admissions policy. The tuition limit might seem to dampen the possibilities for increasing the amount of resources available to schools, but it need not. First, schools are free to raise funds from sources other than tuition. Second, more families would have a stake in increasing public school funds (families with students now in parochial schools, for example). They would perhaps be less likely to oppose needed tax increases. Most important, the tuition limitation prevents public subvention of economically exclusive schools. Public funding of such schools could well usher in a system of education even more segregated by family income, not to mention race or class, than the present sorry situation.

The admissions restrictions also aim to preserve equality of access to voucher schools. Other approaches, quotas for one, might protect against invidious racial discrimination. Yet other, more subtle, forms of grouping could lead to the same undesirable results. Random admissions to at least half the places in an oversubscribed school protects against other less easily identified, yet equally destructive, practices, such as discrimination against slow learners. Note that the proposed random admissions requirement applies only to *applicants.*

Finally, the information requirement is critical. Parents must be well informed about available schools and their differences. Creation of more diverse school opportunities would otherwise serve little purpose. With that information, plus the economic power to choose among schools, the assumption is that parents will make wise decisions for their children. This assumption is not universally shared, but it is at least as believable as the assumption that inflexible geographic zoning is a wise and equitable way to dole out educational opportunities.

Vouchers and Racial Discrimination

Voucher critics have expressed genuine concern that financing education by payments to parents would lead to racial segregation in the schools. This charge must be faced squarely, even though it is disingenuous not to balance it against the reality of our already highly segregated schools. While some voucher systems (such as the Friedman unregulated model) might well lead to more racial segregation, a happy coincidence of education and legal policy appears to prevail in this area. Such systems seem as constitutionally suspect as they are educationally undesirable.

Six Southern states, at one time or another, have attempted to establish "tuition voucher programs." They were designed to avoid dismantling segregated "dual" public school systems by channeling public funds to segregated private schools. The more significant historical fact, however, is that all six efforts were held unconstitutional by the courts; there is every reason to predict the same fate for any similar attempts, either in the North or the South.[4]

First, past case decisions firmly hold that government may not avoid providing citizens with the equal protection of the laws by conducting essentially public functions behind an artificial veil of "private" sponsorship. Under this policy (known as the "state action doctrine") various "private" organizations have been held subject to the constitutional obligations usually imposed on the state by the equal protection clause of the Fourteenth Amendment: a political party which prevented blacks from voting in the party primary;[5] a restaurant located in a state building;[6] a community park;[7] and a hospital which received federal and state subsidies.[8] While few private schools have so far been held subject to the equal protection clause,[9] a "private" school which received public funds via vouchers would seem inexorably subject to that provision of the Fourteenth Amendment.

Once subject to the state action doctrine, a private school would be treated essentially like any public school with regard to racial discrimination. This leaves unresolved the difficult issues of legal differences between "accidental" (*de facto*) segregation and governmentally fostered (*de jure*) segregation.[10] But it strongly argues that whatever decisions affect public schools would also apply to private schools accepting voucher funds. Thus if a voucher school were found to discriminate unconstitutionally against the admission of minority students, it would be ordered to "desegregate" itself. Alternatively, the transfer of public funds to such a school might be enjoined.[11]

A third remedy might also be available in the case of a discriminatory voucher school.[12] The courts could look not only to the school itself, but to the local or state education agency which adopted the voucher plan. This approach was taken in the Southern voucher cases. Courts held that if the adoption of a voucher system had been motivated by a desire to further racial discrimination, the entire plan should be enjoined. This approach avoids dealing with private discrimination, for a court sees itself as testing the action of a governmental body (be it state or local). If that action furthers discrimination, the entire program can be voided.

What if a state does not intend to fund racially discriminatory schools under a voucher system, yet the system in fact supports some discriminatory schools? Would the entire program still be voided? While there is little case law which speaks to this point, two trends emerge. First, in testing the "purpose" of the governmental body which adopts a voucher plan, courts have tended to look at the actual or probable effect of the plan.[13] If either would aid discriminatory schools, then the courts are likely to find that was the intended purpose of the plan, and the entire program would be suspect.

But even if the courts did not find governmental purpose to aid discrimination, they might nonetheless enjoin any program which lacked sufficient safeguards against discrimination. Thus in *Griffin v. State Board of Education,*[14] a federal district court held unconstitutional a state legislated tuition voucher plan, despite arguments that grants to individual schools which discriminated could be stopped without enjoining the entire program. In the words of that court:

> The canvassing and policing of the tuition law to confine its enjoinment to instances [which do not further segregation] would be a Herculean task. It could hardly give full assurance against the abuse of the law. A law may of course survive despite its unacceptable consequences, if the valid portions may be independently enforced. Here, as we see, there can be no such separation and the entire law must go.[15]

The court's language could mean that no voucher plan will ever be acceptable because of the danger of aiding discriminatory schools. More reasonably, however, the decision places a heavy responsibility on any governmental body about to adopt a voucher plan. It must devise one in which the state itself polices discrimination to the satisfaction of the courts.

The Center proposal which includes both a random admissions process for at least half the places in participating schools and state enforcement machinery for detecting and eliminating invidious discrimination in voucher schools is one good approach to the problem. Even if racial discrimination by the state or by individual voucher schools is forbidden, however, a voucher school might, in fact, have a racially segregated student body if students of only one race applied to the school. A state or local agency could adopt a racial balance requirement to prevent this, of course, but such action may not be mandated by the Constitution. Genuine freedom-of-choice plans have not been found unconstitutional except in areas which previously had school systems segregated by law. In those jurisdictions the Court has held freedom-of-choice plans are unconstitutional if there are reasonably available other ways "promising speedier and more effective conversion to a unitary, nonracial school system."[16] In those jurisdictions, a voucher plan might not be held constitutional until the courts were satisfied that the dual school system had been abolished.

How big a segregationist "loophole" is the voucher system's reliance on parental choice? If minority parents are assured admission to any school (e.g., if a large portion of the places in any school are allocated randomly among applicants), those who desire integrated schools for their children can make that choice. Some, of course, will not. There will likely be some all-white or all-black schools, a not uncommon situation in the North and the South. Indeed, financial incentives combined with better quality programs, which should attract both black and white students to all schools, may do more than any of the attempts made so far in Northern cities to provide more students with an integrated experience. To suggest that parents might consider educational factors at least as important as racial ones strikes some as ingenuous. But it may be the most pragmatic basis on which to resolve the deepening racial schism in education. Certainly, past practice, where choice has been restricted to the financially favored, is a weak basis on which to judge.

Finally, an analysis of the relationship between voucher schools and the equal protection clause must also consider the extent of the protection provided. Judicial concern for equal educational opportunity has, until now, focused primarily on prohibiting racial discrimination. But other children may need protection too. The rationale of *Brown v. Board of Education*[17] could apply with equal, if not greater force, to poor children as to black children.[18] The extent to which courts will give the same careful attention to poor children, however, remains unclear. Present cases do not extend this far. Proponents of egalitarian voucher systems must, at least for the present, voluntarily build such protection into their plans. Otherwise, they may be disappointed when the courts do not come to the rescue of poor children, even though persuasive legal and educational arguments can be made for such action.

Religion and Vouchers

If misplaced identification of the voucher concept and aid to segregated schools fail to kill the proposed voucher plans before they are tried, then fallout from the ancient battle over aid to parochial schools could provide the coup de grâce. The temptation is strong to avoid this fight by excluding parochial schools entirely from the first voucher programs. Yet it is conceptually, politically, and perhaps even constitutionally difficult to justify their exclusion from a plan which is supposedly based on the policy of allowing parents more choice in the education of their children.

Unfortunately, while the law on racial discrimination is fairly clear, the constitutionality of aid to parochial schools is very much in flux. Two cases now before the Supreme Court may soon provide clues: *Lemon v. Kurtzman*,[19] in which a three-judge federal district court upheld the Pennsylvania "purchase-of-secular-services" plan of aid to nonpublic schools; and *DiCenso V. Robinson*,[20] in which a three-judge federal court struck down the Rhode Island purchase-of-services plan. If the Court were sweepingly to hold purchase-of-services plans unconstitutional, parochial schools might also be legally excluded from the voucher plan. But since it is likely to rule narrowly, even a decision against purchase-of-services plans will probably not resolve the issue of parochial school participation in a voucher plan.

Traditional case law in the area, unfortunately, leaves much room for speculation. Only two important Supreme Court cases deal directly with aid to parochial schools. In *Everson v. Board of Education,*[21] the Court upheld public payment of the costs of transporting students to parochial as well as to other nonpublic schools. In *Board of Education of Central District No. 1. v. Allen,*[22] the Court similarly upheld the loan of textbooks. *Walz v. Tax Commission,*[23] the most recent Supreme Court pronouncement on church-state issues, is also relevant. Although it dealt with tax exemptions for churches rather than school aid, it proclaimed new church-state guidelines.

In *Walz,* Chief Justice Burger noted, with a pragmatism that will delight some and anger others, that no perfect or absolute separation of church and state is really possible; the very existence of the First Amendment is an involvement of sorts—one which seeks to mark boundaries which avoid excessive entanglement. In past decisions, including the *Allen* textbook case, the First Amendment was interpreted to require that an aid program have: 1. a secular legislative purpose and 2. an effect which neither advances nor inhibits religion. In *Walz,* by contrast, the Supreme Court held that:

> Each value judgment under the Religion Clauses must . . . turn on whether particular acts in question are intended to establish or interfere with religious beliefs and practice or have the effect of doing so.[24]

This modified test seems to narrow the range of activities prohibited by the establishment clause. Legislation which "advances" religion is no longer necessarily barred unless it actually helps to "establish" it. Such aids as busing or loaning textbooks are permissible, in the opinion of the Court, for any activity which "realistically" establishes religion can be stopped "while this Court sits."[25] The *Walz* decision seems to make more constitutionally palatable a voucher program directed at improving the quality of secular education in private as well as public schools.

Walz also placed new importance on the need to avoid excessive entanglement of the state in the affairs of the church. Tax exemptions were upheld in *Walz* in part because they involved less entanglement than would taxing churches. But what constitutes excessive entanglement, as one would suspect, was not clarified. According to the Court, the "test is inescapably one of degree." "The questions are whether the involvement is excessive, and whether it is a continuing one calling for official and continuing surveillance leading to an impermissible degree of entanglement."[26]

The traditional approach to aid to parochial schools has attempted to separate the "secular" from the "sectarian." In the *Everson* busing decision, this was relatively easy for no one seriously charged that bus rides were so inherently "permeated" with religiosity that religion was being directly aided. Indirect aid is apparently acceptable if the direct impact is permissible. Otherwise, one faces the problem that any government service or tax reduction frees private funds which might or might not be devoted to religious activity. Thus if providing bus rides to *all* children is itself an acceptable governmental objective, the "savings" from general busing which accrue to parochial schools (or parents) are also acceptable. It is presumably something like a 5 percent tax reduction for all taxpayers, which might eventually result in a greater contribution to religious activities in the form of personal gifts or bequests.

In *Allen,* permeation was more of a problem, for textbooks are not as obviously secular as are bus rides. But the case had come to the Court on a very meager record. On a limited factual basis, the Court found that the books involved were "secular" and upheld the aid.

Many states have recently passed purchase-of-secular-services legislation. This proliferation of aid to religious schools is based on the notion that the state can purchase secular educational services for its children from religious schools. Sponsors argue that the approach is a reasonable extension of the secular-sectarian line drawing embodied in the *Allen* decision.

Whether their argument is right should be decided soon. The *Lemon* and *DiCenso* cases previously mentioned, which both involve such legislation, are now before the Supreme Court. The Pennsylvania plan, tested in *Lemon,* typifies the purchase-of-services approach. It empowers the State Superintendent of Public Instruction to contract for the purchase of "secular educational services" from nonpublic schools in the state. Secular education services are limited by the act to courses in mathematics, modern foreign languages, physical science, and physical education.[27] The decisions implicit in drawing this list are interesting to contemplate, i.e., Latin is out, but so is Greek. Perhaps the Greeks were considered too religious for the educators of Pennsylvania?

In a voucher system the secular-sectarian approach would mean that vouchers cashed by parochial schools would be limited to strictly secular activities. A less onerous approach might require the participating schools to split the school day explicitly between secular and religious activities. This would presumably decrease the state's burden of policing expenditures.

But whatever one concludes as to the educational wisdom of a plan which skews the curriculum of nonpublic schools by limiting aid to courses which are considered religiously "safe," its constitutionality is in doubt for two reasons.

First, the attempt to police such a line may necessarily entangle the state excessively in the affairs of the church in violation of the *Walz* standard. This appears to be the conclusion reached by the three-judge federal district courts which held unconstitutional both the Rhode Island and the Connecticut purchase-of-services laws.[28] There is, however, an even more serious problem with this type of secular-sectarian distinction. Even if successful, it may not sufficiently protect against the establishment of religion forbidden by the First Amendment. Assume for a moment that religious schools did in some satisfactory way separate secular and sectarian activities for the purpose of spending public funds. Suppose the state were to provide schools of one denomination with many times the funds provided to those of another denomination. Even if those funds were only available for expenditure on secular educational activities, most would agree that the state was helping to establish the religion of the favored schools by helping them to attract more students, and therefore, more potential converts.

This argument depends on assuming some correlation between the amount of resources available and the quality of education provided in a school. The truth of this assumption is not self-evident, particularly in light of the Coleman report.[29] A good teacher may be willing to teach for less money than a poor teacher; expensive equipment may not be as important as skilled instruction. But extreme differences in the amount of educational resources available will tend to create differences in the quality of education provided in different schools, if only because it will become more difficult to keep salaries competitive or equipment up-to-date as the relative differences between the resources of schools increase. While not as restrictive as a law requiring attendance at the schools of one particular denomination (or of any denomination as opposed to secular nonpublic schools for that matter) unequal state funding of schools looks suspiciously like unconstitutional establishment of religion. Relevant in this regard is *Sherbert v. Verner*.[30] The Supreme Court there held that withholding unemployment benefits from a Seventh-Day Adventist who refused to work on Saturday contrary to her religious belief unconstitutionally interfered with her religious rights. The Court said:

> The Governmental imposition of such a choice (between giving up unemployment benefits or violating her religious precepts) puts the same kind of burden upon the free exercise of religion as would a fine imposed against appellant for her Sunday worship.[31]

Similarly present purchase-of-services plans place the state in the position of favoring some nonpublic schools while discouraging attendance at others because the plans fail to relate funding to enrollment. In Pennsylvania, for example, statistics for the first year of the program reveal some schools received more than ten times as many funds for each child enrolled than other schools.[32] Such a disparity must violate the neutrality in religious matters mandated by the Constitution.

But what alternatives are there to the pitfalls of trying to separate the secular from the sectarian? Not surprisingly, we think that the voucher system is one alternative. There are two constitutional arguments for allowing parochial schools to participate in voucher programs. First, in a voucher system money is transferred to parents who are then permitted to transfer the funds to schools; this may mean that the funds are no longer subject to the constraints of the establishment clause. Alternatively, even if the religion clauses of the Constitution do apply to voucher funds, the state remains neutral if it provides roughly equivalent support to the education of a child whether or not the child attends a religious or nonreligious nonpublic school.

The first argument is appealing on its face and gains plausibility from such programs as the G. I. Bill. Under the bill thousands of veterans used government funds not only to attend church-related schools, but for seminary training at that—presumably because the G. I.'s rather than the state chose which school would be "aided."[33]

Other analogies have been proposed. Would it be unconstitutional to support the religious education of children with money provided to parents under family assistance plans or a negative income tax? Would anyone argue that the faithful parishioner violates the Constitution when Social Security payments find their way, at least in part, to the collection plate on the Sabbath? Probably not, for the choice is private and personal; the government is in no way involved in the allocation decision.

The difficulty with this reasoning is that the state is still involved to a certain extent in any voucher program. It requires, for example, that funds be expended only on schools—people cannot choose to use the vouchers entirely at their will. Indeed, the state may place other restrictions on which schools are eligible to cash vouchers, such as the restrictions on admissions embodied in the Center's proposal. With these strings riding with the vouchers, it is more difficult to argue that they somehow become entirely "private" once "given" to parents. Furthermore, in the area of racial discrimination, courts have not hesitated to overlook procedural distinctions in arguing that constitutional limitations apply even though funds are channeled through "private" hands in the form of vouchers. Perhaps racial equality is inherently subject to more stringent constitutional protection and scrutiny than religious rights, but the distinction may be hard to maintain.

The second argument, which might be termed the neutral funding argument, rests on the notion that the state expends no more to educate a given child in a religious nonpublic school than it would expend to educate the same child in a secular nonpublic school.

Isn't this the same argument parochial schools have been trying to make—with notable lack of success—for years? No. For one thing, it is not an argument that the state *must* fund nonpublic schools. Rather, it is an extension of the doctrine that the judiciary should overrule legislative judgments only when a constitutional principle is clearly violated. If a state legislature has decided that the value of funding *all* nonpublic schools to improve the quality of educational opportunity available to all children outweighs possible establishment dangers, that judgment should not be lightly overturned. This is especially true in light of the Supreme Court's apparent willingness to reject only those programs which "realistically" establish religion.

But what of the prayers and other religious activities that may go on in parochial schools which receive funds? Isn't this a clear violation of the cases outlawing prayers or Bible reading? No. Those cases all arose with regard to practices in the public schools, which children of many religions are forced to attend. In a voucher system as long as secular public (and perhaps secular nonpublic) schools are open to any child, then no child will be in a parochial school except at the choice of his parents. Indeed, past Supreme Court decisions restricting prayers in public schools rested in part on the fact that parents were still free to choose a religious education for their children. In the words of Mr. Justice Brennan:

> Attendance at the public schools has never been compulsory. Parents remain morally and constitutionally free to choose the academic environment in which they wish their children to be educated. In my judgment, the First Amendment forbids the State to inhibit that freedom of choice by diminishing the attractiveness of either alternative—either by restricting the liberty of the private schools to inculcate whatever values they wish, or by jeopardizing the freedom of the public schools from private or sectarian pressures.[34]

Absent public regulation or subsidy, poor families cannot exercise this theoretical freedom of choice. A voucher plan, in this sense, does nothing more than extend to all families the same opportunity to make a religious choice which was previously available only to the relatively affluent.

But even if it is constitutional to allow parents to send their children to publicly subsidized parochial schools, does it not violate the constitutional rights of other taxpayers to make them bear the cost of that subsidy? Two arguments suggest not. First, as long as the state spends no more to educate the child at the parochial school than it would to educate the child in a public school, the taxpayer is not shouldering an unconstitutional religious burden. Without public aid, most children in parochial schools will soon seek admittance to the public system, at perhaps even greater cost to the taxpayers. Secondly, even if aid to parochial schools nevertheless infringes in some way upon the religious rights of taxpayers, that infringement may be less than the infringement of freedom which no aid causes to families who are thereby kept from enrolling their children in parochial schools. The conflicting interests may require balancing, as in other difficult constitutional areas, such as free speech. The balance may well favor aid once an important secular purpose, such as raising the quality of secular education in all schools, is added to the scales.

In summary, the fate of participation by religious schools in voucher programs may be determined by the position adopted by the Supreme Court with regard to purchase-of-services legislation. There are several important ways, however, in which voucher plans appear more in keeping with the fundamental policies embodied in the religion clauses than do existing purchase-of-services laws. Therefore, the constitutionality of the parochial school participation in voucher plans will probably remain unresolved until a specific constitutional test of vouchers occurs. In the meantime, educational policy and state laws should guide decisions on this matter.[35]

Quality In Education

Critics of the voucher plan also charge that it may lower the quality of education. They claim the voucher plan would, on the one hand, allow fly-by-night schools to open and flourish. On the other hand, it would allegedly drain the most talented students from the public schools, leaving them only the most difficult children. While these complaints are not the most consistent charges ever raised, they point to two potential problem areas.

First, supporting nonpublic schools could lead to the exodus of the most talented, or the most wealthy, from the public system unless strong guarantees of open admissions are enforced in nonpublic as well as public schools. The restrictions on racial discrimination discussed earlier are important but incomplete safeguards. It is equally important to prevent nonpublic schools from arbitrarily denying entrance to poor students or to those with learning problems. Because the protections of the Fourteenth Amendment are unlikely to go far enough, administrative or statutory guarantees are necessary. The Center proposal that any school should allocate at least one half of its open places *randomly* among the students *who apply* to that school is one approach. Consideration should also be given to possible frustration of open admissions requirements that could arise if nonpublic schools could arbitrarily suspend or expel "undesirable" students. The Center proposal suggests that all students should be entitled to at least the same due process protections in suspension or expulsion proceedings that they are accorded in the public system. Appropriate legislation can accomplish these results. With genuine open admissions, public schools should not be at a disadvantage with regard to serving students of all needs and abilities.

The problem of maintaining quality in nonpublic schools remains. Financial hucksterism should be relatively easy to avoid. If nothing else, voucher funds might be issued at intervals during the year, thereby preventing a school from opening, collecting all of its funds, and disappearing into the night.

But what of educational hucksterism? First, whether or not public funds are provided, states have a clear right to regulate all nonpublic schools. As the Supreme Court explained in *Allen:*

> Since *Pierce* [*v. Society of Sisters*] , a substantial body of case law
> has confirmed the power of the States to insist that attendance
> at private schools, if it is to satisfy state compulsory-attendance
> laws, be at institutions which provide minimum hours of instruc-
> tion, employ teachers of specified training, and cover prescribed
> subjects of instruction. [These] cases were a sensible corollary
> of *Pierce v. Society of Sisters:* if the State must satisfy its interest
> in secular education through the instrument of private schools, it
> has a proper interest in the manner in which those schools perform
> their secular education function.[36]

In exercising this right to regulate all schools, public and nonpublic alike, many states demand certification of nonpublic school teachers. Others specifically define required courses, or various measures of equivalence between nonpublic and public school instruction.[37]

Indeed, the legal precedent for state control of nonpublic schools is so clear that the real danger is not lack of regulation but overzealous regulation. The end result could be to turn nonpublic schools into carbon copies of the most restricted public schools unless freedom for diversity and from unnecessary regulation is carefully protected.

Relevant legal precedent is again available. In *Pierce v. Society of Sisters,* a decision which might be viewed as the magna charta of nonpublic schools, the Supreme Court struck down an Oregon statute which would have required all children to attend public schools. It held that "the fundamental theory of liberty upon which all governments in this Union repose excludes any general power of the State to standardize its children by forcing them to accept instruction from public teachers." [38]

Similarly in *Meyer v. Nebraska,* the Court struck down a Nebraska statute which prohibited teaching any language but English to anyone who had not passed the eighth grade. It held that the statute violated the teacher's "right thus to teach and the right of parents to engage him so to instruct their children." [39] Finally, in *Farrington v. Tokushige,* [40] the Court struck down a Hawaii statute which both taxed and heavily regulated the Japanese foreign language schools. The Court found that the law deprived parents of a fair opportunity to procure for their children instruction which they thought important.

In a voucher system parents are the responsible arbiters of quality. While the state should certainly continue to be vigilant in denying funds to educationally dangerous schools, the real danger is that the state may instead become a vigilante driving out diversity in nonpublic schools. Overzealous effort to "protect children" and their parents from their mistakes could destroy what little diversity now exists.

In Conclusion

In this examination of some major legal aspects of a voucher plan, three characteristic relationships between legal and educational policies have emerged. With racial segregation, legal constraints and educational wisdom run parallel. In church-state matters, federal law remains unclear. State law is often restrictive and may hamper the free play of educational choice. In the regulation of quality, there is a wide variety of choices. Power to regulate is clear, and the critical issue is how state and local officials will use their considerable authority.

The law does erect firm barriers to some types of voucher plans. Plans aimed at furthering racial discrimination, for example, would be forbidden. But for the most part, courts have avoided educational policy-making, stepping in only in those instances, such as racial discrimination, where efforts at self-regulation have failed. This is as it should be, for the other side of imposing apparently desirable principles by judicial fiat as a loss of flexibility, of maneuverability in shaping the education of our children and ourselves. It also means that difficult issues of religion, of quality, and ultimately the way in which we finance education will not be resolved by judges, they remain for us to decide.

___

Walter McCann is chairman of the program in educational administration and associate professor of education, Harvard. Judith Areen, at the Center for the Study of Public Policy, Cambridge, was a member of the team that prepared the feasibility study on vouchers for the Office of Economic Opportunity.

1   *Illinois ex. rel. McCollum v. Board of Education,* 333 U.S. 203, 237 (1948) (concurring opinion).
2   *Brown v. Board of Education,* 347 U.S. 483 (1954).
3   For a more complete discussion of the plan, *see, Education Vouchers: A Report on Financing Education by Grants to Parents.* Prepared by the Center for the Study of Public Policy, Cambridge, Massachusetts, December, 1970.
4   *See, Coffey v. State Educational Finance Commission,* 296 F. Supp. 1389 (S.D. Miss. 1969); *Griffin v. State Board of Education,* 296 F. Supp. 1178 (E.D. Va. 1969); *Brown v. South Carolina State Board of Education,* 296 F. Supp. 199 (D.S. Car. 1968), *aff'd per curiam,* 393 U.S. 222; *Poindexter v. Louisiana Financial Assistance Commission,* 275 F. Supp. 833 (E.D. La. 1967), *aff'd per curiam,* 389 U.S. 571 (1968); *Lee v. Macon County Board of Education,* 267 F. Supp. 458 (M. D. Ala. 1967); *Hawkins v. North Carolina State Board of Education,* 11 Race Rel. L. Rep. 745 (W.D.N.C. 1966).
5   *Smith v. Allwright,* 321 U.S. 649 (1944).
6   *Burton v. Wilmington Parking Authority,* 365 U.S. 715 (1961).
7   *Evans v. Newton,* 382 U.S. 296 (1966). For a subsequent case holding that because the park could not be run on a segregated basis as requested in the donor's will, ownership must revert to other heirs, *see, Evans v. Abney,* 90 S. Ct. 628 (1970).
8   *Simkins v. Moses H. Cone Memorial Hospital,* 323 F. 2d 959 (4th Cir. 1963), *cert. denied,* 376 U.S. 938 (1964). *Accord, Cypress v. Newport New General and Nonsectarian Hospital Assoc.,* 392 F. 2d 89 (4th Cir. 1967).
9   For an important case holding Girard College subject to state action, *see, Pennsylvania v. Brown,* 270 F. Supp. 782 (E.D. Pa. 1967), *aff'd* 392 F. 2d 120 (3rd Cir. 1968), *cert. denied,* 391 U.S. 921. *Cf.* the holding of J. Skelly Wright: "At the outset, one may question whether any school or college can ever be so 'private' as to escape the reach of the Fourteenth Amendment. Institutions of learning are not things of purely private concern. . . . No one any longer doubts that education is a matter affected with the greatest public interest. And this is true whether it is offered by a public or private institution. Clearly the administrators of a private college are performing a public function. They do the work of the state, often in the place of the state. Does it not follow that they stand in the state's shoes? Reason and authority strongly suggest that the Constitution never sanctions racial discrimination in our schools and colleges, no matter how 'private' they may claim to be." *Guillory v. Administrators of Tulane University,* 203 F. Supp. 855, 858-59 (E. D. La. 1962), *opinion vacated on other grounds,* 207 F. Supp. 554, *aff'd,* 306 F. 2d 489 (5th Cir. 1962).
10 *De jure* segregation has been held unconstitutional by the courts; *de facto* segregation, by contrast, has generally not. *See, Offerman v. Nitkowski,* 378 F. 22 (2nd Cir. 1967); *Deal v. Cincinnati Board of Education,* 367 F. 2d 55 (6th Cir. 1966), *cert. denied,* 389 U.S. 847 (1967); *Springfield School Committee v. Barksdale,* 348 F. 2d 261 (1st Cir. 1965). *Contra, Blocker v. Board of Education,* 226 F. Supp. 208, 229 F. Supp. 709 (E.D.N.Y. 1964); *Branche v. Board of Education,* 204 F. Supp. 150 (E.D.N.Y. 1962). While there is little sign of this distinction changing, it is

becoming less important as courts appear more willing to label situations in the North and West as *de jure*. Recently, for example, *de jure* segregation has been found, and held unconstitutional, in Colorado, Illinois, California, and Michigan. *See, Bradley v. Milliken,* Civ. No. 20794 (6th Cir. 1970); *Davis v. School District of Pontiac,* Civ. No. 32392 (E.D. Mich, 1970); *Keynes v. School District No. 2,* 303 F. Supp. 280 (D. Colo. 1969); *United States v. School District 151 of Cook County, Illinois,* 301 F. Supp. 210 (N.D. Ill. 1969); *Crawford v. Board of Education of Los Angeles County,* Civ. No. 822854 (Cal. Sup. Ct. 1970).

11   The extent to which courts will go to prevent any aid going to discriminatory private schools is indicated by the recent rulling in *Green v. Kennedy,* 309 F. Supp. 1127 (D.D.C. 1970). There a three-judge court granted a preliminary injunction against tax benefits (which are tradi. ᵢnally sacrosanct) because they were going to segregated private Mississippi schools.

12   The term "voucher school" or "nonpublic school" is used throughout this article to call attention to the fact that the traditional labeling of schools as public or private is often misleading. The term "public" is applied to colleges even when they charge tuition many people cannot afford; or to academically exclusive high schools even when they have admission requirements few can meet; or to entire school systems even though they refuse to give out information about what they are doing or how well they are doing it. Conversely, the term "private" is applied to schools run by private organizations even when they are open to all applicants on a nondiscriminatory basis, charge no tuition, and willingly provide information about their operation. In other words, definitions have focused too much on *who* runs schools and not enough on *how* they are run.

13   *See, Gomillon v. Lightfoot,* 364 U.S. 339 (1960), in which the Supreme Court considered a law establishing municipal boundaries. On the surface, the law was unobjectionable. Nonetheless, the Court ruled that if the *effect* of the law was to deprive black citizens of the benefits of municipal residence, including the right to vote in municipal elections, then it was unconstitutional. For a more complete discussion of the role legislative motivation should play in constitutional adjudication, *see,* Ely, "Legislative and Administrative Motivation in Constitutional Law," *Yale Law Journal,* Vol. 79, 1970.

14   *Griffin v. State Board of Education,* 296 F. Supp. 1178 (E.D. Va. 1969).

15   *Ibid.*

16   *Green v. County School Board,* 391 U.S. 430. 441 (1968).

17   *Brown, op. cit.*

18   *See,* John E. Coons, William H. Clune III, and Stephen D. Sugarman, *Private Wealth and Public Education.* Cambridge: Harvard University Press, 1970; Kirp, "The Poor, the Schools and Equal Protection," *Harvard Educational Review,* 1968, Vol. 38, p. 635; Michelman, "Forward to the Supreme Court Term of 1969: On Protecting the Poor through the Fourteenth Amendment," *Harvard Law Review,* 1969, Vol. 83, p. 7. *Cf.* James Coleman, *et al., Equality of Educational Opportunity.* Washington, D.C.: U.S. Department of Health, Education and Welfare, 1966: "It appears that variations in the facilities and curricula of the schools account for relatively little variation in pupil achievement insofar as this is measured by standard tests. . . . A pupil's achievement is strongly related to the educational backgrounds and aspirations of the other students in the school."

19   *Lemon v. Kurtzman,* 310 F. Supp. 35 (E. D. Pa. 1969), *prob.juris.noted,* 90 S. Ct. 1354 (1970).

20   *DiCenso v. Robinson,* 316 F. Supp. (D.R.I. 1970), *prob.juris.noted,* 39 U.S.L.W. 3194, Nov. 10, 1970.

21   *Everson v. Board of Education of the Township of Ewing,* 330 U.S. 1 (1947). *See* also, *Quick Bear v. Leupp,* 210 U.S. 50 (1907), a case upholding public funding of parochial schools attended by Indians.

22   *Board of Education of Central District No. 1 v. Allen,* 392 U.S. 236 (1968).

23   *Walz v. Tax Commission of the City of New York,* 90 S. Ct. 1409 (1970).

24   *Ibid.*

25   *Ibid.*

26   *Ibid.*

27   Pa. Stat. Ann. Tit. 24, 5601-09 (1968).

28   *DiCenso v. Robinson, op. cit.; Johnson v. Sanders,* Civ. No. 13432 (D. Conn. Oct. 15, 1970).

29   *See,* Coleman, *op. cit.*

30   *Sherbert v. Verner,* 374 U.S. 398 (1963).

31   *Ibid.*

32   Pennsylvania Office of Aid to Nonpublic Schools, An Analysis of Significant Data (1969).

33   72 Stat. 1177 (1958), 38 U.S.C. 1620. Approximately 36,000 veterans used the G. I. Bill to pay for training as Protestant ministers.

34   *Abington School District v. Schempp,* 372 U.S. at 242 (concurring opinion).

35   For an example of more restrictive state provisions, *see,* New York Constitution, Art. 11, 3 (known as the Blaine Amendment): "Neither the state nor any sub-division thereof shall use its property or credit or any public money, or authorize or permit either to be used, directly or indirectly, in aid of maintenance, other than for examination or inspection, of any school or institution of learning wholly or in part under the control or direction of any religious denomination, or in which any denominational tenet or doctrine is taught, but the legislature may provide for the transportation of children to and from any school or institution of learning." But the textbook program upheld in *Allen* was also upheld against this provision of the New York State Constitution. For discussion of the theory that just as the free exercise clause may limit the application of the establishment clause, now that it had been applied to the states, so it may also limit state constitutional provisions which are more restrictive of free exercise rights, *see,* A. M. Bickel, *The Supreme Court and the Idea of Progress.* New York: Harper & Row, 1970; Drinan, *"Public Aid to Parochial Schools," 75 Case and Comment* 13 (1970). *Cf. Mulkey v. Reitman,* 387 U.S. 369 (1967).

36   *Board of Education of Central District No. 1 v. Allen, op. cit.*

37   For a detailed history of state regulatory statutes, *see,* Elson, "State Regulation of Non-public Schools: The Legal Framework" in Donald Erickson, *Public Controls for Non-Public Schools.* Chicago: University of Chicago Press, 1969.

38   *Pierce v. Society of Sisters,* 268 U.S. 510, 535 (1925).

39   *Meyer v. Nebraska,* 262 U.S. 390, 400 (1923).

40   *Farrington v. Tokushige,* 273 U.S. 284 (1927).

PART II

The Education Voucher Report

The Alum Rock experiment (discussed in Part III), as implemented during 1972-1973, is "transitional." That is, the Office of Economic Opportunity is hoping for a larger and more complex voucher plan during 1973-1974.

Education Vouchers, *a study conducted for OEO by the Center for the Study of Public Policy, of which Christopher Jencks was the director, serves as the Bible of the OEO effort with vouchers. Judith C. Areen has succeeded Christopher Jencks to become Director, Educational Voucher Project.* Education Vouchers *explains eleven models of voucher plans. The study advocates a "regulated compensatory model." But it gives qualified acceptance to other models, including the "Vouchers confined to public schools model." Alum Rock's 1972-1973 plan is an example of the "vouchers confined to public schools model." OEO hopes that the first year's experience will justify a transition to a "regulated compensatory model."*

In order to make this transition, legislation is needed in California, as explained in Appendix C of Education Vouchers. *Such legislation failed to reach the floor of the legislature during 1971-1972 but was reintroduced in 1972-1973. A recommended statute appeared as Appendix D of the study. A similar statute has been legislated in Connecticut. Enabling legislation is advanced in the states of Indiana, New York, Pennsylvania, Washington and Wisconsin. A number of other states are in the preliminary stages of education vouchers enabling legislation.*

Those sections of Education Vouchers *with direct impact on the Alum Rock experiment are reproduced here. Chapters 3 and 4, not reproduced here, and chapters 7, 8, and 9, explore more technical aspects of voucher plans: matching pupils to schools, serving children with special needs, and financial matters. The entire study is available from the Office of Economic Opportunity.*

1. AN OVERVIEW

The Case for Competition and Choice

Conservatives, liberals, and radicals have all complained at one time or another that the political mechanisms which supposedly make public schools accountable to their clients work clumsily and ineffectively. Parents who think their children are getting inferior schooling can, it is true, take their grievances to the local school board or state legislature. If legislators and school boards are unresponsive to the complaints of enough citizens, they may eventually be unseated, but it takes an enormous investment of time, energy, and money to mount an effective campaign to change local public schools. Dissatisfied though they may be, few parents have the political skill or commitment to solve their problems this way. As a result, effective control over the character of the public schools is largely vested in legislators, school boards, and educators, not parents.

If parents are to take responsibility for their children's education, they cannot rely exclusively on political processes to let them do so. They must also be able to take *individual* action in behalf of their own children.

At present, only relatively affluent parents retain any effective control over the education of their children. Only they are free to move to school districts with "good schools" (and high tax rates). Only they can afford non-sectarian private schooling. The average parent has no alternative to his local public school unless he happens to belong to one of the denominations that maintains low-tuition church schools. Only a few denominations do.

The system of education vouchers proposed in this report will, we believe, encourage the development of many new alternatives, open to *every* parent. This would make it possible for parents to translate their concern for their children's education into action. If they did not like the education their child was getting in one school (or if the child did not like it), he could go to another. By fostering both active parental interest and educational variety, a voucher system should improve all participating schools, both public and private.

Under the proposed voucher system, a publicly accountable agency would issue a voucher for a year's schooling for each eligible child. This voucher could be turned over to any school which had agreed to abide by the rules of the voucher system. Each school would turn in its vouchers for cash. Thus, parents would no longer be forced to send their children to the school around the corner simply because it was around the corner. If the school was attractive and desirable, it would not be seriously affected by the institution of a voucher plan. If not, attendance might fall, perhaps forcing the school to improve.

Even if no new schools were established under the voucher system, the responsiveness of existing schools would probably increase. But new schools will be established. Some parents will get together to create schools reflecting their special perspectives or their children's special needs. Educators with new ideas — or old ideas that are now out of fashion in the public schools — will also be able to set up their own schools. Entrepreneurs who think they can teach children better and cheaper than the public schools will also have an opportunity to do so.

None of this ensures that every child will get the education he needs, but it does make such a result more likely than at present.

All these arguments have, of course, been used over and over to justify the maintenance of free markets and competition in areas other than education. Why, then, have virtually all American communities allowed elementary and secondary education to remain a monopoly . . . ?

Monopoly situations are usually justified by one of three arguments:

- "Competition would be technologically inefficient in this field."

- "Consumers are not competent to distinguish between good and bad products in this field, so competition would lead only to more imaginative forms of fraud."

- "Competition in this field would encourage consumers to maximize their private advantages in ways that are inimical to the general welfare."

Let us examine the applicability of these three arguments to education.

The "technological" argument for educational monopoly may have had some relevance in the days when most Americans lived in sparsely settled rural areas. It was hard to get enough children together in one place to pay a single teacher's salary. Competition could (and sometimes did) prevent *any* school from being established. Today, however, most Americans live in densely populated areas, where it is perfectly feasible to maintain several competing schools within reasonable distance of any family. Logistical arguments against diversity, competition, and choice in education have therefore become irrelevant.

Proponents of public monopoly also talk a good deal about economies of scale, especially at the high school level. There is, however, no solid evidence that such economies are real. Big schools can provide certain resources (a physics lab, a Spanish teacher, a swimming pool, etc.) at less cost than small schools. But nobody knows whether these resources increase the likelihood that a school will turn out competent, civilized adults. Recent disorders in many big high schools suggest that massing large numbers of adolescents together in the same place may actually be dysfunctional. The possibility that competition might result in smaller schools need not, then, be viewed with alarm. It could be very healthy.

The "gullible consumer" argument for educational monopoly is only slightly more persuasive. There are instances (e.g. prescription drugs) where consumers really cannot judge the products offered them. Rather strict regulation seems appropriate in these areas. In order to justify governmental regulation, however, it is necessary to show that the government is harder to gull than the individual consumer. This is fairly easy to do in the case of drugs. The government presumably has access to scientific evidence about the effects of each drug, and this evidence is not readily available or comprehensible to laymen. Analogous arguments with respect to schooling seem more tenuous. The government can obtain "expert" opinions about the effects of any given school on various types of children, whereas the average parent cannot obtain such opinions. But there is no evidence that "experts" really know any more than parents about the likely effects of specific schools on specific children. There is no consensus about what causes what in education, much less any scientific evidence to back a consensus. This makes it hard to argue that the government should protect children from their parents' naivete by denying the parents choice about their children's schooling and imposing what the government's experts happen to think "best."

Even if we were to accept the argument that "experts know best," it would not follow that the best solution would be to make education a public monopoly. We do not, after all, have a public monopoly on the production or distribution of drugs, even though we assume that "doctors know best." Instead, we have a publicly regulated market, in which the patient is free to choose both a doctor and a druggist. It would be perfectly possible to establish a similarly regulated market in education. Indeed, such a market already exists—but only for the affluent. The state establishes certain basic rules about what a school has to do before opening its doors to the public. These rules cover physical safety, teacher qualifications, and the like. But in most respects affluents parents are free to send their children to any kind of school they want. It is hard to see why affluent parents should be judged competent to select their children's schools from a wide range of alternatives while poorer parents are given no options.

The final argument against competition and consumer sovereignty is that if parents are encouraged to make educational choices strictly in terms of private advantage, the cumulative result of these choices will be at odds with the general welfare. Unlike the two previous arguments, this one is in some ways persuasive. Creating a completely free market for schooling would almost certainly result in more segregation by race, income, and ability. It would also result in a redistribution of educational resources from disadvantaged to advantaged children. Taken together, these changes would probably leave students from low-income families further behind students from high income families than they are now. This increase in inequality would in turn tend to widen the gap and intensify conflict between racial groups, between economic groups, and between political interests.

But monopolistic control over educational choices is not the only way to avert these evils. Proponents of smog control, for example, argue that so long as the choice is left to individual consumers, not many auto purchasers will elect to pay for expensive exhaust systems whose benefits go largely to other people. But few proponents of smog control claim that the only alternative is to nationalize the automobile industry. Most simply urge legislation which forbids the sale of automobiles that pollute the air. Similarly, we can ensure integration and equitable resource allocation in education without having the state operate 90 per cent of the nation's schools. It would be perfectly possible to create a competitive market and then regulate it in such a way as to prevent segregation, ensure an equitable allocation of resources, and give every family a truly equal chance of getting what it wants from the system.

Criteria for Regulating the Educational Market

Those who want to give parents more voice in shaping their children's educational destinies can be found almost everywhere on the political and educational spectrum. Their objectives are almost as diverse as the objectives of education itself, and their proposals for breaking the present public monopoly therefore cover an extraordinary range of alternatives.

In recent years many advocates of competition and choice have united around a single slogan: "education vouchers." The idea of an education voucher is relatively simple. The government issues the voucher to parents. The parents take the voucher to the school of their choice. The school returns the vouchers to the government. The government then sends the school a check equal to the value of the vouchers. As a result, government subsidies for education go only to schools in which parents choose to enroll their children. Schools which cannot attract applicants go out of business.

Beyond this, however, differences of opinion begin. Who would be eligible for vouchers? How would their value be determined? Would parents be allowed to supplement the vouchers from their own funds? What requirements would schools have to meet before cashing vouchers? What arrangements would be made for the children whom no school wanted to educate? Would church schools be eligible? Would schools promoting unorthodox political views be eligible? Once the advocates of vouchers begin to answer such questions, it becomes clear that the catchphrase around which they have united stands not for a single panacea, but for a multitude of controversial programs, many of which have little in common.

These diverse voucher schemes can be viewed merely as different approaches to the regulation of the educational marketplace. Some schemes propose no regulation at all, counting on the "hidden hand" to ensure that the sum total of private choices promotes the public good. Others involve considerable economic regulation, aimed at offsetting differences in parental income and at providing schools with incentives to educate certain kinds of children. Still other schemes involve not only economic regulation, but administrative regulations aimed at ensuring that schools which receive public money do not discriminate against disadvantaged children. Finally, some schemes would establish extensive regulations to ensure that schools provided the public with usable information about what the school was trying to do and how well it was succeeding in doing it.

In order to deserve support from the Office of Economic Opportunity, a voucher plan should have two objectives:

- To improve the education of children, particularly disadvantaged children;

- To give parents, and particularly disadvantaged parents, more control over the kind of education their children get.

These two objectives are not identical. For the most part we will assume that they are compatible, but this will not be true in every instance.

These broad generalizations require some elaboration. First it is important to decide whether "improving the education of the disadvantaged" means improvement relative to the education offered advantaged children today. We believe that, at least in education, closing the gap between the advantaged and the disadvantaged is of paramount importance. This conviction is central to our proposals for regulating the educational marketplace, so the reasons for it require explanation.

A generation ago the average American finished school with roughly eighth-grade reading competence, while the bottom quarter of the population was at about sixth-grade level. Mass circulation newspapers, being aimed at the "middle majority" of the population, also assumed something like eight-grade reading competence. This meant that most people in the least competent quarter of the population could, with some difficulty and a bit of misunderstanding, follow a daily newspaper. Today the schools have boosted the average reading competence of people finishing school to the twelfth-grade level. They have boosted the average competence of the bottom quartile to the ninth-grade level. The gap between the bottom quartile and the average for the population has thus widened. A comparison of today's mass circulation newspapers with yesterday's indicated that they too have raised their standards, using larger vocabularies and more complex prose than before. The net result could easily be that the least competent quarter of the population is less likely to read the same papers as the "middle majority." If this were in fact the case, the cultural, political, and social isolation of the bottom quarter would have increased, even though their absolute competence had risen.

Man is indeed a social creature. His capacity to do most of the things he cares about depends on his relationship to his fellow men. If he is less competent than they, he will find himself frustrated at every turn. If he is more competent than they, he will be in a good position to get what he wants from life. In a society of illiterates, a man who knows the alphabet is a scholar and a gentleman. In a society of college graduates, he is an illiterate. Translated into practical terms, this means that a man's satisfaction in life depends more on relative advantage than absolute attainment. We judge that this is particularly true in education. It follows that the well-being of American society depends less on its wealth, power, and knowledge than on the way these things are distributed among the population.

We recognize that many Americans reject this view. Nonetheless, if the upheavals of the 1960's have taught us anything, it should be that merely increasing the Gross National Product, the absolute level of government spending, and the mean level of educational attainment will not solve our basic economic, social, and political problems. These problems do not arise because the nation as a whole is poor or ignorant. They arise because the benefits of wealth, power, and knowledge have been unequally distributed and because many Americans believe that these inequalities are unjust. A program which seeks to improve education must therefore focus on inequality, attempting to close the gap between the disadvantaged and the advantaged.

Having said that regulatory machinery ought to help close the gap between the advantaged and the disadvantaged, we must also say something about how this might be done.

First, America must *reallocate educational resources* so as to expose "difficult" children to their full share of the bright, talented, sensitive teachers, instead of exposing them to less than their share, as at present. Merely equalizing expenditures will not suffice to achieve this. Teachers are human, and most of them instinctively prefer children who learn quickly and easily over children who learn slowly and painfully. In order to change these values, society must make working with disadvantaged children a prestigious and highly paid career. This means that if schools that enroll disadvantaged children are to get their share of able teachers, they must be able to pay substantially better salaries and provide substantially more amenities (e.g., smaller classes, more preparation time) than schools which serve advantaged children.

Second, America must alter *enrollment patterns* so that disadvantaged children have more advantaged classmates. A student's classmates are probably his most important single "resource," even though they do not appear in most calculations of per-pupil expenditure. Children learn an enormous amount (both for better and for worse) from one another. Equally important, a student's classmates determine how much, if anything, he will get from his teachers. If, for example, a disadvantaged child attends a school in which most children never learn algebra, his teachers will not expect *him* to learn algebra, even if he is perfectly capable of doing so.

All this implies that a competitive market is unlikely to help disadvantaged children unless it is regulated so as to:

- provide substantially more money to schools that enroll disadvantaged children than to schools which enroll only advantaged children; and

- prevent an increase in segregation by race, income, ability, and "desirable" behavior patterns.

The second general requirement of a regulatory system is that it give parents more control than they now have over the kind of education their children receive. We assume that increasing parents' sense of control over their environment and over their children's life chances is an end in itself both because it makes parents' lives less frustrating and because it makes them more effective advocates of their family's interest in non-educational areas.

Increasing parents' control over the kind of education their children receive should, however, also increase the chances that their children get a good education. The more control parents have over what happens to their children, the more responsible they are likely to feel for the results. This could easily make them take a more active role in educating their children at home. In addition, parents tend to care more than public servants about making sure that their child gets whatever he needs. The intensity of the typical parent's concern is, of course, often partially or entirely offset by his naivete about what would actually be good for his child or by his inability to get what he thinks the child needs. Nonetheless, we think that on the average parents are unlikely to make choices that are any worse than what their public schools now offer.

For parental choice to make a difference, however, genuine alternatives must really be available. "Good" education will always be in short stupply, even if the parents are given money to buy it. Most (though not all) disadvantaged parents will want the same kinds of education as advantaged parents. When the two groups apply to the same "good" schools, disadvantaged children will not normally get their share of places. If disadvantaged parents are to feel that they also have control over the kinds of education their children receive, the market must be regulated in such a way that disadvantaged children have a fair chance of being admitted to the school of their choice.

The foregoing criteria do not exhaust the possible yardsticks for evaluating alternative regulatory systems. Before presenting our proposals it may therefore be useful to review the principal objections that others have raised to vouchers as a device for promoting competition and choice.

First, integrationists fear that vouchers would make it harder to achieve racial integration. This might result in a voucher system's being declared unconstitutional, as has already happened in four Southern states. Even if the system were not declared unconstitutional, it would be undesirable if it intensified rather than alleviated racial separation.

Second, civil libertarians fear that vouchers would break down the separation of church and state. Again, this might result in a voucher scheme's being declared unconstitutional. Even if it did not, it could unleash a series of bitter political struggles from which America has in the past been relatively exempt.

Third, egalitarians have emphasized that an unregulated market would increase the expenditures of the rich more than it increased those of the poor, exacerbating present resource inequalities instead of reducing them.

Fourth, public school men have feared that the public schools would become the "schools of last resort" and hence dumping grounds for students no other schools wanted.

Finally, some educators have argued that parents are not qualified to decide how their children should be educated and that giving parents a choice would encourage the growth of bad schools, not good ones.

The next sections show how these problems might be solved.

A Model Voucher System

In order to understand the proposals made in this report, the reader must begin by reconsidering traditional definitions of the terms "public" and "private" in education. Since the nineteenth century we have classified schools as "public" if they were owned and operated by a governmental body. We go right on calling colleges "public" even when they charge tuition that many people cannot afford. We also call academically exclusive high schools "public" when they have admissions requirements that only a handful of students can meet. And we call whole school systems "public" even though they refuse to give anyone information about what they are doing, how well they are doing it, and whether children are getting what their parents want. Conversely, we have always called schools "private" if they were owned and operated by private organizations. We have gone on calling these schools "private" even when, as sometimes happens, they are open to every applicant on a non-discriminatory basis, charge no tuition, and make whatever information they have about themselves available to anyone who asks.

Definitions of this kind conceal as much as they reveal, for they classify schools entirely in terms of *who* runs them, not *how* they are run. If we want to understand what is really going on in education, we might well reverse this emphasis. We would then call a school "public" if it were open to everyone on a nondiscriminatory basis, if it charged no tuition, and if it provided full information about itself to anyone interested. Conversely, we would call any school "private" if it excluded applicants in a discriminatory way, charged tuition, or withheld information about itself. Admittedly, the question of who governs a school cannot be ignored entirely when categorizing the school, but it seems considerably less important than the question of how the school is governed.

Adopting this revised vocabulary, we propose a regulatory system with two underlying principles:

- No public money should be used to support "private" schools.

- Any group that starts a "public" school should be eligible for public subsidies.

Specifically, we propose an education voucher system which would work in the following manner:

1. An Educational Voucher Agency (EVA) would be established to administer the vouchers. Its governing board might be elected or appointed, but in either case it should be structured so as to represent minority as well as majority interests. The EVA might be an existing local board of education, or it might be a new agency with a larger or smaller geographic jurisdiction. The EVA would receive all federal, state, and local education funds for which children in the area were eligible. It would pay this money to schools only in

return for vouchers. (In addition, it would pay parents for children's transportation costs to the school of their choice.)

2. The EVA would issue a voucher to every family in its district with school-age children. The value of the basic voucher would initially equal the per pupil expenditure of the public schools in the area. Schools which took children from families with below-average incomes would receive additional payments, on a scale that might, for example, make the maximum payment for the poorest child double the basic voucher.

3. In order to become an "approved voucher school," eligible to cash vouchers, a school would have to:

a. accept a voucher as full payment of tuition;

b. accept any applicant so long as it had vacant places;

c. if it had more applicants than places, fill at least half these places by picking applicants randomly and fill the other half in such a way as not to discriminate against ethnic minorities;

d. accept uniform standards established by the EVA regarding suspension and expulsion of students;

e. agree to make a wide variety of information about its facilities, teachers, program, and students available to the EVA and to the public;

f. maintain accounts of money received and disbursed in a form that would allow both parents and the EVA to determine whether a school operated by a board of education was getting the resources to which it was entitled on the basis of its vouchers, whether a school operated by a church was being used to subsidize other church activities, and whether a school operated by a profitmaking corporation was siphoning off excessive amounts to the parent corporation;

g. meet existing state requirements for private schools regarding curriculum, staffing, and the like.

Control over policy in an approved voucher school might be vested in an existing local school board, a PTA, or any private group. No governmental restrictions would be placed on curriculum, staffing, and the like except those established for all private schools in a state.

4. Just as at present, the local board of education (which might or might not be the EVA) would be responsible for ensuring that there were enough places in publicly managed schools to accommodate every school-age child who did not want to attend a privately managed school. If a shortage of places developed for some reason, the board of education would have to open new schools or create more places in existing schools. (Alternatively, it might find ways to encourage privately managed schools to expand, presumably by getting the EVA to raise the value of the voucher.)

5. Every spring, each family would submit to the EVA the name of the school to which it wanted to send each of its school-age children next fall. Any child already enrolled in a voucher school would be guaranteed a place, as would any sibling of a child enrolled in a voucher school. So long as it had room, a voucher school would be required to admit all students who listed it as a first choice. If it did not have room for all applicants, a school could fill half its places in whatever way it wanted, choosing among those who listed it as a first choice. It could not, however, select these applicants in such a way as to discriminate against racial minorities. It would then have to fill remaining places by a lottery among the remaining applicants. All schools with unfilled places would report these to the EVA. All families whose children had not been admitted to their first choice school would then choose an alternative school which still had vacancies. Vacancies would then be filled in the same manner as in the first round. This procedure would continue until every child had been admitted to a school.

6. Having enrolled their children in a school, parents would give their vouchers to the school. The school would send the vouchers to the EVA and would receive a check in return.

We believe that a system of the kind just described would avoid the dangers usually ascribed to a tuition voucher scheme.

- It should increase the share of the nation's educational resources available to disadvantaged children.

- It should produce at least as much mixing of blacks and whites, rich and poor, clever and dull, as the present system of public education.

- It should ensure advantaged and disadvantaged parents the same chance of getting their children into the school of their choice.

— It should provide parents (and the organizations which are likely to
affect their decisions) whatever information they think they need to
make intelligent choices among schools.

— It should avoid conflict with both the Fourteenth Amendment prohibition against racial discrimination and with First Amendment
provisions regarding church and state.

The voucher system outlined above is quite different from other systems now
being advocated. It regulates the educational marketplace more than most
conservatives would like, and contains far more safeguards for the interests
of disadvantaged children. We recognize that such restrictions will be considered undesirable by some people. But we believe that a voucher system which
does not include these or equally effective safeguards would be worse than no
voucher system at all. Indeed, an unregulated voucher system could be the
most serious setback for the education of disadvantaged children in the history
of the United States. A properly regulated system, on the other hand, could
inaugurate a new era of innovation and reform in American schools.

2. SEVEN ALTERNATIVE ECONOMIC MODELS

The merits of the voucher system for distribution of educational funds depend in part on how the value of the voucher is determined and how schools
are allowed to raise additional funds beyond the value of their vouchers. All
the plans discussed in this chapter resemble one another in that they guarantee every voucher school enough money to offer a program comparable in
cost to what the public schools provide. They differ in their approach to the
question of how (or whether) voucher schools might increase their incomes
beyond this level.

We shall consider seven alternative education voucher plans, i.e., sets of ground
rules for distributing money to voucher schools. As noted above, the plans
resemble one another in that per pupil spending in the voucher schools would
at least equal what was spent in the public schools in the district before the
voucher plan went into effect. The plans, however, regulate schools' efforts
to get extra money in different ways. The seven basic models are set forth
in Table 1.

TABLE 1

Seven Alternative Education Voucher Plans

---

1. *Unregulated Market Model:* The value of the voucher is the same for each child. Schools are permitted to charge whatever additional tuition the traffic will bear.

2. *Unregulated Compensatory Model:* The value of the voucher is higher for poor children. Schools are permitted to charge whatever additional tuition they wish.

3. *Compulsory Private Scholarship Model:* Schools may charge as much tuition as they like, provided they give scholarships to those children unable to pay full tuition. Eligibility and size of scholarships are determined by the EVA, which establishes a formula showing how much families with certain incomes can be charged.

4. *The Effort Voucher:* This model establishes several different possible levels of per pupil expenditure and allows a school to choose its own level. Parents who choose high expenditure schools are then charged more tuition (or tax) than parents who choose low-expenditure schools. Tuition (or tax) is also related to income, in theory the "effort" demanded of a low-income family attending a high-expenditure school is the same as the "effort" demanded of a high-income family in the same school.

5. *"Egalitarian" Model:* The value of the voucher is the same for each child. No school is permitted to charge any additional tuition.

6. *Achievement Model:* The value of the voucher is based on the progress made by the child during the year.

7. *Regulated Compensatory Model:* Schools may not charge tuition beyond the value of the voucher. They may "earn" extra funds by accepting children from poor families or educationally disadvantaged children. (A variant of this model permits privately managed voucher schools to charge affluent families according to their ability to pay.)

We will make several basic assumptions about the economic context in which any voucher system should operate:

— We will assume that the level of tax support for education usually would rise at about the same rate under a voucher system as it has under the present system. Where this assumption is unjustified it will be discussed in connection with a specific plan. In general, however, it seems wisest to assume that the basic level of the voucher would be roughly comparable to what the public schools are now spending per pupil. Some models would augment the basic voucher by making special payments for disadvantaged children. Since expenditures on middle-class children are unlikely to decline, these special payments for the disadvantaged would increase overall expenditures, at least in the short run.

— We will assume that the sources of tax support for education would change in much the same way under a voucher system as under the present system. We anticipate a gradual increase in the federal share of education

---

spending, and a gradual decline in the local share. Some federal share would indeed probably be essential if the vouchers for disadvantaged children were to be set higher than the norm for all children, because only the federal government seems to have the capacity to provide such supplements on a large scale.

— We will confine our discussion to "comprehensive" voucher systems in which the amount of public money going to any given school, whether publicly or privately managed, is almost entirely determined by the value of the vouchers it receives. This could be achieved in one of two ways:

1. A local board of education might become the EVA for its area. It would then receive the federal, state and local funds to which the local public schools had traditionally been entitled, plus whatever additional funds were available. It would disburse all its money in the form of vouchers. A variety of complex accounting arrangements must be required to ensure that certain funds went only to public schools, but the net effect would be to make overall tax support for each voucher school in the area a function of the number and kinds of pupils it enrolled, not whether it was publicly or privately managed.

2. The EVA might be independent of the local board of education. The local board of education would continue to operate schools in its area. The EVA would make payments to the local board for the vouchers it collected from parents in the same way that it would make payments to private groups. Ideally the EVA would become the sole recipient of tax funds for education. If however, it were politically necessary, a local board could continue to receive some direct support from the local property tax. The EVA would have to ensure that these funds did not give publicly managed schools an unfair competitive advantage over privately managed schools. In order to do this, the EVA could simply require that when a local board of education submitted its children's vouchers for payment, it also reported its receipts from local tax funds. The EVA could then deduct these direct payments from the check it sent to a local board for its vouchers. This approach would eliminate local incentives to boost property taxes, however. Instead of deducting the public schools' local property tax receipts from its voucher payments, therefore, the EVA might make the overall value of vouchers in an area a function of local property taxes. The EVA could do this if it had federal or state money to augment the value of private schools' vouchers by the same amount that local taxpayers voted for public schools. If taxpayers voted an increase in local property taxes, expenditures in *all* voucher schools would increase. A voucher would thus end up having two parts, one of which was determined by local taxpayers, and one of which was determined by

federal and/or state legislators. This would, of course, be similar to the current situation.

In addition to these assumptions there are certain economic issues which arise under any voucher system but which do not affect the relative merits of alternative systems. These include the following:

— Some existing federal and state aid programs might be subsumed into the voucher program. The purpose of Title I of the Elementary and Secondary Education Act, for example, might well be achieved by using Title I funds to augment the value of voucher payments for low-income children. Similarly, special programs for the handicapped might take the form of augmenting these children's vouchers.

— In order to encourage diversity, a voucher system ought to help new schools to get started. One way to do this would be to establish a loan fund that would lend schools money at low interest rates. A loan fund of this kind ought if possible to be large enough to help publicly, as well as privately, managed schools deal with capital costs.

— In order to ensure genuine choice, a voucher system would have to enable parents to send their children to schools that were beyond walking distance from their homes. This means that a voucher system must pay transportation costs for children who attend schools outside their neighborhoods. Such payments should be added to the basic voucher, and should go directly to parents. It is not desirable to make transportation costs part of the basic voucher, since this has the effect of penalizing a school economically for enrolling children from outside its immediate neighborhood.

— Assuming they are held constitutional, payments to church schools would be roughly comparable to payments to other schools. It might be desirable for legal reasons to make payments to church schools somewhat smaller (80 percent?) than payments to secular schools, and to require that churches contribute the balance to cover the cost of religious instruction. The impact of such a policy on the overall level of school expenditures would be negligible.

— We assume that vouchers would be tax exempt. We will apply four basic criteria to each model:

1. *What would the model do to school expenditures?* This question has two parts:

— How would the model affect *private* expenditures?

— How would it affect *public* expenditures?

The overall effect of a model on school expenditures involves a calculation of trade-offs between the two.

2. *How would the model affect the allocation of school resources among different kinds of pupils?* Again, this question has two parts:

— Would the new pattern of resource allocation be more or less *efficient,* i.e., would it increase or decrease overall school input?

— Would the new pattern be more or less *equitable,* i.e., would it benefit the currently advantaged more or less than the currently disadvantaged?

3. *Would parents who are dissatisfied with the education currently available to them be able to choose an option they preferred under the proposed model?* This question has three variants:

— To what extent would parents who are dissatisfied with the *level of resources* now devoted to their child's education be able to enroll their children in schools with more resources?

— To what extent would parents who are unhappy about the *racial, socio-economic, academic, or cultural mix* of pupils in their children's present school be able to enroll their children in schools that had different mixes of pupils?

— To what extent would parents who are unhappy about the *philosophy and style of education* in their children's present schools be able to enroll their children in schools which were more to their taste?

4. *How would various political interest groups, and especially the public school system, react to the proposed scheme?*

We pay more attention to some of these criteria than to others. In part this is because certain criteria are extraordinarily difficult to apply. The reader will discover, for example, that we make few firm predictions about the overall effect of any model on the tax rate. This reflects the fact that a firm prediction would require not just an enumeration of the various factors that would push tax rates up or down, but an estimate of the relative magnitude of these factors. Similarly, we have said almost nothing about the effect of reallocating educational resources on the overall level of school output. Once again, the reason is that educational research has turned up no solid evidence about the relationship between school resources and the outcomes of schooling. There is even less basis for estimating the marginal return to investment in the education of different *kinds* of students. Lacking such evidence, we cannot say whether the nation's overall level of intellectual or social competence would be higher if we allocated additional resources to students who already do fairly well with the resources they have or to students who do relatively badly.

It would, however, be disingenuous to pretend that technical difficulties were the only reason for our putting more emphasis on some criteria than others. We think some criteria more important than others, and we think some outcomes of a voucher plan desirable while others are undesirable.

The impact of any given economic model on the overall character of the educational system will also depend in part on the ground rules regulating the recruitment, admission, and expulsion of students to various kinds of voucher schools. In Chapter 3 therefore we propose ground rules which would treat publicly and privately managed schools in precisely the same way, and which would prevent any school from discriminating against disadvantaged applicants. Most other advocates of education vouchers have proposed less regulation of the admissions process. Many have assumed that privately managed voucher schools would be free to take the most easily educated students, leaving the hard-to-educate students for the public schools. Economic models which look quite satisfactory if admissions procedures are closely regulated often look far less satisfactory if schools are given more leeway to pick and choose among applicants. The reader should keep this problem in mind when looking at the alternatives.

1. Unregulated Market Model

Perhaps the simplest and certainly the commonest proposal for vouchers is to provide every child with a flat grant or tax credit which his family could use to pay tuition at the school of its choice. The amount of the grant would be determined by legislators, but most advocates of the plan assume that the grant would be roughly equal to the present level of expenditure in the public schools. Most advocates also assume that public schools would continue to exist, and that they would charge tuition equal to the amount of the grant. This is the version of vouchers advocated by Milton Friedman and others.[1]

The effect of a free market on the level of taxation is unpredictable. The initial effect would be to raise the tax rate, since the taxpayers would have to pay for children now being educated at private expense. Nationally, this would increase the tax burden about ten percent, but the jump would be much sharper in some areas. This increase may, of course, take place whether or not a voucher system is established. If public money is not made available to Catholic schools, many of them are likely to close in the next few years. Their pupils will enroll in the public schools, pushing up public expenditures in precisely the same way that a voucher system would.

Since a voucher system would allow more parents to benefit from public expenditures for education, it probably would lead to broader political support for such expenditures. Under present arrangements, parents with children in private schools are seldom enthusiastic about higher taxes for support of public education. If their children were likely to benefit from such taxes, their attitude would perhaps change. This might push public expenditures up over the long run.

An unregulated voucher system would, however, set in motion other forces that might work *against* increased public expenditures. If affluent taxpayers took a consistent, long-run view of their self-interest, they would presumably try to keep the level of voucher payments low and finance their children's education from private supplementation. This would spare them the necessity of subsidizing the education of poor children. If affluent taxpayers all reacted in this way, the result would probably be a powerful political bloc dedicated to holding down the value of the vouchers.

Affluent taxpayers may, however, not take a consistent, long-run view of their interests. Instead, the primary conflict of interest at any given moment may be between those people who have or expect to have children in school, and those who do not. If a family, however well-off, has several children in school, higher vouchers would almost always serve its immediate interest. Conversely, if a family has no children in school, vouchers of a high value would *never* serve its interest, no matter what its income.

If the primary conflict of interest turned out to be between "parents" of all incomes and "non-parents" of all incomes, there could easily be more effective pressure to increase tax subsidies for education than at present. The number and character of the families that gained or lost from raising school taxes would remain much as at present, except that families who now have their children in private schools would acquire an interest in increasing rather than limiting public subsidies. But affluent parents with school-age children would have more interest in raising the level of public subsidies than at present. Today, the parent with a child in public school usually favors "better schools," but his interest in higher expenditures is often tempered by his doubts that higher spending is really going to benefit his children as much as educators claim. But if a parent had enrolled his child in a school that charged tuition in addition to the value of the basic voucher, he would view proposals for increasing the size of the voucher as a way of reducing his current out-of-pocket expenses. The reduction in his private spending would exceed the increase in his taxes so long as he had children in school. Direct help of this kind is likely to generate considerable enthusiasm.

All in all, the effect of an unregulated market on tax levels would probably depend on the relative importance to affluent parents of their long-term interest as tax-payers and their short-term interest as parents. This is hard to predict. Still, it is quite possible that the voucher would gradually lag further and further behind total expenditures per pupil.

The effect of an unregulated market on overall expenditures for education would depend mainly on its effect on tax support for education. An unregulated market would probably increase private contributions to the cost of education. While some parents who now pay the full cost of private schooling would get partial or full subsidies, many parents who now get full subsidies would probably start supplementing their vouchers with private money. The increase in private expenditures could, however, easily be offset by a relative or absolute decline in public expenditures. Whether overall expenditure levels would increase or decrease is thus unclear.

A scheme of this kind would result in a reallocation of educational resources so that a smaller percentage went to the poor and a larger percentage to the well off. Families of varying income would all receive the same subsidy. This would increase slightly the share of public expenditures on education going to the poor, since current expenditure patterns show a moderate bias in favor of schools with middle-class pupils. But this redistribution of public funds would be more than offset by the capacity of affluent families to pay substantial additional tuition. Admittedly, many schools would make an effort to provide scholarships for poor applicants, but it would be unreasonable to expect that any significant number of poor children would attend these expensive schools on scholarships. An applicant who can pay full tuition will almost certainly have a better chance of going to most private schools than an applicant who requires a subsidy.

An unregulated market would shift the decision about how much to spend on education from local school boards to families but only to affluent families, not poor ones. If large numbers of affluent families chose to spend more, an unregulated market would lead to increasing segregation along economic lines. Indeed, this is one reason many middle-class families favor voucher plans. They want to send their children to school with other middle- or upper-middle-class children, and they see vouchers as an easy and apparently legitimate way to do this.

Some have argued that resource reallocation is of limited importance so long as the basic voucher is high enough to provide an adequate educational program for everyone. This is a naive view of the educational process. First, as we have seen, an unregulated market offers no assurance that the basic voucher could be kept high; it might well tend to decline relative to the overall price of education. Second, even if the basic voucher remained high, the absolute level of expenditure in a school does not determine the resources it can command. Rather the critical question is often how the school's resources compare with its competitors' resources. Suppose, for example, that schools attended by poor children were to double their teachers' salaries over the next five years. Suppose that schools attended by middle-class children tripled their salaries over the same period. The quality of the teachers in schools atteneded by poor children would probably decline under these circumstances. It follows that the quality of education provided by a school does not depend simply on its per pupil expenditure, but also on how this expenditure compares with that in competing schools. In addition, if segregation increases, the relative cost of providing a given service to disadvantaged schools will increase, while in an advantaged school its relative cost will decline. We conclude, then, that no politically practical level of basic payments will assure quality education for the disadvantaged so long as other schools can spend more and can exclude the disadvantaged.

Within this context, an unregulated market could give upper-income families an almost unlimited range of potential program options. Low-income families would have a more restricted range of choices, since (a) they could not afford any program that cost more to operate than the value of their voucher, and (b) they could not generally hope to find a school where the majority of their child's classmates were from other than low-income families.

An unregulated market is likely to commend itself to middle- and upper-income families and to existing independent and parochial schools. It may also commend itself to certain low-income black groups who are interested in starting their own schools and cannot seriously believe that *anything* could be worse for their children than the existing public schools. The plan would be opposed by the public schools. Elimination of middle-class children from the public schools would make the lives of public school men even more difficult than at present. It might lead to a reduction in the public schools' financial resources and it could certainly lead to a reduction in the quality of teachers available in the public schools.

Our overall judgement is that an unregulated market would redistribute resources away from the poor and toward the rich, would increase economic segregation in the schools, and would exacerbate the problems of existing in public schools without offering them any offsetting advantages. For these reasons we think it would be worse than the present system of public schools.

2. Unregulated Compensatory Model

In order to protect the poor against an unregulated marketplace, some advocates of vouchers have proposed making the value of vouchers higher for children from low-income families.

Theodore Sizer and Phillip Whitten have proposed one version of this plan.[2] Families with incomes below $2,000 would receive $1,500 vouchers. The value of the voucher would decline to zero as the family's income approached the national average. Families with incomes above the national average would receive no subsidy. Sizer and Whitten clearly do not envisage this plan as an *alternative* to the present system, but rather as a *supplement* to it. They do not explain whether a child who stayed in an existing public school would bring that school the full value of his voucher, or whether he would only bring the difference between his voucher and what the public school was already receiving from other public sources for the student. Were publicly controlled schools to receive the voucher *in addition* to other public monies, it would be extraordinarily difficult for privately controlled schools to compete. We will therefore assume that the value of the voucher would be reduced by the amount of current tax subsidy to any given school, putting publicly and privately controlled schools on the same footing.

If this were done, the Sizer proposal would have the effect of giving the poor some opportunity to buy their way into privately controlled schools, just as the rich now do. It would *not* give the middle classes such an opportunity, since they would receive little or no subsidy and would not be able to pay $1,000 or $1,500 tuition from their own resources. A scheme of this kind would almost certainly be rejected out of hand by legislators.

To make the plan politically acceptable, it would be necessary to enable *all* parents to send their children to privately controlled schools if they chose. The simplest way of doing this while preserving the basic features of the Sizer proposal seems to be to establish a system rather like the one we proposed in Chapter 1. Each child would receive a basic voucher of $750, regardless of family income. Schools taking children from families with incomes below the national average would receive additional payments. Unlike the model proposed in Chapter 1, however, this model would allow schools to charge tuition in addition to the voucher, at whatever level they saw fit. Since few of the regulations on admissions policies proposed in Chapter 1 would be workable if students had to pay tuition, we will assume that privately controlled schools could select their students in any way they wanted, while the public system would have to provide spaces for anyone the privately controlled schools did not accept.

In order to appraise the likely effects of the unregulated compensatory model, we must first estimate the likely effect of the system on the overall purchasing power of various income groups. Overall purchasing power will be the sum of the voucher provided by the EVA, (which would decline as income increased) and private tuition payments (which would tend to increase as income increased). As one moves up the income scale, the value of the voucher might decline faster, slower, or at the same rate that private contributions increased.

If education is sold on the open market, like housing or food, legislators are likely to take their usual attitude toward subsidizing the poor. Low-income families may be given somewhat larger vouchers than middle-income families, but the difference is unlikely to be as large as the difference in private purchasing power between low- and middle- income families. Food stamps, for example, help equalize the purchasing power of rich and poor in a grocery store, but not enough to ensure that the poor eat as well as the rich. The same pattern is repeated in housing, where the poor are sometimes given modest subsidies, but never enough to outbid the wealthy. So too in education, legislatures may provide poor parents with slightly larger vouchers than rich parents, but (as the legislation discussed in Chapter 4 illustrates) the difference is not likely to compensate the poor for their inability to spend private funds on education.

If legislatures behave as they have in the past, then, the "compensatory" features of this model would be of limited importance. Well-to-do families would be able to spend far more on their children's education than poor families. The effects of a compensatory free market model would therefore be similar to those of a completely unregulated market. There would be differences in the *degree* to which the two models promoted segregation and the *degree* to which they widened the gap between rich and poor, but the basic pattern would be the same.

Suppose, however, that a legislative body chose to establish a compensatory voucher system which actually equalized the average purchasing power of families in different income groups. In order to do this, it would need empirical data on the willingness of families at various income levels to spend their own money for private tuition. The result of such studies would vary dramatically, according to what the family would actually buy for different prices, which would in turn depend on local market conditions at the time. Nonetheless, let us suppose that a formula were developed for predicting the *average* private contribution that a family with any given income will make from its own funds. Let us also suppose that a legislature fixed the value of the voucher so as to bring each income group's average purchasing power up to some specified level, say $1,000.

This would have a serious impact on the continued political acceptability of the plan. Suppose, for example, that families with $5,000 annual incomes were found to spend an average of $50 per child on tuition and therefore received vouchers worth $950 per child. Some of these families might be willing to spend as much as $100 of their own money to get their child into a better school, while other families might not be willing to spend anything. The overall difference in purchasing power between the most and least motivated parents in this bracket would still be only $100. This means that most schools which were open to one $5,000 family would also be open to the other. Now suppose the average contribution of a family with $15,000 is found to be $500 per child, entitling it to a $500 voucher. Under these circumstances some $15,000 families might be willing to spend only $250 per child of their own money, while others might be willing to spend another $1,000 per child. The net effect would be that the most motivated parents had $1,500 per child, while the least motivated had $750. This would mean that some children of the well-to-do would not be in schools as expensive as their indigent neighbors, while others would be in more expensive schools.

This picture actually seems somewhat far-fetched, however. If legislation were designed to ensure that every family could end up with $1,000 per child by making "reasonable" effort, almost all schools would probably set their tuition at or near $1,000. Every family would then *have* to spend this much in order to get its children into a satisfactory school. Since the bulk of these payments would be coming from middle-income families, it seems reasonable to anticipate continuing pressure from these families for increases in the value of their vouchers. The effect over time would probably be to eliminate the differential between vouchers paid to middle- and lower-income families. Once again, then, what began as an unregulated compensatory plan would probably end up as a completely unregulated plan, in which almost all parents received roughly equal payments and were free to supplement them from their own funds. We have already analyzed the consequences of such a plan in the previous section.

3. Compulsory Private Scholarship Model

The Compulsory Scholarship model resembles the unregulated market in that schools would be allowed to charge whatever tuition they wished. But they would also be required to provide enough scholarships so that no applicant's family had to pay more than it could afford. Several well-endowed private schools follow this policy, as do a number of wealthy private colleges. The colleges calculate parents' ability to pay from formulae developed by the College Scholarship Service. They then guarantee every successful applicant enough financial aid from one source or another so that he can pay tuition, room, and board without getting any more help from home than required by the CSS formula.

If a scheme like this were adopted as public policy, legislative bodies would presumably establish formulae equivalent to those of the CSS. In theory, any public or private voucher school would apply these formulae to raise additional funds from its more affluent parents. If this money were allocated evenly to all sorts of pupils, the effect would be to "overcharge" the rich and "undercharge" the poor, relative to costs. There are, however, a number of practical difficulties which make it unlikely that the actual effects of this plan would differ appreciably from the effects of an unregulated market.

The basic problem is that all schools want to increase their incomes. If the basic voucher is fixed, and if the permissible level of tuition depends on a family's income, then the only way to increase the school's income is to admit richer students. If schools are required to admit a random sample of applicants, they will develop programs and recruitment policies which appeal mainly to applicants from appropriate economic backgrounds. If all else fails, schools may set higher academic standards for "scholarship" than for "non-scholarship" students *after* admission, encouraging mediocre students to withdraw if they are getting financial aid and to stay if they are not.

The foregoing analysis suggests that it is impractical to require voucher schools to subsidize needy applicants from their own funds. All schools feel they need more resources than they have. If they are allowed to charge tuition based on ability to pay, most schools will decide that they need a fairly affluent student body to provide these resources. And if that is what they want, most schools will be able to get it. The "compulsory" private scholarship model is thus likely to end up almost indistinguishable from a "voluntary" private scholarship model, i.e., the unregulated market.

4. The Effort Voucher

While it seems to be impractical to force schools to subsidize needy students from their own receipts, it might be possible to establish a system in which the EVA did so. At first glance the simplest way to do this is for each family to pay what it can afford, based on some official formula, and for the EVA to pay the rest. The difficulty with this is that if a family's liability for tuition depends exclusively on its income and not at all on what the school spends, the market no longer puts any check on school expenditures. Schools will raise tuition higher and higher in an effort to improve their programs, but parents will pay a fixed amount of tuition based on their income. The rising cost of education will therefore be absorbed entirely from the public treasury. At this point legislators will almost certainly intervene and put upper limits on what tuition a school can charge.

The most practical approach to this problem is probably the one outlined by John Coons and his associates.[3] The Coons' model gives every school a choice between four different levels of expenditure, ranging from roughly the present public school level to 2-3 times that level. Schools at the lowest level would be almost completely subsidized by the state, although at each level parents are expected to pay at least a token charge. The size of their contribution would depend *both* on the family's ability to pay *and* on the cost of the school the family chose. The government would contribute the difference between what a family paid and what the school spent per pupil.

Coons assumes that the charges for attending expensive schools, while only covering part of these schools' extra costs, would keep the overall tax burden under control by keeping the number of applicants moderate. Affluent families would be charged more for attending expensive schools than these schools actually cost. If, for example, schools were allowed to spend no more than $1,500, some families might nonetheless pay $2,000 or more to send their children there. The model could, however, also limit costs for affluent families to the level of expenditure in the school of their choice. Such a maximum might make the model more politically acceptable.

Coons' model seeks to allocate educational resources on the basis of parental "willingness" to pay rather than "ability" to pay. Ideally, then, schools operating at any given expenditure level would attract an *economically* representative student body. Schools demanding different levels of economic sacrifice would, however, attract students from very different *cultural* backgrounds. Schools which demanded economic sacrifices for education would attract families in which the parents were better educated than the norm for their income group, more likely to hold regular jobs, and more likely to be doing non-manual work. The values and atmosphere of these children's homes would usually support the values and atmosphere of the school, and the children would mostly be diligent, disciplined, and easy to teach. Schools which demanded lighter economic sacrifices and provided a lower level of resources would attract the opposite sorts of families.

Evaluating this proposal in terms of the criteria outlined at the beginning of this chapter, we conclude that:

— The model's impact on the tax rate is problematic. The average tax subsidy per pupil would probably rise, but this would depend on the formulae adopted to ensure "equality of sacrifice." The model is designed to increase overall education expenditures, and it would probably succeed.

— The model would redistribute resources away from children whose parents had relatively little interest in education and toward children whose parents had an intense interest in education. The effect of this would be to accentuate the advantage already enjoyed by children whose parents are willing to make sacrifices in the children's behalf, and to accentuate the disadvantage of children whose parents are not willing to make such sacrifices.

Whether the model would redistribute resources between rich and poor families would depend on the precise formula adopted. Coons argues that a formula could be developed which made the cost of attending a high-expenditure school so great that many upper-income families would not take this option. He believes, indeed, that the correlation between school expenditures and family income could be kept at zero. If so, this would thus represent a modest improvement over the status quo.

— The model would allow parents considerable latitude in determining how much they wanted spent on their children's education. In this respect it is superior both to the present system for financing public education and to the other voucher models discussed in this chapter.

— The model might well reduce the amount of segregation by race and income. It would presumably increase the amount of segregation by ability and behavior patterns. It would thus give some parents more choice about the race and socio-economic background of their children's classmates. It would ration the supply of able, well-behaved classmates by charging families more if they sent their children to schools with "advantaged" student bodies. This charge would, however, supposedly be related to ability to pay.

— The model would allow parents a wide variety of program options, including options of varying cost.

— The model would almost certainly be unpopular with publicly controlled schools. This is because publicly controlled schools would still be politically constrained to operate at the lowest expenditure level allowed in the model. The public schools would thus find themselves both with the children whose parents were least willing to make sacrifices for education and with the least adequate resources.

Overall, our conclusion is that while the effort voucher would lead to a substantial increase in parental choice, it would also lead to a much greater spread between the "best" and the "worst" schools than exists within most public school systems today. This would exacerbate inequalities in the outcomes of schooling, insofar as these outcomes are at all influenced by the quality of schools. Politically, the model may be attractive because it would give interested parents a better chance of getting what they want. Children with uninterested parents, on the other hand, would be much worse off than today, first because they would go to schools with less resources, and second because they would have more disadvantaged classmates. While a system like this might be popular in the short run, its long-term effect on the next generation seems to us undesirable.

5. "Egalitarian" Model

What we have called the "Egalitarian" approach to vouchers would provide vouchers of equal value to all children and would prohibit any school which cashed the vouchers from charging tuition beyond the value of the voucher. It seems reasonable to assume that the value of vouchers would resemble the present and projected levels of per pupil expenditure in public schools.

Both publicly and privately managed schools would, of course, be able to solicit money for special programs from federal and state agencies and from foundations. Privately managed schools might also be able to obtain money from their church if they were affiliated with one, from rich alumni if they had any, and from rich parents of children in the school if there were any.[4] Both publicly and privately controlled schools could, of course, also obtain the additional funds by working together to persuade legislators to increase the value of the vouchers.

An Egalitarian voucher would tend to equalize the allocation of educational expenditures among children from different income groups. It might not eliminate disparities between districts, but it would equalize expenditures within districts. Since most studies of resource allocations within districts indicate that rich children get slightly more than their share of the money, while poor children get slightly less, the Egalitarian model would produce a small improvement over the status quo in this respect.

It does not follow, however, that the Egalitarian voucher would actually equalize the allocation of educational resources, as distinct from educational expenditures. There is considerable evidence that it costs more to provide a given resource to a poor child than to a middle-class child. Teachers, for example, often prefer to teach middle-class children, and many will accept a job with such children at a lower salary than they would accept if they were going to have to teach lower-class children. Similarly, physical resources seem to last longer in middle-class than lower-class schools. This means that equal expenditures do not ensure equal resources; on the contrary, equal expenditures ensure unequal resources.

The Egalitarian voucher would not change the locus of control over educational expenditures. The basic level of expenditure would still be determined by a combination of federal, state, and local legislators. Individual parents and small voluntary groupings of parents would still have relatively little influence on expenditure levels.

The effect of an Egalitarian voucher on parental ability to choose a school with a desirable mix of pupils would depend on the extent to which schools were allowed to exercise discretion in selecting among applications. If schools received exactly the same amount of money per pupil, they would in most instances want to recruit and admit those pupils who cost least to educate. School administrators also know they can get better teachers and make their resources stretch further if they can recruit talented, well-behaved students than if they cannot. A school administrator's most rational strategy, given limited fiscal resources, would therefore be to make his school as exclusive as possible. Exclusion would, however, tend to be based more on the characteristics of students and less on the characteristics of parents than in the models discussed up to this point.

Were this to happen, parents with talented and well-behaved children would clearly have more choice than they now do about the mix of pupils to whom their children would be exposed. Parents with children who have trouble in school would have relatively little choice, since they would be excluded from over-applied schools, both public and private. This would be less sure if strict regulations were put on discriminatory admissions policies, but even then the pattern would persist to some extent. Parents with talented, well-behaved children are not, however, always advantaged economically. It is not easy to tell whether a system that promoted segregation along academic and behavioral lines would give low-income families more or less choice than the present system of neighborhood assignments.

Within the limitations imposed by equalization of per pupil expenditure, the Egalitarian voucher would shift the locus of control over school programs away from the local board of education to a combination of parents and semi-public schools. It seems clear, for example, that an Egalitarian voucher would encourage the survival and growth of Catholic schools. It would also encourage the growth of all-white schools unless administrative and constitutional prohibitions against discriminatory admission policies were energetically enforced.

It is important to emphasize, however, that an Egalitarian voucher scheme would *not* provide unlimited program options, because it would not provide enough money to do what many parents and educators think necessary. Existing independent, non-parochial schools almost all spend more money per pupil than do the public schools. Since most of these schools have no significant source of revenue other than tuition, accepting all voucher students would mean cutting their expenditures to about the same level as the public schools. Such a cut would mean abandoning what most independent schools regard as their most important asset, namely their high ratio of staff to students.[5] Most independent schools would probably accept only a limited number of voucher students. (If, as we propose in Chapter 3, cashing vouchers was contingent on a non-discriminatory admissions policy, most independent schools would probably decline to take *any* voucher students.)

While the refusal of independent schools to accept vouchers is not in itself a problem, it does suggest that the Egalitarian voucher fails to satisfy the interests of one group of parents who are now acutely unhappy with the public schools. These are parents whose fundamental complaint is that spending on public education is too low. Such parents complain that public school facilities are inadequate, that classes are too large, and that children receive insufficient personal attention in the public schools. There is no way to solve these problems without spending more money, and an Egalitarian voucher does not offer parents this option. Such parents' only recourse under an Egalitarian voucher scheme would be the same as at present: enroll in a private school at one's own expense, or move to a district which supports education more generously.

If we assume that relatively few independent schools would choose to become voucher schools under an Egalitarian voucher scheme, we must ask whether any appreciable number of *new* voucher schools would be established. The answer to this question is not obvious. We suspect that most of the upper-middle class parents who patronize existing independent schools want a brand of education which requires substantially more resources than the electorate is willing to vote for public education. Such parents would probably not be much interested in creating voucher schools that had to stay within the budget limitations established by taxpayers.

But not all dissatisfied parents are preoccupied with the level of resources available for their children. Some are dissatisfied with the way in which these resources are used. Many black parents seem to fall into this category, in that their primary demand is for schools they can call "ours" rather than "theirs."

A number of business firms have also shown interest in trying to operate schools at roughly the same cost as the public schools. Some claim that innovative staffing and instructional patterns could achieve considerably more at about the same cost as the present public system. There is no way to determine whether this claim is really accurate except by letting them try.

If an Egalitarian voucher appealed mainly to Catholics interested in parochial schools and blacks interested in black-controlled schools, it would probably not have a major disruptive effect on the existing public schools. Nor would it necessarily arouse intense political opposition from school boards and school administrators. If public school men were assured that privately managed schools would (a) have to operate on more or less the same budget as the public schools, and (b) have to take their share of "hard to educate" children, they might well expect to hold their own in competition with these schools. Public school systems in cities with large black populations might reasonably anticipate the departure of substantial numbers of black children to privately managed schools, but if this exodus reduced the political turmoil now engulfing public education, many public school men might think it a net gain. Public school opposition to vouchers usually derives from fear of a massive exodus of the middle-class students. An Egalitarian voucher scheme would probably not have this effect.

Taking all these observations together, we reach the following conclusions:

— The Egalitarian model would produce less segregation by race, income, and ability than any of the unregulated models. But unless stringent restrictions were placed on the right of over-applied schools to select their own students, the Egalitarian model would still produce more segregation by ability than most existing public school systems.

— The Egalitarian model would result in a much more equitable allocation of educational resources between rich and poor than the unregulated models. But because it would probably increase segregation by ability, the Egalitarian model would also increase cost differentials for many resources. As a result, it might produce a less equitable distribution of actual resources between rich and poor children than the present system, and it would almost certainly produce a less equitable allocation of resources between quick and slow learners.

— The Egalitarian model would do less than the unregulated models for parents who dislike the existing public school system because the public schools devote inadequate resources to their children. On the other hand, the Egalitarian model would provide more satisfaction than the present system to those parents whose complaints have to do with the way schools are run rather than the resources at their command.

6. Achievement Model

All of the foregoing models assume that the value of a voucher is determined by the characteristics of the family or the child receiving it. There is another possible approach, however, under which the value of a voucher is determined not by how much the school "needs" to educate the child, nor by how much the parents "want to spend" on the child, but by whether the school actually succeeds in teaching the child what the state (or the parent) wants taught. This approach, traditionally known as "payment for results," has recently been revived by a number of business firms. Such firms have sought (and in several cases received) contracts with school boards. Under these contracts the firm teaches specified subjects to certain children and is paid more if the children then do unusually well on some standard achievement test.

The basic assumption behind this model is that society can measure the effects of schooling and that we should therefore reward schools which produce good effects while penalizing schools which produce bad effects. We do not accept this assumption. We do not believe it is possible to measure the most important effects of schooling, and we do not believe it is desirable to reward schools for producing relatively unimportant effects.

The only reliable measures of elementary schools' effects are standardized cognitive tests. These measure such things as vocabulary, reading comprehension, arithmetic skills, and so forth.

Attitude measures are not generally thought to be very reliable at this age level and their validity for predicting subsequent behavior is almost completely unknown. The question, then, is whether elementary schools should be rewarded for producing high test scores. The answer to this depends first on the intrinsic importance of test scores, and second on the effect of such a reward system on the overall character of schools.

We know very little about the importance of elementary school children's test scores to their later lives. Test scores predict subsequent grades in school with moderate accuracy, but that is hardly a basis for taking them seriously. A child's scores also predict the number of years of school he is likely to complete with considerable accuracy. His scores predict his subsequent occupational success rather poorly, though the relationship is still significant, at least for whites.

The difficulty is that test scores measure both a general aptitude factor that is unaffected by schooling and specific skills that are subject to school influence. One cannot tell from available data whether the general aptitude factor or the specific skills lead to later success. Thus we cannot tell whether a school that boosts a child's test scores is appreciably improving his life chances. This kind of research could be carried out, but it is far from obvious what it would show. In general, even if we were to assume that schools which boost test scores also boost life chances, the available data show such a weak relationship between test scores and adult success that it would be foolish to make boosting scores the primary goal of schooling.[6]

Our skepticism about test scores is reinforced by repeated findings that the correlation between years of schooling completed and later success is much higher than the correlation between test scores and later success. Employers, in other words, pay more and give more important work to people with low scores and a lot of schooling than to people with high scores but little schooling. People who have spent a long time in school appear to have values, habits, and attitudes which make them more useful to the average employer than dropouts, even if the dropouts are good readers, verbalizers, counters, and so forth. The available data do not tell us whether people actually *learn* these habits, values, and attitudes in school, or whether schools simply retain people who already have them while screening out people who lack them. One thing *is* clear, however. The difference between the educated and the uneducated is not primarily a matter of test scores, at least as far as employers are concerned. This being so, it seems foolish to encourage schools to act as if test scores were their most important output.

Some advocates of payment for results accept the view that test scores are not very important in themselves, but argue that a school which maximizes test scores is also likely to develop other characteristics that will give students more control over their lives. This argument may be correct, but we have seen no evidence for it. We have already seen that the *individuals* who do well on tests are not especially likely to be the individuals who do well in later life. We can therefore see no reason for assuming that *schools* which produce high test scores will be the same as schools which produce high incomes, happy parents, concerned citizens, or whatever else a school ought to produce.

One final difficulty deserves attention. We know very little about the non-school influences that affect students' test performance. Socio-economic status and race are known to be important, but a *precise* measure of their importance is not available. Yet if schools are to be paid on the basis of how much they boost students' test scores, some system must be devised for ensuring that this does not induce schools to take white, middle-class children whose test scores are likely to rise rapidly, and to reject black, lower-class children whose test scores are likely to rise more slowly. There is no theoretical obstacle to developing equations which predict individual achievement on the basis of diverse non-school factors. We could then reward schools when their students exceeded the predicted level, and penalize them when their students fell below the predicted level. But this would be extremely difficult to do politically.

Our overall conclusion, then, is that we need far more research on the validity of test scores as measures of school output before we initiate a program which encourages *all* schools to place more emphasis on such scores and less emphasis on other outputs of schooling that both parents and educators have traditionally thought important. This does not, of course, mean that *no* school should be encouraged to establish contractual arrangements in which payments were proportional to gains on standard tests. But this would be a matter of choice, not a district-wide requirement.

7. Regulated Compensatory Model

The Regulated Compensatory Model resembles the Egalitarian Model in that every child would receive a voucher roughly equal to the cost of the public schools of his area. No voucher school would be allowed to charge tuition beyond the value of the voucher. If schools wanted to increase their expenditure per pupil beyond the level of the vouchers, they could seek subventions from churches or from federal agencies and foundations for special purposes. They could also increase their incomes by enrolling additional children who were in some way disadvantaged. The extra costs of educating these children would be defrayed by the EVA. The EVA would pay every school a special "supplementary education fee" for every child with special educational problems.

The most difficult question about the Regulated Compensatory Model is how to decide which children have special problems. Some cases are obvious, such as the physically handicapped. But no family wants its child officially labelled a "behavior problem" or a "slow learner," even if this means that the child's school gets more money to spend on his education. We have considered several solutions, none of which is entirely satisfactory.

The first possibility would be to approach the problem directly. An over-applied school is likely to discriminate against applicants whom it expects to have trouble — and hence to cause trouble — in the school. In most cases this means that the school expects the child to be a slow learner; in some cases it means the school expects misbehavior. The most direct way to help slow learners would be for the agency administering the vouchers to give every child a standardized test (e.g., Metropolitan Readiness) before he entered first grade. The agency would not reveal the child's score on this test to the child, his parents, or the schools to which the child applied. His score would simply be placed in his file. A formula would then be adopted for adjusting the value of each child's voucher according to his test score. Vouchers might, for example, start at $750 for children who scored at or above the national average. They might rise to $1500 for children at the very bottom of the scale. But nobody would know the value of any specific child's voucher. When a school turned in its vouchers, the administrative agency would compute their total value and send the school a check. It would not tell the school which of its students were "worth" more and which were "worth" less. (A school could, of course, institute its own testing program if it wanted to do so, and this would give it a rough idea how much any given child was bringing in.)

It is important to emphasize that while the amount of money available to specific schools would depend on the initial ability of their pupils, the amount of money the school spent on any particular pupil would not necessarily depend on his ability. The school could, for example, use its extra resources to provide *every* child with small classes. This might encourage parents with able children to enroll them in these same schools. Such students could, in turn, both ease the school's problems in attracting staff and serve as directly useful resources to less adept classmates.

The principal difficulty with this scheme is that mental tests are understandably unpopular with many parents. Minority groups are particularly likely to reject their use. Whether such objections would be muted by the fact that the testing program resulted in spending more money on minority children is uncertain.

If direct testing of pupils were impractical or politically unacceptable, the next best alternative would probably be to collect socio-economic data from families with children in each school. Families might, for example, be required to state their taxable income for the previous year when turning in their vouchers. If this were a sworn statement and was supposed to correspond with figures submitted to IRS, cheating would probably not be a major problem. The agency administering the voucher scheme could then make additional payments for each low-income child.

The difficulty with this scheme is that children from low-income families are not necessarily hard-to-educate children. The correlation between income and scores on the Metropolitan Readiness Test, for example, seldom exceeds 0.4 and is considerably less in many populations. If a school had a large number of applicants among whom it could pick and choose, it could quite easily choose a first grade whose average score on most standard tests was quite high, even though its median family income was low. This possibility would be only slightly reduced if statistics were also collected on parental occupations and education.

The best way around this problem would be to insist that schools admit applicants randomly. This would not, of course, rule out selective recruitment and publicity. But schools whose location, program, or publicity attracted large numbers of poor applicants would almost certainly also attract large numbers of low-IQ applicants. Thus a combination of non-discriminatory admissions and incentives for enrolling low-income pupils might achieve the same result as direct incentives for enrolling low-IQ pupils.

Another version of the Compensatory Model might be more acceptable to those who take a strict view of the First Amendment "establishment of religion" clause. This version would inflate the value of each child's voucher if he came from a low-income family. The difficulty with this approach is that it might be harder to sell politically than a system which paid bonuses to schools for enrolling the same children. Suppose, for example, that family income were deemed the only practical way of discriminating between the advantaged and the disadvantaged. Many middle-income families would probably object to having their vouchers worth less than vouchers assigned to indigent neighbors. They would rightly cite innumerable cases in which their indigent neighbors' children were no more difficult to educate than their own, and would argue that they were being discriminated against simply because they worked harder and earned more. If, on the other hand, the bonus was paid to the school rather than to the individual, and if schools were not allowed to discriminate on the basis of ability, many of these inequities might even out. Barring deliberate selection, schools with low median incomes will almost always have a harder overall job than schools with high median incomes. This is fairly easy to demonstrate to any interested parent – though demonstrating it obviously does not ensure that parents will accept the principle that the schools with the toughest problems should get the most money.

If the EVA wanted to place primary emphasis on economic sanctions and incentives and did not want to regulate admissions procedures at all closely, another version of the Regulated Compensatory Model might be appropriate. If admissions procedures were left unregulated, privately-managed schools would have a considerable advantage over their public competitors in attracting middle-class parents, because they would be freer to exclude students whom they judged undesirable for some reason. In order to offset this advantage, it might be desirable to charge middle-class parents for attending a privately-managed voucher school. Charges would be based on an official formula which determined ability to pay, but could not exceed the basic voucher (e.g., $750). Parents who sent their children to a publicly managed voucher school would be admitted free, no matter what their income. Children from families with below-average incomes would be admitted free to either publicly or privately managed voucher schools.The net effect would be to penalize affluent families for leaving the public system, but not to penalize others. This seems appropriate if other regulations place the publicly managed system at a competitive disadvantage. It would not be appropriate if publicly and privately managed schools were all on the same competitive footing, as we have urged.

In the short run, a compensatory scheme of this kind would substantially increase both the tax burden and the overall level of expenditure on education, since it would involve spending more money on the disadvantaged and could hardly involve spending less money on the advantaged. In the long run, on the other hand, it might have the opposite effect, since it might reduce the interest of advantaged parents in increasing expenditures for education.

Such a scheme would also lead to an increase in the percentage of educational resources going to the poor. If, as seems likely, it also led to a greater measure of socio-economic integration than the present system, a Regulated Compensatory Model would presumably result not only in redistributing expenditures but also in redistributing resources.

The Regulated Compensatory Model would give schools considerable latitude in determining their own expenditure levels. It would also give parents considerable choice about the expenditure level of the school in which they enrolled their children. In both cases, however, the price of choosing high expenditures would be dealing with large numbers of disadvantaged children.

A scheme of this kind would also be likely to produce more racially, economically, and academically mixed schools than the present system, giving more parents a choice as to the kinds of classmates they wanted their children to have. But again, the price of choosing more advantaged classmates would be that the school had less adequate economic resources.

This is not to say that integration is likely to be complete. We doubt, for example, that any politically feasible system of economic incentives could induce over-applied schools, public or private, to enroll their share of the children with severe behavior problems or severe mental retardation. Economic incentives might, on the other hand, persuade over-applied schools to accept children whose only fault was an IQ of 95 or an unusually large repertory of four-letter words. We expect, in other words, that economic incentives could reduce or perhaps even eliminate discrimination against pupils who belong to the "middle majority." Since incentives will not suffice for dealing with extreme cases, special schools, which might be either publicly or privately managed, would still have to take responsibility for most of these children.

Finally, the Regulated Compensatory Model would provide parents of all kinds with a fairly wide range of program alternatives. The only real option that would be excluded is the school which combines unusually affluent children with unusually ample resources. While this is doubtless the option many people really want, it is not an option that can possibly be available to most people under *any* system. Furthermore, a system that makes such schools available to a privileged few cannot hope to attain the other goals which we think important.

The basic difficulty with the Regulated Compensatory Model, of course, is political, but even this difficulty may not be as serious as it looks. Its principal political virtue is that it might well be attractive to the public schools. This could be especially true in cities where large numbers of parents have already deserted the public schools for independent or parochial alternatives. The Regulated Compensatory Model would offer all voucher schools substantial additional funds for undertaking to educate the most disadvantaged segments of the population. Instead of exacerbating the flight of the middle classes, a model of this kind might help the public schools finance a program that would hold such parents.

A Regulated Compensatory Model might not be as attractive as the Egalitarian Model to most parochial schools, since they seldom enroll many really difficult children. Nonetheless, the compensatory model would give the parochial schools substantially more public money than they are getting now. It would also give them more than they would get under most proposed "purchase of services" schemes. The only important reason for them to oppose it would be if it imposed unacceptable restrictions on their admissions procedures.

The major opponents of the Regulated Compensatory Model are likely to be middle-class parents who would like to be able to take their children out of the public schools, get a voucher of a certain value, and then be able to use their own money to make the child's new school more affluent than the public system. In the long run, such parents could be a potent political force.

Conclusions

In weighing the seven alternatives outlined above, four general conclusions stand out:

   — The effects of various models on the tax rate and on the overall level of educational expenditure are uncertain without detailed estimates of the schedule of payments for different categories of schools and children, and detailed projections of likely parental choices among the alternatives available under each scheme.

   — While most of the proposed schemes appear at first glance to give the poor a larger share of total educational resources than the present system, this appearance is often deceptive. While the more adequately regulated models would lead to more equal expenditures, most would also lead to more segregation by ability and/or income. A scheme which leads to more segregation will raise the relative price of most resources for disadvantaged children. Such relative price increases would probably offset the effect of equalizing expenditures. Only the Regulated Compensatory Models seem likely to give the poor a larger share of the nation's educational resources.

   — Any system which gives schools discretion in choosing among applicants will inevitably reduce the range of choices open to parents whose children are deemed "undesirable" by most educators. Lotteries and quota systems might partly offset the effect of educators' preferences for certain kinds of children. But some system of economic incentives is also needed to ensure that schools give disadvantaged students a reasonable chance of getting into the school of their choice.

   — The fundamental political and pedagogic danger posed by most voucher plans is that a few publicly managed schools would become dumping grounds for the students whom over-applied schools, both public and private, did not want. The over-applied schools would become privileged sanctuaries for students whom educators enjoy teaching. In order to avoid this danger, a voucher system must provide economic incentives for enrolling "undesirable" children.

The seven models analyzed in this chapter by no means exhaust the full range of possibilities. Neither have we examined all the possible consequences of each model, especially given the variety of possible assumptions about admissions regulations to accompany each economic model. We hope to cover these issues more fully in our final report.[7]

---

1 See Milton Friedman, *Capitalism and Freedom*, N.Y. 1962, Chapter 6.

2 Sizer, Theodore, and Whitten, Phillip, "A Proposal for a Poor Children's Bill of Rights," *Psychology Today*, August, 1968.

3 Coons, John; Clune, William; and Sugarman, Steven; *Private Wealth and Public Education,* Harvard University Press, May 1970. Coons and his associates have developed a model statute for California.

4   The possibility of obtaining contributions from rich parents and alumni would presumably make schools somewhat more favorable to applications from such pupils than to applications from the less affluent. So long as contributions remained voluntary, however, the experience of existing private schools and colleges suggests that wealth would have a significant effect on admissions policy only when the size of the anticipated contribution was very large. Existing private schools and colleges do not appear to be influenced by the fact that Parent A could be expected to contribute $200 to the building fund whereas Parent B can not be expected to contribute more than $20. They *do* appear to be influenced by the fact that Parent C can be expected to contribute $20,000 to the building fund whereas Parents A and B can only be expected to contribute $200 and $20 respectively. The number of parents sufficiently rich to influence admissions decisions through potential capital contributions is small. We doubt that any politically practicable system can be devised for offsetting the advantage of being born with such parents. The bureaucratic machinery and regulations needed to eliminate this injustice would almost certainly cause more problems than it would solve.

5   Independent schools almost all have smaller classes and hence spend more money per pupil for teachers' salaries than do the public schools. Teachers' salaries in private schools are generally lower than in public schools, because many teachers are willing to take lower salaries in return for smaller classes and other advantages. The expenditure *per pupil* on teachers' salaries nonetheless usually exceeds public school expenditure.

6   For an analysis of the best available data, see Otis Dudley Duncan, "Ability and Achievement," *Eugenics Quarterly,* March 1968.

7   Three alternatives at least deserve brief mention:
(a) The "California" Model. This model makes eligibility for a voucher conditional on the local public school's having mean reading scores substantially below the national average.
(b) The "Escalator" Voucher. This model makes the overall level of tax support for the EVA contingent on the overall level of private expenditures for tuition, by guaranteeing a fixed ratio between the two.
(c) "Incentives for Integration." This model makes the value of a school's voucher partially contingent on how close its student body comes to some "optimal" racial, economic, or academic mix.

5. THE DEMONSTRATION PROJECT[1]: SPECIFICATIONS AND EVALUATION

This chapter proposes specifications for a meaningful experiment with education vouchers. These specifications are derived in part from the preceding discussion and in part from arguments outlined here. The effects that these specifications would have on both the form of the demonstration and the ease of evaluating its success or failure will be apparent. The first section of the chapter describes general specifications for a demonstration; the second section outlines the evaluation mechanisms which we believe would make it possible to judge the relative success or failure of the demonstration with some confidence.

Specifications

Duration

1. *The demonstration should continue for a minimum of five years and probably should last for eight years.*

Parents in the demonstration should be convinced of the relative stability of the voucher program. Although sophisticated parents will realize that the Federal government cannot guarantee that money will be available for more than one year, some public commitments should be made to ensure at least minimum consumer confidence.

A demonstration of less than five years would discourage applications for admission to schools other than those run by the board of education. Parents would consider it too much bother to transfer children both into and then out of an elementary school. Further, parents might believe that their children would be harmed by changing schools too often.

Moreover, commitment to less than five years would make it extraordinarily difficult to establish new schools. Even if there were adequate funds to cover initial starting costs, and experts available for advising would-be school founders on how to get started, the task of finding a building, personnel, and clients for a short-lived operation would put off all but the hardiest reformers and businessmen. Because it would take several years for new schools to establish themselves and build reputations, it would be several years before parents could make intelligent choices among new schools. If, at that point, the new schools were already phasing out of existence, no real tests of parental preferences would be possible.

Although five years is the minimum acceptable project length, eight years would be preferable. At the beginning of the demonstration period parents would need time to become familiar with their alternatives. Toward the end of the demonstration, parents would be naturally reluctant to enroll their child in a school which might not exist in one or two years. Eight years would ensure full participation for at least one complete "class" of students. We estimate that a demonstration longer than eight years would yield only slight gains in information. Hopefully, the effects would be large and unambiguous. In that case they should be evident after eight years. If the effects were small, the correct strategy would be replication, not extension.

2. *There should be a planning period of at least one year preceding the demonstration.*

A variety of tasks would be required before the demonstration begins. Political machinery responsive to the interests of the parents in the area should be established to control the experiment. Specifically, mechanisms for distributing and redeeming vouchers should be arranged. An information gathering and disseminating agency should be established to collect information about participating schools and to ensure that all parents have access to that information. Educators and parents should be given time to organize and to establish new schools. Time would be required for building or remodeling, hiring staff, and attracting students. Finally, the organizations carrying out evaluations should be given time to collect preliminary information.

Location

Every effort should be made to have more than one demonstration site. There is no substitute for even a partial replication. Whatever the number of sites, certain criteria are relevant for each.

1. *If possible the demonstration should be carried out in an area with a population that is heterogenous with regard to social class and race.* Such an area would be desired for two reasons.

First, unless vouchers were available to both black and white children and to both rich and poor children, the effect of a voucher system on segregation by race and class could not be tested.

Second, the greater the heterogeneity of the population, the more diverse the demand for schools would be and the greater the range of choices for individual parents.

2. *The demonstration area should be confined to the boundaries of a single municipality.*

For one thing, the task of negotiating with more than one school district or municipal government seems impossibly complex. In addition, the impact of the program on local politics, while difficult to appraise under any circumstances, would be easier to appraise if a single municipality, or a self-conscious, self-defined area within a large city, were covered.

3. *Because alternative schools might be difficult to establish even in an eight year period, demonstration should probably be located in an area where a number of existing private schools were willing to become voucher schools for the duration of the project.* In this way, some assessment of parental choice

would be assured. Further, the prior existence of alternative schools is an indication that parents would be interested in such options.

Eligibility of Pupils

1. *The demonstration should include only kindergarten through sixth-grade pupils.*

Many people believe that the early years of a child's education are the most crucial in determining what he will eventually achieve or become. Perhaps because of this, parents seem to be most ·concerned about the quality of education received by their children when they are young. They are, therefore, likely to be more willing to accept the responsibility of choosing schools implicit in a voucher program at the elementary level.

In addition, the costs of elementary schools are less than those of secondary schools. Assuming limited funds, a demonstration project confined to elementary schools would therefore reach more students. Moreover, elementary schools are easier to set up than secondary schools. Accreditation requirements and the need for special facilities are less extensive. Elementary schools are generally smaller than secondary schools. Both these points suggest that more schools would be established in a limited demonstration if secondary schools were excluded.

2. *All children of appropriate age in the demonstration area should be eligible for vouchers.* A random or stratified random sample of children within the demonstration area does not seem politically possible.

Type of Voucher

The compensatory formulae for determining the value of vouchers and levels of tuition described in Chapter 2 should be used in the demonstration. No voucher schools should be allowed to charge tuition over and above the value of the vouchers. Pupils attending parochial voucher schools should receive vouchers worth no more than the cost of their secular education. All schools should be eligible for compensatory funds if they enroll disadvantaged students.

Admissions Procedure

The discussion of admission procedures in Chapter 3 applies to a demonstration as well as to a large-scale project.

1. Voucher schools should be allowed to fill a limited number or percentage of their places in any way they see fit.

This percentage, although it should be no more than half, should be large enough to ensure that children of parents who helped establish a school would be admitted, as would pupils with siblings already in a school. We also believe that schools should be able to select certain pupils according to non-discriminatory criteria based on educational objectives.

2. Voucher schools should be required to fill at least half their places by a lottery among applicants. A lottery seems to be a practical system for ensuring that voucher schools take their share of "difficult" children. It is also important that parents perceive that their children have an equal chance. Many parents now assume that their children have no chance of getting into a selective school, and therefore do not bother to apply. If significant numbers of places were known to be distributed by lot, more disadvantaged parents might apply to such schools.

3. Children should not be arbitrarily expelled from a school during the school year. Appropriate mechanisms are outlined in Chapter 3. The suggested procedures include a review board to ensure that pupils are guaranteed due process rights, and economic incentives to schools to keep students.

Mechanisms For Aiding Parental Choice

An agency should be set up to collect information about schools and to distribute this information to parents. All schools participating in the demonstration should be required to make this information available. The information-gathering agency should collect and validate two types of information on a continuing basis throughout the demonstration. First, certain common information should be collected from all schools participating in the demonstration. This information probably would include descriptive characteristics of the school (size, pupil/staff ratio, racial and social class composition, age of building, etc.). It might also include some objective measures of pupil performance (test scores). The nature of this information should be determined by the agency administering the experiment by taking into account: (a) the information desired by parents, which should be made available to the public, and (b) the information desired solely by OEO, which could be confidential.

A school should also be able to define its own criteria of "quality" or success (tests of musical or artistic performance, data about special extra-curricular activities) and request the information-gathering agency to verify this data and include it in publications about the school. The information-dispensing agency should devise ways, probably involving personal contact, to make all collected information available and understandable to *all* parents in the demonstration.

Administration

Some agency should have overall responsibility for administering the voucher plan. This education voucher agency (EVA) should be representative of the community. Its particular form would depend on the nature of the site chosen for the experiment. Above all, it should have legitimacy in the eyes of the parents and educators. It would have two basic functions:

    — It would have overall fiscal authority. This would include overseeing the administration of vouchers to all parents. It would also include allocating funds to the information collecting and dispensing agencies, to the review board and to any other agency set up for the demonstration, and allocating funds for starting costs to new schools, and for transportation costs to all students in the demonstration requiring such funds. Last, it should redeem vouchers and distribute funds to eligible schools. In addition, it might wish to fund its own local evaluation effort. OEO's overall evaluation should, however, be funded directly by OEO.

    — It would have authority to make necessary administrative decisions. It would have final authority over each of the agencies to which it allocates funds. It would also certify schools for participation in the demonstration. This is likely to be a complicated problem. Guidelines for certification should be established. Participating schools should accept a voucher as full payment of tuition. They should agree to a lottery system if they are over-applied. They should agree to the decisions of the review board on expulsions. Aside from these requirements, schools would presumably have to meet the established state and local criteria for accreditation with regard to building codes, teacher certification, curriculum, etc. *We strongly recommend that the EVA obtain waivers of unnecessarily restrictive state and local education regulations.* The reason is clear. If extensive curriculum and teacher certification requirements were imposed on every participating school, the trend would be toward uniformity rather than diversity. This would discourage innovative schools and would reduce the overall level of choice available to parents.

Costs

It is impossible to estimate the cost of a demonstration project with any accuracy before selecting a site, contacting existing schools, and surveying the likely choices of parents in the area. For illustrative purposes, however, let us make the following assumptions:

1. In order to find out very much about parental choices and the character of the "education market in one area," we would need at least 10 privately controlled secular voucher schools, several parochial voucher schools, and several neighborhood public schools. This mix would allow the development of genuine competition and "product differentiation," and would test the capacity of parents to discriminate between a fairly wide variety of alternatives. If the average voucher school enrolled 200 children, 2,000 families would need to be willing to remove their children from public or parochial school for the experiment.

2. In order to obtain 2,000 families interested in such schools, we assume that we would need an area in which there were at least 12,000 children between 5 and 11 years old. We assume, in other words, that about a sixth of the population would choose privately controlled voucher schools under the ground rules we have proposed. This figure is arbitrary but enables us to develop rough estimates.

3. Let us suppose that the area were 30% Catholic. Assume further that 1/3 of the Catholics in the area would attend public school, and 2/3 parochial schools, all of which would elect to become voucher schools in order to cash vouchers.

4. Let us assume that the basic voucher were set at $750 per child. Assume also that "compensatory" payments for low-income children began when the parents' income falls below the national median, and that such payments rose to a maximum of $750. Let us assume that two-thirds of the demonstration area children were from families with below-average incomes, and that they carried an average compensatory payment of $300 per child. This would make the average expenditure in the demonstration area $950 per pupil. If 12,000 pupils were covered, the overall annual expenditure in the area would be $11.4 million.

5. Let us assume that per pupil expenditure in the public schools at the beginning of the experiment were $500 per pupil, and that 80 percent of the children in the area were in public schools at the beginning of the demonstration. The public schools are thus presumed to be spending $4.8 million at the beginning of the experiment. They would be required to commit themselves to maintaining this level of effort.

6. Let us assume that parochial schools would not be entitled to a full voucher because their audited expenditures for secular purposes (exclusive of

compensatory benefits) come to only $500 per pupil rather than $750. This would save $250 apiece for some 2400 children, reducing the original $11.4 estimate by $600,000 to $10.8 million.

7. The overall cost of the school programs being $10.8 million, and the local contribution being $4.8 million, the cost to OEO would be $6.0 million, plus administration, evaluation, planning, etc., per year.

It must be recognized that these estimates are very rough. Different assumptions would have great influence on the estimates. Also, we must assume that costs would rise steadily from year to year.

Summary

We have sketched some initial specifications for an OEO voucher project. We suggest that wherever possible, a demonstration should follow the guidelines set out in the previous chapters for a large-scale project. We therefore argue for a compensatory voucher program, for a partial lottery for admissions, and for mechanisms aiding parental choice. In addition, we recommend that a demonstration continue for a minimum of five and preferably eight years; that it be located in an area heterogeneous with respect to social class and race and within the boundaries of a single municipality; and that only elementary school children be eligible for vouchers. We estimate that a demonstration area should include about 12,000 eligible children. We estimate the annual costs to OEO of such a demonstration would be in the range of $6 to $8 million.

In addition, we have set out a very tentative administrative structure. But we anticipate that this would be modified once a site had been selected.

Evaluation

An evaluation of a voucher demonstration project should include three components:

- A political and educational history of the demonstration,

- An evaluation of the specific objectives of the program, and

- An assessment of criticisms of the voucher plan.

This section suggests criteria, mechanisms, and designs for carrying out these three tasks.

1. General Recommendations

— An OEO demonstration project might become the model for future large-scale voucher projects. This suggests that mechanisms for the demonstration should be similar to those regarded as desirable for future projects. It should be recognized, however, that it might be easier to ensure equal opportunities for poor parents in an OEO demonstration than in a large-scale system. The proposed mechanisms for establishing equal choice and access to schools (i.e., restrictions on tuition, a lottery to allocate scarce places, compensatory grants, and an efficient information gathering and dispensing agency) may be less important to legislators than to OEO, and therefore might be abandoned entirely in a non-OEO project. It might also be easier to get temporary suspensions of building codes, certification requirements, and the like for a demonstration project than for permanent legislation. Nonetheless, a demonstration should try to demonstrate what ought to be done, rather than being a prototype of what is most likely to be done. If any other approach were followed there would be little likelihood of evaluating the full potential of a voucher system.

— Any demonstration would be idiosyncratic. The political climate, the racial, ethnic, and social class mix of the area, the number of available alternative schools, and the amount of dissatisfaction with the public schools would all affect the findings of an evaluation. Great care must therefore be taken in making inferences from the results of any one demonstration. It is unlikely that the results would be the same in a permanent, large-scale project, even if it were carried out in the same area. *This suggests that more than one demonstration area should be funded.*

— Any single evaluation of a demonstration would have certain shortcomings. Evaluators, no matter how hard they try, must still make somewhat arbitrary decisions about which objectives they examine, and what methods of evaluation they use. OEO should, therefore, retain several groups of evaluators. Each group should independently define objectives and the way they are to be evaluated. At least one of the evaluation groups should be particularly responsive to the interests of the parents. None should be fiscally dependent on the agency administering the project.

— Even if these recommendations were followed, a demonstration might appear more conclusive than it really is. Claims of what it proves about any particular issue, therefore, should be kept to a minimum.

2. Monitoring the Political and Educational History and Consequences of the Demonstration

July 1970 — August 1971 — The Planning Year

Political conflict might be great. Many groups would be attracted by the Federal and state monies available for the demonstration. Each group might have its own ideas about the desirable form of demonstration. Though political pressures might force the abandonment of the recommended voucher plan during the planning year, it is more likely that compromises in the structure of the demonstration would be reached to appease powerful groups. An analysis of the political situation during this period would be critical for an understanding of what people expect, want, and will get from a tuition plan. If the demonstration were seriously altered or terminated prematurely, this analysis might suggest why and how to establish a new demonstration in another location.

Other data also should be available to evaluators. People would want to start new schools, to decide whether to send their children to alternative schools in the following year, and to understand the implications of the "new" scheme. The information collecting and dispensing agencies should set up early in the "planning" year, and should keep complete records. These records should be available to evaluators as baseline data for the overall evaluation.

September 1971 - June 1980 — During and After the Demonstration

During this period similar evaluations should be carried out. A political history should be kept and descriptive information gathered about the demonstration. To a large extent the information gathered by the information-collecting agency should suffice. As the demonstration progressed a number of potential problems could be examined.

— The admissions mechanism could be examined. By the second year of the demonstration, the evaluators should begin to be able to estimate the importance of over-application to specific schools and the overall effect of the lottery mechanism on parental choice, levels of enrollment, segregation, etc.

— The economic model could be examined. Again early in the demonstration evaluators should be able to estimate the equalizing effect of the "compensatory" model on the services children receive in schools.

— The adequacy of the information collecting and dispersal agencies could be examined. Early in the project there should be some indication as to the overall effectiveness of the mechanisms in making pertinent information available to all parents.

These evaluations should have a feedback effect on the demonstration. If they suggested that the agencies were not performing efficiently, it would seem reasonable to alert people and to attempt to correct performance. This path, however, should be taken with caution. Preliminary indications of a problem might be misleading and corrective measures, therefore, inappropriate. Further, substantial tinkering would complicate the already difficult business of generalizing from the results of the demonstration to other voucher projects. We think, however, that a demonstration of the voucher project should attempt to set an "ideal." The benefits of such corrective measures then should generally outweigh possible costs in generality. It should be noted that the amount of "corrective" action required to keep the agencies performing efficiently would in itself be an important subject for evaluation.

The effects of the voucher plan on parts of the education system other than parents and students should also be examined. An analysis of the attempts to establish new schools should be made. The role of teachers' professional organizations in the history of the demonstration should be analyzed. Some estimate should be made of the effect of the plan on the salaries, turnover rate, and attitudes of teachers in the demonstration area.

Finally, the introduction of a new scheme for financing schools would have effects reaching beyond the schools. If parental feelings of efficacy were increased, this might be reflected in higher registration and voting rates. Local political candidates might have to take a stand one way or another on the value of the voucher scheme. Financial incentives tested in a demonstration might create opportunities for new political alignments. Assessment of these changes would be valuable in estimating the overall impact of the voucher scheme.

In summary, there should be a descriptive and historical component in the evaluation of the demonstration. Although this is not a typical evaluation function, special circumstances demand it. To many, the demonstration would be considered a "success" when the first voucher was administered. Yet, until the demonstration was operating, no amount of talking or writing would convince people either that a voucher scheme was feasible, or that it would create outcomes different from those of the present system. Even when the demonstration was going, there would be little hope of accurately evaluating its influence unless careful attention was paid to its effects on the surrounding environment.

3. Evaluation of Specific Objectives of the Demonstration

An evaluation should assess the success of a voucher demonstration in reaching the two stated objectives:

— A voucher system should improve the education of children, particularly disadvantaged children.

— A voucher system should give parents more control over the kinds of schooling that their children receive, particularly the parents of disadvantaged children.

Two general strategies could be used to assess these objectives (which were discussed in detail in Chapter 1). The first might be labeled the "black box" approach. Measures of the quality of education available in the demonstration area could be taken before, during and after the demonstration. The problem with this approach is that it would not show whether or not the voucher scheme itself influenced the outcomes. We would not know, for example, whether the situation would have changed without the voucher scheme, whether the reason for change was the experimental nature of the program, or whether the increase in expenditures for education was the cause of change.

This second strategy involves testing the validity of the assumptions underlying the argument that the voucher plan would lead to improved education and greater parental control. If the assumptions were found to be valid, we would have some assurance that the plan, rather than the circumstances surrounding the demonstration, was causing any changes. We suggest using the second strategy. It requires gathering additional data and greater expense than the "black box" approach, but we think the advantages outweigh the costs.

The arguments for the voucher plan rest on three assumptions which should be evaluated:

(1) A voucher scheme would lead to a greater diversity of educational alternatives.

(2) Poor parents, given financial resources and insured equitable admissions treatment, would be able to exercise greater choice among the alternatives, thereby requiring the schools to be more responsive to their children's needs. This should result in parents' having greater control over the education that their children receive.

(3) The diversity of educational alternatives and the increased

responsiveness of schools to children's needs would lead to improved education, particularly for poor children.

(1) A voucher model would lead to a greater diversity in education.

There are three possible sources of diversity. First, given freedom and financial resources, educators might create large numbers of schools that are significantly different from those now operated by local boards of education. Second, through the exercise of choice, parents might force schools to be more responsive (accountable) to their particular interests, thereby increasing diversity. Third, the decentralization of fiscal control might increase the number of administrators making decisions and, therefore, potentially increase diversity.

In the evaluation, it would be important first to consider whether the voucher scheme increased diversity, then the sources of the increase could be investigated. Three categories for assessing diversity seem helpful:

— Diversity in conventional inputs, e.g., adult/pupil ratio, qualifications of teachers, characteristics of student body, age and nature of building and equipment, curriculum characteristics.

— Diversity in the objectives of schools: Do they focus on the three R's? on "learning to learn"? on music? on discipline?

— Diversity in the outputs of schools: Do some schools teach math better than others? Do some schools produce better informed citizens?

A distinction can be made between "perceived" and "real" diversity. Either might occur without the other. That is, parents and educators might "perceive" that the voucher scheme had spawned diverse schools without "objective" measurement finding the diversity and vice versa. Both types of diversity are important. "Perceived" diversity can lead to "perceived" choice, which in turn might lead to parents' feelings of greater control over their environment; "real" diversity might lead to greater choice and, therefore, greater control. The measurement of "perceived" diversity is relatively straightforward. Parents, educators, and other interested persons should be asked which differences were apparent and whether the new scheme was in part responsible for them.

The measurement of "real" diversity is somewhat more difficult. Although there is a large body of literature dealing with the problem, most previous attempts have been inadequate. Nevertheless, it would be important to obtain objective measures of the three categories suggested above.

Assessment of the three sources of "real" diversity does, however, present problems.

In the demonstration project, it would be important to assess whether the market structure of the voucher scheme would encourage educators to set up new and different schools. As noted earlier, the limited duration of the demonstration would discourage many innovators from starting schools. Specifically, educators starting new schools would need to consider what to do when the demonstration was over; they would have to take into account the large starting costs of new schools; and they would have to consider the problems in building a reputation for the school in a short time. For these reasons, extensive aid should be given to help the development of new schools. Thus, although it would be possible in a demonstration to determine whether the new schools were different from the old, it would be impossible to assess whether educators would set up new and different schools in a larger-scale project.

The second potential source of "real" diversity might be easier to examine in the demonstration because the responsiveness of schools to the wishes of the parents probably would not be greatly influenced by the fact that a demonstration was limited in duration and scope. The measurement problem would be, however, nonetheless difficult.

Multiple measures of schools' responsiveness should be made. A school might be responsive either to the wishes of individual parents or to the collective wishes of parents with regard to hiring and firing of teachers, to curriculum introduction and modification, etc. A number of control groups should be used for comparison purposes. Specifically, at least three sets of comparisons should be made. The responsiveness of schools in the voucher area during the demonstration should be compared (a) to the responsivneness of the schools in the area prior to the demonstration; (b) to the responsiveness of the schools in a nearby and similar non-voucher area; (c) to the responsiveness of schools in an area where decentralization legislation is just going into effect. Furthermore, the schools in the voucher area should be divided into "old" and "new", publicly and privately controlled, etc., for comparisons with the control schools.

The third possible source of "real" diversity is, in part, a given. That is, because financial control would be decentralized, there would probably be greater diversity than before in certain decisions: e.g., teacher salaries, textbook purchases, amount of time devoted to certain curriculum matters. Judging just how much of the overall diversity is due to fiscal decentralization, however, might be very difficult.

In summary, it does *not* appear possible in a demonstration of limited duration to test the proposition that new schools would automatically spring up in reaction to the new buying power of parents. It would be possible, however, to examine whether the "new" schools that did arise differed significantly from the old schools. This would be itself a partial test of whether parents had more choice. It would then be possible to examine whether parents were aware of the available choices and whether they reacted to the choices. It should also be possible to assess whether schools in the demonstration were more responsive to parental pressure.

Finally, it might be possible to assess whether decentralization of fiscal control led to greater diversity of schools. There would be, however, great problems in considering each of these issues — perhaps the greatest being the definition of diversity and thereby the definition of choice.

(2) Parents would have more choice about the education that their children receive. This would lead to parents having greater control.

The second argument has two parts. First is that the voucher plan would extend to all parents, rather than just the rich, the opportunity to send their children to alternative schools. This would allow parents both *actually to place* their children in new or different schools and to *threaten* to place their children in new and different schools. Therefore, both the old and the new schools would have an incentive to be more responsive to the wishes of the parents. The second part of the argument is that parents would exercise their choice in such a way as to obtain greater control over their children's education.

Unless choice exists, there is no reason to believe that the schools would be more responsive to the needs of the child and certainly no reason to think that parents could exercise choice. The economic model, the admission mechanism, the information collecting and dispensing agencies, and the review board were all designed to encourage "real" choice.

Real choice for parents can be presumed to exist if:

— Real diversity exists.

— Everyone can afford alternative schools. The guidelines in our preferred model are designed to accomplish this, but there is no guarantee that they would succeed. If other economic models were used, or the value of the voucher were set too low, the poor might not be any better off than they are in the present system.

Choice, however, would not lead to greater control on the part of parents unless two further conditions were present. First, parents would have to realize that they had a choice and would have to be prepared to use it, both individually and in groups. (The extent of parents' "perception" of choice and of their willingness to exercise their choice, therefore, should be measured.) Second, teachers and principals would have to be aware that parents could and would choose different schools. Otherwise they would have no incentive to be responsive to the wishes of the parents. (Some assessment of teachers' and principals' perceptions, therefore, also should be made.)

Evaluating these issues might take great ingenuity. The task, however, would be necessary if the effects of the voucher scheme were to be estimated. In order to attribute changes in the quality of education to the establishment of a voucher plan, we would have to be able to demonstrate that diversity of educational alternatives led to parental choice, which in turn led to increased parental control and increased school responsiveness to the needs of children.

(3) Children, particularly poor children, would receive improved education.

Improvement presumably would occur because parents would be able to choose from a range of alternatives, and could, therefore, either select more appropriate schools for their children or force their present schools to be more responsive to the needs of their children. Before we could relate diversity in choice and parental control to improved education, however, some way of measuring "improved" education would have to be developed.

One way of measuring improved education would be simply to ask parents and children whether things had gotten better. The response of various types of parents could be contrasted and control groups set up, tested, and studied. Teachers and principals could be similarly questioned.

It is unlikely, however, that this would be entirely satisfactory. Everyone likes to think that objective measures tell us more than subjective perceptions. To "objectively" examine the question of "improved" education, however, would require that some prior value judgments be reached as to what was "improved" education. This suggests, as we noted earlier, that multiple evaluations are important and that the judgments of each evaluator should be made as independently as possible.

Presumably, multiple evaluations would lead to the collection of large amounts of data. Although the evaluators would be independent, attempts should be made to reduce duplication and bother to parents, students, and school personnel.

The analysis of school quality should not be limited to a study of conventional measures of inputs and standardized tests of achievement. The longitudinal nature of the project would allow for a much more detailed and comprehensive approach. Specifically, samples of students might be systematically followed throughout their school years. Measures might be taken of their early achievement and ability, and data gathered on their home environments and on their school experience. These measures could be related to the later achievement of the students, to their admission to high school or college, to their completion or withdrawal from high school, to their attitudes and aspirations.

Many problems, of course, would remain. Specifically, parents would have exercised their choice of schools, thereby mingling the effects of schools with the effects of choice. Some schools might not wish to divulge certain information. The sample size would be small, at least in comparison to some recent surveys. Control groups might not be comparable in certain ways. Finally, the experimental nature of the demonstration might have unexpected effects on the students, the parents, and the schools. Nonetheless, the suggested data should provide an adequate base for estimating changes in the quality of education.

4. Assessment of Criticisms of the Voucher Plan

Three particular aspects of a voucher demonstration should be reviewed:

— The effects of the demonstration on segregation by race, social class and ability should be assessed. This assessment could be made without collecting data beyond that already suggested. The extent of each type of segregation among schools before, during, and after the demonstration could be measured. These measures could be compared to each other and to comparable measures gathered in control locations. All of this is relatively straightforward. Difficulties would arise if subjective criteria were applied.

— The effect of the voucher plan on church/state relations might be easier to examine in a demonstration. In the context of the demonstration, suits holding that the voucher plan was unconstitutional might be brought before the courts. If the courts were to decide to hear the cases, much of the ambiguity presently surrounding the constitutionality of the plan might be removed. Of course, information should also be gathered about the effects of the plan on parochial schools.

— The effects of the voucher scheme on the allocation of resources within a single school district could also be examined without collecting data beyond that already suggested. No estimate, however, of the effects of the plan on resource allocation over a large area would be possible.

Summary

Three general evaluation tasks have been proposed. First, a political and educational history of the demonstration should be maintained. The history should include an analysis of the political pressures for and against the voucher plan. It should also include information about the effectiveness of the mechanisms proposed for admission to schools, for the distribution of vouchers, and for the collection and dissemination of information. We suggest that this latter information should be used as feedback to the demonstration. If agencies were not performing adequately, they should be so informed, and their performance corrected.

Second, the evaluation should test the success of a demonstration in reaching two objectives:

— A voucher scheme would improve the education of children, particularly disadvantaged children.

— A voucher scheme would give parents more control over the kinds of schooling that their children receive, particularly parents of disadvantaged children.

Although the demonstration would not provide definitive answers to these hypotheses, we argue that analyses of the assumptions underlying them would indicate the probable effects that the voucher plan had on school quality and parental control.

Third, an assessment of the principal criticisms of the voucher scheme should be carried out. Specifically, the effects of the voucher plan on segregation by race, social class, and ability, on church-state relations, and on resource allocation in the demonstration area should be monitored. The results of these analyses should not, however, be automatically generalized.

---

1 In the text we use the terms "demonstration," "project," and "experiment" interchangeably. We generally employ the singular form, although as the text makes clear, we do recommend that more than one area be used for demonstration purposes.

6. FOUR ADDITIONAL ECONOMIC MODELS

A. Vouchers Confined to Public Schools

One of the most common criticisms of the voucher system proposed in Section I is that it makes public money available to privately managed schools. Some object to this on constitutional grounds, fearing that it will break down the wall that is supposed to separate state and church. Some object on ideological grounds, fearing that it will result in the creation of large numbers of second-rate profit-seeking schools. Some object on administrative grounds, arguing that it would be much simpler to plan and operate a voucher system if parents' choices were confined to the public sector.

Section I suggested that the distinction between the "public" and "private" sectors would be very different under a voucher system than under the present system of school finance. Privately managed schools which chose to participate in the voucher system would not only receive public money, but would also be subject to public regulation. Specifically, they would have to open their doors to all races, income strata, and levels of ability, in a way that private schools have seldom been willing or able to do in the past. Nonetheless, privately managed voucher schools would still differ in some important ways from publicly managed voucher schools, and a system which excluded privately managed schools would certainly differ in important respects from the system advocated in Section I.

A voucher system which was confined to the public sector might take one of two forms. In its simplest form, the board of education and the superintendent would undertake to develop a variety of "alternative schools" in the public sector. These schools would exist alongside a network of neighborhood schools operated along more or less traditional lines. Parents would be free to enroll their children either in an "alternative school," if they found the program of such a school attractive, or in the neighborhood school. The "voucher system" would simply be a bureaucratic mechanism for allocating money among alternative schools and neighborhood schools on an equitable basis.

A second kind of voucher system confined to the public sector would involve "alternative schools" managed by private groups under contracts with the board of education. In such a system the local board of education would retain ultimate control of program, but would contract with universities, private corporations, community groups, or others to run innovative programs of various types. As in the first version, alternatives would exist alongside a network of traditional neighborhood schools. Parents would have a choice between enrolling their children in the new alternative schools or the traditional neighborhood schools. Again, the "voucher system" would be a mechanism for allocating funds among various schools on an equitable basis.

As usually conceived, both these models differ in one critical respect from the voucher system proposed in Section I. They both allow the Board of Education (or its administrative staff) discretion in determining what kinds of innovation should receive public subsidy and what kinds should not. Both models are therefore attractive to many professional educators, and unattractive to many who distrust the educational profession.

The voucher system proposed in Section I would allow the EVA to regulate the kinds of schools eligible for public subsidy. But the EVA's criteria for determining eligibility would have to be explicit and quasi-legal. The EVA could bar subsidies to schools which charged tuition for voucher students, or schools which discriminated in their admission policy, or schools which refused to disclose specified kinds of information to the public. But it could not withhold subsidies simply for doing a poor job, or for offering a curriculum which offended the taste of the EVA's board, or for any other idiosyncratic reason. It could, of course, invent seemingly "neutral" criteria whose actual purpose was to justify exclusion of a particular school. But the very necessity of doing this would normally lead to a far more just policy than would a system in which the public authorities could give or withhold public monies without offering any explicit justification for the decision.

The difference between the systems is best understood by looking at a hypothetical example. Let us suppose that several young teachers decide that they would like to operate a school along the lines pioneered in Leicestershire, England. In the regulated voucher system proposed in Section I these teachers must meet state requirements for private schools, must demonstrate that their school is open to everyone on a non-discriminatory basis, and must make a full description of their school available to the public. Then, if parents enroll their children, the school can cash their vouchers. If the EVA wants to withhold the money, the burden of proof is on the EVA to show that the school is ineligible to cash vouchers because it violates some previously promulgated regulation.

Now let us suppose that this same group of teachers wants to run the same kind of school in a voucher system confined to the public sector. Under the first version of such a system, the group would go to the superintendent and seek permission to take over an existing public school. The teachers would all be directly employed by the public schools, and their school would differ from existing public schools only insofar as the central administration gave it permission to differ. Under the second version of such a system, the teachers would form a corporation and would contract with the board of education to manage a public school.

Unfortunately, boards of education and superintendents have not usually been very responsive to such proposals for innovative schools. There is nothing in existing law in most states to preclude the establishment of alternative public schools, either within the public system or on contract, and yet only a handful of boards of education have moved in this direction. So long as the burden of proof for demonstrating the value of a proposal is on someone else, boards of education and school administrators are likely to be extremely cautious. The political cost of having said "no" to a good proposal is seldom as great as the cost of having said "yes" to a proposal that then turns out badly.

Furthermore, so long as the criteria for accepting or rejecting a proposal need not be made precise and explicit, most potential innovators will simply assume that their proposals stand no chance of acceptance, and will not bother to develop them into workable form. The board will therefore receive few proposals, and will feel sure that no new ideas or competent leaders exist outside the public system.

Many of these difficulties could be avoided if the local board of education made an official commitment to fund *any* alternative school which met certain explicit criteria. The board might, for example, agree to designate as "public" any school that met minimal state requirements, agreed to open its doors on an equitable basis to everyone, and agreed to disclose fully what it was doing. The board could promise such schools space and fund them on the basis of a per capita formula derived from what it was spending in other schools. In this way the board could in effect become an EVA. With luck, this might convince educational innovators that they had an excellent chance of getting financial support if they followed the official ground rules laid down by the public system for receiving public money, and might lead to a greatly diversified public system.

This approach would presumably rule out the participation of certain kinds of schools. In particular, church-related schools would probably not want to participate, since once they had been designated as legally "public", they would be subject to the Constitutional prohibition against prayers in the same way as existing public schools. Profit-making schools might also be ruled out, although the public system could perhaps allow profit-making groups to *manage* a public school.

The full range of existing procedural and substantive restrictions on public schools would presumably apply to all schools in a voucher system restricted to "public" schools. This might discourage or prevent many innovative educators from participating, and it might seriously restrict the range of alternatives that would become available. Suitable enabling legislation might, however, eliminate this problem.

We conclude that a voucher system confined to the public sector could result in a substantial increase in parental choice *if* the school administration and board of education were willing to take risks. But we expect this would be the exception rather than the rule. A voucher experiment confined to the public sector would almost certainly be some improvement over the status quo, but it would probably mean far more cautious and limited innovation than the system described in Section I.

B. Vouchers Confined to Private Schools

Many people think of an educational voucher system as a proposal for financing private education through "scholarships". The regulated voucher system proposed in Section I goes much further than this, in that (1) it also proposes mechanisms for introducing diversity and choice within the public sector, and (2) it proposes rather stringent conditions for private schools' cashing vouchers. As indicated in Chapter 1, a system of this kind would change the traditional meaning of the terms "public" and "private." On the one hand, even publicly managed schools would presumably have more budgetary and administrative autonomy *vis-à-vis* the school board and the central school administration than at present, and in this respect would be more like private schools. On the other hand, both publicly and privately managed schools would have to commit themselves to genuinely open, non-discriminatory admissions policies, letting in all students without regard to race, and letting in at least half without regard to test scores or neighborhood residence. Many public school administrators have said that they could not or would not try to make neighborhood schools "public" in this sense. This reluctance reflects the fact that parents in many white neighborhoods regard the nearby public school as "theirs," and resist any proposal which would open their school to "outsiders," especially black outsiders. This resistance is likely to be particularly fierce when a large number of "outsiders" is expected to apply. Accepting them would mean severe crowding, double sessions, temporary classrooms, and the like. Restricting enrollment would mean resorting to a lottery or some similar device for choosing among applicants, and would in some cases exclude some neighborhood children from their "own" school. Foreseeing this, some politically sensitive school administrators and mayors have concluded that a voucher system ought to leave the neighborhood public school untouched, and should make vouchers available only to children who want to go elsewhere.

The limitations of this approach are obvious, but not necessarily overwhelming. First, such a system offers little help to public school principals and teachers who would like to try one or another innovative program, but cannot do so because it would be unpopular with some part of their neighborhood clientele. Under a voucher system confined to the private sector, the neighborhood public schools would provide the non-innovative alternative, while the private sector would provide new options to families that wanted them. This is, of course, a traditional division of labor between the public and private sectors in America, but it is probably not one which ought to be encouraged. Since the majority of children will probably remain in public schools no matter what system is adopted, forcing the public schools to remain in a traditional mold and leaving innovation to a few private schools seems unfortunate.

A second major objection to excluding neighborhood schools from voucher system financing and voucher system regulation is that such a policy severely restricts the choices available to black families. Many such families are anxious to enroll their children in racially integrated schools. There is little chance of integrating existing public schools in black neighborhoods. For most black parents the only plausible way to achieve integration is to enroll their child in a school in an integrated or white neighborhood. Most of these schools are now public neighborhood schools. If they continue to admit only neighborhood children, black parents living in all-black neighborhoods will be left with no integrated alternatives.

Despite these limitations, a voucher system which is confined to the private sector has obvious political advantages. While it threatens the existing public school system ideologically, in that it challenges the legitimacy of confining public subsidies to publicly managed schools, it does not threaten the public system politically, since it does not require important rearrangements of financial and staffing arrangements or of attendance patterns. A "private only" voucher system would enable dissatisfied community groups to establish their own schools, and it would also enable principals, teachers, universities, and others with educational ideas to set up their own schools. If church-related schools were allowed to cash vouchers, a "private only" voucher system would also keep the parochial school system going, and would forestall the influx of Catholic children into the already overburdened public system. If profit-making schools were allowed to cash vouchers, a "private only" system would also allow private enterprise to try its hand at education. Even if profit-making schools were barred, non-profit private schools could presumably contract with profit-making firms to provide specific services, operate part of the curriculum, or whatever.

A voucher system confined to the private sector is, then, far less likely than a comprehensive voucher system to result in major changes in the range and quality of choices available to most children. But perhaps for that very reason it may be more politically palatable. Properly regulated, it would certainly represent a modest step in the right direction.

C. Vouchers Confined to the Poor

A number of people have suggested that OEO should conduct an experiment in which the use of vouchers is restricted to the poor. The primary reasons for this suggestion are (1) a feeling that the poor are the ones whose children need special help, especially from OEO, and (2) the hope that if only poor parents received vouchers, the white middle-class could not use the system to maintain segregation. Many of the difficulties with this approach were touched on in Chapter 2 of Section I, especially in the discussion of the "Unregulated Compensatory Model". This part of this chapter deals in more detail with some of the problems with a "poor only" system.

The fundamental problem raised by making vouchers available only to poor children is that *all* children must have access to free schools. If middle and upper income families are denied vouchers, then their children must be able to attend the same neighborhood public school they have always attended. Since most families are not officially defined as poor, most neighborhood public schools, particularly those in middle income neighborhoods, would continue to operate much as they always have. They would presumably not have budgetary autonomy. Thus they would not have any real incentive to find room for applicants from outside the neighborhood. (Even if these applicants had valuable vouchers, the money would go to the central school administration, not the local school.) If public schools in middle-class neighborhoods have no incentive or obligation to make room for disadvantaged children, and if middle-class children have no opportunity for free education except in these schools, the disadvantaged child will have almost no opportunity to use his voucher in an economically integrated school.

Indeed, a voucher system designed exclusively for the poor would involve only a small fraction of the children in *any* public school, even in a relatively poor neighborhood. All existing public schools, including those in the poorest neighborhoods, would therefore have to continue their present operations on much the same financial and administrative basis as at present. This would make it almost impossible to generate new educational alternatives in existing public school buildings or with existing staffs, since these schools and staffs would for the most part be committed to their traditional clientele and could not hold out any alternative to parents who disliked any given innovation.

The public sector could theoretically establish new experimental schools, especially designed for voucher holders, but it would hardly find this politically attractive if vouchers were confined to the poor. For one thing, the new schools would be economically segregated. For another, they would exclude the vast majority of children whose parents are actively dissatisfied with their children's education.

New private schools might be created to cater to voucher holders, but these schools would also labor under great difficulties. No genuine "community schools" would be possible, because no urban community is composed primarily of people who fit any official definition of poverty. Most potential leaders of community school movements would discover that their children and many of their friends' children were not going to qualify for help, and would lose interest in creating a new school. New private schools catering to voucher holders would thus tend to be schools run *by* the middle classes *for* the disadvantaged. They would also be economically segregated.

A voucher system designed exclusively for poor children would probably create few new educational alternatives. It would, however, give some poor children access to *existing* private schools, whose tuition is now beyond the means of poor families. Some of these private schools would, of course, be reluctant to expand their low-income enrollment appreciably, even if the cost of the children's education were largely or entirely covered by vouchers. But some private schools, especially some Catholic schools in poor neighborhoods, would jump at such an opportunity. Such schools now enroll a number of poor children, including many non-Catholics. Many charge these children little or nothing. Vouchers for poor children would enable them to expand their low-income enrollment. Vouchers would also increase these schools' overall income, enabling them to cut class size and make other improvements.

We conclude, then, that a voucher system confined to poor children would enable a moderate number of disadvantaged children in urban areas to attend Catholic schools that are currently underutilized and might otherwise go out of business. Some low-income parents, both Catholic and non-Catholic, would regard this new option as an improvement. The cost to the federal government would also be modest. But a formula for revamping urban education it is not.

D. Vouchers Confined to Non-Profit Schools

One of the most common objections to a voucher system is that it would encourage profit-hungry "hucksters" to open schools which spend most of their income attracting customers and paying back investors rather than educating children. One device for solving this problem is to bar profit-making organizations from cashing vouchers. The California legislature inserted such a provision when it considered enabling legislation for a voucher demonstration during 1970, and similar restrictions have been attached to some other legislation aiding private schools.

This part of this chapter considers three questions:

(a) Would profit-making schools be likely to attract large numbers of students under a voucher system?

(b) Would profit-making schools be likely to provide substantially worse education than non-profit schools?

(c) What would be the practical effect of barring profit-making schools from a voucher system?

(a) Probable Prevalence of Profit-Making Schools

Much of the discussion of "hucksters" in a voucher system seems to be predicated on the notion that vouchers would create an entirely unprecedented opportunity for profit-making groups to open schools. This is hardly so. There are already some six million American children enrolled in non-public schools. Very few of these children are in profit-making schools. In part this is because most of the parents who enroll their children in private schools cannot afford to pay as much tuition as a profit-making school would have to charge.[1] But even those parents who have enough money and choose to buy private education at full cost seldom choose profit-making schools. While no exact statistics are available, several hundred thousand children are enrolled in unsubsidized private elementary schools. Only a handful of these schools are operated for profit.

We have no simple explanation for the prevalence of non-profit rather than profit-making elementary schools. Several factors seem to play a role. When elementary schools operate for a profit, the owner is almost always the principal, rather than some outside individual or corporation. In many cases it is not even obvious to outsiders that the school is operated for profit. Parents often just think of the school as being synonymous with the individual who runs it, and ask no questions about its finances. This suggests that while parents are probably not very sophisticated about school finance, they may be suspicious of schools where profit is an *overt* objective.

The scarcity of profit-making schools is, however, probably attributable to other factors as well. Parents tend to seek schools which have a good reputation, and reputations depend heavily on what educators say about a place. Educators in non-profit schools have a strong prejudice against profit-making schools. In some cases this prejudice is so strong that accrediting associations refuse to consider profit-making schools as even potentially reputable, although this is more common at the college level.[2]

It is true that when students begin to make their own decisions about their education, they are more likely to enroll in profit-making institutions. Driver training schools, foreign language schools, computer programming schools, secretarial schools, beauty schools, and a host of others testify to people's willingness to attend institutions which operate for a profit when they want specific skills rather than more general education. But this is not very relevant to elementary schooling, which is primarily concerned with socialization and general training of a kind that most parents do not seem to think a profit-making school is likely to provide.

These judgments are reenforced by looking at higher education. There are a handful of proprietary colleges, and a much larger number of proprietary technical training institutions. When the G.I. Bill gave large numbers of young men a chance to attend the institution of their choice, a small number enrolled in "fly-by-night" institutions which took their money and taught them little or nothing. Most of these institutions purported to teach some marketable skill. Very few purported to offer liberal education or even professional-level training. They managed to defraud their students largely because there was no professional group or regulatory agency designated to police their activities. Whenever serious regulatory efforts were instituted, the problem diminished to a negligible level. Furthermore, even when regulation was non-existent, fraudulent institutions got only a tiny fraction of the market. The great majority of GI's, even those who were in no way sophisticated about differences between "good" and "bad" colleges, applied to reputable institutions. While there seem to have been plenty of GI's who learned little of value from their post-military education, most of them were enrolled in fully accredited colleges, often under public control. This would probably be true in a voucher system too.

Some critics of vouchers argue that while middle-class parents and students may have enough sense to avoid schools run by profiteers, disadvantaged parents are not equally shrewd. The poor are now the most frequent victims of business fraud, and a voucher system is often expected to make this equally true in education. If the present non-profit system were serving the poor at all adequately, this argument would be very telling. Given the actual distribution of benefits from non-profit schools, the case is less clear. Our field work suggests that the initial educational preferences of disadvantaged parents in a voucher system would probably be quite traditional. The idea that schools should teach manners and morals is as strong among the disadvantaged as among the advantaged, and distrust of business is even more widespread among the poor than among the affluent. This makes it hard to imagine large numbers of poor parents turning their children over to schools which they *perceive* as primarily profit-oriented.

Large corporations that wanted to break into an educational market might try to deal with such suspicions by linking up with some respected local non-profit group which wanted to start a voucher school. The corporation might then contract with the local group to manage part or all of the school program. Most non-profit schools already make such arrangements for certain services. Both public and private schools normally contract with profit-making firms to do their construction work, for example, and many do the same to obtain school lunches, to have their buildings maintained, and so forth. Even on the instructional side, most schools contract with profit-making firms to obtain instructional materials such as textbooks and audio-visual equipment. In the past two years, a number of public schools have also entered into contracts with profit-making firms to train teachers, set up new classroom arrangements, and so forth. Such contracts would presumably be permissible even in a system which barred profit-making schools from cashing vouchers.

Of course, profit-making schools need not be operated by national corporations. Small local groups, including bona fide educators, may also start proprietary schools. We suspect, however, that the disclosure requirements proposed in Section I would have a very adverse effect on enrollment in any proprietary school that made large profits. If an individual wanted only modest profits, and if he planned to manage the school himself, he would probably find it easier to attract students if he made himself principal and paid himself a good salary than if he tried to operate as a profit-making enterprise.

The foregoing considerations suggest that even if a voucher system allows profit-making schools to participate, the number of parents using such schools is likely to be small. This prediction could be wrong, however. Furthermore, even if it is right, it does not answer the question of whether profit-making schools *should* be allowed to participate. The answer to that question does not depend on whether profit-making schools are likely to get one percent of the market or fifty percent, but on whether children who attend such schools are substantially more likely to be miseducated than children in non-profit schools.

(b) Quality of Profit-Making Schools

It is more or less an article of faith among non-profit enterprises in any particular field that they offer services superior to those provided by profit-making enterprises in the same field. This assumption may well be correct, but it is hard to find much evidence to support it, either in education or elsewhere. Persuasive evidence about the quality of services offered by different enterprises is simply not available in most fields, including education. Generalizations about the quality of profit-making schools must therefore be deduced from theoretical arguments rather than being built up on the basis of empirical evidence. This is a risky business.

Critics who argue for exclusion of profit-making schools offer two justifications for this position. First, they assert that all schools are plagued by inadequate resources, and any arrangement which allocates some of these resources to profit inevitably leaves less for education. Second, the critics argue that the profit motive will affect the way in which a school is operated, to the detriment of the students.

The first argument is unpersuasive. If schools were shoe factories, in which a well-understood technology was being applied in a relatively consistent fashion, it might be reasonable to assume that any reduction in the resources available for the enterprise would reduce output. But schools are not shoe factories, and the factors affecting their output are virtually unknown. The available evidence indicates that expenditures have very little impact on such outputs as standardized test scores, college entrance rates, and student attitudes. This suggests that the amount of money a school spends is less important than the way the money is spent. A profit-making school which diverts ten or even twenty percent of its income to profit, but which uses the other eighty or ninety percent wisely, will produce better results than a school which spends all its money in the school but uses it less imaginatively.

The question, then, is whether non-profit schools are more likely than profit-making schools to use their money imaginatively. We have no clear basis for answering this question. Supporters of profit-making schools claim that the profit motive generates efficiency, but this argument seems unpersuasive, since competition between non-profit schools should serve the same purpose. Supporters also argue that the possibility of making a profit will attract individuals to education who are more willing to take risks than the average educator. This may be true, but it is not necessarily desirable. There is no evidence that the kinds of risks businessmen are willing to take have any relationship to the education of children.

The critics of profit-making schools argue that attempts to maximize profits lead to a variety of corner-cutting arrangements within a school. Unfortunately, attempts to balance non-profit budgets have precisely the same result. It may be that money is less of a consideration on a day-to-day basis in non-profit schools. But this may simply be another way of saying that people who run profit-making schools are likely to have different preoccupations from people who run non-profit schools. Profit-making schools may be more willing to alter established procedures in order to cut costs, and less concerned with the effect of such alterations on the internal tranquility of the school. Whether this would be an argument for or against proprietary schools is unclear.

The most visible difference between profit and non-profit schools is likely to be the staffing pattern. All schools allocate the bulk of their budget to staff, and there is little room for economy in any other area. If a school is to make a profit while operating at the same budgetary level as a non-profit school, it must either pay its staff less or hire fewer of them.

Neither of these economies would automatically reduce the quality of children's education. There has been considerable research on the relationship between teacher salaries and school effectiveness. It shows the relationship to be extremely erratic. Likewise, two generations of research have shown that while teachers, students, and parents almost all prefer small classes to large ones, students who are educated in small classes emerge almost indistinguishable from those educated in large ones.[3] Thus it is hard to see any compelling evidence that profit-making schools would turn out worse educated children if they economized on staff costs while innovating in other ways.

Overall, we doubt that profit-making schools would be more effective than non-profit schools. But the evidence that profit-making schools would necessarily be less effective is also unpersuasive.

(c) Practical Problems

Let us suppose that a state or the local EVA decides that only non-profit schools can cash vouchers. What are the results likely to be?

First let us consider a situation where there is a very large unmet demand for certain kinds of education. Under these circumstances there might be a good deal of potential profit in setting up a suitable voucher school. If profit were forbidden, firms which thought they could meet the demand would probably try to establish non-profit subsidiaries to operate schools. They would then have these subsidiaries contract with the profit-making parent organization to manage the school, supply textbooks and equipment, train the teachers, or whatever. If the EVA barred such arrangements, the entrepreneur would presumably seek a local "front" which would establish the school on a nominally independent basis, but which would contract with the entrepreneur to provide specified services. The EVA could, of course, forbid all schools to contract with profit-making firms to provide instructional services. A restriction of this kind would, however, seem to defeat the primary objective of the voucher system, namely the encouragement of flexibility and diversity in education.

In addition to educational skills, profit-making firms might be able to provide risk capital. If the EVA put up seed money for new schools and provided adequate loans to rehabilitate facilities, there would be no need for private capital. But if public funds were not readily available for getting new schools started, and if the demand for new schools were substantial, private capital would be essential. In some cases, such capital might simply be borrowed and then repaid from voucher income. But starting a new school is a risky business. Unless there were a chance of making a substantial profit, few private investors would loan large sums to a school which still had no customers. Investors might be persuaded to put up money for initial staffing and rehabilitating facilities if they were guaranteed a share of the school's profits. If profit-making schools were prohibited, all kinds of loan and mortgage agreements could be devised to achieve the same result. A non-profit school might, for example, borrow a large sum from a private investor at a very high interest rate, with repayment contingent on the schools' getting a certain number of students. The main difference between such a loan and the sale of stock would be that the investor would have no formal control over the day-to-day management of the school. But even this might not be true, since the investor might insist on representation on the school's board in return for the initial loan.

The foregoing discussion assumes that a voucher system restricted to non-profit schools would leave many demands for new kinds of schooling unmet, and that profit-makers would therefore be eager to enter the field. This need not be true. If technical assistance and risk capital are fairly readily available to individuals and groups wanting to start non-profit schools, such schools will proliferate to meet almost any widely felt need. If non-profit schools are competitive, flexible, and relatively efficient, the potential profit margin for entrepreneurs will inevitably be low. Under these circumstances it would be relatively simple to enforce regulations which excluded profit-making enterprises from the system. When potential profits are high, ingenious businessmen and attorneys will devote endless hours to getting around official restrictions. But when potential profits are low, they no longer think it worth the bother to circumvent official regulations, and turn to other fields.

The best way to prevent profit-making schools from entering a voucher system may, then, be to make rules which facilitate the creation of non-profit schools. Specifically, the EVA must find ways to provide the risk capital needed to get new non-profit schools off the ground. Otherwise, such capital will have to come from those seeking a profit.

(d) Conclusion

We can see no prima facie case for excluding profit-making schools from a voucher system. The arguments against their participation are all unproven and for the most part illogical. Yet the case for allowing profit-making schools to participate is also far from conclusive. There is no evidence that profit-making schools are more effective than non-profit schools, and some reason to suspect that they might be less so. In the absence of conclusive evidence on either side, it seems wisest to err on the side of permissiveness and let profit-making schools participate. This leaves the decision about whether to trust such schools up to the parents, instead of having the state make up parents' minds for them. Tight regulation of a voucher system seems both necessary and appropriate in those areas (e.g., admissions policy, tuition charges, information disclosure) where past experience has demonstrated that an unregulated system is inadequate or inequitable. But where past experience is inconclusive, as in the case of profit-making schools, it seems more reasonable to avoid regulation and create a system which generates a wide variety of options.

---

1 The overwhelming majority of private schools are affiliated with a religious denomination. Most of these church-related schools spend less per pupil than nearby public schools. In good part this is because they are at least partly staffed by religious teachers who work for subsistence. In addition, some church-related schools receive direct subsidies from the churches with which they are affiliated. Most church-related schools have thus been able to keep tuition relatively low, in a way that proprietary schools cannot. All this is changing, but it makes past parental preference for church-related schools irrelevant when considering the likely future demand for places in profit-making schools.

2 The Middle States Association of Colleges and Secondary Schools, for example, will consider proprietary secondary schools for membership but not proprietary colleges. It accredits three such schools. The Western Association of Schools and Colleges also accredits proprietary schools.

3 See, e.g. James Coleman *et al., Equality of Educational Opportunity,* U.S. Government Printing Office, 1966. While the "Coleman Report" has been widely criticized on methodological grounds, the Report's conclusions on these issues have been supported by much other research and by reanalyses of the EEO data. See, e.g., the articles to be published in Daniel Patrick Moynihan and Frederick Mosteller, *On Equality of Educational Opportunity,* Random House (forthcoming).

PART III

The Alum Rock Experiment

SENATE BILL No. 120

Introduced by Senators Harmer and Alquist
(Coauthors: Assemblymen Campbell and Ryan)

January 25, 1972

Senate Bill No. 120 represents the philosophical enabling thrust to provide educational alternatives to the children of the State of California through the use of education vouchers. Of four proposed "Demonstration Scholarship Programs," the Alum Rock Elementary School District in San Jose is the first. Indeed, it is the first "Education Voucher Project" in the nation. However, California was not the first state to pass *voucher legislation. That distinction belongs to the State of Connecticut where Public Act No. 122 was passed into law on April 28, 1972.*

An act to add Chapter 2.5 (commencing with Section 31175) to Division 22 of the Education Code, relating to the Elementary Demonstration Scholarship Act of 1972.

Legislative Counsel's Digest

SB 120, as introduced, Harmer. Elementary Demonstration Scholarship Program.

Enacts Elementary Demonstration Scholarship Act of 1972, authorizing no more than four school districts or groups of districts of specified a.d.a. to participate in demonstration programs whereby the districts would make educational scholarships available to school pupils in kindergarten and grades 1 to 9, inclusive, residing in a demonstration area. Declares legislative intent. Prescribes standards for determining amount of scholarship. Provides that the scholarship may be used at any school, including private schools, meeting prescribed standards. Prescribes method of computing a.d.a. of a demonstration district.

Permits demonstration school districts to contract for demonstration funds.

Limits duration of such programs from 5 to 7 years.

Vote—Majority;   Appropriation—No;   Fiscal Committee—Yes.

The people of the State of California do enact as follows:

SECTION 1. Chapter 2.5 (commencing with Section 31175) is added to Division 22 of the Education Code, to read:

Chapter 2.5. The Elementary Demonstration Scholarship Act of 1972

Article 1. General Provisions

31175. This chapter shall be known and may be cited as the Elementary Demonstration Scholarship Act of 1972.

It is the intent of the Legislature to enable one or more school districts in the State of California to participate in no more than four demonstration programs designed to develop and test the use of education scholarships for schoolchildren.

The purpose of the Elementary Demonstration Scholarship Program is to develop and test scholarship programs as a way to improve the quality of education by increasing the level of academic achievement of the pupils involved by making schools, both public and private, more responsive to the needs of children and parents, to provide greater parental choice, and to determine the extent to which the quality and delivery of educational services are affected by economic incentives. The demonstration scholarship program authorized by this chapter shall be used exclusively to aid students.

31176. As used in this chapter:

(a) "Elementary Demonstration Scholarship Program" means a program for developing and testing the use of education scholarships for schoolchildren in kindergarten and grades 1 to 9, inclusive, or any combination thereof.

(b) "Demonstration area" means the area designated by the participating local board for the purposes of a demonstration program.

(c) "Demonstration board" means a board established by the participating local board to conduct an elementary demonstration scholarship program. In the event the local board designates a board other than itself to act as the demonstration board, public hearings on appointment procedures to assure community acceptance shall be held. The demonstration board shall consist of no fewer than five or more than 15 members, who shall be residents of the participating local district, and shall be representative of the population of the participating district. The members of the demonstration board shall serve for the terms established by the appointing power.

(d) "Participating local board" means an elementary or unified school district governing board or two or more elementary or unified school district governing boards contracting with a state or federal governmental agency to conduct an elementary demonstration scholarship program.

(e) "Public school" for the purposes of this chapter means any school which admits students to kindergarten and grades 1 to 9, inclusive, or any combination thereof, residing in the demonstration area without distinction to location of residence, race, color, national origin, economic status, or political affiliation, and which is otherwise qualified to negotiate vouchers under the provisions of this chapter.

(f) "Contract" for the purposes of this chapter means the agreement entered into by a local board and a state or federal governmental agency for the purpose of conducting an elementary demonstration scholarship program.

Article 2. Establishment and Administration of Demonstration Programs

31180. There is hereby established the Elementary Demonstration Scholarship Program, to exist for a period of at least five and not more than seven years commencing upon the effective date of this section.

31181. A school district governing board, or combination of school district governing boards, may contract with a state or federal governmental agency for funds to establish an elementary demonstration scholarship program. There shall be no more than four elementary demonstration scholarship programs. Each district in which a program is established shall have had no fewer than 1,000 students in average daily attendance in the year preceding the demonstration program. The overall population of any demonstration area shall include a substantial number of disadvantaged children.

31182. The demonstration board shall control and administer the demonstration program, and shall adopt rules and regulations for the efficient administration of the demonstration program. These rules and regulations shall provide for the following:

(a) The scholarship funds shall be expended exclusively for the secular education of students.

(b) Comprehensive information on all eligible schools, as defined in Section 31185, shall be disseminated by the demonstration board to the parent or guardian of each eligible child in the demonstration area no later than six months preceding the commencement of the school year for which the elementary demonstration scholarships are to be issued. Provision shall be made to advise all eligible recipients of the opportunities available to them under this chapter.

(c) Eligible schools shall be required to file with the demonstration board a statement of financial responsibility in compliance with standards established by the demonstration board.

(d) The demonstration board may review and approve the expulsion or suspension of any student by any eligible school, so that no arbitrary action by any school would invalidate the admissions standards established in this chapter.

31183. The scholarship funds may be made available for the school year beginning after the effective date of this chapter, and for each subsequent year of the demonstration; provided that at least six months prior to the initial issuance of the elementary demonstration scholarships the demonstration board has undertaken comprehensive planning for the demonstration project.

31183.5 The demonstration board shall award a scholarship to each school-child residing in the demonstration area, subject only to such age and grade restrictions which it may establish.

The scholarship funds shall be made available to the parents or legal guardian of a scholarship recipient in the form of a voucher, drawing right, certificate, or other document which may not be redeemed except for educational purposes which satisfy the requirements of Sections 31185 and 31186. All scholarships are exempt from state income taxes.

31184. The demonstration board shall establish the amount of the scholarship in a fair and impartial manner, as follows:

(a) There shall be a basic scholarship equal in amount to every other basic scholarship for every eligible student in the demonstration area. In no case shall the amount of the basic scholarship fall below the level of average current expense per pupil in all the elementary schools governed by the participating local board in the year immediately preceding the demonstration program.

(b) In addition to each basic scholarship, compensatory scholarships shall be given to disadvantaged children. The amount of such compensatory scholarships and the manner by which children may qualify for them shall be established by the demonstration board.

(c) In determining the amount of the compensatory scholarship, consideration shall be given to the needs of children intended as recipients of categorical or special aid funds and in-kind materials.

(d) Adequate provision for the pro rata or incremental redemption of scholarships shall be made.

31184.5 The contract shall provide sufficient money to pay all actual and necessary transportation costs incurred by parents in sending their children to the school of their choice within the demonstration area, subject to distance limitations imposed by existing law.

31184.7 The contract shall specify that the contracting state or federal governmental agency shall hold harmless the participating local board from any possible decreased economies of scale or increased costs per pupil caused by the transition to a demonstration program.

31185. The demonstration board shall authorize the parents or legal guardian of scholarship recipients to use the demonstration scholarships at any school in which the scholarship recipient is enrolled which also:

(a) Meets all health and safety standards required by law.

(b) Does not discriminate against the admission of students and the hiring of teachers on the basis of race, color, national origin, economic status, or political affiliation and has filed a certificate with the State Board of Education that the school is in compliance with Title VI of the Civil Rights Act of 1964 (Public Law 88-352); and provides that students from minority and ethnic groups be admitted in proportion as such students make application; and takes an affirmative position to secure a racially, ethnically, and socio-economically integrated student body which shall, to the greatest possible extent, reflect the racial, ethnic, and socioeconomic composition of the demonstration area. Any school that receives applications in excess of enrollment capacity shall fill at least 50 percent of its enrollment capacity by a lottery among the applicants, to further assure nondiscriminatory admissions procedures. Enforcement of this subdivision shall be vested in the demonstration board. The demonstration board shall immediately investigate all complaints of violations of this subdivision and, after adequate notice and hearings, shall suspend redemption of any scholarships by any school in violation of this subdivision. The decision of the demonstration board shall be final, except that nothing in this subdivision shall be construed so as to deny judicial review. In the event an otherwise eligible school is subsequently found to be ineligible, the demonstration board shall immediately notify the parents of the students in attendance of such ineligibility.

(c) In no case levies or requires any tuition, fee, or charge above the value of the education scholarship.

(d) Is not controlled by any religious creed, church or sectarian denomination except as provided in Section 31186.

(e) Provides public access to all financial and administrative records and provides to the parent or guardian of each eligible child in the demonstration area comprehensive information, in written form, on the courses of study offered, curriculum, materials and textbooks, the qualifications of the teachers, administrators, and paraprofessionals employed, the minimum school-day, the salary schedules, the actual amount of money spent per pupil and such other information as may be required by the demonstration board. In no case shall the public have access to personal information concerning individual pupils. The demonstration board shall determine the form and manner in which this information shall be submitted and may suspend redemption of any scholarships by any school not complying with the provisions of this subdivision.

(f) Provides periodic reports to the parents on the average progress of the pupils enrolled, including the administration and reporting of any state-wide examinations required by law for the public elementary schools of California.

(g) Offers a comprehensive course of study in the basic skill areas of reading; mathematics; and the English language, whether as a second language or the language of instruction.

(h) Maintains a register of reports, including monthly attendance, and any other information as may be required by the demonstration board.

(i) Prohibits instruction in, or advocacy of, the violent overthrow of the United States or California state government.

(j) Is a public school as defined in subdivision (e) of Section 31176.

31186. In compliance with the constitutional guarantee of free exercise and enjoyment of religious profession and worship, without discrimination or preference, schools may be exempted from subdivision (d) of Section 31185 if they meet all other requirements for eligibility including the provision in subdivision (a) of Section 31182.

31187. The participating local board, after public hearings, may request the Superintendent of Public Instruction to selectively waive any restrictive or limiting provisions of this code for the schools under his jurisdiction in the demonstration area, except the provisions of this chapter. The Superintendent of Public Instruction may waive provisions pursuant to this section, as in his judgment will improve the educational opportunities of the students participating in the demonstration program.

31187.2. The participating local board may also request the Superintendent of Public Instruction to waive any restrictive or limiting provisions of this code for any school within its jurisdiction not participating in the demonstration program, except the provisions of this chapter.

The purpose of this section is to permit the establishment of a control group of schools of comparable characteristics and size with the flexibility to innovate in education without using education scholarships. This may be done in order to compare the progress of students and the type and variety of educational offerings of control group schools with that of schools participating in the Elementary Demonstration Scholarship Program.

No statutory financial penalties shall be assessed during the period of the demonstration which are associated with those sections of the Education Code which may be waived by the participating local board for the purposes of the demonstration.

31187.5. The participating local board may rent or lease any of its property, equipment, buildings or other facilities for the duration of the program.

31187.7. The participating local board may authorize any certified or classified employee to take a leave of absence for the duration of the demonstration program for the purpose of accepting employment directly related to the demonstration program.

31188. The demonstration board may:

(a) Employ a staff for the demonstration board.

(b) Receive and expend funds to support the demonstration board and scholarships for children in the demonstration area.

(c) Contract with other government agencies and private persons or organizations to provide or receive services, supplies, facilities, and equipment.

(d) Determine rules and regulations for use of scholarships in the demonstration area.

(e) Adopt rules and regulations for its own government.

(f) Receive and expend funds from the state or federal governmental agency necessary to pay for the costs incurred in administering the program.

31188.7.   The meetings of the demonstration board shall be open to the public, and the residents of the demonstration area shall be afforded the regular opportunity to express themselves before the demonstration board.

31189. An impartial, private or public, nonprofit institution, foundation, or university shall research, evaluate and report on the Elementary Demonstration Scholarship Program to the Governor and Legislature of the State of California by the fifth calendar day of each regular session of the Legislature for the duration of the demonstration program.

The research model, and the contractor, shall be selected by the contracting governmental agency and the demonstration board prior to the commencement of the first school year in which scholarships will be issued.

The contractor shall evaluate the demonstration program and compare it to programs conducted in schools in districts not participating in the demonstration program. The contractor may select control group districts with reasonably similar characteristics to those of the demonstration area. Such characteristics shall include size, enrollment, wealth, expenditures per pupil, and the socioeconomic mix of the district. Other control group districts with substantially different characteristics may be selected by the contractor for the purpose of measuring and comparing various kinds of programs in varying types of learning environments.

The contractor shall have access to the records of the schools in the demonstration area and in the control group districts and is authorized to conduct necessary surveys and tests within the districts for the purposes of this evaluation.

The research and evaluation shall focus upon the identification of measurable change in the progress of students in the demonstration area, and changes in the type and variety of education offerings in the demonstration area.

Special attention shall be given to the achievement of students as measured by standardized tests which are free of cultural bias. Relative and absolute gains in growth rates and achievement of students shall be determined by the contractor. The contractor shall report on variations in class size, staff salaries, teacher-administrator ratios, and the qualifications of staff, and the impact that they have on the progress of students.

The contractor may report on the cost effectiveness of the various programs, and may make necessary adjustments to accounting data to insure comparability between programs.

The research and evaluation shall also compare changes in the demonstration area to changes in any schools qualifying under Sections 6493, 6497, or 31187.2 or any other provision which authorizes a waiver of this code. The research and evaluation shall identify the actual amount of money spent per pupil by each school. The contract shall provide for and specify the amount of funds necessary to accomplish this research.

Article 3. Attendance

31190. For purposes of state and local financial support, the Superintendent of Public Instruction and local officials responsible for the allocation of funds to schools in the demonstration area shall compute the average daily attendance in the demonstration area as follows:

(a) The average daily attendance in the elementary schools governed by the participating local board in the demonstration area for the five years immediately preceding the demonstration shall be determined; and

(b) The total enrollment in all elementary schools in the demonstration area shall be determined; and

(c) The ratio of average daily attendance in the elementary schools governed by the participating local board to the total enrollment in all elementary schools in the demonstration area shall be computed for each of the five years immediately preceding the demonstration and the average of the five ratios so derived shall be determined; and

(d) For each year of the demonstration program the total enrollment in all elementary schools in the demonstration area in that year shall be multiplied by the average ratio computed in subdivision (c) to determine the total number of students in average daily attendance.

31191. The participating local board shall receive all public funds allocable to the demonstration area, and shall transfer these funds to the demonstration board.

These funds shall include moneys apportioned to the district from the State School Fund and the proceeds of the property taxes levied for the district. For the purpose of this chapter, the participating local board shall not take any discretionary action to reduce the local property tax rate.

The demonstration board shall use these funds for the demonstration program as provided in this chapter and the terms of the demonstration contract.

Nothing in this section shall prohibit public schools, as defined in subdivision (e) of Section 31176, from receiving grants or gifts from foundations, charitable trusts, governmental agencies, or other public or private sources. Eligible schools shall maintain financial records which clearly report all income, trusts, bequests, gifts, grants, or donations which are used to defray the actual costs of educating students in attendance.

Article 4. Construction of Act

31192. The provisions of this chapter shall be liberally construed with a view to effect its objects and promote its purposes.

31193. If any section, subdivision, sentence, clause or phrase of this chapter is for any reason held to be unconstitutional, such decision shall not affect the validity of the remaining portions of this chapter. The Legislature hereby declares that it would have enacted this chapter and each section, subdivision, sentence, clause or phrase thereof, irrespective of the fact that any one or more of the sections, subdivisions, sentences, clauses or phrases be declared unconstitutional.

The Alum Rock feasibility study was a small study, more suggestive than conclusive in its findings. Nevertheless, its conclusion was accepted that sufficient support exists, in Alum Rock, to proceed into the planning stage. Critics (see for example, "Vouchers on the Rocks" in Part IV) have been quick to find fault with the study. Here are the germane portions of that study:

FINAL REPORT
ALUM ROCK UNION ELEMENTARY SCHOOL DISTRICT
VOUCHER FEASIBILITY STUDY

SANFORD J. GLOVINSKY, Ed.D.
Study Coordinator

April, 1971

Edited and Reprinted
September, 1971
Richard Ruiz
CPE Associate, Editor

Supported by a Grant from the
Office of Economic Opportunity

Introduction

The report which follows presents a chronology of events and activities which were part of the study aimed at determining the feasibility of the Alum Rock Union Elementary School District as a potential site for a voucher demonstration. The study resulted from a grant to the District from the Office of Economic Opportunity.

In the summer of 1970, OEO had issued a general nation-wide request for proposals from interested districts. At that time Alum Rock contacted the Center for Planning and Evaluation and requested assistance in the development of a proposal, and, in the event that the grant was awarded, help in planning and conducting the study. The grant was officially awarded early in February, 1971, although CPE, at the District's request, began preliminary planning at the end of December, 1970.

When the grant had been officially accepted by the Alum Rock Board of

Trustees, the task at hand was the formation of an Education Voucher Committee which would serve as the main working body at this stage of the study. Its function would be to represent the views of the community concerning the different aspects of a Voucher experiment as well as to generate and report its own opinions. The committee was recruited by means of a letter to all segments of the community requesting the designation of representative citizens. To provide direction in the development of an Education Voucher Committee, CPE produced a set of guidelines for the selection of the committee and presented these in the form of a report.

An Overview, Rationale for Selection, Tasks and Bylaws for an Education Voucher Committee

The Education Voucher Committee: An Overview

An education voucher program represents a significant departure from traditional means of financing and managing public elementary education. Such a program will alter financial and organizational structures in public education that have existed since the beginning of the twentieth century. It is essential, therefore, in considering such a change, that the planning and policy-making body to be created be broadly representative of the racial, ethnic, social, economic, occupational, and political segments of the affected community. Without meaningful and widespread community involvement, it is unlikely that a voucher progam would be successful, and furthermore, it would fail to provide a demonstration and test of the program's underlying theoretical principles.

It appears, then, that two qualities should characterize the planning and policy-making group—the Education Voucher Committee: It should be visionary and it should be representative. A committee with vision will recognize the significance of the proposed test and will demand that the operational program reflect, as closely as possible, an "ideal" that could serve as a model for implementation in districts throughout the country. A committee that is representative, in a heterogeneous district, will demonstrate the nature and degree of conflict that can develop in the process of determining the objectives and economic and educational specifications of a voucher program.

Individuals should be chosen for the Education Voucher Committee who possess insight into the philosophical, economic, social, and political issues that are inherent in the proposed program for financing and managing public education. Committee members should have the capacity to consider the total community effects of the voucher project. In addition to a view of the whole community, members should understand and be able to represent the interests of their constituencies. Finally, committee members should be willing to devote long hours to planning the program and resolving conflicts that arise.

Rationale for the Selection of the Education Voucher Committee (EVC)

The rationale for the selection of members of the EVC which will advise the Local Education Agency in the pre-planning (two months) and planning (seven months) stages of the project must reflect the primary goals of the entire Demonstration Voucher Project, i.e. "to improve the education of children, particularly disadvantaged children and to give parents, and particularly disadvantaged parents, more control over the kind of education their children get."[1]

Although the people who comprise the initial EVC during the two-month term of the Feasibility Study may not be the same people who eventually sit on the Education Voucher Authority (EVA) during the years of the demonstration, they should be as widely representative of the many segments of the entire community as the legislation which will establish the group allows. (The total number of members and their representative make-up may be specifically stipulated.)

Although it may be assumed that legislation will probably limit the Education Voucher Authority (EVA), which will function during the demonstration period, to 9 or 10 members, the early EVC need not be restricted in membership. The purposes of the pre-planning and planning stages will be better served by having a broad representation which can then be reduced to the required and less unwieldly number. The following categories of representation are suggested. If all the segments are involved, the EVC would have 24 participating members and 21 voting members for the pre-planning and planning stages. When the project moves to the demonstration stage, the number of voting members would be reduced to 9 (one from each category).

---

1 *Education Vouchers: A Preliminary Report on Financing Education by Payments to Parents,* Center for the Study of Public Policy, Cambridge, Mass., 1970.

The following categories and initial numbers for EVC and EVA are suggested.

Nine Categories for EVC and EVA

Category	Number of Participants	Total Voting Members
1. Minorities:		2
La Confederaction de las Raza	1	
NAACP	1	
2. Community Action Programs		2
E.S.O.	1	
Model Cities	1	
3. Teachers		3
CTA	1	
AFT	1	
Private Schools	1	
4. School Board (Alum Rock)	2	2
5. Educational Administration		1
Alum Rock	1	
*County Office	1	
*State Dept. of Ed.	1	
6. Business		3
Banking/Finance	1	
Business Adm./Mgt.	1	
Unions	1	
7. Community		4
Religious Groups	1	
Service Organizations	1	
Ad Hoc Citizens Groups	2	
8. Parents		2
PTA	1	
Students	1	
9. State Administration & Legislature		1
Local Assemblyman or his Representative	1	
*A Member of the Governor's Office	1	
Total	23	20

*These participants to serve in an ex-officio capacity.
NOTE: County Counsel will be available to advise on legal matters.

These nine categories represent an arbitrary definition of the segments of the society which should be represented. The rationale for why certain groups are placed under a given category may be debatable. Minority and disadvantaged representation are a must for the purposes of the project as outlined by O.E.O. The agencies, organizations, and groups listed in the first two categories seem to represent these segments. The other seven categories likewise will allow these segments to be heard.

The placement of these groups in their various categories is an attempt to further the goals of the project. Although they may at first glance appear to be more divergent than similar in their outlooks, the "areas of concern" are in truth similar. For example, private schools are placed with the "teachers" groups because under the "voucher plan" all schools become "public" to the extent that they become able to cash vouchers. This concept, which reduces public school monopoly to provide parents with new alternatives, also makes necessary a realignment of educational resources.

As stated, these categories and groups represent one viable option for the formation of the initial EVC. By adding additional categories and/or groups, an infinite number of options would be possible. The EVC, once constituted, may wish to augment its membership and should have the freedom to do so.

Experience would seem to demand that some cautions be pointed out. The two-month period designated for the pre-planning stage presents a most formidable constraint. To convene a widely representative group which will then coalesce into a working team capable of consensus recommendations within a two-month period will indeed be difficult. If, after the two-month feasibility study, the Board decides to move into the planning stage, hopefully what should happen is a merging of the pre-planning into the planning stage so that the EVC will have the advantages of continuity. This EVC would function during the planning year and provide overall direction for the project.

Other factors need consideration in a selection process which claims "representativeness." Racial and ethnic percentages in the district show the Spanish surname population to be 47.2% and total minority population nearly 60%. Thus representation based on this factor alone would mean the composition of the EVC (and later EVA) would have to reflect this population makeup. Income levels, having or not having school age children, geographic location, sex, age of citizens, and other factors may also require consideration. It seems improbable that all such considerations can be equitably included in EVC composition although the attempt should be made. A given individual may be asked to serve because he or she represents a "variety of concerns" rather than one.

Role and Tasks of the EVC

Groups, agencies, and organizations invited to provide members to the EVC should have a clear understanding of what the goals of the education voucher program are and what their role in the pre-planning stage is to be. With the acceptance of the pre-planning grant from O.E.O. by the Alum Rock Union Elementary School District Board of Education, the decision to test the feasibility of such a voucher project in the school district has been made.

The task which the new EVC will have will be to make recommendations on the basis of the results of their feasibility study to the LEA about whether or not to continue the project.

The tasks in which the members of the EVC will be involved during the two-month feasibility study will include the following:

1. To familiarize themselves with the goals of the Education Voucher Program.

2. To modify and/or adapt by-laws for their own organization.

3. To respond to and advise on the collection of feasibility data by the outside subcontractor, the Center for Planning and Evaluation.

4. To arrange for and conduct a minimum of three public forums on the education voucher program.

5. On the basis of their deliberations, to recommend to the Alum Rock Union Elementary School District Board of Trustees by March 31, 1971, whether or not to apply for a planning grant.

These activities constituted an integral part of the Study and the framework for this discussion.

Tasks To Be Accomplished
During the Pre-Planning Period

I.   Assessment of Alternative Potentials

A. Existing Schools

1. Orienting *present* public schools in Alum Rock Union Elementary School District

2. Contacting *existing* public schools *outside* present boundaries to determine their willingness to participate, number of spaces likely to be available

3. Contacting *existing* private (parochial and non-sectarian) schools *within* present boundaries to determine willingness to participate and number of spaces likely to be available

4. Contacting existing private schools *outside* present boundaries to determine willingness to participate and number of spaces likely to be available

B. New Schools

1. Within present boundaries

2. Outside of present boundaries

II. Assessment of Attitudes

A. Public Forums and Small Group Meetings

1. Preparation of literature to be distributed

2. Questionnaire to be distributed, tabulated, summarized

3. Record of questions raised, development of answers

4. Summary report to EVC of meeting outcomes

B. Other Populations

1. Teacher groups: questionnaire and selected follow-up

2. Parents with school age children: questionnaire and interview

3. Adults with no children of elementary school age

4. Assessment of populations represented by nine categories of EVC: Can some categories be excluded? Will the EVC member represent his group or his own view?

III. Report to the EVC: Development of a preliminary regulatory system with alternatives

IV. Report to EVC: Development of preliminary plans for phasing in and phasing out with alternatives

V. Development of Rationale and Criteria for Identification of Education-
    ally Handicapped Child

    A. Conferences

    B. Report with alternatives to EVC

VI. Information Program

    A. Preparation of printed material for dissemination to various popu-
       lations

    B. Conducting of search for relevant materials for use by district
       personnel, EVC members, consultants

    C. Arrangements for dissemination of materials through other media
       (press, radio, television)

    D. Determination of present status of hardware (films, slides, etc.) and
       staff (printers, graphic artists, etc.)

    E. Beginning of planning for future stages of project: drawing up
       specifications for obtaining necessary hardware and personnel

    F. Establishment of "headquarters" for administrative and informational
       activities

VII. Preliminary Planning for the Establishment of the Parent Counseling
      Program: Staff needs, space needs, location

VIII. Preliminary Planning for Computer Needs Based on Possible Require-
      ments for Data Processing. Consideration of these needs in the design of
      the various data-gathering instruments and techniques.

I. Assessing Alternative Schools

A. Existing Schools

1. School Districts — Six school districts bordering Alum Rock were contacted. Of the six districts, one (San Jose Unified) mentioned a possible
   200 to 1000 openings which could be made available to voucher students.
   The only other possibility is Franklin-McKinley and that is doubtful. Of
   the remaining districts, all stated they could see no possible voucher
   student openings at this time. Two school officials expressed their
   personal disapproval of the voucher concept, but all but one were

careful to not shut the door on their district's possible future involvement. All of the districts except San Jose Unified are in areas of substantial growth and most are having a difficult time just keeping up
with the demand for services in their own district.

2. Private Schools — The responses of the non-denominational private
   schools are impossible to generalize. They run the whole spectrum from
   very hostile negative responses to promises to live by any and all EVA
   restrictions. While all existing private schools within a 20 mile radius of
   Alum Rock were not surveyed, enough schools were contacted to gather
   an accurate picture of the private school sector. There are two factors
   which should be pointed out. First, we located no non-denominational
   private schools within 10 miles of Alum Rock. Second, most of these
   schools have a tuition charge which is greater than the proposed basic
   voucher, and some have a tuition charge which would exceed the total
   of the basic voucher and the proposed increment for "disadvantaged"
   students.

   The responses of the parochial schools have been very similar. Whether
   the schools are Baptist, Adventist, Catholic, etc., they have all been
   interested in *possibly* taking part in a voucher experiment. They do,
   however, have two questions of major concern. The first involves fears
   of whether or not they will begin to lose control of their curriculum
   under a voucher experiment. The second and perhaps the greater concern is about admissions policy. The parochial schools all feel a need
   to give admission preference to members of their own faith. If over-
   applied, they are willing to use a lottery system, but only to make
   decisions *among* church members. All have been willing to admit nonchurch members after church member needs have been met. Unlike non-
   denominational private schools, there are a number of parochial schools
   in the immediate Alum Rock area.

B. New Schools

Most of the information gathered on the possibilities of new schools
emerging under a voucher experiment is the result of an article in the
March, 1971, *Superintendent's Bulletin,* a publication of the Santa Clara
County Superintendent's office. The efficacy of this article is questionable.
First of all, it is a very imperfect way of spreading information. Not only
did it reach present school employees of Santa Clara County, but the
tentative nature of the article might have kept a number of concerned
individuals from calling. Second, it was not always easy to judge the commitment of responding individuals to actually open their own schools. All

of the respondents were very sincere, but it would be impossible to predict how many of them would follow through with their ideas.

Despite the above qualifications the results were very encouraging. 50 to 75 inquiries about the article were received. Most of the callers are presently employed in the public schools; most were teachers, but a few were principals and one was a former assistant superintendent of a Santa Clara County School District. Virtually all could be classified as very dissatisfied with the lack of diversity in their present school districts. Their ideas for alternative schools were varied and for the most part well thought out. Reported on the chart is a limited, but representative sampling of some of the more developed ideas.

If a voucher experiment were to be funded in Alum Rock, it appears that a number of alternative schools would develop. From the data on the following pages, we can predict two characteristics of these schools: 1) they would be varied in size, curriculum, philosophy, etc.; and 2) most would be located within the present boundaries of the Alum Rock School District.

Other than private individuals, Behavioral Research Lab has indicated they would begin a school in Alum Rock which would stress individualized instruction; Westinghouse Learning Corporation is interested either in supplying their educational materials to an existing school or beginning a school of their own.

The results of research with possible alternative schools are summarized in the tables which follow.

TABLE 1

ASSESSING EXISTING ALTERNATIVE SCHOOLS

Name	Definitely not interested	Definitely interested	Uncertain, would like more information	Miles from Alum Rock	Total School Population	Number of Grades	Curriculum	Tentative number of slots for Alum Rock Students	Per pupil expenditure	Tuition charge	Comments
Berryessa Union School District			✓	Bordering	5,800	K-8	traditional	Probably None	$600	N/A	At present, the district already has 2,000 students on double sessions and it is highly unlikely they could take any Alum Rock students.
Evergreen School District			✓	Bordering	4,200	K-8	traditional	Probably None	$600	N/A	The district is overcrowded now according to a district official. In all probability, they will not participate.
Franklin-McKinley School District			✓	8 miles	6,600	K-8	Primarily traditional. They are experimenting with some open-space classrooms	Uncertain	N/A	N/A	The district appears interested in the voucher experiment. It appears they would like to participate if they had openings available. They are experiencing rapid growth, however, and actual Alum Rock participation is doubtful.
Mt. Pleasant School District			✓	Bordering	3,500	K-8	traditional teacher/pupil ratio (1-28)	Probably None	$582	N/A	At present, the elementary grades are full and 7-8 are in double sessions. There is little chance of their participation.

Part II

TABLE 1—*Continued*

Name	Definitely not interested	Definitely interested	Uncertain, would like more information	Miles from Alum Rock	Total School Population	Number of Grades	Curriculum	Tentative number of slots for Alum Rock Students	Per pupil expenditure	Tuition charge	Comments
Orchard School District				11 miles	250	K-8	traditional	Probably None	$800	N/A	The district was interested in receiving more information. Their schools are full and they have a growing population. Slim chance they would be willing to participate.
San Jose Unified School District				Bordering	37,067	K-8	traditional – with some special programs	200-1,000	$712	N/A	The district was very supportive of a voucher experiment. Formal approval, however, would rest with the board. The number of slots would be a function of how many vacancies they had.
St. John Vianney				in Alum Rock	619	1-8	traditional with religious instruction pupil/teacher ratio (40-1)	most students presently from Alum Rock	$185	$180/ family	All denominational schools have two major concerns: 1. *Control over their curriculum* - if they were forced to unite their religious instruction in any way they would not take part.

TABLE 1—*Continued*

Name	Definitely not interested	Definitely interested	Uncertain, would like more information	Miles from Alum Rock	Total School Population	Number of Grades	Curriculum	Tentative number of slots for Alum Rock Students	Per pupil expenditure	Tuition charge	Comments
St. Victors			✓	3 miles	336	1-8	traditional with religious instruction pupil/teacher ratio (44-1)	unspecified number at 1st grade level	$291	$180/family	2. *Control over admissions* – all three schools feel it is necessary for them to give first priority to parishioners. If they still have openings after them, they are willing to use a lottery system of some type.
Most Holy Trinity			✓	Border-	300	1-8	traditional with religious instruction pupil/teacher ratio (40-1)	2/3 of pupils are from Alum Rock	$185 $400/family	$180/family	Same as above
Apostle Lutheran Church School		✓		5 miles	47	K-8	"traditional equivalent of the public school"	N/A	N/A	Sliding scale	Same as above

TABLE 1–Continued

Name	Definitely not interested	Definitely interested	Uncertain, would like more information	Miles from Alum Rock	Total School Population	Number of Grades	Curriculum	Tentative number of slots for Alum Rock Students	Per pupil expenditure	Tuition charge	Comments
Valley Christian School			✓	15 miles	650	K-12	traditional college prep with Bible classes teacher/pupil ratio (12-1)	N/A	$600	$600	Same as above
United Baptist Church School			✓	in Alum Rock	230	K-10	traditional college prep teacher/pupil ratio (23-1)	most students from Alum Rock. Presently 25 openings	$500	$500	Same as above "Both the students and teachers must believe in God and the Bible."
Seventh Day Adventist Schools (3 schools)				1-20 miles 1 close to Alum Rock	600	1-8	traditional college prep with religious instruction, student/teacher ratio (22-1)	uncertain	church students $480 non-church $536	$480 $536	All three schools would have to have the approval of the district supt. before they would participate. They are definitely interested but have raised the same two control issues as the other denominational schools.

TABLE 1—Continued

Name	Definitely not interested	Definitely interested	Uncertain, would like more information	Miles from Alum Rock	Total School Population	Number of Grades	Curriculum	Tentative number of slots for Alum Rock Students	Per pupil expenditure	Tuition charge	Comments
Denman Private School				15 miles	100	K-8	college prep	probably very few	$650	$650	The school official went to great lengths to stress the independence and rigor of his school. He has grave doubts about the voucher system and he would probably be opposed to any lottery requirement.
Palo Alto Military Academy				25 miles	156	1-9	traditional with a special military program in leadership	25 openings at present	$1125	$1125	They wanted to stress they are only willing to take "good boys." They would demand the freedom to expel those who couldn't meet their standards.
Ford Country Day School				20 miles	200	K-8	traditional college prep	definitely none	$1125	$1125	They support the position of the *Calif. Association of Independent Schools*, who oppose the voucher concept.
Hillbrook School				20 miles	275	K-8	traditional college prep student/teacher ratio (20-1)	about 25	$930	$930	The school is very interested in taking part and sounded like they would try and live with any and all restrictions.

TABLE 1–Continued

Name	Definitely not interested	Definitely interested	Uncertain, would like more information	Miles from Alum Rock	Total School Population	Number of Grades	Curriculum	Tentative number of slots for Alum Rock Students	Per pupil expenditure	Tuition charge	Comments
Astro-land Montessori School				15 miles	100	K-6	Montessori	N/A	$550	$550	No real concern at this time. They are very interested in the possibility.
Montessori Day School Western				15 miles	60	pre-school & K	Montessori	N/A	$600	$600	Would like more information.
Daystar School (Christian Science)		✓		13 miles	25	pre-school to 4th	traditional with religious training	N/A	$750	$750	They all were interested. A student, however, must be a member of the church and must attend Sunday School.
Lutheran Church School (3 campuses)			✓	15 miles	225	1-8	traditional with religious training	25 potential openings	$300	$300	The school principal was very interested. If a tentative go ahead is given, he would like to have a presentation made to his Board.
San Jose Christian School	✓			15 miles	N/A	N/A	N/A	N/A	N/A	N/A	Very concerned about regulations. Offered almost no information.

TABLE 2

CORPORATIONS INTERESTED IN DEVELOPING AN ALTERNATIVE SCHOOL

Name	Definitely not interested	Definitely interested	Uncertain, would like more information	Miles from Alum Rock	Total School Population	Number of Grades	Curriculum	Tentative number of slots for Alum Rock Students	Per pupil expenditure	Tuition charge	Comments
Behavior Research Laboratory				in Alum Rock	up to 500	what-ever the voucher included	individualized instruction, using teachers, paraprofessionals, and individualized materials	probably as many as they could recruit		the amount of the voucher	Behavior Research Lab has stated they will definitely open a school if a voucher experiment takes place. They will live with any and all restrictions which the EVA specifies.
Westinghouse Learning Corporation				in Alum Rock	N/A	N/A	their own materials "Project Plan"		N/A	N/A	At the present time they are thinking primarily in terms of selling their educational materials to an existing or new school. If, however, they felt they could attract at least 500 students, they would probably consider operating their own school in Alum Rock.

251

TABLE 3

NEW SCHOOL POTENTIALS

Name	Participation		Miles from Alum Rock	Total School Population	Number of Grades	Curriculum	Tentative number of slots for Alum Rock Students	Per pupil expenditure	Tuition charge	Comments
	Reasonably committed	Thinking about it								
Community Worker	✓		in Alum Rock	100	whatever voucher included	traditional elementary curriculum with black history & culture included	100		amount of voucher	In the past he has run classes with the curriculum, but he was forced to discontinue them for lack of funds. He appeared to be genuinely committed to re-opening.
Montessori teacher	✓		in Alum Rock	N/A	"	Montessori technique	N/A		amount of voucher	She is presently holding classes for free in an empty churchroom for about 10 pre-school, east side children who cannot afford to pay. She is stopping in June for lack of funds. With voucher funds she would either open her own school or begin with someone else.
Former Superintendent	✓		in Alum Rock	125	"	traditional with less bureaucracy and much more in the way of experimental program	125		amount of voucher	He has a lot of administrative background and there are other teachers who are also interested. They are very disenchanted with their present position.

TABLE 3—Continued

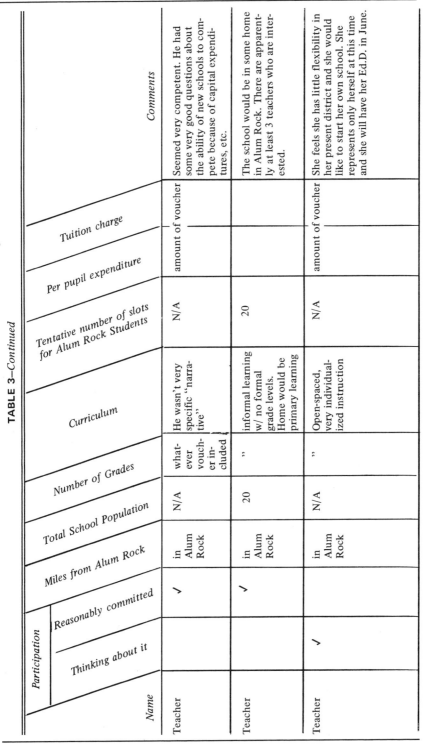

Name	Participation: Reasonably committed	Participation: Thinking about it	Miles from Alum Rock	Total School Population	Number of Grades	Curriculum	Tentative number of slots for Alum Rock Students	Per pupil expenditure	Tuition charge	Comments
Teacher	✓		in Alum Rock	N/A	whatever voucher included	He wasn't very specific "narrative"	N/A		amount of voucher	Seemed very competent. He had some very good questions about the ability of new schools to compete because of capital expenditures, etc.
Teacher	✓		in Alum Rock	20	″	informal learning w/ no formal grade levels. Home would be primary learning	20			The school would be in some home in Alum Rock. There are apparently at least 3 teachers who are interested.
Teacher		✓	in Alum Rock	N/A	″	Open-spaced, very individualized instruction	N/A		amount of voucher	She feels she has little flexibility in her present district and she would like to start her own school. She represents only herself at this time and she will have her Ed.D. in June.

TABLE 3—Continued

Name	Participation		Miles from Alum Rock	Total School Population	Number of Grades	Curriculum	Tentative number of slots for Alum Rock Students	Per pupil expenditure	Tuition charge	Comments
	Thinking about it	Reasonably committed								
Principal in Santa Clara County		✓	N/A	100	whatever voucher included	modeled after British infant School—very child-centered w/ individualized instruction	100		amount of voucher	He has become very disenchanted with his own school district and they with him. He feels his school board is too rigid and he would like to begin his own school which would be much more flexible.
Student teacher	✓		in Alum Rock	N/A	united to K-4	primarily for Spanish-speaking children. A combination program of Montessori techniques and bilingual education				He is now doing his student teaching and will have his teaching credential in June.

II. Assessing Attitudes

A. Public Forums and Small Group Meetings

The EVC requested four "public hearings" to be conducted during the two month study period. Evening hearings were held at the Sheppard School, Cureton School, and Fischer School. The fourth hearing was an afternoon meeting at the Mathson School.

Also, five small group evening meetings were held at several locations: two were regular meetings of the PTA groups at Painter and Goss Schools; two were meetings of parent groups at St. John Vianney and Most Holy Trinity Schools; and one set of data was collected, at the EVC chairman's suggestion, at one of the EVC's scheduled open business meetings.

The attitudes expressed by the people who attended the forum held at the Sheppard School are presented here, followed by a short summary of personal comments from those attending the other hearings and group meetings. It should be pointed out that many of the same people attended each of the public hearings and small group meetings and that they undoubtedly completed more than one questionnaire form. Since possible "change of attitude" as well as anonymity were factors in this data, no attempt was made to refuse a questionnaire to any adult attending any of the public hearings. It should also be noted that many of the attendees voluntarily refused to fill out another form because they had "already done it at the last meeting."

Center for Planning and Evaluation

SANTA CLARA COUNTY
OFFICE OF EDUCATION

TELEPHONE 299-3731
1110 NORTH TENTH STREET
SAN JOSE CALIF 95112

Sheppard School

The Alum Rock Education Voucher Committee and the Center for Planning and Evaluation would appreciate your taking a few minutes now to complete this questionnaire. Thank you.

1. Please fill in the appropriate blanks. Today's date February 22, 1971

   SEX: __21__ male __56__ female
   AGE: __See Attached__

2. What is your present job? See Attached

3. Do you have youngsters in the Alum Rock Schools?
   yes _____ no _____ ; if yes, how many? <u>See Attached</u>

4. Did this meeting answer your questions and concerns about the Education Voucher study?
   <u> 1 </u> all questions were answered
   <u> 37 </u> some questions were answered
   <u> 36 </u> no, I need more information
   If *no,* what specific questions do you have?

   <u>See Attached</u>

5. Would you want the Education Voucher Committee to examine the Voucher study further in a planning phase?
   <u> 35 </u> yes
   <u> 18 </u> need more information
   _____ don't care
   <u> 18 </u> no

6. How did you learn of this meeting?
   <u> 37 </u> newspaper
   <u> 1 </u> TV
   _____ radio
   <u> 20 </u> letter home from school
   _____ other (please indicate) <u>   See Attached   </u>

7. We would appreciate your comments on this meeting.

   <u>See Attached</u>

Place	Sheppard School
Tally Sheet Date	February 22, 1971
Attendance	Approx. 200
Returned Questionnaires	77

1. SEX: Male 21   Female 56

   AGE: 18-20   22-30   31-45   46-55   56-
            1   7   41   11

2. Present Job:

Housewife	35	Florist
Office Clerk	1	Computer System Analyst
Substitute Teacher	2	Engineer-Ford Co.
Salesman		Real Estate Broker
Teacher	7	Self-Employed
Cartographic Techn.		Superintendent (School)
Electronic Eng.	1	School Principal
Wholesale Produce		Maintenance Man
Program Mgr. IBM		Cement Mason
Research Eng.		School Student
School Secretary		Retail Clerk
Alum Rock Dist. Emp.		Accounting Mgr.
Bus Driver		Professor
Bank Teller		School Administrator

3. Youngsters in Alum Rock Schools

   0   1   2   3   4   5   6   more
   23   11   17   13   6   5   2

4. Were questions answered?

   All   Some   No, need information
    1   37   36

5. Shall the EVC go into a further planning stage?

   Yes   Need more info   Don't care   No
    35   18   18

6. How did you learn about meeting?

Newspaper	TV	Radio	Letter from School
37	1		20

Others:	PTA	A.A.O.W.		Friend
15		Church Bulletin	3	Committee for State
		Previous Meeting	7	Aid Investigation
				Confederacion de
				La Raza Unida

4. What specific questions do you have?

How can any school district plan for buildings, materials, programs, teachers equipment and curriculum design children's needs adequately and good educational program in the provided time? __4__

Where does money for voucher come from and what will it be used for? __1__

Will special education be provided for deaf and retarded? _____

How will you avoid overcrowded classes? _____

How will you avoid segregation to keep white parents from taking their children out of a school because negro children get enrolled? _____

How much money is going to be siphoned off by politicians? __1__

How can a parent know one school is better than another? __4__

Who will decide which children will get voucher and why? _____

What is the goal of the voucher system? _____

Why should parochial schools be considered? _____

Why aren't these questionnaires sent home from school? _____

How will it affect us after the time limit is over for voucher? _____

What is the problem in Alum Rock and how will the voucher solve it? __3__

5. What are your comments? ⎯

Would like to see a more open mind from part of audience   1

Very informative   ⎯

Since monies have been made available for planning voucher program and groups have begun vocational support and high level public relations program to sell the voucher program in California I wonder if the voices of concern will be heard over the political appeal the voucher system holds   ⎯

Voucher system is answer to the tossing issue for affluent parents. I am opposed to voucher system   4

What would happen if our private school children were placed on public school rolls because of lack of funds?   ⎯

No control group the opposition has already pre-judged the economic problem formidable   ⎯

Too much contradictions among speakers   3

We should be more objective on the general concern of O.E.O.   ⎯

Questions not clearly answered   6

Fear of only one school system especially when teachers strike and cause double session   ⎯

Parents should be allowed to vote on this matter   3

Information should be readily available to inform the public   ⎯

Parents should be better informed on the overall—and what is O.E.O. doing with taxpayers money   ⎯

In addition to the foregoing comments, those attending the various evening forums and small group meetings had several insightful comments and questions about the Voucher program. They represent some of the issues an Education Voucher Committee should thoroughly treat in the course of discussion and deliberation.

1. Will the Voucher system really improve the quality of education? (Some wanted to know specifically about raising test scores, improving reading skills, etc.)

2. What would be the effect on private/parochial education?

3. What about transportation of children to another district?

4. Would the program really improve the variety of curriculums?

5. What would be the effect on the cost to the taxpayer? What happens when the O.E.O. grant runs out?

6. What are the results in other similar experiments?

7. What happens to schools not chosen to participate?

8. How stable would a program like this be once started?

9. How can schools plan for the year if they don't know their approximate enrollment beforehand? Would the school with too small an enrollment face a financial crisis?

10. How will competition affect public schools?

11. Can some people take it and others leave it?

12. Who decides whether we have a Voucher system or not?

13. What about children who transfer from another school?

14. Could the voucher be used as punishment, in the same way as suspension or expulsion?

15. We need more information before we can decide.

16. We want equal representation on the board.

17. Don't change the system—improve it!

Introduction

B. Other Populations

The survey segment of the Feasibility Study was conducted over the four day period of March 30th through April 2, 1971. It consisted of two separate questionnaires. One was administered to all school district personnel. The procedures for the parent survey incorporated a computer generated random number list which was applied to the class lists within each school of the district. Once the subjects were selected, each child was given a questionnaire to take home for his parents to complete and return the following day. Those who did not return a questionnaire by the second day were given another copy with the same instructions. On day three, children still not returning the questionnaire were given another copy and the same instructions. On day four, all questionnaires were collected from each individual school.

The questionnaire administered to the district staff was delivered to each school on day one and distributed by school personnel. Every person employed by the District was asked to complete a questionnaire. These were collected on day four along with the parent survey.

Of the parents selected, 57 percent responded. This response ratio is considered high when the demographics of the school district are taken into consideration. Of the staff surveyed, a 72% response was received.

The results of the survey are quite clear. While there was a strong favorable reaction to the concepts that underlie the proposed voucher plan, there existed a substantial segment of the community that had no opinion about the term, "voucher", at the time of the survey. It can reasonably be concluded that any sales effort on behalf of the Voucher Plan should be conducted through the medium of those underlying concepts that received a favorable reaction on the survey.

An analysis of the parent and school district personnel surveys follows.

TABLE 4
ALUM ROCK VOUCHER ASSESSMENT
PARENT SURVEY

A. Years resident in the Alum Rock School District

	No.	*Percent*
0-1	42	11
2-3	73	19
4-5	65	17
6-10	94	25
11-15	91	24

B. Type of residence

single family	296	79
duplex	16	4
apartment	19	5
other	20	5

C. Do you own or rent?

own:	245	65
rent:	127	34

D. Age

15-20	3	8
21-25	10	3
26-30	88	23
31-40	182	49
41-50	73	19
51 and over	9	2

E. Sex

Male	134	40
Female	200	60

F. Number of children attending public schools

0	2	5
1	16	61
2	88	23
3	85	23
4	81	22
5	32	9
6	11	3
7	8	2
8	6	2
9	1	2

G. Number of children in private schools

0	363	96
1	9	2
2	2	5
3	1	2

H. Your education (nearest year)

grade 5	13	4
8	67	18
12	223	61
16	46	13
post grad	15	4

TABLE 4—*Continued*

QUESTIONS

1. I am well informed about the voucher plan.

	No.	*Percent*
yes	117	32
no	189	51
undecided	62	17

2. I would want my children to participate in this program.

yes	93	26
no	83	23
undecided	180	51

3. The voucher plan is a good idea for the district to explore.

yes	143	40
no	58	16
undecided	153	43

4. My children would benefit from participating in voucher.

yes	82	23
no	73	21
undecided	198	56

5. Parents should be the ones to decide what types of elementary school education their children should receive.

yes	199	57
no	69	20
undecided	83	24

6. Parents have the abilities to make appropriate decisions about their children's elementary education.

yes	196	56
no	73	21
undecided	82	23

7. The schools should try new ideas.

yes	270	76
no	22	6
undecided	63	18

8. The schools are not doing as good as they can.

yes	130	37
no	85	24
undecided	133	38

TABLE 5
ALUM ROCK VOUCHER ASSESSMENT SURVEY
TOTAL STAFF SURVEY

1. Your current position:

	No.	*Percent*
Aide	67	9
Counselor	6	8
Project Dir.	2	2
Teacher	417	58
Consultant	2	2
Administrator	41	6
Other	173	24

2. Age

20-29	197	27
30-39	241	33
40-49	162	23
50-59	78	11
60 or over	22	3

3. Years of prior teaching or administrative experience (not counting this school year):

0	101	14
1-5	208	29
6-10	146	20
11-15	78	11
16 or more	95	13

4. Years of prior experience at this school:

0	175	24
1-5	360	50
6-10	96	13
11-15	30	4
16 or more	14	2

5. Number of children in Alum Rock School District

0	383	53
1	32	4
2	32	4
3	21	3
4	8	1
5	7	9
6	2	2
7	0	0
8	2	2
9	1	1

6. Highest educational level completed:

Less than BS degree	150	21
BS or BA	71	10
BS + 15 semester hrs.	293	41
MA	39	5
MA + 15 semester hrs.	100	14

TABLE 5—*Continued*

7. Grade level currently taught:

		No.	Percent
	Kindergarten	46	9
	First	46	9
	Second	46	9
	Third	40	8
	Fourth	40	8
	Fifth	42	8
	Sixth	25	5
	Seventh	18	4
	Eighth	15	3

8. Sex:

	Male	183	25
	Female	501	70

QUESTIONS

1. I am well informed about the voucher plan.

	No.	Percent
*SA	63	9
A	317	44
NA	112	16
D	136	19
SD	55	8

2. The voucher plan has potential for enhancing education.

SA	70	10
A	258	36
NA	140	19
D	140	19
SD	88	12

3. Educational changes as a result of voucher could be positive.

SA	71	10
A	276	38
NA	136	19
D	133	18
SD	72	10

4. School personnel should attend public meetings about voucher.

SA	221	31
A	394	55
NA	63	9
D	21	3
SD	9	1

5. Parents should decide the type of elementary school education.

SA	94	13
A	231	32
NA	83	12
D	202	28
SD	81	11

*SA—Strongly Agree; A—Agree; NA—No Opinion/Does Not Apply; D—Disagree;
SD—Strongly Disagree.

TABLE 5–*Continued*

6. Parents have the ability to make decisions about their children's education.

	No.	*Percent*
SA	52	7
A	234	33
NA	97	13
D	223	31
SD	78	11

7. New alternatives are needed in the public and private schools.

SA	153	21
A	358	50
NA	72	10
D	34	5
SD	21	3

8. Voucher could jeopardize administrative and teaching jobs.

SA	81	11
A	224	31
NA	182	25
D	133	18
SD	31	4

9. Experimental schools are healthy for education.

SA	121	17
A	353	49
NA	84	12
D	58	8
SD	31	4

10. I would work in an experimental school if the salary was compatible with my present job.

SA	131	18
A	312	43
NA	111	15
D	58	8
SD	27	4

11. I would want my children to participate in the voucher program.

SA	65	9
A	120	17
NA	251	35
D	100	14
SD	109	15

12. The Alum Rock School District should continue to explore the voucher plan as a possible course of action.

SA	113	16
A	249	35
NA	82	11
D	107	15
SD	99	14

Several other questions were asked of the data. For example, we wondered whether or not parents of better economic circumstances responded differently to the survey than did parents from poorer circumstances. On only two questions did there appear to be a difference. On question 8, parents with greater financial resources tended to agree to a greater extent (significant at the .001 level) than the poorer parents that "The schools are not doing as good as they can." On question 7, the same difference existed, although to a lesser degree, with the financially secure parents more readily agreeing that "the schools should try new ideas."

We wondered if younger parents (under 30) would respond differently than parents over 40 to the questionnaire. No significantly different responses were obtained. Neither did years of schooling affect responses on the parent survey.

On the parent survey, men tended to be more favorably disposed toward the voucher concept than the women. A larger percentage of women responded with "don't know" than did men of the sample. No significant difference existed in the way men and women responded to question 5: "Parents should be the ones to decide what types of elementary school education their children should receive."

In terms of parents education, those with sixteen years or better felt more informed about voucher (significant .001), however, they were negative (at a statistically significant level) about all other questions except question 7, "The schools should try new ideas." Here there were no differences.

In regard to the teacher survey, we wondered if years of teaching experience would affect the way the second question was answered. However, there was no difference in the way teachers responded to "The Voucher plan has potential for enhancing education." On the other hand, the teachers with 6-15 years experience felt they were "well informed about the voucher plan" compared to the new teachers or the teachers who had been on the job 16 years or more. On question 5, the "well informed" group felt parents should not decide the types of elementary school education their children should receive, while teachers with the least experience felt that the parents should decide. This trend continued with question 6, where the least experienced teacher agreed most that "Parents have the ability to make decisions about their children's education;" with teacher experience, the degree of agreement decreased.

The most experienced teachers saw the voucher as jeopardizing administrative and teaching jobs while the least experienced teacher was the most undecided on this issue.

Conclusions

There is significant community interest in the possibility of the Alum Rock Union Elementary School District becoming a demonstration site for the development of a workable Voucher System. The data gathered from both the small and large group open meetings and the parent and staff survey show a definite edge on the side of those who favor the trial over those who are opposed, but the large segment of undecided or uninformed indicates a need to further inform the public. The time and financial constraints on this Feasibility Study made it difficult to adequately reach the large number of people in the community. Continuing efforts aimed at disseminating information about the proposed trial would dispel this indecision.

Although the concern that "not enough people had been contacted" was voiced many times at the open meetings, the amount of interest generated by the study exceeded any similar involvement in the District in recent times. Opponents of the voucher concept were noticably better organized and more vocal than those who favored the concept even though the data collected indicated more favorable than unfavorable interest.

It would be desirable, in the event that such a study be replicated, that it be preceded by an extensive pre-planning phase during which the primary activity would be that of informing the community. Such an approach could allow for the establishment of the EVC only after the various involved segments of the district had had adequate time to familiarize themselves with the issues. The problem of obtaining equitable representation of voting members on the EVC could thus be minimized. Such a pre-planning period would also allow for refinement of the specifics of the model of the voucher system under consideration. Questions raised about such specifics could then be answered precisely rather than ambiguously as was too frequently the case in presentations made during this study. Further exploration of the variables generated by this study would provide additional insights into the complexities of the voucher concept.

Appendix B

The Voucher System — Some Cons and Pros

Cons

Pros

1. The neighborhood school concept would disappear.

1. Those parents who wanted their children to go to the "neighborhood school" because it was close to home, could still send them there. But they would also have a choice of sending them to any other school taking part in the system because they felt that school met their needs better.

2. Freedom of choice of school would promote segregation of pupils, not only on an ethnic, religious, or political basis, but also on a socioeconomic basis. Schools would not necessarily be picked because they offered quality education.

2. The reasons that a family might use for picking a given school will be as varied as there are families. Part of the plan requires that information and counseling be available to all parents about all voucher schools. Schools would have to follow the rules established for the system in their policy of admitting students. These rules could be designed to minimize segregation.

3. Regardless of the desires of O.E.O. and the Alum Rock School District, the final decision to try the voucher system would rest with the state legislature.

3. New legislation would be needed to allow for the trial of a voucher system in Alum Rock. The legislature, however, should reflect the desires of the people involved.

4. The student whose voucher has been refused at the first, second, and third choice schools would have no place to go.

4. The State code requires that children go to school. The Education Voucher Authority (EVA), would have to comply with this law by making certain each student found a place in a school.

5. Students have great mobility, no school would be able to ascertain its enrollment at any given time.

5. This is a management problem in all large organizations. The use of computerized student information data for all schools is planned. The actual procedures would be established by the EVA.

6. The voucher system would compound staffing problems, budgets, contracts and credentials, and booking for transfers.

6. Just as in the need for a computerized student information system (SIS), there will be need for a management information system (MIS) to provide current awareness of all activities. Staffing problems would continue to be handled by the individual schools involved in compliance with the regulations of the voucher system and the enacting legislation.

7. Parents would not be aware of the specific amount budgeted for purposes of busing.

7. Information on all aspects of the system will be available to the public. If the suggested levels of funding are realized, up to $300,000 might be allocated for busing.

8. Parents would not be aware of the amount of money budgeted for parental counseling.

8. All expenditures would be public information. Since parental counseling is an integral part of the voucher system under study, the present budget might allow up to $1.7 million per year for this activity. Information and involvement on the part of parents would be crucial to the system.

9. Schools would have a tendency to "teach to the test" so that they would "look good." This is not *quality education.*

9. Evaluation of the accomplishments of the schools taking part in the system would be done by an outside agency under the direction of the EVA. This would prevent "teaching to the test." Results would then be compared

both within the system and with national and state standards. Such results would be publicly disseminated as part of the information program.

10. Vouchers would break down the separation between church and state. Statistics show that 12% of the nationwide student population attend non-public schools. 95% of the 12% are in religious schools, mostly Catholic. Therefore, strong church schools in a given community would have first crack at voucher money.

10. All schools taking part in the system would have to follow the rules as established by the controlling EVA. Religious schools would have to maintain open books which showed that no voucher funds were being spent on religious instruction. It is likely that the value of a voucher for a student would be reduced by the percentage of time the school devoted to religious instruction. For example, if 1/5 of the day was assigned for such instruction, the school would receive only 80% of the amount that a student would being to a "non-religious" school.

11. The voucher system would intensify racial separation. Integration would be impossible to accomplish.

11. Schools with a high percentage of educationally handicapped students would be able to offer enriched programs because the vouchers they would be cashing would be worth more in the regulated compensatory system which is being studied. This could actually encourage integration. Also, a parent who chose to send his children to an integrated school outside of his area could afford to do so. These options are not possible under most systems presently in use.

12. The mis-fit or "late bloomer" that no one wants would have no place to go.

12. Quite the contrary. It is the present system which produces the "mis-fit" because he has no choice. Parents could shop for a school that best meets the needs of each of the children and afford to send them there.

13. High I.Q. students, athletes, and those artistically talented would group together.

13. The purpose of education is to meet the needs of the individual. Such groupings may result in better education for those students.

14. The demonstration would not be effective unless all schools in the Alum Rock District took part.

14. This is true, however, experiments must always attempt to account for variables. The broader the amount of data collected, the more that can be inferred from it. Schools would have to agree to the rules of the demonstration or they could not be part of it. Although their participation would be voluntary, hopefully most would be in the system.

15. The Education Voucher Authority would determine the policies for students rather than the appointed Superintendent or the elected school board.

15. The EVA would only direct and monitor the system to insure that the schools were operating in accordance with the agreed upon regulations. These regulations should be minimal so as to permit as many different kinds of schools as possible to operate whatever way they felt would most benefit their students. Too many regulations would make all the schools "the same" and there would be no trial.

16. Picking the members of the EVA will be difficult. Some will want them to be appointed, others will want them to be elected.

16. Picking the EVA will be difficult. The present EVC will have to develop the method that seems to best reflect the wishes of the community.

17. The leading educational organizations (NTA, CTA, PTA) are opposed to the voucher system.

17. People and organizations generally resist change. If the system as it is conceived is determined to have merit as an alternative to our present systems, only a test will answer the questions being raised.

18. Wilson Riles, newly elected Superintendent of California Schools "condemns the voucher proposal as destructive."

18. In the same article cited, (*San Jose Mercury,* January 21, 1971) Dr. Riles is quoted as saying he didn't oppose the plan as a "limited controlled" experiment.

19. Prestigious education writers such as Fred Hechinger in the June 7, 1970 *New York Times* says the only way to solve public education is to reform the public schools, not abandon them to a voucher system.

19. There are many different voucher systems. The regulated one being studied does not abandon the public schools but requires them to compete in a way that will stimulate them out of their complacency and rigidity. They will become more accountable for the educational growth of children. Major reform is not possible without major change. The last few years of unrest have resulted in the need to seek alternatives to what we have available today.

20. If the number of students in a given public school drops sharply, there will be an excess of teachers whose contracts will have to be honored.

20. The plan under consideration has a contingency fund which would allow for such a condition. The excess teachers would be used to reduce class size and thus make that school perhaps more attractive. They might also seek new positions in other public or private voucher schools without losing seniority or tenure during the years of the demonstration.

21. The voucher system will strain public financing of education beyond the point already reached.

21. During the years of the demonstration, no tax increases would be sought. O.E.O. would be subsidiz-

ing the system until the end of the trial which could extend for 5 to 7 years.

22. Without control over textbooks, schools would have no uniform offerings. The courses would not be relevant.

22. Meeting the needs of its students is the paramount concern of each school taking part in the system. If their books and courses are not relevant, the students will go elsewhere.

23. Many new private schools will spring up. Who will regulate them?

23. The demonstration encourages the development of new schools. They would be regulated in the same way as existing schools and would have to follow the rules prescribed by the EVA.

24. The voucher system would mean the death of public school education as we have known it for the past 200 years.

24. More schools would be "public" than ever before. The change would be extensive and is one possible way that improvement may come to a system which many feel no longer meets our needs.

25. This system would give parents carte blanche decision making authority in determining the education of their children.

25. This is true, but parents would have to be far better informed than most are today to know whether or not they were "getting their money's worth." This is seen as one of the most valuable aspects of the voucher systems.

26. Parents are not of equal ability intellectually or socially.

26. Parent involvement through the counseling program would attempt to equalize this need. There is virtually no provision for such service to parents under our present systems.

27. There would be too many new ideas, too many people involved.

27. This is the essence of education.

28. The system would cause further unrest among teachers.

28. Teachers would have to compete in a new way. They would be part of a team which had to be accountable to its students and parents or the school would lose them to other schools.

29. Some method would be needed to determine the length of the school year. Who would be responsible?

29. Hopefully, the parents, students, and faculty would, with the approval of the EVA, determine how they would operate. If the parents and students were not content, they would look for another school.

30. Even increased funding cannot guarantee that parents will become more involved.

30. This is true, but many will. They have never had a choice to express before. One must assume that parents are interested in their children and do want the best for them.

TRANSITION MODEL VOUCHER PROPOSAL

A proposal to the Office of Economic Opportunity
from the Alum Rock Union School District
for funds to support a two-year demonstration
of an education voucher transition model

*April 12, 1972, the School Board in Alum Rock approved this proposal;
it was submitted to OEO and quickly accepted. Says Joel Levin, Project
Director for the Alum Rock voucher experiment, this proposal is the
definitive description of the history and intent of the 1972-1973
voucher plan.*

Contents

Title	Page

I. Introduction and Summary

The Alum Rock Union School District requests a grant of $ _____
from the Office of Economic Opportunity to support the implementation of a
transitional model of a voucher system over a two-year period. We request
this funding for two years to insure the District against any possible disrup-
tions resulting from policy decisions at the federal level. Furthermore, we wish
to specify at the outset that our participation in this federally funded demonstration in no way should be construed to imply that there will be any dilu-
tion in the local control of education in our District. Final authority for all
educational decisions in the District will remain with the Alum Rock School
Board.

The main features of this proposal are summarized below. Cross references
appear in brackets.

I.1   The parents of each participating child will receive a voucher (or
certificate) which will be worth the current average cost of educating a
child in the Alum Rock School District. [See Section III.1]

I.2   Each participating public school will develop two or more alternative,
distinct educational programs. These alternatives will be developed with
the active cooperation of the participating community. During the course
of the experiment, we will cooperate in the development of programs
sponsored by groups not currently in the public school system, and

these programs, through individual contracts with the School Board, will be governed by the same rules as the public schools. [See Section III.2, III.7, III.9]

I.3　Each parent will select for his child an educational *program* and school building in accordance with his evaluation of the educational needs of his child, and each child will be assured of placement in the first choice program. Students currently enrolled, and their incoming siblings also, will be guaranteed the right to remain in the school building they are presently attending. [See Section III.3, III.4, III.5]

I.4　Admissions to each program and building will be made in a way that will maximize the satisfaction of each participant. Each new enrollee will have equal access to every program and building in the demonstration. If a *building* is over-applied, additional capacity will be created, whenever possible. If a *program* is over-applied, additional capacity will be created somewhere in the system so that each child will be accommodated in his or her first choice program. [See Section III.5]

I.5　The vouchers of disadvantaged children will be enhanced by a "compensatory" voucher both to help the schools meet the special needs of these children, and to encourage schools to develop programs to meet these needs. [See Section III.1]

I.6　The budget of each program will be determined by the voucher money brought by the children who enroll in that program. In the event of transfers, a child's voucher money will be divided equitably between the two programs that he has attended. [See Section II.1, III.5]

I.7　Each program will be required to provide information about its philosophy, practices and finances, and this information will be made available to all participating parents. In addition, community counsellors will be provided to consult with parents about program offerings and their children's needs. [See Section III.4]

I.8　A representative advisory board will be formed to advise the School Board and Administration on decisions relating to the demonstration. [See Section III.1]

I.9　The community will participate actively in the operation and governance of the transitional voucher demonstration. Individual schools and programs will encourage parental participation at a meaningful level in their respective decisionmaking processes. [See Section III.1, III.2, III.3, III.9]

I.10 An on-going evaluation of the transitional voucher demonstration project will be conducted. [See Section III.11]

The goals of this program are:

I.11 To offer all parents in the demonstration area a range of choices for the education of their children. In particular, it is hoped that the right of educational choice presently available only to the affluent will be extended to the poor and middle income sectors of the community.

I.12 To allow schools to become more responsive to the needs of their communities and to involve parents more meaningfully in their decision-making processes as a consequence of this revised procedure for allocating educational resources.

I.13 To stimulate parents to take a more active interest and become more involved in the education of their children.

I.14 To improve the educational achievement of the participating students.

I.15 To increase the level of parental satisfaction with their schools.

I.16 *Funding Commitment*

The Alum Rock Union School District requests that O.E.O.'s initial funding commitment be for two years. This request is made to insure the District sufficient time to phase out of the demonstration without adverse consequences in the event that the program proves unworkable or the agency's funding should be imperiled.

We recognize that the first year of this project will be a "transition" year, and this is one of the reasons for limiting the participation to six pilot schools. In the absence of unforeseen problems we anticipate a significant expansion of the program. We commit ourselves to expand the program to include approximately 8,000 to 10,000 students during the second year if the demonstration is successful; if not, we will phase out the project at the end of the second year. If the program is successful and enabling legislation is passed, we will survey the community and school personnel to assess the desirability of moving to a full voucher program. If the project is sufficiently expanded in the second year, we request O.E.O. to commit itself to fund the program at least through June, 1977, if this is consistent with its legal authority, so that a full five-year demonstration of the voucher concept can be carried out and evaluated. If this commitment is not legal, we require that O.E.O.

guarantee at least one year of *advance* funding at all times in order to assure the District of an orderly phase-out in the event that decisions at the federal level should endanger funding for the project.

II. Background

On July 15, 1970, a representative of the Center for the Study of Public Policy (C.S.P.P.) made a presentation to the Special Study Committee of the California State P.T.A. on the projected O.E.O. demonstration of educational vouchers. The Superintendent of the Alum Rock Union School District attended this meeting and invited the C.S.P.P. representative to come to Alum Rock in order to explore the possibilities of developing a demonstration. After a sequence of meetings between representatives of the C.S.P.P., O.E.O., Alum Rock Union School District, and community representatives during the summer, a decision was made to apply to O.E.O. for a grant to study the feasibility of undertaking an education voucher pilot project. The Alum Rock School Board approved this application by a unanimous vote of the members present at its meeting on September 3, 1970.

This application was accepted by O.E.O. and funds to carry out the feasibility study became available to the District in February, 1971. An Educational Voucher Committee (E.V.C.) was convened consisting of representatives of the public and private schools, business community, Governor's Office, existing community groups, and a student. The Center for Planning and Evaluation of the Santa Clara Office of Education (C.P.E.) was hired to provide technical support for the E.V.C. C.P.E. developed and distributed informational brochures, conducted opinion surveys, arranged for media coverage of the study, and generally provided staff work for the E.V.C., its chairman, and its executive director, the Deputy Superintendent of the Alum Rock Schools.

A series of public meetings was announced to discuss the issues with community residents and to solicit their reactions. The public meetings generated earnest and, at times, heated discussions and tended to draw the same group of interested people each time. It was difficult to assess the community's opinion from these meetings.

Surveys were then conducted which indicated a significant level of support from parents, teachers, and administrators. The surveys also revealed that many members of the community felt that they were not sufficiently informed to make a decision. An important feature of the study was the willingness of the Alum Rock teachers and their organizations to consider the proposal on its merits. Full details of the conduct and conclusions of the feasibility study can be found in the final report of C.P.E. to O.E.O. [Final Report – Alum Rock Union School District Voucher Feasibility Study]

In trying to draw up a recommendation to the School Board, the E.V.C. was faced with two crucial areas of uncertainty. First, in order to develop a full voucher demonstration, California state enabling legislation was required. Second, a School Board election was pending within a month of the end of the Study, and there was some reluctance to impose a decision of such magnitude on new Board members. Therefore, the E.V.C. recommended that the Board postpone making a decision until enabling legislation had been passed.*

In the interim, the District applied to O.E.O. and received a continuing planning grant to fund a staff training program to explore the issues of increased decentralization and autonomy for principals and teachers in six pilot schools. The District hired the Center for Human Resources and Organization Development of San Jose, which began to conduct this training sequence in the fall of 1971. Its activities concentrated on developing the abilities of the various groups to improve communications and evaluate their own group processes. As a result the principals and staffs became eager for greater autonomy, with full awareness of the risks inherent in such a position.

In January, 1972, convinced that greater decentralization was desirable, but unable to move towards a full voucher system in the absence of legislation, the principals and central staff developed a plan which embodied many of the key features of the voucher model developed for O.E.O. by the C.S.P.P., and yet did not require enabling legislation for initial implementation.

The plan was further refined with the assistance of C.S.P.P. staff, and O.E.O. was asked to fund the modified plan. The Division of Experimental Research of O.E.O. indicated an interest in the project, provided that certain basic features of the original model were maintained. Subsequently, the staffs of each of the six pilot schools voted to participate in the proposed demonstration.

On March 8, 1972, the Alum Rock School Board unanimously authorized the Superintendent to develop a proposal to O.E.O. for the demonstration. Recognizing the need for community and staff participation in the development of the project, a three-day conference was held at Santa Clara University from March 21 to March 23 to write the first draft of the proposal. Fifty-five people participated in this conference: principals, teachers, and parents from the six pilot schools, representatives of the teachers' organizations (A.R.T.A. and A.F.T.), P.T.A. representatives, central staff, and representatives from the C.S.P.P., H.R.C., and O.E.O. Small groups were formed and each was assigned to develop a position on one facet of the program. Each committee's preliminary results were typed and distributed to the whole conference and then new groups reviewed these outputs and suggested modifications. This sequence was repeated; final positions were negotiated by all the participants and adopted by consensus. This effort was extremely productive, and the recommendations produced by this conference provided the basis for the present proposal which was presented to the Alum Rock School Board at its meeting on April 12, 1972.

---

*Time was also a factor, since California legislation does not take effect until sixty-one days after signing. This stipulation implied that even if enabling legislation did pass after the middle of July, no demonstration could be conducted during the following school year. Subsequently, the bill was defeated in committee, although similar legislation has been re-introduced in the current session.

III. Operations

III.1 *Voucher Mechanism*

The voucher mechanism is a new system for allocating educational funds. Its underlying purpose is to improve the quality of a student's education by making schools more responsive to student needs and accountable for educational performance. Central administration, instead of transferring fixed amounts of money to individual schools, will issue vouchers worth a prescribed amount to the parents of all students who will be attending participating schools. The parents will select an educational program from the alternatives available and give their child's voucher to the school of their choice. In turn, schools will receive their financial support by redeeming the vouchers collected from students enrolled.

This process will permit families to express confidence in a given program by choosing to enroll their children in it, thereby allocating their educational dollars to support it. Schools and programs which are not attracting students will continue to lose resources until they respond to the needs perceived by the parents.

The vouchers will be issued in two parts. The first, or basic voucher, will be equal in value to the amount of money spent per child by the District in the preceding year, excluding the special funds indicated in Exhibit I.

The second, or "compensatory" voucher will be allocated to disadvantaged students to permit schools to meet the special needs of these children, and to encourage schools to develop programs to meet those needs. The compensatory voucher will defray the additional expense of educating children who traditionally have fared most poorly in the schools. It will provide for additional services without adding to the financial burden of the school they attend. The confidentiality of children receiving the compensatory vouchers will be preserved. It is important that the recipients of compensatory vouchers not be publicly identified. The creation of a special class of "compensatory" students would be likely to produce adverse educational and personal reactions among students and faculty. When schools redeem vouchers, they will receive the amount attributable to the compensatory students enrolled. Guidelines for confidentiality will be developed locally. Compensatory voucher recipients will be identified solely for educational and management purposes.

A school may then provide the educational services its students require without reference to whether or not a specific student is a recipient of a compensatory voucher. The net effect of this will be to help remedy the somewhat arbitrary test of eligibility described in the conclusion of this section and provide equitable educational opportunity for all children enrolled in the school.

III.1.1. *Computation of Basic Voucher*

As noted above, the first or basic voucher will be equal in value to the amount spent per pupil in the preceding fiscal year. The amount budgeted in 1971-72 was $678.98 for K through 6th and $966.54 for 7th and 8th grades. The difference in amounts is due to higher program costs in 7th and 8th grades because of departmentalization.

In determining the amount of actual per pupil expense we omitted special program funds, such as Building Fund, Repayment Funds, and Miller-Unruh Funds, to identify the on-going cost of education in the District. Exhibits I and II are based on the final budget, 1971-72, Alum Rock Union School District, dated August 9, 1971, and student enrollment data as of February 28, 1972, taken from Alum Rock Union School District enrollment report from A-104.

EXHIBIT I — BASIC ENROLLMENT DATA AND EXCLUSIONS
FOR CALCULATING BASIC VOUCHER VALUE

Enrollment Report as of 2/28/72   Total Enrollment   15,890

                                            Enrollment minus
                                            Special Education
                                            Students   15,192

Voucher School Enrollment   w/Special Ed. Students

Cassell	701	734
Pala (M.S.)	547	558
Meyer	707	750
Miller	542	566
McCollum	578	630
Goss	651	651
Total	3,726	3,889 (3,331 elementary + 558 middle school)

1971-1972 Budget

    Total Budget $14,156,976

Deductions

OEO + PL 874	112,756
Federal Funds	912,351
Preschool Aid	85,151
Special Education	638,185
Miller-Unruh	96,530
Mentally Retarded	79,281
Bldg. Fund Repayment	40,761
Public School Bldg. Fund Repayment	729,151
Educ. Handicapped	27,656
Children's Center	4,000
	$2,725,822

    Budget — minus deductions $11,431,154

EXHIBIT II — PER PUPIL COST ANALYSIS BY ELEMENTARY SCHOOL
COSTS, MIDDLE SCHOOL COSTS AND GENERAL
ADMINISTRATION COSTS

(Excluding Federal Funds and Special Education)

Total Students (including Special Ed.)	15,890
Middle School	4,297
Elementary School	11,593

Elementary School Costs

Salaries & expenses ($4,995,410/11,593 students)	$430.90
Music (67,283/11,593 students)	5.80
Miller-Unruh (Local contribution 38,679/11,593)	3.33
General Administration costs (see below)	238.95
Total Elementary School PPC	$678.98

EXHIBIT II—*Continued*

Middle School Costs

Salaries & expenses ($1,427,166/4,297 students)	$332.13
Art (83,138/4,297)	19.35
Foreign Language (34,780/4,297)	8.09
Home Economics (94,944/2,149 girls)	44.18
Industrial Arts (96,407/2,149 boys)	44.86
Math (175,407/4,297)	40.82
Music (114,485/4,297)	26.64
P.E. (165,108/2,149 boys)	76.83
P.E. (160,587/2,149 girls)	74.73
Reading (38,483/4,297)	8.96
Science (73,283/4,297)	17.05
Interscholastic sports (10,100/4,297)	2.35
Library (67,306/4,297)	15.66
Counselling (70,218/4,297)	16.34
Subtotal	$727.99
General Administration costs (see below)	238.95
Total Middle School PPC	$966.94

General Administration Costs

Summer Session ($79,945/15,890)	$ 5.03
Home and Hospital (10,575/15,890)	.67
Mentally Gifted Minors (85,307/15,890)	5.37
Basic Supplies (68,000/15,890)	4.28
Educ. Media (118,540/15,890)	7.46
Instruct. Admin. (36,435/15,890)	2.29
R & D (8,490/15,890)	.53
Special Services (Local costs) (62,630/15,890)	3.94
Central Dupl. (18,660/15,890)	1.17
Inservice Education (115,199/15,890)	7.25
Meals for Needy Pupils (32,918/15,690)	2.07
Home-School Busing (163,467/15,890)	11.55
Nursing Service (187,233/15,890)	11.78
Psychological Services (94,688/15,890)	5.96
Governing Board (261,043/15,890)	16.43
Attendance Service (43,438/15,890)	2.73
District Administration (56,103/15,890)	3.53
Leave Program (7,000/15,890)	.44
Personnel Services (97,532/15,890)	6.14
Business Services (209,295/15,890)	13.17
Fringe Benefits (787,759/15,890)	49.58
Maintenance (340,639/15,890)	21.44
Operations (793,111/15,890)	49.91
Community Relations (14,850/15,890)	.93
Community Relations (12,642/15,890)	.80
Community Use of Facilities (25,990/15,890)	1.64
Community Action Program (3,000/15,890)	.18
Community School (Local costs) (13,258/15,890)	.83
Total General Administration PPC	$238.95

III.1.2 *Computation of Compensatory Voucher*

We propose that the amount of the compensatory voucher be one-third of the amount of the basic voucher, and that the test for eligibility for the compensatory voucher be the self-declaration by the family of eligibility for free federally funded lunch programs. The purpose for establishing this means test for compensatory vouchers (rather than educational criteria) is the relatively high correlation between student performance and family income and the relative ease of determining eligibility. In addition, the annual income eligibility for receipt of free lunch in California is $4,000 for a family of four which approximates the income poverty guidelines used by the Office of Economic Opportunity.

We have discarded one seemingly convenient index of family income, eligibility for AFDC, because upon examination it is of limited utility. Typically, AFDC eligibility is contingent on the absence of the head of the household, and we believe that any criterion which tends to exclude families with both parents contradicts the objectives of the program. The use of AFDC case-load figures skews the statistics purporting to represent the actual number of disadvantaged students in Alum Rock.

The maximum amount of money for distribution to participating disadvantaged children in the form of compensatory vouchers is $442,070. This dollar amount is determined by estimating the percentage of children who would be eligible to receive free lunches if they ate in school. For computational purposes, we have assumed that roughly the same percentage of children who now receive free lunches would be eligible for them in the demonstration and therefore eligible for compensatory vouchers.

This $442,070 represents the maximum number of dollars available for distribution for initial year compensatory funds for the six school demonstration. Eligibility for a compensatory voucher will be determined solely by eligibility for the free lunch program, not participation in it. No child may receive a compensatory voucher worth more than one-third of the value of the basic voucher as projected in this proposal. In the event that there are more children eligible for compensatory vouchers than we have projected, the amount of each compensatory voucher will be reduced so that each eligible child can receive his share of compensatory funds within the fixed budgetary figure. Any unutilized money in the compensatory voucher fund will be carried over to the compensatory voucher funds for the next year of the project, but that year's grant will be reduced by that amount.

Exhibit III displays the calculations used to arrive at the amount of the compensatory voucher.

EXHIBIT III — COMPENSATORY VOUCHER COST ANALYSIS

Five Elementary School Enrollment + 6th Grade Pala	3,423	
50% Eligible for Compensatory Voucher	1,711	
1/3 of Elementary School Basic Voucher	226	
Eligible Students x Comp. Value (1,711 x $226)		$386,686
One Middle School Enrollment (7th & 8th Pala)	466	
27% Eligible for Compensatory Voucher*	126	
One 7th Grade (Goss)	92	
50% Eligible for Compensatory Voucher	46	
Total Eligible Middle School Students	172	
Eligible Students x Comp. Value (172 x $322)		$ 55,384
Total Compensatory Voucher Value		$442,070

Per Pupil Compensatory Voucher:	K-6	$226
	7-8	$322

*As defined by eligibility for free lunches

An inconsistency appears to exist between the first two exhibits and Exhibit III because of the limitations of the existing accounting system; current records do not display any excess costs for sixth graders enrolled in Middle Schools. We treat sixth grade costs as equal to the cost of every other grade, K through five, because the permissive override tax monies used to support middle schools are restricted by law to seventh and eighth grades.

III.2   *Participating Schools and Programs*

Six schools* within Alum Rock District have been selected for the initial demonstration project, with a target date of September, 1972.

The six schools with the number of faculty, administrators, classified employees and students as of February, 1972, are:

		Faculty	*Admin.*	*Class.** *	*Students*
Cassell	(K-5)	29	1	13	734
Miller	(K-6)	22	1	11	566
McCollum	(K-5)	24	2	9	630
Meyer	(K-5)	32	2	12	750
Pala	(6-8)	29	2	14	558
Goss	(K-7)	26	1	9	651
					3,889

These six schools and their attendance areas comprise a nearly contiguous geographic area approximately 3 miles long and 2 miles wide.

---

*Throughout this proposal we shall consistently distinguish between "schools" (meaning buildings) and "programs" referring to the distinct educational alternatives within each building.
**Includes part-time paraprofessionals.

III.2.1 *School Autonomy*

The single most important change in the six participating school buildings from the standpoint of school administration will be the emergence of autonomy. The need for this is clear: because a program derives income by redeeming vouchers submitted by students enrolled, its staff members must be in a position to tailor their offerings to their students' needs; otherwise, this form of accountability is meaningless. Thus, we foresee the program administration and staff as exclusively responsible for their own policy and curriculum.

III.2.2 *Program Management*

The requirement that each school offer at least two distinct programs presents interesting organizational challenges and opportunities, and we have explored the idea of programatic organization rather than building organization. In this case, a "principal" would become an educational program manager who would be responsible for one or more programs which would be conducted simultaneously in several buildings. Although this does run counter to a literal interpretation of building autonomy, it correctly emphasizes the primacy of educational programs in this proposed pilot project.

Because we have no actual experience in inter-building program management of the kind we visualize, we cannot project a final model of school organization. It is likely, however, that some blending of styles will emerge as the dominant form. The more traditional, which leaves the building principal in charge of all programs within his school, embodies the disadvantages inherent in a situation in which loyalties conflict. Can a principal adequately manage two programs when he is personally convinced one is superior to the other?

Alternately, can a principal do any program justice if he is not wholeheartedly committed to the educational superiority of a single program?

The other organizational style consistent with multiple program offerings, the program manager, provides unitary management of the single program in the building or buildings in which it is offered. The principal program manager would retain a "home base", but he would not manage a building as a whole. In turn, routine building administration would be handled by a "building" manager, similar to business managers.

Theoretically, the use of program managers and building managers has much to recommend it. Program managers can ration time in response to teaching and administrative responsibilities. For example, programs that are modest in size, or that require relatively small administrative supervision can be conducted by a teaching program manager. As programs enlarge or become complex, the program manager's direct teaching duties can be reduced. The important point is that program management, as we envision it, provides needed flexibility in an experiment of this kind and may provide a new form of school organization.

Similarly, a building manager's services can be provided under contract for one or several buildings, freeing program managers to invest more time and energy in the instructional program.

The theoretical advantages and disadvantages of each method are several; the program management concept may lend vitality to the various programs, but it could create a larger administrative overburden than the traditional arrangement. Questions of this kind cannot be answered in the abstract and should be treated as one of the many issues that the experiment itself will help to resolve.

III.2.3 *Middle Schools*

A special problem exists for our proposed demonstration with regard to middle school children. Only one of the six participating pilot schools is a middle school, and consequently the choices available to these children would seem to be rather limited. Nevertheless, we believe that this school (Pala) should be included for several reasons:

1)   The fact that only one middle school will participate during the first year does *not* imply that middle school children will have no choice; the transitional voucher model is set up to create program alternatives within existing buildings, and therefore program options will be available to participating middle school children.

2) Other participating K-6 schools have indicated a strong interest in developing programs to attract middle school students during the first year, and this development will provide additional options for these children.

3) In the anticipated expansion of the transitional voucher model during the second year, additional middle schools will probably participate; we would consider this to be a highly desirable development, and *we believe that Pala's participation in the first year will make it more likely that other middle schools will enter the program next year.*

4) The problems of middle school education are some of the most pressing ones facing American educators, and every effort should be made to encourage innovation in this area; Pala's participation will certainly contribute to such exploration.

5) The principal and staff of Pala are very eager to participate in the project, and it would be a tangible loss to dissipate this support by excluding Pala from the first year of the program.

III.2.4 *Program Development*

In order to develop alternative programs within the limited time available before September, 1972, we foresee the need for intensive program development work throughout the spring and summer. We expect parents to be involved extensively in this development process, and funds must be available from OEO to pay school personnel and parents for the extra time which they contribute to this planning process. Further discussion of this aspect of the program will be found in Section III.6.2, *In Service,* and Section III.12, *Finance,* which includes the proposed budget.

III.2.5 *New Schools*

We foresee additional educational alternatives being offered by groups within our present system as well as groups not currently associated with our public schools. We will encourage such outside groups to participate in order to enrich the range of choice being offered to students and to allow new approaches to enter the system without unnecessary obstacles.

These new programs could arise in the following ways:

a) Existing schools could "spin off" new programs in response to needs emerging during the year.

b) Additional public schools could opt to enter the transitional voucher program.

c) Community groups could develop new programs in cooperation with local or outside educators by making their proposal to the E.V.A.C. (III.6.4).

d) Outside groups could develop programs and try to interest parents in supporting them.

An extended discussion of the rules and procedures governing new schools will be found in Section III.9, *New Schools.*

III.3 *Participating Children and Their Families*

The children participating in the voucher program will be those who would normally attend the six pilot schools. The population is heterogeneous with significant minorities of Spanish surname (48.9%), Black (10.7%), and Asian (3.7%) students.

III.3.1 *Guarantees of Real Choice*

In principle, the voucher mechanism offers a choice to all participating students, but it is clear that this choice could be illusory because of the absence of alternative programs, parents' unawareness of the existence of certain programs, difficulty in obtaining transportation to the program of choice, limitations of capacity in popular programs, or preferential admissions procedures that might exclude "undesirable" children. In order to guarantee a real choice to each child, we propose the following safeguards.

III.3.2 *Existence of Alternatives*

Each participating public school building shall offer at least two (or more) distinct programs. These programs will be chosen and developed by the staffs of each school in cooperation with the people of the community which they serve. We propose that OEO provide funds to support these planning efforts (see Section III.6.2 for further details). In subsequent years new offerings could be developed by groups of educational innovators from inside or outside of the public school system. The conditions under which outside groups would be permitted to participate are described in Section III.9, *New Schools.*

III.3.3 *Transportation*

In order to assure that each child can attend the school of his choice, transportation must be provided to supplement the busing services presently being offered by the Alum Rock School District. Any incremental busing costs will be paid by OEO.

III.3.4 *Counselling and Information Dissemination*

In order to guarantee that each parent will be fully apprised of the nature of the demonstration and the alternatives available to his child, we propose to inform parents through written notices, public meetings, media presentations, and existing community organizations. Furthermore, we propose to create a group of knowledgeable community counsellors with bilingual capacity who will conduct an outreach program to assure that every eligible parent will be contacted. The details of this effort are described in Section III.5, *Information and Counselling.*

III.3.5 *Open Enrollment*

All newly entering children (either kindergarten or transfers) will be free to apply to any program in any school in the demonstration and will have equal chance of access to any program and school. For children presently attending these schools, however, we recognize the strong feelings of parents (both majority and minority) that their children should not run the risk of being uprooted unwillingly from their present schools because of this demonstration. Therefore, we intend to guarantee to every child presently enrolled the right to remain in his present building. This still leaves such a child with the choice of alternatives within his present school or the option to voluntarily apply to another school. Younger siblings entering kindergarten should also enjoy preferential admission to the schools which their older siblings attend.

III.3.6 *Variable Capacity*

In order to maximize the possibility for each child to gain access to the education of his choice, we intend to encourage the development of a variable capacity in each program. In particular, we envision the possibility of staggered scheduling, use of portable classrooms, intensive use of underutilized space, and, when necessary, the extension of programs into other buildings. The six schools selected for the pilot project currently have 10% excess capacity on the average. Finally, if a group of parents is still not satisfied with the choices available, the voucher mechanism offers the realistic possibility for them to start new programs. We propose that OEO provide start-up money to assist such groups through their planning phases. While we have not reached a final conclusion on the precise mechanism for making start-up funds available, we do believe that vouchers should be used for start-up as well as operating funding. A start-up fund will be set aside and money will be allocated to a new school in an amount proportional to the number of children who commit themselves to attend it. In addition, a group of parents interested in starting a new school might be permitted to draw a fixed amount against anticipated vouchers to provide start-up funding. "Voucherizing" the start-up system is highly desirable in that it reduces the likelihood of whimsical or capricious requests for new programs. At the same time it will maintain a constant relationship between prospective program size and funding for program planning and program implementation. More detail is provided in Section III.6.

III.3.7 *Special Education*

Many features of the voucher concept are already standard practice in the field of special education. Parents of children eligible for special education programs can choose whether or not to enroll their children in special education classes. Furthermore, the special education funds allocated to these programs are proportional to the number of children enrolled.

Several of our participating pilot schools currently operate programs for approximately 165 special education pupils, and the question has been raised whether or not these children should be included in the voucher demonstration. We believe strongly that they should be included for the following reasons:

1) Special facilities have already been set up with special state funds in some of the participating schools, and these could not be moved.

2) Furthermore, we believe that for most of these children segregating them at all times is educationally unsound; we currently make considerable effort to assure that a significant amount of their time in school is spent in regular classes. Because of these

two factors a very awkward situation would be created if the special education children were excluded from the voucher process.

3) Since one of the goals of the OEO project is to improve the education of disadvantaged students, we believe that it would not be sensible to exclude special education students from the benefits of the voucher program, particularly the additional funds that would be available through the compensatory voucher.

We wish to specify that funds earmarked for special education will be available only at schools where special education programs are offered; if a parent of an eligible child chooses a different program in the demonstration, that child's special education funds will not be permitted to follow him.

Finally, special education funds will not be included in the computation of the compensatory voucher for special education children; their compensatory vouchers will have the same dollar value as those of other children in the demonstration.

III.4   *Counselling and Information Dissemination*

III.4.1 *Information Agency*

A thorough program of informing the parents about both the nature of the voucher mechanism and the educational alternatives available is essential for the effective operation of this pilot project. Therefore, we propose to establish a single, centralized educational information unit to collect and verify information about the participating schools and transmit this data in a comprehensible way to parents. In order to carry out this task, we shall require each participating program to submit detailed information about its programs and finances to the information unit.

III.4.2 *Required Information*

In particular, we shall require the following information:

a) Educational philosophy and program: Each program will submit a statement describing its method, emphasis, techniques, philosophy, and objectives.

b)   Staff profile: A description of the teaching and administrative staff, including years of service, educational background, specialties, etc.

c)   Budget: A breakdown of the program's budget indicating amounts and percentages spent on salaries, equipment, materials, etc.

d)   Governance: A description of how policy decisions are made in the program, including the extent to which parents are involved in the process.

e)   Class size: The number of children per certified teacher, the number of aides, and the total number of children per adult.

f)   Evaluation: A statement of how the students, teachers, and the program itself will be evaluated. For example, will students be graded? How will parents be informed of their child's performance—report cards, conferences, written evaluations, or not at all? Will children and/or parents participate in the evaluation of staff and program?

g)   Communications: A description of how the school intends to communicate with parents (written notices, meetings, conferences, home visits, telephone conversations). This statement should include some indication of the desired level of parent involvement, (e.g., one hour per month during school hours, supervision of homework assignments, attendance at P.T.A. meetings, etc.).

h)   Other information: Each school should be entitled to submit additional information which it considers important for parents to know. Furthermore, as the demonstration proceeds, additional information may be required in response to requests from parents or suggestions from participating schools.

III.4.3   *Channels of Information*

Recognizing the difficulty and importance of reaching every parent, the information unit will use a number of communication channels to assure that each parent is informed, including:

a)   School meetings: Meetings to present the voucher concept and discuss the available educational alternatives will be held in each of the six schools. The scheduling of these meetings will be staggered to allow parents who miss their meeting to attend one at another school. Announcements of these meetings will be in English and Spanish and an interpreter will be present at each meeting to present the information in Spanish.

b)   Written material: Written information explaining the demonstration and providing information on available programs will be distributed to each parent. This material will be available in Spanish and English; it will be presented in a short form at a simple reading level, and also in a more extended and detailed format. Each parent will receive both of these documents.

c)   Media: Every effort will be made to use radio, television, and newspapers to present basic information about the demonstration and the alternative programs.

d)   Individual meetings: Parents who do not respond to the foregoing measures will be individually contacted by community counsellors. Furthermore, parent conferences may be arranged including combinations of the following people: parents, children, teachers, principals, community counsellors, or other interested parties.

III.4.4   *Timetable for Parent Counselling*

We intend to devote the entire month of May to providing information and counselling to the approximately 3,000 sets of participating parents. These parents will first be contacted by a mailed letter which will briefly outline the nature of the proposed demonstration and the alternative programs of all of the six schools and will also include an invitation to parents to attend a meeting which will attempt to further explain the program. In addition other available sources of information will be identified such as home visits, or individual school contact. The parent meeting will be followed by parent-teacher conferences and counselling to determine the best possible placement of the individual child, and we will encourage the child to participate in this. We will contact all parents by mail, phone, or personal meetings by the end of May.

Before June 9 all parents will be required to submit their preferences for the programs and school buildings of their choice. The details of this procedure will be discussed in Section III.5, *Admissions.*

A team of bilingual counsellors will continue to deal with problems directly related to this program throughout the year.

The counselling staff will consist of counselling teams with bilingual capacity, each including one professional and several para-professionals.

III.4.5 *Expected Questions from Parents*

The following questions are some of those to which counsellors should be prepared to respond:

a) What will the role of the teacher be in counselling?
b) What will the role of the parent be in counselling?
c) What is the program about?
d) Where is it going to be located?
e) Which schools are involved and why?
f) Is participation voluntary?
g) What happens to parents who don't want to be involved?
h) Will it be possible to transfer from alternative programs to traditional programs?
i) Why is *Pala* the only middle school involved?
j) What effect will this have on primary school graduates?
k) Will the program include kindergartens?
l) Is it possible to expand participating K-5 or K-6 to K-8?
m) How are the children going to be transported?
n) What happens if a parent is not satisfied with his choice?
o) How difficult will it be to switch a child if a program does not suit him?
p) Is there cost to the parent?
q) Will this affect our taxes?
r) Will there be a quota in schools or programs?
s) How will the admissions procedure work?
t) What happens to a child who can't adjust?
u) Where can I get more information?
v) How will this affect special education classes?
w) Will children be in reading groups?
x) How do we assimilate volunteers into alternative schools?

After the children have been placed in the programs of their choice, an ongoing counselling effort will be maintained during the year to inform new residents, advise transferring students, and prepare parents whose children will be coming into the program during the 1973-74 academic year.

The para-professional counsellors will be residents of the demonstration area who know many of the people in their communities. Spanish speaking para-professionals will be employed as needed to ensure adequate communication with Spanish speaking families.

III.5   *Admissions*

Because one of the key elements of a voucher system is the maximization of parental choice in selecting a student's school, a carefully designed admission procedure is essential. We propose a system of open enrollment within the six participating schools subject to the constraints listed below.

III.5.1   *Current Enrollment*

Children currently in attendance at a given school building must have a right to continued attendance. We are convinced that any system that would "bump" otherwise satisfied students and their families would be wholly unacceptable in Alum Rock. Moreover, preferential treatment of siblings must be included if the experiment is to succeed. The prospect of members of the same household involuntarily attending different schools is unacceptable.

Beyond this, we believe that each incoming or transferring student should have equal access to every program and building in the demonstration. Furthermore, we believe that each child should be guaranteed access to the *program* of his choice, although we cannot necessarily guarantee that he will be able to attend this program in the school building of his choice. In the event that a given program in a given building is over-applied, presently enrolled pupils and their siblings who apply will be admitted, and the remaining places will be allocated on the basis of a fair and impartial selection procedure among the rest of the applicants. Those students who are not selected will have the right to enter the same program in a different building or else apply to a different program in the original building or some other building.

III.5.2   *Integration*

From the figures presented in Section III.3 on the ethnic makeup of the participating schools, it is clear that they are presently well integrated. Therefore, by guaranteeing present enrollees the right to remain in their present schools, we minimize the possibility of increasing segregation. While we are firmly committed to prevent racial polarization from developing, we believe that this admissions procedure will maintain a high level of integration in each school and provide parents with the opportunity to demonstrate their commitment to good education rather than to racial bias. In the unlikely event that segregated enrollment patterns do emerge during this demonstration, we are prepared to assure racial integration in whatever way is necessary. It will be the responsibility of the Educational Voucher Advisory Committee to report quarterly to the School Board on the racial and ethnic composition of the various schools.

III.5.3 *Excess Capacity*

Each of the six participating schools at the current time has approximately 10% excess capacity. This fact will be of great importance in the initial period of the pilot project. While we do not know in advance the number of transfers that will result, the excess capacity of the various schools will minimize dislocations.

Nevertheless, it is possible that one or several schools and programs will receive excess applicants and we propose that program expansion to accommodate these applicants be required. This device will eliminate the necessity for lottery selection at the program level, for each student will be assured placement in the program of his choice.

The requirement that each school offer at least two programs will make this possible; similar programs conducted simultaneously at several different sites will permit a greater degree of variable capacity because the program limit will not be the physical capacity of a single building. Thus, a program with students in two or more buildings can expand or contract more easily than one which is confined to one site.

Because the number of participating students is fixed, and the prospective enrollment in any given program is variable, it is physically possible to guarantee each student his first program choice. Any program with excess applicants can expand by using another site. Thus, although a given student cannot be guaranteed assignment to a given program in *a given building,* he can be assured of his ability to pursue the program of his choice at one of several locations.

III.5.4 *Program Assignment*

Guaranteeing program assignment will not compromise a student's right to remain in his current school building. Thus, families which attach primary importance to continuous attendance at the original school of enrollment will be satisfied. Exercising this right, however, will limit the student's choice to the programs offered in that building. This device will hopefully decrease the significance of attending a given school building and increase family awareness of program options by encouraging consideration of educational trade-offs. Is the convenience of attending the school of original enrollment of greater value to a family than transferring to a building which provides the educational program the family prefers?

The mechanism to implement placement of students must be direct and easily understood, and the program organization discussed above lends itself to a straightforward placement system.

III.5.5 *Placement Procedure*

Students currently enrolled in a given building who wish to stay there will exercise their option to do so. Incoming siblings who wish to follow older siblings in the same building will exercise their option. In addition, these students will be placed in the program offered in "their" building which they wish to attend.

All parents not exercising "squatters" rights, including incoming kindergarten students, new students from outside the demonstration area, and transfer students from outside the demonstration area, and transfer students within the demonstration area will be required to identify both program and building choices. Because of the program expansion requirement discussed earlier, all of these students will be assured of placement in their first choice program. They may, however, face some uncertainty about building assignment depending upon the demand for a given building.

Each incoming parent will be asked to make a maximum of three program/building choices. In the unlikely event that none of these combinations can be satisfied, the *program* choice expressed in the first combination will be guaranteed. An outline of our proposed selection and placement procedures follows:

1. Central administration will provide all voucher families with application forms.

2. Families will complete these forms and return them.

3. All children who were previously enrolled may exercise their

right to remain in the same building, but their program choice will then be limited to the alternatives being offered in that school. Within this constraint, these children (and any of their younger siblings who so desire) will be placed in their first-choice program.

4.   The remaining students will indicate three preferred building/ program choices. If no school building receives more applications than its expanded capacity can accommodate, each child will be assigned to his first-choice building and then the capacity of each program within that building will be adjusted so that each child can attend his first-choice program as well.

5.   If some buildings are over-applied beyond their capacity to expand, first choice building/program combinations will be satisfied for as many children as possible by some impartial selection procedure such as a drawing.

6.   For children who do not receive their first choice building/ program preference, the same procedure will be followed with their second and third choices. In the event that a child cannot be accommodated in any of his first three building/program preferences, he will be guaranteed his first choice *program,* although this placement may not be in one of his preferred buildings.

7.   All participating program administrators will be required to guarantee the enrollment of children who list their program as their first choice. Excess demand will be met in the following way:

a)   If the program is only being offered in one building the program administrator will attempt to secure sufficient additional space in that building.

b)   If no additional space exists in that building, the administrator will attempt to secure portables, if the Governing Board deems it financially feasible.

c)   If (b) is not feasible, staggered scheduling will be instituted with the concurrence of the program's Governing Board.

d)   If such scheduling is considered unacceptable, the program administrator will secure additional space either in other pilot school buildings or in other buildings in the school district.

e)   If any parent is dissatisfied with the placement of his child and in concert with the administrator of the desired program can arrange to place his child in a more preferable situation, the parent may do so within ten days after the results of the admissions procedure are announced.

For families with strong program interests, and only moderate interest in a given building, there will be no problem. We recognize, however, that some new families will attach great significance to attending a given school building. There is no way at present to project the extent of such demand, and our comments must, of necessity, be regarded as speculative. However, we are confident that the rate of placement in a preferred building will be high. Because programs will be distributed among several buildings, there will be no compelling educational reason for one building to enjoy excessive "popularity." Furthermore, if most parents prefer their neighborhood school, the probability of having over-applied buildings will be reduced even more. Thus, building preferences are more likely to be distributed, leading to a high incidence of families securing placement in the building of first choice. The extent to which families do not secure their first place building choice—even though they secure first choice of program—will have to be carefully monitored.

III.5.6 *Random Selection*

In the unlikely event of heavy over-application among new students and transfer students to certain buildings, we will undertake random selection procedures to guarantee fairness. A drawing for new students would institutionalize an impartial selection procedure, and eliminate the arbitrary exclusion of any student. One "spin-off" of an impartial drawing is to put "unchosen" schools on record that they must change their program offerings if they wish to attract students.

To recapitulate, throughout this discussion we have assumed that each school has at least two program offerings, as we described earlier. It is possible that some schools will have three or more, and that several schools will have similar offerings. Thus the range of choice to a given family will be quite large and the prospect of family satisfaction quite high.

III.5.7 *Transfers*

The potential problem in transferring students is a difficult one to assess at this point in time because there is no reasonable way to anticipate the volume of transfers. However, the policies and procedures governing the allocation of a transferring child's voucher funds will in themselves shape transfer practice and incidence. Straightforward and routine *pro rating* of the voucher over the ten months of the school year would be likely to encourage transfers; a prohibition against *pro rating* would discourage transfers. A middle course we propose calls for a sliding "front-loaded" scale which favors the child's original school. The intent of this mechanism is to permit reasonable budget planning within programs in order to reduce the possibly disruptive financial effects of transfers during the year. The chart below describes how a transferring child's voucher money will be divided between his two schools:

(Cumulative Total)

Quarter of Attendance		*Percentage of Voucher Remaining with First School*	*Percentage of Voucher Which Follows Transferee*
1st	September October November	40	60
2nd	December January	50	50
3rd	February March	70	30
4th	April May June	100	0

The rationale behind this pro rata schedule is to provide compensation for the loss of a budgeted student, but at the same time to make it financially possible for receiving schools to accept transfers even though the amount may not, theoretically, offset the additional cost associated with the transfer student's attendance. The receiving school will have the additional incentive of getting the transferred child's entire voucher allotment during the subsequent year. Furthermore, a program's reputation will be enhanced if it keeps attracting new students.

A new student coming into the demonstration site will be eligible to apply for any vacancies at any of the schools. If he is eligible for a compensatory voucher, and if monies remain in the compensatory voucher fund, the receiving school will be credited with the compensatory voucher pro-rated on a quarterly basis. Students leaving the demonstration leave their compensatory funds behind; the loss of ADA revenues for these students will be handled by the District in accordance with its present procedures.

III.6 *Administration*

III.6.1 *General Considerations*

We perceive the voucher system of allocating resources to schools as the ultimate form of decentralization. The object of decentralization is to make the educational decision-making units more accountable to the parents and communities which they serve. While we recognize that creating smaller, local boards is an important step in this direction, we believe that replacing one large bureaucracy by a few smaller ones avoids coming to grips with the fundamental problem—that many parents are reluctant to "tangle" with *any* bureucracy, even a locally controlled neighborhood council. We believe that true accountability and community control may be achieved by placing the power of the purse—the control of the flow of dollars—in the hands of the individual parents of school children. This mechanism obviates the necessity for a dissatisfied parent to approach the school bureaucracy as a supplicant. He has the right to determine what group of educators will be entrusted with his child's educational dollar, and if they are unable or unwilling to be responsive to his needs, the parent, without requiring the approval of any bureaucracy, can decide to reallocate his child's educational funds to another program. For this procedure to be functional, most of the educational decision-making power must reside in the individual schools and programs which are competing for the child's support. If a program is losing support, it must have the flexibility to change without requiring multiple approvals from "above".

Because of these considerations, great care must be taken in establishing a voucher system "administration" to protect against the possibility of creating another bureaucracy which will undermine the basic objectives of the program. Certain functions clearly must be centralized, such as operating the admissions process, collecting and disseminating information on the system and its component programs, processing the vouchers and allocating the corresponding funds to programs, pupil accounting and financial accounting, and, in the case of this demonstration, overall evaluation of the implementation of the internal voucher system. It is equally important to specify, however, the functions which are not the province of the central administration but which must remain with the individual programs; some of these areas are educational philosophy, curriculum, staffing, texts and materials, program governance, and budgeting, with the clear understanding that this discretionary power must be exercised within the limits imposed by the California State Education Code.

III.6.2 *Proposed Administrative Structure*

For the purposes of this demonstration project we foresee the need to provide the following administrative functions:

a) information collection and dissemination,

b) counselling — to assist parents in understanding the program and familiarize them with the options available,

c) accounting; fiscal and pupil — matching pupils to the program of their choice and keeping track of their location and records,

d) evaluation — conducting an in-house evaluation of the implementation of the project and also providing an interface between the District and the contractor performing the national evaluation for OEO,

e) hearing procedures — establishing fair, impartial hearing procedures for transfers, dismissals, suspensions and expulsions,

f) coordination — a project director will be required to coordinate these functions.

The following preliminary organization chart indicates how this administrative unit would be structured:

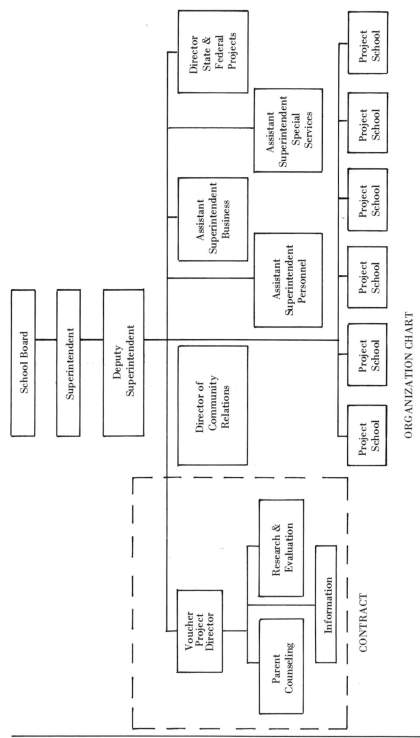

ORGANIZATION CHART

Further details regarding the cost and staffing of this administrative structure will be presented in Section III.12, Budget and Finance.

III.6.3 *Local Board*

The legal responsibility for the schools participating in this experiment remains with the locally elected School Board and Superintendent. The responsibility of the Board to establish District policy cannot be delegated. The Board and Superintendent can, however, provide for the principal or program manager to assume much greater responsibility in the development and operation of the educational program.

The Board can authorize the use of vouchers by students as the delivery mechanism for school funds rather than transferring lump sums to the school. Concurrently, the Board can require the development and presentation of budgets by program, with the corollary requirement that program expenditure be tied to program review. The Board can also authorize the admission procedures described above.

III.6.4 *Education Voucher Advisory Committee*

There are a variety of new issues associated with the voucher demonstration, and because of the heavy work load of the existing Board, we recommend that an advisory group be created to deal with these questions. This advisory group, the Education Voucher Committee (EVAC), would have no legal status or responsibility but should ask as a sounding board and community resource while the program is being developed and implemented. Its function will be to make policy recommendations to the School Board regarding the demonstration, and to work closely with the project director and his staff in making decisions about the implementation of the program. EVAC will also review and comment upon the design and performance of the voucher administrative unit. In the transition model EVAC will consist of twelve members representing the parents and staff of each school. The method of selection at each school will be determined at the school level. The new administrative unit will be responsible for providing staff support to the EVAC.

III.6.5 *Jurisdictional Limits*

EVAC and the administrative unit working with it would be explicitly prohibited from making curricular and fiscal decisions that are properly the role of the individual principals or program managers.

III.6.6 *Central Services*

In all public school systems there is a central administration which provides services in such areas as counselling, curriculum, payroll, personnel,
purchasing, etc. Usually, the motivation for providing these services centrally is the considerable economics of scale which ensue. However, considerable frustrations often emerge at the building level because of the
lack of flexibility imposed by the centralization of services. We would
argue that the same accountability principle inherent in the voucher
concept - that parents should have the option to choose the school which
they feel is providing the best service for their child——should also be
applicable in the relationships between the individual school programs
and the provision of services to them by the central administration.
Ideally, each program manager should have discretionary authority over
the expenditure of all administrative costs for the children in his program.
Each program manager then would determine which servicing are needed
and whether or not they should be purchased from the control administration or some outside supplier. In turn, each service of the central administration would have to demonstrate that the services which it offered
were valuable enough to a child's education that a school program would
be willing to purchase their services for some of the child's voucher money.

However, to protect the District during the demonstration, certain central
services such as accounting, payroll and fringe benefits must be assessed
against each pupil's basic voucher value, but we have identified three
central functions, psychological services, curriculum coordination and
audio-visual materials, which can and should be purchased at the discretion of the individual schools and programs. In the event that the central office personnel associated with providing these services are not
utilized adequately by the schools, the District may lose the funds to pay
their salaries (since this money will be distributed in the vouchers and
some of it may be spent elsewhere). Since we are obligated to protect
our personnel during the demonstration, we can "voucherize" these central services only if OEO guarantees to reimburse the District for any
losses which are incurred from this aspect of the program. The liability
of OEO in this area will in no case exceed 25% of the total budget of the
Alum Rock School District for the personnel providing these services
(based on the projected figures for 1972-73, this maximum figure will
be approximately $70,000).

III.7 *Development of Alternatives within Existing Schools*

Initially, the development of alternatives is likely to be expensive and
time consuming. Traditional school district practice, state mandated
curriculum, and state adopted textbooks lead inevitably to the substantial

uniformity among the schools of a district. The success of the voucher model we propose depends on the development of alternatives. Given a long history of homogeneous schools within a given system, it would be unrealistic to expect viable alternatives to spring to life full blown. In addition, out short lead time makes it unlikely that many new schools will be created during the first year to stimulate competition. We believe it would be a serious, even fatal error to leave the development of alternatives to chance.

At the same time, it would seriously weaken the experiment if it became necessary to channel operating revenues into large scale planning and development. Although the use of current operating revenues can be made in terms of long term development, such a course is costly in a short term demonstration. This presents special problems in light of the short lead time that is available. Thus, we are committed to the notion that adequate funding for inservice training is essential for the development of real alternatives in the six pilot schools during the first year.

Funding for alternatives should be provided as a separate category of expense, and should not be commingled with voucher revenues. We propose that OEO provide funds to support an in-service program to develop alternatives. In the initial years these funds will be divided equitably among the six participating schools. The processes of choosing which alternatives will be offered and planning for their implementation will be carried out with the maximum feasible participation of the parents in the community.

The EVAC staff should function as a clearing house and liaison to prevent costly and unnecessary overlap, but the program development role and in-service planning should be the primary responsibility of the individual school. Clerical and support staff may be purchased centrally, and the individual school should have the authority to employ consultants, conduct workshops and seminars, and undertake in-service training as needed.

III.8   *Certified and Classified Employees*

Full protection as provided by the California State Education Code and Alum Code and Alum Rock School Board Policy will continue to be extended to all participating certified and classified employees in the demonstration project. If any legislation is passed to permit changes regarding certified employees rights these shall be negotiated through the Certified Employees Council.

III.8.1 *Tenure and Seniority*

Certified employees who participate in the demonstration shall retain all tenure and seniority rights, and shall continue to accrue these rights during their participation in the demonstration.

III.8.2 *Transfers*

Any certified employee in a participating school who does not wish to participate in the program may transfer to a non-participating school, provided that such vacancies exist. Furthermore, teachers in non-participating schools who wish to participate may apply for any vacancies in the participating schools. Participating certified employees should have maximum freedom possible to choose to teach in a program that is compatible with their own educational philosophy.

III.8.1 *Displaced Certified Employees*

In the event that shifting enrollment patterns decrease a program's budget to the point where the salary of one or more staff members cannot be covered, surplus certified employees will be removed from that program. If a certified employee is displaced from the program, the following procedure will be followed:

(a) The administrator of the demonstration will assist the certified employee to find another program within the demonstration which has additional staff needs and which is mutually acceptable to the certified employee and the program.

(b) If no such position is available, the Alum Rock School District will undertake to find a suitable position in the remainder of the District.

(c) Prior to a commitment to move to step (d) (teacher contract buy-up) written documentation shall be provided to OEO as assurance that steps (a) and (b) have been pursued in good faith.

(d) In the extreme case that there is no position available in the entire school district, funds will be provided to support thay certified employee at his present salary level until another position can be found. In no case will this support be extended for more than the remainder of the school year plus one full academic year. A maximum dollar value for these contract buy-ups appears in the budget. During the period when a certified employee is being paid without working, he will be required to negotiate with the demonstration board a plan for the constructive use of his time in a way which will improve his ability to provide services needed by the District.

III.8.4   *New Teacher Role*

In the event that the staff of a program determines the need for additional management, they may select a member of their program to provide such services. This position would entail additional responsibilities and, consequently, additional remuneration to be determined by the planners of the program in conjunction with the staff member selected, within the constraints of the program's budget.

III.8.5   *Counselling and Evaluation of Teachers*

(a)   A counselling service shall be established to assist certified employees on any aspect of the demonstration. All certified employees who wish shall be interviewed by an impartial party selected by the local teachers' organization and approved by the Superintendent to establish their position on remaining in the demonstration or transferring.

(b)   Since free and open experimentation has been encouraged by the demonstration plan, any failure in a program will not be held against a certified employee for dismissal purposes except for any of the 14 reasons of cause outlined in the State Education Code and Stull Bill.

(c)   Any procedures for evaluating public school teachers must also be applied to the certified employees in any non-public schools participating in the project.

(d)   Certified employees evaluation shall take into consideration the involvement in an experimental program. The evaluation procedure shall be mutually accepted by the evaluator and the teacher.

(e)   Private organizations or individuals sponsoring or establishing schools shall provide opportunity for qualified Alum Rock certified employees to fill positions before hiring others.

(f)   Funds will be made available to compensate participating personnel for the additional time which they spend in planning for the demonstration.

(g)   Any grievances over teacher rights, working conditions, evaluation or dismissal shall be conducted through regular District and teacher organization channels. All certified staff in the six experimental schools shall have all rights of grievance procedure guaranteed under the Winton Act.

(h)   Any changes in the opening and closing dates of schools will be uniform and determined with community involvement. In-service days will be taken at the discretion of each school.

III.8.6   *Classified Employees*

Classified employees who participate in the demonstration shall be governed by the existing District policy for classified employees. All new positions crested by the project will be classified according to the existing pay scale.

III.8.7   *Planning*

Classified employees will be paid at their regular rate for any additional time which they work because of planning and development of the program.

Parents participating in planning activities will be paid at the beginning classified rate, subject to prior agreement of the principal and the constraints of the in-service funds available.

III.9   *New Schools*

We explicitly agree to cooperate with groups trying to establish new schools. In the absence of legislation, however, these schools can participate only if the School Board contracts with them to provide services.

III.9.1   *Rules Governing New Schools*

New schools must be willing to abide by the rules governing all voucher schools. They must:

(a)   be open equally to all participating students,

(b)   make no charges to students beyond the voucher funds,

(c)   supply the same financial and program information as other voucher schools,

(d)   submit to the same evaluation procedures as other voucher schools,

(e)   participate in the same admissions and counselling procedures as other voucher schools.

(f)   abide by all state laws now governing the public school system.

III.9.2   *Procedures for Starting New Schools*

The establishment of new schools will require at least the following:

(a)   Demonstration of parental support - An interested group of educators will be required to demonstrate that the level of parental interest and commitment in sufficiently high to guarantee that enough voucher revenue will be generated through enrollment to support the program.

(b)   Burden of proof - If a new school can demonstrate sufficient parental commitment, upon recommendation of the EVAC the School Board will enter into a contract with the new group to permit its participation in the demonstration. If the School Board refuses to allow a new school to participate in spite of a demonstratable level of parental commitment, the burden of proof for justifying this decision will rest with the School Board. Unless there are substantial reasons to the contrary, a sufficient level of parental support will imply approval of the program by the School Board.

(c)   Staffing - In hiring staff, new schools will give priority to employees of the Alum Rock School System, if there are such employees who are qualified to teach in the new program. The affirmative action program of the District will be followed in hiring new staff.

III.9.3   *Space*

New schools may be housed in the following facilities:

(a)   Available space in the Alum Rock Public Schools (including non-participating schools),

(b)   portable classrooms set up for the purpose,

(c)   any other physical facility in close proximity to the demonstration area which complies with Field Act standards.

III.9.4   *Start-up Funds*

If community groups are interested in starting new schools, start-up grants will be available for planning, organizing, equipping, and, if necessary, leasing the school site. This start-up money will be provided as part of the OEO grants, and will be "voucherized," as explained in Section III.2 of this proposal. In the event that profitmaking schools should participate, they will not be eligible for start-up grants.

III.10 *Transportation*

We have previously indicated that in order to guarantee all eligible children participating in the demonstration access to the school of their choice, additional bussing will be required. In addition, however, we believe that some additional transportation must be provided to parents to assure them of the means to attend meetings or conferences at schools which are more than one mile from their homes.

The incremental transportation costs will be paid for by OEO. Incremental transportation costs will occur if there is an increased number of children being busses.

Extra busses to provide additional transportation services may create additional unscheduled bus availability during the day; participating schools may utilize this excess capacity, at their own cost, for field trips or other educational purposes.

III.11 *Evaluation*

III.11.1 *National*

We understand that OEO will engage an outside contractor to conduct an evaluation of the demonstration. OEO and its analysis and survey contractor will coordinate its efforts with the Alum Rock School District administration, and with individual principals taking part in the demonstration. The School District and individual schools will provide access to personnel and records to supply basic program data. OEO will make the analyses of these data available to the school system with the proper safeguards to assure confidentiality to all participants. Some data gathering activities such as classroom observation and achievement testing are necessary to the full evaluation of this demonstration. OEO will coordinate these activities with the school district to assure minimal obtrusiveness consistent with one chain of useful information.

III.11.2 *Local Evaluation*

In addition to the OEO evaluation, however, we have a number of questions which we as a District want to be answered during the demonstration for the purposes of our own assessment of the project. The questions to be answered are:

(a)   To what extent will parents exercise choice if it is available to them?

(b)   What effects, if any, will the availability of choice have on the attitudes and achievement of children?

(c)   Will new programs emerge which are more effective than the present ones for some children?

(d)   Will parent involvement and contact with the schools increase as a consequence of the increased financial power that parents will have towards their children's schools?

III.11.3 *Evaluation of Implementation of the Demonstration Project*

Because the voucher concept is untried, and setting up a demonstration is complex, we believe that an evaluation of our implementation procedures would provide valuable information to other school systems which might be considering voucher mechanisms. In particular, we believe that the following aspects of the program would be worth evaluating:

(a)   in-service and planning
(b)   counselling
(c)   management
(d)   admissions procedures
(e)   material utilization
(f)   personnel
(g)   transportation
(h)   finance

III.11.4 *Cost Evaluation*

How will the costs of operating the voucher system (exclusive of special costs related to the experimental nature of the program) compare with the costs of operating the present system? The following variables should be included:

(a)   pupil achievement
(b)   pupil attitude
(c)   parent involvement
(d)   teacher satisfaction
(e)   parent satisfaction
(f)   attendance (pupil and staff)
(g)   vandalism
(h)   transfers - both incidence and reasons

(i)   effect on parent and pupil satisfaction of transfers

(j)   costs of programs and their effectiveness

III.11.5 *Selection of Local Evaluation and Methodology*

The Superintendent in conjunction with the project manager must select the evaluation coordinator and plan the evaluation at an early date to provide adequate evaluation.

III.11.6 *Final Evaluation*

Finally, we must ask whether or not the voucher concept was a good idea. In particular, we must decide whether we want to continue with a voucher approach after the demonstration, and, if so, can we afford to do so? Clearly the evaluation information must permit us to make this crucial decision during the final year of the demonstration.

III.12 *Accounting*

To insure the success of the proposed transitional voucher model, two basic needs must be met: financial accounting and pupil accounting. The voucher concept permits movement of the students among the six schools, or within a school itself. Our present manpower cannot meet the complex problems that will arise from the proposed program. Therefore, we recommend an amount of $69,931 to meet anticipated costs of the project.

III.12.1 *Financial*

We will assume an obligation for reporting financial transactions among the six schools. This will require an expanded accounting system. The number of transactions and the need to report to the community, Board, staff and OEO will be an important part of the program. To accomplish this we will need additional manpower, equipment, supplies, and the use of additional manpower, equipment, supplies, and the use of additional computer time.

The full time accountant and secretary, furniture and equipment are required to achieve the goals mentioned. The equipment lease for bookkeeping purposes and additional computer are preliminary estimates at this time.

The amounts displayed are based on a preliminarty investigation made by District staff office with limited available information. It is suggested that we be allowed flexibility to amend these requests as additional needs arise.

III.12.2 *Pupil*

The District is currently using a hand accounting system for students. We are barely able to meet our present needs with this outdated system.

IV.   BUDGET

IV.1   *Budget by Program*

VOUCHER ADMINISTRATIVE COSTS

	First Year	Second Year
— Directo		
— Director	$ 24,000	$ 24,000
— Secretary	7,000	7,000
— Advisory Board Costs	1,000	1,000
— Furniture and Equipment	1,000	—0—
— Supplies	1,000	1,000
— Travel	2,000	2,000
— In-service for Advisory Board . . .	1,000	1,000
	$ 37,000	$ 36,000

COMPENSATORY VOUCHER

	First Year	Second Year
— Cost of Comp. Voucher	$ 442,090	$ 442,090
— Administrative Costs — School . .	90,000	90,000
— Cost of System		
— mail out — reception, etc.	3,000	3,000
	$ 535,090	$ 535,090

PARENT COUNSELING

	First Year	Second Year
— Professional Counselors (2) . . .	$ 26,000	$ 26,000
— Paraprofessionals (8 positions) . . .	15,000	15,000
— Travel	2,000	2,000
— Furniture and Equipment	1,000	—0—
— In-service	1,000	1,000
	$ 45,000	$ 45,000

RESEARCH COORDINATION

	First Year	Second Year
— Coordinator	$ 20,000	$ 20,000
— Clerk-Typist	5,000	5,000
— Computer Time	—0—	—0—
— Travel	1,000	1,000
— Furniture and Equipment	1,000	—0—
	$ 27,000	$ 26,000

IN-SERVICE EDUCATION	First Year	Second Year
— $30,000 per school — 9 schools . .	$180,000	—0—

TO BE USED FOR —
- Teacher payment
- Parent payment
- Consultant
- Facilities
- Travel
- Education expenses
- Supplies

INFORMATION DISSEMINATION

	First Year	Second Year
— Coordinator	$ 20,000	$ 20,000
— Public Information Specialist	10,000	10,000
— Travel	2,000	2,000
— Reproduction	3,000	3,000
— Furniture and Equipment	5,000	5,000
— Supplies	2,000	2,000
— Art work and photo	2,000	2,000
— Translator	5,000	5,000
	$ 48,000	$ 49,000

FISCAL MANAGEMENT

	First Year	Second Year
— Accountant	$ 12,000	$ 12,000
— Accounting Clerk	8,000	8,000
— Furniture and Equipment	1,000	—0—
— Computer Time	2,000	2,000
— Lease of Equipment	4,000	3,500
— Supplies	1,000	1,000
	$ 28,000	$ 26,500

PUPIL ACCOUNTING (Contract to Evaluator)

	First Year	Second Year
— CEIS Contract	$	$
— Development costs (forms, etc.) . . .		
— Attendance Acct.		
— Furniture and Equipment		

MANAGEMENT/STAFF TRAINING	First Year	Second Year
— Component for Present Pilot Schools	$ 29,000	—0—
— Component for Additional School — Fiscal Year 1973	—0—	—0—
— Component for Central Staff, Psychologists, Coordinators in Operations of Internal Voucher System	$ 21,000	—0—
— Development of Internal Counseling Team to Carry on Project in Remaining Three Year Period	—0—	—0—
	$ 50,000	$ —0—

ADMINISTRATIVE COSTS		
— Incremental Transportation Costs . .	$ 10,000	$ 10,000
— Fringe Benefits for Staff (12%) . . .	15,600	15,600
— Overhead costs of project (8%) . . .	11,720	11,540
— Rent and Utilities	5,400	5,400
— Contingency	10,000	10,000
	$ 52,720	$ 52,540

RESERVE		
— Teacher Salary Guarantee	$ 38,000	$ —0—
— Central Service Salary Guarantee . . .	30,000	30,000
— Grants to New Schools	13,000	15,000
	$ 81,000	$ 45,000
	$1,082,810	$ 812,130

— First Year	$1,082,810	
— Second Year	812,130	
	$1,894,940	$1,894,940
— Less operation costs of Interim grant		49,700
— Total Grant for two years . . .		$1,845,240

IV.2   *Budget by Categories*

		Fiscal 72-73	Fiscal 73-74	Line Total
Category I - Salaries & Expenses				
A.	Full-time Employees			
	Director 25,000			
	Operations Director . . . 20,000			
	Research Director. . . . 20,000			
	Accountant 12,000			
	2 Counselors @ 13,000 . . 26,000			
	Public Info. Spec. . . . 10,000	112,000	112,000	224,000
	Secretary 7,000			
	Accounting Clerk 8,000			
	Clerk Typist 5,000	18,000	18,000	36,000
B.	Personnel Expenses (12% of IA) (Fringe Benefits)	15,600	15,600	31,200
C.	Part-time Employees			
	9 Paracounselors (138 manweek @ 60 per week)	15,000	15,000	30,000
	Translator secretary	5,000	5,000	10,000
	Total Category I	165,800	165,600	331,200
Category II — Travel		7,000	7,000	14,000
Category III — EVAC Costs		3,000	3,000	6,000
Category IV — Operations				
A.	Purchase & rental of things (furniture 10 x 500 + typewriters, xerox, calculator, computer use)	15,000	10,500	25,500
B.	Printing	5,000	5,000	10,000
C.	Rent and utilities	5,400	5,400	10,000
D.	Supplies	7,000	7,000	14,000
E.	Student and financial accounting	90,000	90,000	100,000
F.	Incremental Bussing Costs	10,000**	10,000**	20,000
G.	Contingency	10,000	10,000	20,000
H.	District Overhead (4% of Categories I – IV)	11,720	11,580	23,250
	Total Category IV	158,120	149,140	203,560

	Fiscal 72-73	Fiscal 73–74	Line Total
Category V — Alternative Education Development			
A. In-Service Training Cost (6 schools & $30,000)	180,000	—0—	180,000
B. HRC — Staff Training	50,000		50,000
Total Category V	230,000		230,000
Category VI* Compensatory Member Fund	442,000	462,000**	684,180
Category VII Reserve for Contingency			
A. Teacher Salary Guarantee	35,000	—0—	38,000
B. Central Services Staff Salary Guarantee	30,000	30,000	60,000
C. Grants to New Schools	15,000	15,000	30,000
Total Category VII	81,000	45,000	128,000
Grand Subtotals	1,082,810	812,130	1,884,900
Less Operational Costs of Interim Grant Previously Granted	49,700		
Grand Totals	1,033,110		1,845,240

* Not Transferable
** To be renegotiated based upon 1972-1973 data

A PROPOSED DEMONSTRATION
IN EDUCATION VOUCHERS

Office of Economic Opportunity
Office of Planning, Research, and Evaluation
April 24, 1972

Within days of receiving Alum Rock's proposal, OEO announced its funding of a series of grants to operate a voucher experiment in Alum Rock. "A Proposed Experiment in Education Vouchers" *distributed April 24th, 1972, and remains the official statement from OEO of its plans and intentions. The reader will note that OEO's emphasis is quite different from that of the Alum Rock proposal, although the wording of the two documents is often very similar.*

Introduction

Since December, 1969, the Office of Economic Opportunity has been working with the Center for the Study of Public Policy of Cambridge, Massachusetts, to devise a system which would:

-- Give poor parents greater influence over the education of their children, and greater choice among the types of education available.

-- Foster educational innovation both within the public schools and outside the public school system.

-- Make schools more accountable to parents at all income levels.

The study evolved from a general concern by OEO that while our public schools are probably performing better today than at any time in the past, they are not meeting the educational needs of the poor. Study after study has indicated the general failure of existing remedial and compensatory programs for the poor. At the same time, the poor, perhaps more than any other group in our society, must depend on public education for future success in life.

One means of improving the education of the poor may be the education voucher system devised by the CSPP and OEO. Under this system, all parents in the community, regardless of income, would be given vouchers with which to purchase their children's education at the school of the parents' choice. This model is explained in detail in this pamphlet, which updates an earlier OEO publication on education vouchers.

Since preparing that earlier publication, OEO has decided to fund a small pilot test of vouchers, described in the chapter entitled, "The Transitional Phase." This decision was made in part because of the lack of state legislation needed to implement the full voucher system envisioned in the original model and in part to permit a pretest of some of the administrative issues surrounding the voucher concept.

Those interested in more details on the voucher concept may also wish to consult:

> *Education Vouchers: A Report on Financing Elementary Education by Grants to Parents* (December, 1970), Center for the Study of Public Policy, Cambridge, Massachusetts, available from the Office of Planning, Research, and Evaluation, OEO, (free)

Reports on feasibility studies conducted in four potential voucher sites will be will be available after June 1 from the National Technical Information Service, U.S. Department of Commerce, Springfield, Virginia 22151. The titles of the reports are:

> *Preliminary Feasibility Study for the Establishment and Use of an Education Voucher System in Gary, Indiana,* Volume I ($3.00) and Volume II (Appendices, $3.00), May, 1971, Institute for the Advancement of Urban Education, New York, New York.

> *Voucher Feasibility Study Final Report,* Center for Planning and Evaluation, San Jose, California ($3.00)

> *The Feasibility of Implementing a Voucher Plan In Seattle,* May, 1971 ($3.00); *The Feasibility of Implementing a Voucher Plan in Seattle, Phase II Final Report,* March, 1972, ($3.00); and *Third Survey: A Summary of Major Findings Concerning Citizen Opinions Toward the Voucher Plan,* March, 1972 ($3.00), Bureau of School Service and Research, University of Washington, Seattle, Washington.

> *A Feasibility Report on Education Vouchers for the San Francisco Unified School District,* February, 1972 ($3.00), Abt Associates, San Francisco, California.

The Issues

Proponents of the voucher concept see it as a means of effecting a number of improvements in education for the poor:

-- Individuals would have greater freedom within the public education system because they would not be required to accept standardized programs offered in assigned public schools. Middle-income and poor parents would have much the same freedom to choose schools that wealthy parents can exercise.

-- Parents would be able to assume a significant role in shaping their children's education, thus renewing the family's role in education and resulting in concomitant improvement in the attitudes of both parent and child.

-- A range of choices among schools would become available. Small new schools of all types could come into operation-- Montessori, Summerhill, open classroom, and traditional style schools, among others.

-- Administrators and teachers could arrange their curricula to appeal to a particular group or to reflect a particular school of thought on education methods. Schools could emphasize music, arts, science, discipline, or basic skills. Parents not pleased with the emphasis of one school could choose another. Thus, public school administrators and teachers would be freed from the necessity of trying to please everyone in their attendance area, a practice that often results in a policy that really pleases no one.

-- Resources would be more accurately channeled directly to a target group, the poor, since funds would follow the child holding the voucher.

-- A form of accountability would be introduced since parents would be free to withdraw their children from any school with which they were not satisfied.

Critics of the voucher system argue that:

-- The voucher system could be used to promote economic segregation within the schools because well-to-do parents could add money to the vouchers and thus be able to choose schools that charge additional fees. If this occurred, the vouchers would, in effect, become a subsidy for the rich and middle-class parents.

-- Vouchers could lead to racial segregation within the schools. The courts have, however, found this attempted use of vouchers to be unconstitutional where it has been tried in the South.

-- The system would lead to public support of religious instruction, in violation of the Constitution.

-- Use of a more nearly free market in education would lead to false claims by educators that would mislead and misinform an unsophisticated public. In short, hucksterism would enter the educational market.

Others also question whether parents, particularly low-income parents, have the capability and desire to choose sources of education for their children. In addition, there is a concern about the feasibility of administering a voucher system and about financing new forms of education as alternatives to existing sources. Finally, many wonder whether a voucher system would jeopardize the public schools, which might be forced to become schools of the last resort.

The Original Model

The voucher model proposed by the Center for the Study of Public Policy seems to retain the advantages cited by advocates of a voucher system while eliminating most of the problems cited by its opponents. This model is based on the premise that an unregulated voucher system could lead to all the problems listed above. The Center, however, indicated that the education marketplace could be regulated so as to eliminate the difficulties and retain the system's popular advantages. The Office of Economic Opportunity, after reviewing the potential merits of a regulated voucher system, has decided to test a system that would include the following regulations:

-- No school may discriminate against pupils or teachers on the basis of race or economic status, and all schools must demonstrate that the proportion of minority students enrolled is at least as large as the proportion of minority applicants.

-- Schools must be open to all applicants.

-- The schools must accept the voucher as full payment for all educational services. In other words, no school may require parents to make additional payments out of pocket. Schools may seek additional sources of funds from the government, foundations, or interested citizens and parents, but in no case can the admission of a child to the school be conditioned upon such contributions on the child's behalf.

-- All schools must make available to parents information about such matters as the school's basic philosophy of education, number of teachers,
teacher qualifications, facilities, financial status, and pupil progress. In
short, schools must provide sufficient information to parents to enable
them to make wise decisions when they select schools.

-- The value of the voucher will be supplemented for the poor. This regulation is designed to help schools develop and operate special programs for
these children.

These regulations would be enforced by a locally selected Education Voucher
Agency (EVA), which also would be responsible for the day-to-day administration
of the voucher system. As shown in Table I, the EVA would distribute vouchers
to all eligible parents and cash the vouchers on presentation by qualifying schools.
The EVA could be the current board of education augmented by members of the
community and representatives of alternative sources of education. Or, it could be
a new board empowered to receive funds from the local system and disburse them
to parents.

The demonstration, to be mounted in ssveral communities, would include only
elementary children. This period is crucial in the development of the child's basic
skills and learning motivation. It is also a time when the parents are particularly
concerned with their children's education. In addition, since it is hoped that additional sources of education will be developed within the community, the elementary level was selected since developing new elementary schools requires less capital. There is substantial evidence to suggest that elementary school facilities are
less expensive than those for the intermediate or secondary grades.

All elementary school children in the experiment areas would be eligible to receive the vouchers, which could be used at any school meeting requirements to be
established by the community. The EVA would make every effort to provide parents with information and counselling, and other types of assistance to facilitate
their choices.

The bulk of the funds would come from existing and projected state and local
education revenues, which would be distributed on a per student basis. The OEO
plans to provide the additional funds for compensatory payments for poor children, and to pay the extra costs of educating students not now in the public
schools. These costs would be roughly equal to current per pupil expenditures.
In addition, OEO would finance the extra costs occasioned by setting up and administering the voucher system, and would provide transportation funds, so that
students would not be limited to neighborhood schools. It is not, however, the
intention of OEO to reduce the burden of local taxpayers by substituting Federal
for state and local funds.

The original model for the voucher system also called for participation and parochial schools, as well as existing public schools, and for the EVA to be representatives of all providers and consumers of education in the community. At the same time, the EVA would be independent of the existing school board (although it might include some or all of its members).

To allow the EVA to distribute public funds to nonpublic schools, however, enabling legislation is necessary in states where the demonstration will be operated. Such legislation is pending in two states -- California and Washington -- but at this time has been passes only in Connecticut.* No state in which a community currently studying vouchers is located has yet passed in the legislation.

*See Part IV of this book.

The Transition Phase

In the absence of state enabling legislation, OEO has decided to consider a transitional tional phase of the voucher demonstration. It would involve only public schools (or private schools operating under contract to the public schools) and would in many ways serve as a pretest for the full voucher demonstration to follow.

Five school districts -- Alum Rock in San Jose, California; San Francisco, California; Gary, Indiana; Seattle, Washington; and New Rochelle, New York -- have been awarded small grants to conduct studies of the feasibility of mounting a voucher demonstration in their communities. After extensive reviews, the Seattle and public school boards decided not to proceed with the voucher demonstration. A vote is expected shortly from the San Francisco school board, while New Rochelle's feasibility study is just as its initial stages. Strong support was found for the voucher system in Alum Rock, however. Thus, because of this strong support and because of the continued efforts by Alum Rock officials to obtain state enabling legislation, a decision was made to implement the transitional phase in Alum Rock in the 1972-73 school year.

The OEO/Alum Rock Voucher Demonstration

Alum Rock school officials first became interested in the voucher plan in July, 1970, after a presentation to the special study committee of the California State P.T.A. by the representative of the Center for the Study of Public Policy (CSPP). After a series of meetings between representatives of CSPP, OEO, and Alum Rock residents, the Alum Rock school board voted unanimously to apply for a feasibility study grant. The grant was awarded by OEO in February, 1971.*

An Education Voucher Committee (EVC) was constituted to guide and review the feasibility study, and to advise the school board on whether to continue or cease voucher activities. The EVC included representatives of the public and private schools, business community, Governor's Office, existing community groups and students. The Center for Planning and Evaluation of the Santa Clara Office of Education was hired to provide technical support for the EVC. The technical group developed and distributed information brochures, conducted opinion surveys, and developed preliminary plans for the voucher model.

As noted above, the surveys indicated much support for educational experimentation and alternative forms of education. Of the parents surveyed, 56 percent felt schools should try new ideas while 74 percent of the teachers, and 78 percent of the administrators felt that experimental schools are healthy for education. In addition, 77 percent of the teachers and 78 percent of the administrators agreed that new alternatives are needed in the public and private schools.

However, most parents felt that they were not well enough informed about vouchers. Even so, 40 percent of the parents, 53 percent of the teachers, and 69 percent of the administrators were favorable to continued exploration of the voucher plan. Some 16 percent of the parents, 42 percent of the teachers, and 32 percent of the administrators felt further study was not desirable.

At the conclusion of the eight-week feasibility study, the EVC recommended that the school board wait to make a decision on whether to proceed until state enabling legislation had been passed.

The Elementary Demonstration Scholarship Act of 1971 (AB 150), which included the necessary enabling provisions, was introduced to the California State Assembly on January 14, 1971. The Alum Rock School District actively supported the passage of AB 150. The school superintendent frequently testified at committee hearings at the request of state legislators, and provided a needed information resource for many of the state assemblymen and senators.

The enabling legislation was not passed during the 1971 session, but has been reintroduced this session. The Alum Rock School District is lending continued support for its passage this spring.

In the interim, the district applied for and received a continuing planning grant for a staff training program that explored increased autonomy for principals and teachers in six pilot elementary schools.

*Excerpts from that study appear later in Part III.

In January, 1972, convinced that greater decentralization was desirable, but unable, but unable to move toward a full voucher system in the absence of legislation, the principals and central staff developed a short-term transitional plan which embodied many of the key features of the original voucher model developed for OEO by the Center for the Study of Public Policy. This plan was submitted to the OEO and, after being discussed with the community, was approved by the teachers and principals of the six pilot schools.

On March 8, 1972, the Alum Rock School Board unanimously authorized the superintendent to develop a specific proposal for the demonstration.* In recognition of the need for community and staff participation in the development of the program, a three-day conference was held at Santa Clara University to write the first draft of the proposal. Fifty-five people participated in the conference: principals, teachers, and parents from the six pilot schools, representatives of the teachers' organizations (A.R.T.A. and A.F.T.), P.T.A. representatives, central staff, and representatives from the Center for the Study of Public Policy, the Center for Human Resources and Organization Development, and OEO.

The proposal was revised and submitted to the school board, which approved unanimously on April 12, 1972.*

The Alum Rock proposal specifies that:

-- Parents in the attendance areas of the six pilot school districts will receive vouchers worth about $680 for children in kindergarten through sixth grade and about $970 for those in seventh and eighth grades. This amount represents the current average cost of educating a child in the Alum Rock School District.

-- Each of the six principals (program managers) with their staff will develop two or more alternative, distinct education programs. The programs will operate simultaneously in one or more buildings. The alternatives will be developed with the full cooperation of the community. Efforts also will be made to encourage private organizations and parent and other public groups to develop programs that would be operated under contract with the public school board.

-- As shown in Table II, each parent will select his child's education *program* and the specific school building he wants his child to attend. Each child will be assured placement in his first-choice program. Children currently enrolled in one of the six schools and their younger brothers and sisters will be guaranteed the right to remain in their present building.

*The proposal appears later in Part III.

-- Admissions to each program and building will be done in such a way as to maximize participant satisfaction. Each new enrollee will have equal access to every program and building in the demonstration. If a *building* is over-applied, additional capacity will be created whenever possible. If a *program* within a building is over-applied, additional capacity will be provided somewhere else in the system, so that each child can be guaranteed enrollment in his first-choice program.

-- The vouchers of poor children will be supplemented by about a third of the value of the basic voucher to help schools meet the special needs of these children.

-- The budget for each program will be determined by the voucher money brought in by its enrollees. The funds of students who transfer from one program to another will be equitably divided between the program they have attended.

-- Each program will be required to provide information about its philosophy, practices, and finances, and this information will be made available to all participating parents. In addition, community counsellors will consult with parents about program offerings and their children's needs.

-- A representative board will be formed to advise the school board and administration on decisions relating to the demonstration.

-- The community will participate actively in operating and governing the transitional demonstration.

The specific goals of the Alum Rock program, as outlined in the district proposal, are:

-- "To offer all parents in the demonstration area a range of choices for the education of their children. In particular, it is hoped that the right of educational choice presently available only to the affluent will be extended to the poor and middle income sectors of the community.

-- "To allow schools to become more responsive to the needs of their communities and to involve parents more meaningfully in their decision-making processes as a consequence of this revised procedure for allocating educational resources.

-- "To stimulate parents to take a more active interest and become more involved in the education of their children.

-- "To improve the educational achievement of the participating students.

-- "To increase the level of parental satisfaction with their schools."

The Alum Rock transition model differs structurally from the original voucher model in essentially four ways:

1. The EVA will finction as an advisory body to the school board rather than an autonomous, publicly constituted body.

2. Interested new school groups will have to contract with the school board to become eligible for voucher funds, rather than apply to the EVA for certification.

3. Six schools and approximately 4,000 students will participate in the first year of operation, rather than the original expected 12,000 to 15,000 pupils.

4. Each of the six schools will offer at least two alternative programs rather than one.

Although the pilot transition phase does differ from the original voucher model, several points should be kept in mind. First, the transition model has been structured to achieve many of the desirable features of the original model:

1. A fairly wide range of alternative pedagogies will be available to parents.

2. Low-income parents will be given the opportunity to make choices between programs, and could in turn begin to exert influence on the system.

3. School principals will be given independent budgets and freedom to experiment, with accountability to parents rather than solely to the system.

4. Groups who want to start schools will be guaranteed the right to become part of the public system if they meet certain specific requirements set in advance by the school board and if they demonstrate that some number of parents want to enroll their children.

Further, as the Alum Rock school district has committed itself to expansion during the second year if the demonstration is successful; if not, the project will be phased out. The school district has also committed to exploring the desirability of moving to a full voucher program should enabling legislation be passed, and the transition program be successful.

The transition model also will allow Alum Rock to test the admissions procedures, parent counselling function, and the fiscal and evaluation systems on a small scale to allow for a smoother transition into the full system.

Transition Model Tentative Costs*

	First Year	Second Year
Administrative.	$ 89,720	$ 88,540
Compensatory Vouchers	535,000	535,000
Parent Counselling	45,000	44,000
Information Dissemination	49,000	49,000
In-service Training/Program Development. . . .	180,000	—0—
Research/Evaluation	27,000	26,000
Fiscal Management	26,000	24,500
Reserves (contingencies and new school grants)	81,000	45,000
Management and Central Staffing Training	50,000	—0—
TOTAL	$1,082,720	$ 812,040

*These additional costs will be covered by a grant from OEO.

The Questions

It is important to emphasize that the Office of Economic Opportunity is not an advocate of education vouchers. Rather, the Agency believes the concept holds enough potential for the poor to merit testing. Among the more important questions to be answered by the demonstration are:

-- Will the parents, and the community as a whole, feel their needs are met by the education offered under a voucher system?

-- Will the education of children be improved?

-- Is a regulated voucher system administratively feasible?

-- Will a voucher system result in improved integration patterns; i.e., are racial and economic integration fostered? Is a voluntary system of this sort more satisfactory to all concerned than involuntary bussing?

Other questions to be answered during both the transitional and full demonstration periods are:

-- Do meaningful alternatives to the existing public school system actually occur under a voucher system?

-- Do low-income parents feel able to exercise this degree of influence over their child's educational future?

-- Is the impact of vouchers on the existing public schools beneficial?

-- Do compensatory payments offer adequate incentives for schools to accept children who are difficult to educate?

The evaluation of this demonstration and an analysis of the policy issues surrounding the concept of education vouchers will be conducted by the Rand Corporation. Most important, however, the judges will be the parents, state and local officials, educators, and representatives of the poor who will participate in the experiment and who will have the opportunity to examine the voucher system on a first-hand basis. They will make the judgment as to the desirability or nondesirability of adopting such a system on a permanent, operational basis.

Of the 4,000 Students in the Program

Almost half are Chicano --
About ten percent are black --
Forty percent are white --
Based on federal eligibility standard for free lunches, about half of the students are from economically disadvantaged families.

Program Managers' Role

1. Develop and manage programs that will be located in two or more buildings in the district.
2. Provide parents with complete information about their programs.
3. Receive vouchers as full payment for education.
4. Work within a budget for each program set by the number of vouchers received for that program.

Parents' Role

1. Receive vouchers to pay for their children's education.
2. Choose the *program* they want their children to attend
   and/or
3. Choose the *school* they want their children to attend.
4. Work separately or with principals to develop new programs.

Alum Rock School Board's Role

1. Reimburses programs for vouchers they receive.
2. *Guarantees* parents that children will be accommodated in their first-choice *program*.
3. Makes every effort to place children in their first-choice *school*.
4. Guarantees that children may remain in their present *school*, and that younger siblings will be placed in same school.
5. Contracts with private firms and/or parent groups wishing to start new programs.

Vouchers Advisory Board's Role

1. Works with principals, parents, and school board to develop new programs.
2. Provides counselling and verifies information given to parents.
3. Encourages development of new programs.
4. Reviews applications from outside groups for new schools.

OEO's Role

1. Monitors demonstration to ensure nondiscrimination and adherence to all other demonstration guidelines.
2. Provides funds for:
    -- Parent counselling
    -- Information dissemination
    -- Start-up grants for new schools
    -- Supplementation of vouchers for poor children
    -- Administrative costs
    -- Transportation

WHY, WHAT AND KINDS OF VOUCHERS

"Why Vouchers?", "What is a Voucher?" and "Educational Choices For Your Child" were published in Alum Rock, in Spanish as well as in English versions, and distributed to parents in the experimental population, as part of the choice-making procedure. A cadre of professional and para-professional counselors and sides were employed during May and June, 1972, to speak personally with every child's parents, inform them of the program, its purpose and procedures, and the choices available.

The information provided to parents about their educational choices is less thorough than had been recommended by the feasibility study. This is due, in part, to the haste required in implementing the program during 1972-1973. It is due also to the fact that many of these educational choices are new in Alum Rock, so that answers to many questions will not be known for one year. In effect, parents were asked to select among **plans** *for school programs. In 1973-1974, of course, parents will choose among operating school programs (plus whatever new programs, if any, have been planned). To aid parents in making their alternative school choice the cadre of professional and para-professional counselors and aides provided answers to the anticipated parental questions presented in III. 4.5 of the Alum Rock's* **Transition Model Voucher Proposal Supra.**

During June, 1972, choices were made for over 2500 youngsters by their parents. Parents overwhelmingly (2400) chose to keep children in the school they had previously attended. However, **within** *those schools, parents had a choice of 3 or 4 programs for their children. Over 1000 youngsters were entered in the new nonconventional choices. At Meyer Elementary School, for example, 189 were enrolled in the Basic Skills program, 104 in the Sullivan Individualized Language Language Arts program, 83 in the Fine Arts-Creative Expression program, and 100 in the School 2000. Moreover, according to project director Dr. Joel Levin, over 200 families in which there are were more than one child (there are at least 750 such families) enrolled in the voucher experiment schools, parents chose different programs for different children. Dr. Levin saw these statistics as suggestive that parents can and will make choices about their children's schooling, when given the opportunity.*

The new school programs, generally, were prepared by volunteers from the faculty of the Alum Rock district. Developmental planning occurred during 1971-1972 and through the summer of 1972.

Documents Distributed to Alum Rock Parents—May, 1972

Alum Rock Union Elementary School District

Why Vouchers?

The Alum Rock School District has decided to start a voucher program in order to give you, the parent, more control over the education of your child. You will decide how your child's educational dollars will be spent. Before this program only wealthy people had any choice over the kind of education their children received, because only they could afford to shoo around among private and public schools until they found one which they liked. Middle income and poor people had no choice; their children were assigned to the nearest public school, and they had to be content with whatever was offered there. Some parents were quite satisfied, but if they were not there was very little they could do about it.

In the voucher system, each parent will receive a certificate or voucher, which is worth the cost of one year of education in the Alum Rock School System. For elementary school children (kindergarten through sixth grade) this basic voucher will be worth $679.00; for seventh and eighth grade students it will be worth $967.00. This voucher can be redeemed only by the principal of a participating voucher school. When you choose a program for your child and he or she is enrolled, you turn your voucher over to the principal, and the money is credited to your child's program. If a program is successful and attracts many children, its budget will be large, and it will expand. If a program does not attract children, its budget will be small; eventually it will either change to attract more children or else close down at the end of the year because no one wants to go there.

A compensatory voucher equal to one-third of the basic voucher will be added to the account of each child who is eligible for the free school-lunch program. The purpose of this compensatory voucher is to help schools to meet the special needs of these children, and to offer an incentive to encourage the development of programs to improve their education. The awarding of compensatory vouchers will be confidential, and the additional funds which they bring to a school will be used to improve the education of all the children in that school.

In order to assure that parents will have real choices between different kinds of education, each of the six participating schools will offer two or more distinct programs.

If parents are not satisfied with any of these, a group of them can get together and start their own "community" school. The simplest way to do this would be for the parents to find some interested teachers in an existing voucher school and encourage them to develop the new program within their school. If this was not possible, the parents could apply to the School Board through the Education Voucher Advisory Committee (EVAC) for a start-up grant to plan their own school, and if they complied with the rules governing all voucher schools, they could obtain authorization to start their own. Another possibility would be to find an existing private school or group of educators who would be interested in coming into one of the voucher schools by making a special contract with the School Board.

We hope that vouchers will help to make the schools more responsive to the needs of children and parents, and that parents, in turn, will become more actively involved in the education of their children.

"Vouchers" — Por que?

El Distrito Escolar Elemental de Alum Rock ha decidido a empezar un programa de certificados de fondos "Vouchers", para la educacion de los ninos para dar a los padres mas control sobre la educacion de sus ninos. Usted va a decidir como vamos a gastar el dinero para la educacion de su nino. Antes de tener este programa los ricos eran los unicos que podian escoger el tipo de educacion para sus ninos porque solamente ellos tenian el dinero para buscar la escuela de su preferencia entre las escuelas privadas y publicas. Los que tienen ingresos medios y los pobres no pudieron escoger; se colocaron sus ninos en la escuela publica mas cerca y no podian quejarse. Algunos padres estaban muy satisfechos, pero si no estaban contentos no podian hacer mucho de su situacion.

En el sistema de "Vouchers", todos los padres recibiran un certificado o "Voucher" que vale el costo de un ano de educacion en el Distrito Escolar Elemental de Alum Rock. Para los ninos de la escuela primaria (de Kinder hasta el grado sexto) este "Voucher", valdra $679.00; para los alumnos de los grados siete y ocho valdra $967.00. La unica manera de redimir un recibo es darlo al principal de la escuela participando en este programa. Despues que escojes un programa para su nino y esta matriculado, usted da el "Voucher" al principal y se acredita el dinero al programa de su nino. Si un programa es muy popular y les interesa a muchos ninos, va a tener mas dinero y se puede extender. Si un programa no es muy popular, no va a tener mucho dinero y para atraer mas ninos tendra que cambiar el programa o estara descontinuado.

Para todos los ninos que reciben el almuerzo gratis se anadira un recibo compensatorio (que equivale un tercero del "Voucher basico). La intencion de esta "Voucher" compensarotio es a ayudar las escuelas a satisfacer las necesidades especiales de estos ninos y a fomentar el desarrollo de programas para mejorar su educacion. El proceso de dar los "Vouchers" compensatorios sera confidencial y se usara el dinero adicional para mejorar la educacion de todos los ninos en la escuela.

Para asegurar que los padres puedan escoger entre diferentes programs de educacion, cada de las seis escuelas que participa va a ofrecer dos o mas programas distintos.

Si los padres no estan satisfechos con ningunos de estos programas, un grupo de padres puede juntarse para formar su propia escuela de la comunidad. La manera mas facil de hacer esto seria hallar unos profesores interesados de la escuela de programa "Voucher" y convencerlos a desarollar un programa nuevo en la escuela. Si esto no era posible, podrian aplicar al Personal de la Escuela por el Concilio Consejero y Comprobante (EVAC) para (dinero) para empezar su propia escuela y si estan en los limites de las reglas que gobiernan todas las escuelas de "voucher" pudieran conseguir la autorizacion para empezarla. Tambien podian encontrar una escuela privada o un grupo de educadores que tienen interes en juntarse con una de las escuelas de recibo por medio de hacer un contrato especial con la Junta Directiva De La Escuela.

Esperamos que los recibos nos ayudaran a hacer las escuelas mas responsivas a las necesidades de los ninos y padres y que los padres tomaran un papel activo en la educacion de sus ninos.

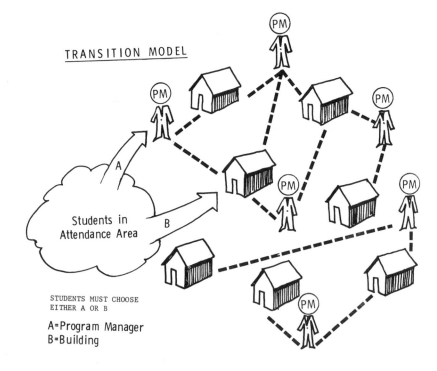

TRANSITION MODEL

Students in Attendance Area

A

B

STUDENTS MUST CHOOSE EITHER A OR B

A=Program Manager
B=Building

What is a Voucher?

¿ Que es un Certificado?
(certificado de fondos.
para educar niños)

Your child will be in the Education Voucher Program next year.

Su niño estará en el programa "certificado" de fondos para educar niños el próximo año escolar.

This means that you will have the right to choose what kind of education he will receive.

Esto quiere decir que usted tendrá el derecho de escoger el tipo de educación que él va a recibir.

Six schools will participate: Cassell, Goss, McCollam, Meyer, Miller and Pala. Each school will offer two or more different kinds of educational programs for you to choose from. You may choose <u>any</u> <u>program</u> in <u>any</u> <u>of</u> <u>the</u> <u>six</u> <u>schools</u> for your child.

Seis escuelas van a participar: Cassell, Goss, McCollam, Meyer, Miller y Pala. Se ofrecerán dos o más diferentes programas en cada escuela. Usted puede escoger cualquier programa en cualquiera de las seis escuelas para su niño.

Some of these programs will be traditional; some of them will be new and different. All of them will be trying to help your child to learn the basic skills that he will need in his life. They will be different from each other in the methods which they use to reach this goal.

Algunos de estos programas serán tradicionales; otros serán nuevos y diferentes. Todos tratarán de ayudarle a su niño a aprender los fundamentos que necesitará en su vida. Se diferencian en los métodos que se usan para lograr este fin.

How will you know which program to choose for
your child?

¿Cómo va a escoger el programa para su niño?

We will have
meetings at each
school to explain
what is offered
in all the schools.

Vamos a juntarnos
en cada escuela
para explicarle
los programas que
se ofrecerán en
todas las escuelas.

We will have counsellors
who will meet with you
either in your home or
at their office, or by
phone, whichever you
prefer.

Habrán consejeros que
estarán para servirle
en su casa, en su oficina,
o por teléfono.

If you want the advice of professional educators who know
your child, teachers, principals, and school counsellors will be
available for conferences at school to help you to decide
what is best for your child.

Si usted quiere consejo de un educador profesional que conoce
a su niño, los profesores, los directores, y los consejeros
de la escuela estarán a sus órdenes en la escuela para
ayudarle decidir lo mejor para su niño.

You will receive an information booklet
which describes in some detail each of
the programs in each of the schools.

Usted va a recibir un folleto que describe
cada parte que compone los programas en
todas las escuelas.

We will try to have the T.V., radio, and newspapers cooperate in presenting
this information to you.

Trataremos de tener la cooperación de la televisión, el radio, y los
periódicos para publicar esta información.

When you have decided what programs are best for your child and what buildings they are offered in, you are ready to fill in your application form.

Después de decidir el mejor programa para su niño y las escuelas en que se ofrece, estará usted listo para llenar la aplicación.

The application form has room for three choices. Each choice must include <u>two</u> items:

    a) the name of the program and,

    b) the name of the school.

Hay tres secciones en la applicación. Cada sección incluye dos partes:

    a) el nombre del programa y,

    b) el nombre de la escuela.

Place your choices in the attached envelope and mail it
before June 8th!!!

Por favor, envíe la aplicación en el sobre antes del
8 de junio.

We will try to place every child
in his first choice school and
program.

Nos esforzaremos en colocar cada
niño en el programa y la escuela
de su primera preferencia.

But what will happen if everyone
wants to go to the same school
and program? Then we couldn't
give everyone their first choice.

¿Qué va a pasar si todo el mundo
quiere ir a la misma escuela?
No pudiéramos dar a todo el mundo
su primera preferencia.

Some parents who like their present school are afraid that their
child might be forced to transfer if too many new children apply
to their school. THIS CANNOT HAPPEN!!!

Algunos padres que están satisfechos con la escuela tienen miedo
de que sus niños tengan que cambiar de escuela si demasiados niños
aplicar a la misma escuela. ¡ESTO NO PUEDE PASAR!

Any child who is presently enrolled in one of the voucher schools will be GUARANTEED the right to stay in his present school IF HE OR SHE WANTS TO STAY THERE.

Cada niño que está matriculado en una de las escuelas de "certificado" tendrá garantizado el derecho de quedarse en su escuela si lo prefiere así.

Younger brothers and sisters who are coming to school for the first time will also be guaranteed a place in the same school if they want it. These children will then be guaranteed a place in the program of their choice, as long as that program is offered in their building.

Los hermanos menores que vienen a la escuela por la primera vez también tendrán el derecho garantizado de ir a la misma escuela. Estos niños tendrán garantizado un lugar en el programa de su preferencia, mientras que esté ofrecido en su escuela.

After these children have been placed, we will try to give the remaining children their first choice of building and program.

Después de colocar a estos niños, trataremos de darles a los demás niños su primera preferencia de escuela y programa.

If that is not possible, we will try to give you your second choice.

Si esto no es posible, trataremos de darle su segunda preferencia.

And if that, too, is already filled, we will try for your third choice.

Si ésa también está ocupada, trataremos de darle su tercera preferencia.

These selections will be made by a fair "drawing" so that no one will
be able to use any influence to get his child into a school more
easily than anyone else.

Las selecciones se harán de un modo de que ninguno de los padres pueda
usar la influencia para que su hijo entre facilmente en una escuela.

If one building becomes very popular, we will not be able to please
everyone who wants to go there. WE CANNOT PROMISE EVERYONE A
GUARANTEED PLACE IN THE BUILDING HE WANTS TO ATTEND.

Si una escuela es muy popular, no podremos satisfacer a todos que quieren
ir. NO PODEMOS PROMETER A TODOS UN LUGAR GARANTIZADO EN LA ESCUELA DE
SU PREFERENCIA.

On the other hand, WE GUARANTEE TO EVERY CHILD A PLACE IN HIS FIRST
CHOICE PROGRAM. If there is no more room in the program you want, we
will expand it until everyone who wants to attend can be included.
If necessary, we will expand a popular program into other buildings
so that everyone can have his first choice.

GARANTIZAMOS A CADA NIÑO UN LUGAR EN EL PROGRAMA DE SU PRIMERA
PREFERENCIA. Si está ocupado el programa que prefiere, lo extenderemos
hasta que todos puedan estar incluidos. Si es necesario, extenderemos
un programa popular en otras escuelas para que todos tengan su primera
preferencia.

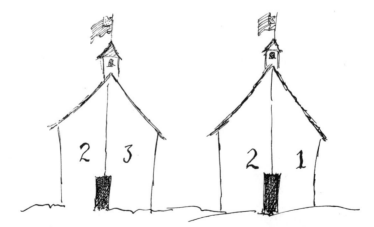

After we receive your selections on June 9th, we will match your choices
to the available spaces. Before June 20th you will receive a letter
telling you the building and program which your child will attend starting
in September, 1972.

Después de recibir sus selecciones el 9 de junio, decidiremos dónde será
colocado su niño. Usted recibirá una carta indicándole la escuela y el
programa de su niño para el año escolar de 1972.

If your child's school is too far to reach by walking, we will provide
free transportation.

Si la escuela de su niño queda demasiado lejos para ir caminando, le
ofreceremos la transportación gratis.

Each school will have some form of parent Advisory Board. This Board will help the principal and his staff to keep in touch with your feelings about your child's program. If you have a problem about school, you can approach your Parent Advisory Board; they will help you to bring it to the attention of the principal and his staff.

Cada escuela va a tener un Comité Consejero de padres. Este Comité le ayudarán al director y a su personal a conocer los sentimientos acerca del programa de su niño. Si usted tiene algún problema sobre la escuela, puede hablar con el Comité Consejero de Padres; le ayudarán a notificar al director y al personal.

Furthermore, each school will select two réprésentatives (either two parents or a parent and a staff member) to the Education Voucher Advisory Council (EVAC). EVAC will consider all issues relating to the voucher project and make policy recommendations to the School Board. EVAC will also:

1) check to make sure that the information you receive about each program is accurate,
2) supervise the school and program assignment procedure to make sure that it is fair,
3) supervise the operation of the voucher administration,
4) establish student transfer and complaint procedures,
5) provide a special communications link between the parents and schools in the voucher project and the School Board.

De cada escuela se van a escoger dos representativos (sea dos padres o un padre y un profesor) para servir en el Concilio Consejero y Comprobante (EVAC – Education Voucher Advisory Council). Este Concilio, EVAC, va a considerar todas las sugestiones que tienen que ver con el proyecto de "certificado" y va a hacer recomendaciones a la Mesa Directiva. Los propósitos de EVAC son:

1) Asegurar que la información que usted recibirá de cada programa es correcta.
2) Dirigir la designación de sus niños a la escuela y al programa para estar seguro de que sea justo.
3) Dirigir la administración del proyecto de "certificado."
4) Establecer transferencias y los procedimientos de quejas.
5) Proveer una comunicación especial entre los padres y las escuelas en el proyecto de "certificado" y la Mesa Directiva.

If you have any further questions about the voucher project or the programs
offered by the schools, call the Alum Rock School District, 258-4923, and
ask the operator for "Voucher Information." We will have bilingual counsellors
available during the day to answer your questions.

Si usted tiene preguntas del proyecto de "certificado" o los programas que se
ofrecerán en las escuelas, por favor, llame Alum Rock Districto Escolar,
258-4923, y pregúntale a la operadora por la información de "certificado."
Vamos a tener consejeros bilingües durante el día que estarán para servirle.

**EDUCATIONAL CHOICES FOR YOUR CHILD
PROGRAM ALTERNATIVES, ALUM ROCK VOUCHER
SCHOOLS, 1972**

Dear Parent:

We hope that this booklet will help you to decide what kind of program to
choose for your child. Unfortunately, we had to collect this information very
quickly in order to get it into your hands by May 20th. This meant that we had
to guess about schools and programs. We want to do a better job next year, so
please tell us what information you would like us to provide. What do you
really want to know about the program you choose for your child? Please write
your comments on this page and return it to school with your child. For more
information, call 258-4923.

Thank you for your help,

Joel M. Levin
Voucher Project Director

Are you satisfied with this information?   Yes   No

What additional information do you want?

Comments:

(Use the back side for additional written comments.)

Program Summary

Name	Program Name	Description
Sylvia Cassell El.	Traditional	Basic skills development, emphasizing reading, writing and arithmetic.
1300 Tallahassee	Daily Living	Basic skills taught by doing.
K – 6	Cultural Arts	Emphasizes study of different cultures.
		(Overall Kindergarten – to place in other programs.)
Mildred Goss	Open Activity Centered	Basic skills taught by doing.
2475 Van Winkle	Developmental Reading	Based on reading – all other subjects relate to reading.
K – 7	Seventh Grade	New 7th grade – based on community involvement.
McCollam	Traditional	Basic skills development, emphasizing reading, writing, and arithmetic
3311 Lucian	Individualized Learning	Learning is tailored to each student. Maximum parent involvement.
K – 6	Enrichment	A program for gifted children, grouped by ability, not age. Open to children who are creative and curious.
	Continuous Progress Non-graded	Emphasizes basic skills; students not grouped by grades; each learns at his own pace.

Name	Program Name	Description
Meyer	Basic Skills	Basic skills development, emphasizing reading, writing, and arithmetic.
1824 Daytona	Sullivan Individualized Lang. Arts	Learning tailored to each student. **BRL** methods used.
K – 6	Fine Arts – Creative Expression	Concentrated on learning through the fine arts.
	School 2000	Prepared students for the future.
Miller	Multi-cultural	Emphasizes study of different cultures. Spanish offered.
1250 So. King	Academic Skill Development	Basic skills development, emphasizing reading, writing and arithmetic.
K – 6	Individualized Leadining	Learning tailored to each student.
Pala	Three "R'"s Plus	Basic skills development, emphasizing reading, writing and arithmetic.
149 North White	Creative Arts	Concentrates on learning through the creative arts.
6 – 8	Fine Arts	Concentrates on learning through the fine arts.
	Math – Science	Concentrates on learning based on a mathematics-science core.
	Girls' Physical Education	Two periods a day of **Physical Education** for girls who want special sports emphasis.

PROGRAM OFFERINGS BY TYPE

Traditional/Academic (7)

Cassell (Traditional)
Goss (Developmental Reading)
McCollam (Traditional)
Meyer (Basic Skills)
Miller (Academic Skill Development)
Pala (Three "R"'s Plus)
Pala (Math — Science)

Learning By Doing (3)

Cassell (Daily Living)
Goss (Open Activity Centered)
Goss (Seventh Grade)

Individualized Learning (3)

McCollam (Individualized)
Meyer (Sullivan — BRL)
Miller (Individualized)

Innovative/Open Classroom (3)

Meyer (School 2000)
McCollam (Continuous Progress —
    Non-graded)
Pala (Gives Physical Education
    Emphasis)

Multi-Cultural (2)

Cassell (Cultural Arts)
Miller (Multi-cultural)

Gifted (1)

McCollam (Enrichment)

Fine and Creative Arts (3)

Meyer (Fine Arts and Creative Expression)
Papa (Fine Arts)
Pala (Creative Arts)

Sylvia Cassell Elementary School (K—6)   Jerry Witt, Principal
1300 Tallahassee Drive
San Jose, California

The Cassell Elementary School will offer three different education programs for
1st through 6th grade this fall as a part of our participation in the internal voucher
project. They are (1) Traditional School — Enriched Approaches to Basic Educa-
tiob, (2) The Daily Living School, and (3) The Cultural Arts School. An over-all
kindergarten, encompassing the three programs, is offered to expose the children
to as many different experiences as possible, and to guide them in the choice of
the program that suits them best. In-coming kindergarten students are tested to
help in class placement. Students, with their families, choose the program in
which they want to enroll.

This report gives you a brief description of the programs. We will hold public
meetings in the future to provide you with more information and answer questions. In addition, more detailed information on each program is being prepared,
and trained counselors and community workers will be available to talk to you.
For more information, call 258-4923.

Cultural Arts Program (Cassell)

Description — This program is based on the belief that education's most important
job is to help each child develop the skills, knowledge and confidence to become a
self-reliant person. Through the study of cultures we hope to show the children
that all people contribute something of value. America is the melting pot of different cultures contribute to the American way of life. The program emphasizes
that each child needs to:

- Learn reading, mathematics and language skills to communicate with
  others.
- Know himself
- Feel successful
- Be able to get along with others
- Understand that all cultures have something of value to offer and that
  we can be proud of our cultural heritage

A variety of teaching methods is offered:
- "Words and Math in Color
- Total reading program
- Team teaching

- Learning centers
- Individualized instruction
- Contract teaching
- Field trips

Various cultures are studied through arts and crafts, music, dramas, puppetry, dance, cooking, assemblies, parents and resource people.

Governance — Policy decisions are made by the teachers with the advice of parents and student representatives.

Evaluation — The Fountain Valley Testing Program for reading is used. Parent conferences are also used. Children are evaluated on the basis of the improvement they make.

Communication with Parents — Written notices, phone calls, parent conferences, home visits, classroom visits. We appreciate as much parent support and participation as is possible.

Other Information — We hope that parents will help in the classroom as resource persons or aides, and will identify people in the community who are willing to help in the Cultural Arts Program.

The Daily Living School (Cassell)

Description — This program's objective is to prepare children to live effectively in our society. The basic skills of reading, mathematics, writing, science, and social studies are taught with a daily living emphasis. Because we believe that children Learn By Doing, we build our learning situation on real life activities. Activities are designed to develop children's understanding of themselves, their family, and their environment. Full parent participation is encouraged.

Reading is stressed, with a total continuous program offered. Overlapping age groups (6 to 8, 8 to 10, and 10 to 12) are formed to group by ability. Individualized learning centers provide English as a second language and a Resource Daily Living Library includes cookbooks, instructional materials, and current popular magazines.

Mathematics is also stressed through a continuous program in the basic math skills. Mathematics enrickment is offered through practical application: cooking, sewing, wood carving, budgeting, school store and grocery shopping

Social Science study is geared to the child's needs and what parents think is important.

Planned activities include field trips, natural science study, and cultural experiences such as dancing, music, art and plays.

Governance — Policy decisions will be made by all the staff of this school with input from the principal, outside resource people and parents. This will be done through group meetings.

Evaluation — The Fountain Valley Diagnostic Program is used to continually diagnose reading progress.

Communication with Parents — Parents are encouraged to participate in the program to the fullest extent possible.

Other Information —

The Traditional School —
Enriched Approaches to Basic Education
(Cassell)

Description — This program's emphasis is on basic learning skills, reading, writing and arithmetic, enriched by a variety of learning techniques and other subjects. It is based on the belief that every child has the right to as much education as he can absorb with the professional guidance of experienced teachers.

Each child is taught at his own pace:
    The tools of learning
    Social development
    Self-discipline and self-respect
    The satisfaction of learning
    To take pride in progress and growth.

Each child's best level is determined by testing in reading and mathematics. The "Total Reading Program" and state texts are used with the most advanced teaching methods. Field trips, extensive use of audiovisual materials, tutoring, supplementary learning centers and contract teaching are used for enrichment.

Governance — Our program plans to select a Parent Advisory Committee from interested parents. This will be set up by the teaching staff. The Parent Committee will offer its suggestions and ideas on policy matters and decisions affecting the operations of our program. The Parent Committee's opinions will be welcomed and considered by the teaching staff and scbool principal in making decisions for the program.

Evaluation — Each child is tested in reading and mathematics to determine his level of development. The Fountain Valley Diagnostic Testing Program is used to show each student's progress.

Communication with Parents — We work closely with parents during the year through a Parent Advisory Committee, parent conferences, social activities to bring school and home close together, and training sessions to help parents help their children.

Other Information — We plan to offer a strong enriched program for all children, and welcome parent cooperation and help.

Mildred Goss Elementary School   Jim O'Berg, Principal
2475 Van Winkle Lane
San Jose, California

The Goss Elementary School will offer three different education programs this fall as a part of our participation in the internal voucher project. They are (1) Open Activity Centered School (Learning by Doing), (2) Seventh Grade School, and (3) the Developmental Reading and Communication School. Students, with their families, choose the program in which they want to enroll.

This report gives you a brief description of the programs. We will hold public meetings in the future to provide you with more information and answer questions. In addition, more detailed information on each program is being prepared, and trained counselors and community workers will be available to talk to you. For more information, call 258–4923.

Open Activity Centered School (Goss)

Description — This program is based on the belief that students learn best by doing. Our motto is: I hear and I forget;

I see and I remember;

I do and I understand.

Students develop competence in reading, writing, mathematics, science, athletics, and the arts by activities. We offer learning centers, open classrooms, multi-age groupings and individually guided education, A team of two (2) teachers and one aide work with sixty students.

Governance — There is an advisory board of four parents, four teachers, and student representatives which considers any necessary changes. The board plans curriculum, finds resources for activities and organizes activities. Parents also participate in open meetings and parent-teacher-student conferences.

Parents participate in an advisory capacity, with final decisions made by the teachers and principal.

Evaluation — Initial objectives for students are based on skill profiles, tests, and other means. Progress is then measured by teacher prepared tests and/or standardized tests. Parents are informed about student progress in conferences, telephone conferences, and/or written evaluations as thought necessary by parents, students, and teachers.

Program evaluation is accomplished by student-parent communications, open meetings and the Advisory Board.

Continuous enrollment of students constitutes another form of evaluation.

Communication with Parents — All means are used, and telephone discussions are encouraged and used frequently. Supplemental conferences are held. Open meetings are also held.

Parents are expected to participate as much as their personal situation permits.

Other Information — Because of the emphasis on activities, members of the community are often involved in arranging or conducting activities. Parents are to arrange a contract with the program for experiences in which the family participates off campus. Parental permission for field trips is given on a total year basis.

Seventh Grade School (Goss)

Description — Goss has been a Kindergarten through sixth (6) grade school. This program expands Goss' offerings to include seventh grade. The main emphasis of the program is upon the total student, as a self-directed, functioning individual. The awareness of individual worth, pride, and respect are critical to this program. This is achieved by involving the community with the student, and the student with the community. Effective use of transportation facilitates this objective.

Outside resources are used, such as parents; aides; businesses; vocational plants; laboratories; recreational plants; communications' media; health centers; clinics; hospitals; law enforcement agencies; and local, state and federal agencies.

A partial list of program goals and objectives includes:
- Develop independent thinking and self-reliance
- Acquire an effective use of reading, writing, speaking and listening skills
- Produce respect for the natural environment and the cultural arts
- Create a sense of responsibility to society through democratic ideals
- Practice and understand ideas of health and safety

Students accept responsibility in a number of significant ways:
- The student must function on an individual, self-directed basis
- The student is accountable for his actions and must justify his self-directed decisions
- The student has direct involvement in curriculum planning
- The student helps establish individual and group performance objectives

The ratio of adults to students is approximately 1–18.

Governance — Policy decisions are made by teachers with the advice of students, parents, and aides. Open meetings, conferences, and individual contact are made to receive this advice.

Evaluation — Students, by testing, observation, interviewing. Both individual and group evaluation is conducted. Teachers, by self-evaluation, students, parents and administrators; the program, by pre and post testing of goals and objectives.

Parents are informed of student progress by conference and written evaluation.

Communication with Parents — Written notices, meetings, conference, home visits, telephone, and any other necessary means are used.

Other Information — The bounds of education should be unlimited and include the community as a laboratory for learning.

**The Developmental Reading and
Communication School**
(Goss)

Description — This program emphasizes developmental reading and communication, which will be the focal point for all other subject areas. Provision will be made for bilingual, ESL* multi-cultural and other educational components as needed. A step by step reading program used for the past 4 years at Goss, is used. Classes are non-graded in reading and mathematics. A variety of techniques are used, including basal readers, social reading materials, S.R.A.** and speed reading. Teaching styles include contract teaching, one-to-one, team teaching, and staggered reading.

Governance — All operating policies will be decided by teachers and the building principal. A parent-teacher advisory board is composed of each classroom teacher and one parent for each class.

Evaluation — Students, by personal growth as measured by commercial and teacher-prepared tests; Teachers, by the building principal, in accordance with district policies; The program, by building principals and teachers in accordance with district policy.

Communication with Parents — Regular student progress reports are given parents, who are expected to acknowledge receipt. A minimum of two face to face conferences are held each year. Written notices, meetings, conferences, home visits, and telephone calls are used. Parents are also encouraged to visit the classroom at least twice a year.

Other Information — To make our program more meaningful and effective for parents, we will provide workshops in reading, math and other subjects to help you to help your children.

* English as a Second Language
**Science Research Associates reading kits

McCollam School   Don Ayers, Principal
3311 Lucian Avenue
San Jose, California

The McCollam Elementary School will offer four different education programs
this fall as a part of our participation in the internal voucher project. They are
(1) Traditional, (2) Individualized Learning, (3) Enrichment, and (4) Continuous Progress-Non-graded. Students, with their families, choose the program in
which they want to enroll.

This report gives you a brief description of the programs. We will hold public
meetings in the future to provide you with more information and answer questions. In addition, more detailed information on each program is being prepared,
and trained counselors and community workers will be available to talk to you.
For more information, call 258-4923.

Traditional (McCollam)

Description — Emphasizes basic subjects, following the recommended state curriculum: reading, arithmetic, English grammar, spelling, writing and social science.
The program uses the Sullivan and Science Research Association (SRA) reading
materials for each grade level as a supplement; learning center; contract teaching;
team teaching; and S.E.E.D. (Discovery Math); Behavioral objectives will be developed after the beginning of school.

Governance — Policy decisions are made by professionals with the approval of
the principal. Department heads serve on a rotating basis. There is close cooperation with other schools. Parents are involved in the selection of text books,
extra-curricular activities and Friday afternoon interest centers.

Evaluation — Students by standardized tests, teacher prepared tests, subjective
evaluation, observation and other professional techniques. Teachers by Stull
Bill requirements, informally by parent conferences, students and other teachers.

Communication with Parents — Written notices, meetings, home visits, phone
calls, folders and conferences. The program expects parents to encourage completion of homework assignments, cooperate in meeting goals and objectives,
and have students at school on time.

Other Comments — The traditional program concentrates on academic subjects,
through a structured program. Parents are encouraged to volunteer, and will be
utilized.

Enrichment Program
(McCollam)

Description — This program is for gifted students, who are grouped according to ability rather than age. Class sizes are small, and students are encouraged to choose their own areas of study.

The purpose of the program is to increase individual student creativity, and a blend of teaching styles will be used. The philosophy is to guide students to appreciate, understand and contribute their unique abilities.

The program goals are described to encourage students to:

- express intellectual curiosity, develop special talents of memory and creativity

- master the basic academic skills

- interact with each other, to acquire the bility to express and receive ideas

- express and create in cultural arts

The program objectives are to:

- excel in academic achievement, through perfecting the skills of reading, writing and the use of numbers, and to create original and worthwhile projects

- become adept at intellectual skills such as definition and analysis of problems, and developing alternative solutions.

Governance — Policy decisions are made by the teachers with the approval of the principal. Parents are invited to make suggestions through spoken and written comments to the school, or through the Parent Advisory Board.

Evaluation — Three forms of evaluation take place:

- students: by tests, teacher observation and parent-child reaction

- teachers: by procedures currently being developed by the Alum Rock School District, as required by the Stull Bill of 1971.

— the program: by child-parent reaction, the Parent Advisory Board and other outside evaluations.

Parents are informed about their child's progress by conferences and written reports. Students and parents participate in program evaluation only, and not the evaluation of teachers.

Communication with Parents — Parents are kept informed by written notices, meetings and conferences. Parents are expected to instill a positive attitude toward school, and support the goals and objectives of the Enrichment Program.

Other Information — To insure a child's success in the Enrichment Program, parents should be sure that their child has some of these characteristics:

- Learns easily and rapidly
- Long attention span; unusual power of concentration
- Advanced ability and interest in reading
- Large vocabulary; verbal proficiency
- Inquisitive mind; intellectual curiosity
- Unusually good memory
- Comprehension in abstract areas
- High energy, alertness, eagerness
- Creative and unusual ideas
- Outstanding talent in special areas

Continuous Progress — Non-Graded
(McCollam)

Description — The curriculum is designed around the basic skills a student should master between kindergarten and 5th grade, with the absence of grade levels and grades. A variety of techniques will be used, including team teaching, small groups, interest centers, departmentalization and field trips. Parent volunteers will be used.

Governance — Policy decisions are made by a governing board consisting of the professional staff and two parent representatives and the involvement of the principal at prescheduled meetings. Parents assist in the selection of supplemental materials, policy for child management, and curriculum materials.

Evaluation — Continuous evaluation is conducted, using culturally unbiased, standardized tests, teacher-made tests, teacher evaluation, and parent-teacher meetings. Teachers are evaluated in terms of Alum Rock guidelines for the Stull Bill.

Communication with Parents — There are periodic newsletters containing student, teacher and parent articles, public meetings, written notices sent home, conferences, home visits and telephone calls.

Other Information — The program incorporates multi-cultural experiences through social science, music, art, creative language, crafts and folk dancing.

Individualized Learning Program (McCollam)

Description — This school encourages your child to progress independently, make meaningful decisions, and realize happiness through successful involvement in school. Emphasis is on the child's individual needs, interests, and choices. These ideas are reflected in the teaching techniques and styles of the staff. Our educational philosophy is tailored to the subject matter and interest areas of each child to assure success at his social and academic level. Learning objectives for the year will be developed individually for each child, and will be flexible throughout the year. There will be one teacher for every thirty students.

Governance — We encourage as much parent participation as possible. We feel the children will benefit from parent involvement, ideas, and talents. For our program to ber successful, we need to know the parent's desires, needs, and feelings regarding their children. We will meet with all interested parents before school opens. We will provide inservice training to help parents feel comfortable with the staff and children. All policy decisions will be made by a majority of the faculty and principal.

Evaluation and Communication — We continually evaluate your child's growth and can tell you what progress he is making at any time. Each parent should evaluate his child's behavior to determine if he is happy, likes his teachers and school, and is learning. We are also concerned about parents' reactions to the program and will stress open communications at all times. Conferences are held whenever the staff or parent feels a need. Each child will evaluate himself with his teacher's help, and this evaluation will be sent home. Teachers are evaluated under the Stull Bill, and parent evaluation of all areas is welcome.

Donald J. Meyer Elementary School   Thomas J. Fay, Principal
1824 Daytone Drive
San Jose, California

The Meyer Elementary School will offer four different education programs this fall as a part of our participation in the internal voucher project. They are (1) Basic Skills Program, (2) Sullivan Individualized Language Arts Program, (3) Fine Arts and Creative Expression, and (4) School 2000. Students, with their families, choose the program in which they want to enroll.

This report gives you a brief description of the four programs. We will hold public meetings in the future to provide you with more information and answer questions. In addition, more detailed information on each program is being prepared, and trained counselors and community workers will be availanle to talk to you. For more information, call 258-4923.

Basic Skills Program — (Meyer)

Description — This program emphasizes each basic skill area equally. Individual teachers decide which teaching methods and style to use. The student-teacher ratio is 30 to 1, with 1 paid aide and 2 volunteers for every 15 students.

Governance — Parents make policy decisions in meetings with teachers, school administration and the voucher program coordinator. Each classroom has a parent representative who is in touch with the teacher. Questions or problems are first raised with the parent classroom representative

Evaluation — Students, by pretesting, progress testing, and final testing; observation; questionnaires; parent-teacher-child conference; and students personal evaluation; teachers, by parents through class room visits and observation; by administration, through classroom visits and observation; the program, by parent, teacher and administration interaction.

Communication with Parents — Written notices, meetings, conferences, home visits, telephone and classroom visits. Parents are expected to support the program by dialogue with the teacher and others involved.

Other Information — The basic skills to be covered include the following: (1) Social, (2) motor, (3) auditory, (4) visual perception, (5) speaking, (6) reading, (7) mathematics, (8) social studies (including multi-cultural studies and family life), (9) science, (10) physical education, (11) fine arts and (12) language arts.

Sullivan Individualized Language Arts System
(Meyer)

Description — This program provides a full range of opportunities for the child to progress academically, socially, and emotionally within his abilities. The goals are improved reading and mathematics ability, enhanced self-interest, and greater parent/community involvement.

Programmed instruction is the main method. It is sponsored by Behavioral Research Laboratories (BRL), and provides solid foundations in reading and mathematics. The teacher may use the materials as he/she desires.

Governance — This is a highly structured program, so there is little opportunity for parents to be involved in policy decisions, but a great deal of opportunity to be involved in operating the program. Possible areas of involvement are tutorial services, material preparation, and encouragement and help at home.

Evaluation — Students, by informal evaluations during tutoring by observation; in-book tests, in the programmed materials; post-tests at the end of every unit; teachers, by self-evaluation, by principal, and by BRL consultant's evaluation. Program, by subjective teacher evaluation; by sponsors; by student progress and enthusiasm; by program directors; and by parent opinion.

Communicating with Parents — Written notices, phone calls, parent teacher conferences, and home visits. We expect parent support for the program including help at home or at the school, if possible.

Other Comments — There are no grades or report cards in this program. Each child proceeds, with direction, at his own pace. BRL materials are designed to meet each student at his instructional level, and provide him with success as he progresses.

Fine Arts and Creative Expression — (Meyer)

Description — This program emphasizes creative expression and basic skill development through arts and crafts. Involvement in field trips, dramatic productions and the creation and sale of arts and crafts are included. Art related material is used for basic skill development. The student-teacher ratio is 30 to 1 with one or two aides per class.

Governance — Policy decisions are made jointly by teachers, parents and administrators, through meetings and individual contacts.

Evaluation — Students, by testing and observation of basic skills, attitude, and social development; teachers, by administrators, parents, and program success; program, by teacher-parent-administrator interaction. Students and parents participate in the evaluation of staff and program.

Communication with Parents — Written notices, meetings, conferences, home visits, telephone and word of mouth. Parent volunteers are hoped for.

Other Comments — A Fine Arts and Creative Expression Program encourages the development of self-understanding, basic learning skills, awareness of likes and differences, creative expression and aesthetic values.

School 2000 — (Meyer)

Description — This program is future oriented, designed to provide students with self-awareness and thought processes necessary to adapt and function now and in the future. It stresses problem solving activities, learning by discovery, inquiry, and doing. It uses large and small group discussions, learning centers, multi-media instruction, and cross level grouping.

Governance — Decisions involving the internal structure are made by representation teachers, and the principal based on communications from parents and students. All other decisions will be made by representation teachers, parents, students and the principal.

Evaluation — Students, by participation and attitude; completion of assignments; progress check list for goals and objectives; progress check list for academic levels; weekly evaluation; and, observation. Teachers, by peers, students and general program success. Program, by structural functioning of program; degree of student success; degree of parent involvement; community feed back; requests for new enrollments.

Communication with Parents — Conferences, parent observation, telephone, letters, visits and demonstrations. Parents are expected to serve as volunteers, help their children function effectively in School 2000, and attend conferences and meetings.

Other Information —
    "When millions share this passion about the future we shall have a society

far better equipped to meet the impact of change. To create such curiosity and awareness is a cardinal task of education. Education must shift into the future tense."

Alvin Tofler,
Future Shock

Grandin H. Miller Elementary School   Frank Wilkens, Principal
1250 So. King Road
San Jose, California

The Miller Elementary School will offer three different education programs this fall as a part of our participation in the internal voucher project. They are (1) Multi-cultural Program, (2) Academic Skill Development Program, and (3) Individualized Learning Program. Students, with their families, choose the program in which they want to enroll.

This report gives you a brief description of the programs. We will hold public meetings in the future to provide you with more information and answer questions. In addition, more detailed information on each program is being prepared, and trained counselors and community workers will be available to talk to you. For more information, call 258–4923.

Individualized Learning Program (Miller)

Description — This program is designed to capitalize on the unique ways that children learn. Experiences will be created to accent this individuality. The motivation to learn is created through the enjoyment and success of tasks.

In this child-centered environment, individualized instruction will predominate. Learning centers, interesting activities, community assistance and varied materials will support the individualized program.

Regular academic subject areas will be taught in a positive and exciting learning environment. The student will be provided successful experiences in learning that will assist in the development of a healthy self image.

Decision Making and Communication — Parent suggestions, reactions and support are encouraged through open communication continuing throughout the year. Program policy decisions will be made by the professional staff.

Evaluation — No decision at this time.

Other Information —

Multi-Cultural Program (Miller)

Description — This program stresses appreciation of the diversity of cultures while sharing the commonality of human needs. Emphasis is on human relations and self-pride, with respect for others. Mexican culture, as well as all other cultures represented by the students enrolled, is emphasized. Basic academic skills are stressed, and are offered in self-contained classrooms: reading, mathematics, English, spelling written expression, science, and health.

Cultural studies are taught by specialized teachers with the aid of community members, college students and special guests: Spanish, English as a second language, music, art, and social studies.

Programs and displays of each cultural unit are used, including folk dancing, food tasting, use of musical instruments, folk art, games of other cultures, field trips, customs, and history.

Basic skills are enriched by multi-cultural materials, and the proper use of English is stressed.

Decision Making and Communication — Parent suggestions, reactions and support are encouraged through open communication continuing throughout the year. Program policy decisions will be made by the professional staff.

Evaluation — No decisions have been made at this time.

Other Information — The multi-cultural program builds on success oriented group teaching.

Academic Skill Development Program (Miller)

Description — This program is founded on the belief that basic skills can best be achieved through consistency, routine and structure. Children learn best with guidance from a teacher and in a success oriented environment. A child succeeds in this program because it is basically geared to his needs and abilities.

The emphasis in this program is on basic skills. Each academic area (reading, mathematics, language arts, social studies, science and health) is taught as well as Enrichment programs such as music, art and physical education.

The Kindergarten program is self contained with emphasis on Reading Readiness. In grades 1-6 reading is completely ungraded. Children's needs are assessed at the beginning of the program, and they are placed according to these needs regardless of grade level. The reading program is staggered at all levels so the children can benefit from personalized instruction at smaller class size. Various approaches to reading are used according to the child's need, such as "Distar," language experience, literature and basic texts. With future evaluation, flexibility prevails and the child advances with his ability.

Subject areas are departmentalized as in junior high school. Teachers have chosen subject areas in which they are skillful and interested, thereby contributing their enthusiasm and talents to their students. In this program, children experience opportunities for success with various teachers and their methods.

Enrichment activities are taught in the same manner as basic skills.

The children will move to designated rooms which are organized according to subject areas: for example, the math teacher sets up the room as a math room which includes all math materials.

Decision Making and Communication — Parent suggestions, reactions and support are encouraged through open communication continuing throughout the year. Program policy decisions will be made by the professional staff.

Evaluation — No decision at this time.

Other Comments —

Pala Middle School   Armen Hanzad, Principal
149 N. White Road
San Jose, California

The Pala Middle School will offer five different education programs this fall as a part of our participation in the internal voucher project. They are (1) Three "R's" Plus School, (2) Creative Arts, (3) Fine Arts, (4) Math Science, and (5) Girls' Physical Education Emphasis. Each of these programs is served by a Resource Center, to provide the student with additional resources and to assist the new programs in motivating students. Students, with their families, choose the program in which they want to enroll.

This report gives you a brief description of the programs. We will hold public meetings in the future to provide you with more information and answer questions. In addition, more detailed information is being prepared, and trained counselors and community workers will be available to talk to you. For more information, call 258–4923.

"Three R's" Plus School (Pala)

Description — This program emphasizes the individual student's mastery of skills traditionally considered important for success in this society: reading, writing, arithematic, science, social studies, music, art and physical education. Reading skills are stressed most heavily, and teachers use diagnostic tests to determine which students require remedial assistance. Children are also evaluated when they enter to determine their language arts ability and units of the program are planned weekly in staff meetings. Teachers choose the techniques they use for teaching social studies.

Governance — Decisions are made with full staff approval, and enacted with administrative support and parental concurrence. Parent input is made at meetings set up for that purpose, and written reports are sent to parents.

Evaluation — Students evaluate themselves, and are evaluated by teachers, parents and groups. Teachers' performance is evaluated by other teachers, administrators, and, possibly, by students. Program evaluation is achieved by beginning and ending diagnostic tests. The rate of return to the program by students is also a form of program evaluation.

Conferences, folders, tests and telephone calls are used to inform parents about student performance.

Communication with Parents — The conferences and reports on student progress are supplemented by group meetings.

We expect parents to provide a high level of interest, cooperation, guidance and support.

Other Information — Our strength lies in the size of our classes and our proximity to each child at least 5 hours daily. Our staff has a wide and varied background.

Creative Arts Program — (Pala)

Description — Our curriculum is geared to the capacities and interests of the student. The educational experience offered is carefully related to their needs and interests. This program is based on three components, that we believe make a complete program of education:

- Traditional knowledge
- Knowledge of practice
- Practice

Knowledge of practice encompasses man's way of doing which brings about, through action, what is of value.

Knowledge of practice requires an organized body of knowledge, a system of concepts and unifying themes which apply to the world of industry and the world of family living.

Practice develops the skills necessary for creation of what is valuable.

Governance — Policy decisions are made by teachers, and the program manager (principal), with advice from parents. Parents have the final decision as to whether or not to enroll their children in the program.

Evaluation — Students are evaluated in terms of the material taught. Teachers are evaluated in terms of goals and objectives worked out with the program manager. Program evaluation is conducted by teachers and the program manager, in connection with "feedback" from the community.

No decision has been reached about informing parents about student performance or involving parents or students in program — staff evaluation.

Communication with Parents — As the need arises, various methods are used: written notices, meetings, conferences, home visits, and telephone.

Other Information — In this program, students receive necessary academic preparation for high school: reading, language arts, and mathematics.

Fine Arts Program (Pala)

Description — This program is based on music and art as special subject areas, with reading, mathematics, language arts and social studies taught using music and art as the point of departure. Each of these areas correlation, to provide continuous educational development.

The influence of historical, social, political, economic and religious effects on music and art through the centuries is also presented.

This program provides students with special interests in music and art to concentrate in these areas without giving up fundamentals. This permits each child to have an opportunity to develop unique talents at his own level of interest and ability.

Governance — Policy and operating decisions are made by experienced teachers. Because this program stresses two subject areas, decisions require a knowledge and understanding of music and art and how they are to be related to other subjects.

Evaluation — Written grades and reports are prepared to assess student progress, and either letter grades or a check list is used. Parent conferences are held at the parents' request.

Communication with Parents — Student progress reports in the form of report cards are sent home regularly. Telephone calls and group meetings are also used.

Parents are expected to support the program and its philosophy, to encourage the highest level of work possible.

Parents are encouraged to visit and observe the program in operation.

Other Comments —

Math-Science Program (Pala)

Description — This program stresses mathematics and science as the core of the program. Reading, language arts and social studies are taught with a math-science orientation.

Class size for math is 30 students per teacher, and 25 per teacher in laboratory sciences.

Governance — Policy decisions are made by teachers and administrators, with advice from parents.

Evaluation — Students are evaluated by teacher observation and quizzes. Teacher evaluation is performed by the program manager. Program evaluation is conducted by student questionnaires and the program manager.

Parents are informed about student performance by written evaluation, conferences, phone calls, and report cards.

Communication with Parents — Parents receive written notices, telephone calls, and home visits, and are expected to attend occasional meetings. Parents are also expected to honor conference requests, and provide feedback on the work of students.

Other Information — Although this is a math-science program, communication skills are emphasized.

Girls' Physical Education Emphasis Program (Pala)

Description — This program is offered two periods a day to all girls interested in lifetime sports. Because each girl differs from every other in her capacities, needs and interests for physical education, it is important that girls with a keen interest in physical education, it is important that girls with a keen interest in physical education be given the opportunity to further develop skills and leadership ability.

The goals are to:

- Provide an effective program which emphasizes physical development in team and individual sports.

- Promote interest and skill in a "lifetime" sport for leisure time.

- Provide a wider variety of activities to help students make an intelligent choice of recreational activities in later years.

- Promote interest, understanding and enjoyment of sports as a spectator.

Two hours of physical education per day are offered. One hour is devoted to team sports, and one hour focuses on the development of "lifetime" individual sports skills.

In addition to daily activities, each student is involved in tutoring and leadership activities with general physical education classes.

Girls from any other program can choose to be part of this PE Emphasis. These girls would spend the morning class time in their regular program and be part of the PE Emphasis in the afternoon. Girls' Physical Education Emphasis Program students should be scheduled in the afternoon for activity periods.

Team sports offered are:

- Volleyball
- Speedball
- Volley-tennis
- Soccer
- Basketball
- Softball
- Flag football

Individual "lifetime" sports offered are:

- Archery
- Badminton
- Tennis
- Bowling
- Paddle tennis
- Swimming

Governance — No decision at this time.

Evaluation — Evaluation is based on individual analysis of efficiency in movement skills, throwing, kicking, stretching, body movement, large muscle movement, fine muscle movement and physical fitness.

Communications with Parents — No decision at this time.

Other Comments —

PART IV

Reactions to the Voucher Experiment

VOUCHERS AT ALUM ROCK

JAMES MECKLENBURGER

America's very first educational voucher experiment is under way. Sort of.

Parents of 4,000 elementary school students in the Alum Rock School District of San Jose, California, "spent" their vouchers early last summer.

What did they buy?

The opportunity to enroll each child this fall in the educational program of the parents' choice. By spending his voucher, a parent directly affected the budget of his child's educational program, because the more students entering a program, the larger the budget. The school system offered a catalog of 21 options. Parents shopped with vouchers worth $680 per child for children in kindergarten through sixth grade and $970 for children in the seventh or eighth grade – an amount equivalent to the average cost of one year's education in the Alum Rock schools.[1]

Last April the U.S. Office of Economic Opportunity agreed to fund the Alum Rock voucher program for two years. But planning had started in Alum Rock long before; teachers and administrators were designing educational programs all last year. Once approval came from OEO, parent selection of educational programs began.

A team of counselors and their assistants visited the home of each child to describe the voucher concept as it would operate in Alum Rock and to assist parents in selecting appropriate programs for their children. Because nearly half the families in Alum Rock speak Spanish, the counseling team was bilingual, as were the materials they left with each family; a brochure, "What Is a Voucher?"; an application blank (which is the voucher); and another brochure outlining the 21 "Educational Choices for Your Child."

The OEO has sought, since 1970, to field demonstrations of the voucher concept. Feasibility studies in Gary, San Francisco, and Seattle during 1971 came to naught. Currently a feasibility study is under way in New Rochelle.

The voucher plan favored by the OEO, the so-called Jencks plan, is advocated in *Education Vouchers: A Report on Financing Elementary Education by Grants*

1. Parents were not made aware that the vouchers of "poor" children were worth $200 to $300 more than vouchers of middle-income children.

to Parents. This report was written in 1970 at the Center for the Study of Public Policy under a grant from the OEO. Christopher Jencks, who directs the center in addition to his faculty duties in the Harvard Graduate School of Education, is a noted advocate of vouchers. As outlined in *Education Vouchers* and elsewhere,[2] the Jencks plan has these features:

— Parents choose between competing schools.

— Schools must be open to all applicants.

— Schools must accept the voucher as full payment for the cost of a child's education. Parents may not add money to the value of a child's voucher.

— Each school must make information available which will enable parents to make wise decisions.

— A new independent agency, the Education Voucher Agency (EVA) enforces these regulations and administers the voucher program.

— The value of the voucher is supplemented for the poor, to enable schools to develop special programs for these children.

— All kinds of schools are included — private and religious schools as well as public schools.

Because the Jencks plan stresses benefit to poor children, the Office of Economic Opportunity, mandated to devise programs to help the poor, finds the Jencks parent-choice scheme attractive. Schematically, OEO represents its ideal voucher plan as in Figure 1.[3]

However appealing the voucher idea was to the OEO, few communities were willing to conduct a feasibility study, much less a full-scale voucher demonstration. Obviously, several provisions of the Jencks plan are very controversial both educationally and politically: that parents, not educators, would choose educational programs for children; that public funds would flow to private and parochial schools; that parents would be prohibited from adding money to the voucher; that school boards would be displaced by the new Education Voucher Authority. Possible effects of voucher plans upon teacher rights and upon desegregation fanned political controversy still hotter.

2. See Christopher Jencks, "Giving Parents Money for Schooling: Education Vouchers," *Phi Delta Kappan,* September, 1970, pp. 49-52, plus commentaries in the same issue by Robert Havighurst and A. Stafford Clayton.

3. This figure comes from an OEO press release titled "A Proposed Experiment in Education Vouchers," OEO Pamphlet No. 3400-8, April 24, 1972.

Figure 1. Full Voucher Model

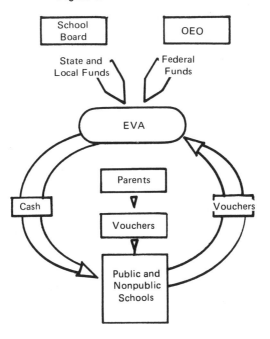

But Alum Rock did not say no. It said maybe, with conditions. So after three disapprovals in four tries, the OEO reluctantly compromised the Jencks plan in favor of trying Alum Rock's less controversial variant of vouchers:

— Only one-third of the school district is involved, and only for one year, after which either the OEO or Alum Rock may cancel the demonstration.

— Only public school programs are involved.

— The Alum Rock Board of Education retains control, although it is advised by an Education Voucher Advisory Committee (EVAC) composed of parents.

— Parents choose between competing school *programs*, not competing schools.

The Alum Rock program nominally retains other features of the Jencks plan: Programs are open to all applicants; vouchers are full payment; information is given to parents; and a supplemental value is added to the voucher of poor children. Schematically, one might represent the Alum Rock voucher plan as in Figure 2.

According to the OEO, the Alum Rock plan for 1972 is "transitional." It trails quite a string of "ifs." *If* the California legislature passes a bill now pending, which would allow the creation of an EVA and the use of public funds for private and parochial schools, and/or *if* the Alum Rock School District is willing to double the school population in the demonstration in 1973, then *if* OEO has the funds it will continue the Alum Rock program for five to seven years.

When the OEO announced the Alum Rock program on April 24, 1972, reporters pressed Thomas Glennan, OEO's director of planning, research, and evaluation, to explain how the 1972 voucher plan was different, in its effect upon students, from open-enrollment plans or minischool plans operating elsewhere. The question is well taken. In Alum Rock, where all programs are public school programs, the voucher (which took the form of a parent's application) can be construed as merely as administrative convenience. The OEO, as the Jencks plan requires, is providing supplemental funds for the vouchers of poor students (who are identified in Alum Rock by the rule of thumb that they qualify for federal school lunch programs); a poor child's voucher is worth one-third more than other children's vouchers. But, since the voucher program remains within the public school, the compensatory voucher can be construed as merely an administrative convenience for distribution of compensatory funds. Seemingly, in Alum Rock the

Figure 2. Alum Rock Voucher Model, 1972

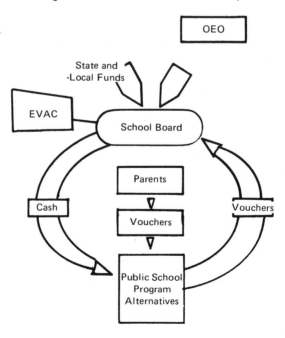

voucher mechanism adds nothing to the process of parental selection which could not have been accomplished as well as conventional administrative techniques.

But Joel Levin, director of the voucher program for the school district,[4] says this is nonsense. Look at it from the parents' perspective, he says. Parents not only have real choice among educational programs, something which has never before existed in Alum Rock, but they perceive that their choice truly influences the financing of school programs. Levin hastens to point out that if a parent becomes dissatisfied with a program he may withdraw his child during the school year and enroll him (and his voucher) elsewhere.

Moreover, the Alum Rock voucher plan may facilitate parent choice better than the Jencks plan in one way: In the Jencks plan the only way a student can change programs is to change schools — that is, be bused from his neighborhood. In the Jencks plan parental choice means, in effect, either that many students will be bused or that most students will remain in their neighborhood school voucher or not. In Alum Rock parents who prefer the neighborhood school (which is 95% of them this year) still have a choice among three or four programs for their children. And if a parent is willing for his child to be buses (at OEO expense), then he may select among all 21 alternatives.

With names such as Traditional, Developmental Reading, Basic Skills, Three R's Plus, Academic Skill Development, and Enrichment, nearly half the 21 alternatives closely resemble conventional schools in Alum Rock. Open-Activity Centered, Individualized Learning, and Continuous Progress Non-graded, while hardly startling to readers of *Kappan* pages, are untried innovations in this district. The Sullivan Individualized Language Arts program uses the Behavioral Research Laboratory methods of individualization.

Six school programs have redesigned the elementary school curriculum to stress one subject area: Fine Arts-Creative Expression, Fine Arts and Creative Arts, Math-Science, Cultural Arts, and Multicultural (which offers bilingual instruction).

The Daily Living School believes that "children learn by doing" and focuses its curriculum around life experiences of children. Seventh Grade School, for seventh-graders only, is a school-without-walls imitation of Philadelphia's Parkway School. And School 2000 offers "passion about the future," taking its lead from Alvin Toffler's exhortation, "Education must shift into the future tense."

When Joel Levin described these programs in a telephone interview last May, he was enthusiastic and proud of the many new programs that would be offered. He

4. From 1970 to 1972, Levin was on the staff of the Center for the Study of Public Policy at Harvard. He served as the center's liaison to Alum Rock and contributed to the *Education Vouchers* study. Now, as a member of a nonprofit organization called Sequoia Institute, he holds a 2-year contract with the school district to direct this program.

marveled at the energy and skill of the teachers and administrators who developed these programs. But he worried that parents might not select the new programs. He estimated that 10 to 14% of parents would select non-traditional alternatives. "Twenty percent," he said, "would demonstrate without question the value of a voucher system. We would have proven our major contention, that many parents would choose differently for their children, if given the opportunity to choose."

In a telephone interview a month later, Levin sounded elated. Of the 2,500 returns then available,[5] closer to 40% than 20% of parents had chosen nontraditional programs. For example, 70 students were enrolled in the Seventh Grade School, 115 in Daily Living, 83 in Fine Arts, 220 in Open-Activity Centered, and 100 in School 2000. Levin cautiously estimated that at least 25% of parents with more than one child had selected different programs for each child - an indication that parents had taken seriously their opportunity to choose programs.

Whether Alum Rock's current plan is a *real* voucher plan or some lesser breed of parent-choice scheme may be academic. Whatever the label, Alum Rock's new program allows the broader educational community to ask three sets of questions about parent choice in the education of children:

— What social and political tensions or benefits emerge when parents usurp this "professional" prerogative?

— Does the educational marketplace function as some might predict, i.e., Do new programs and options develop? Are the customers satisfied? Does the cost of education change?

— Do students learn more, or differently, or worse, than under conventional school patterns?

The Rand Corporation has contracted for nearly $1,000,000 with the OEO to pursue these three sets of questions with persistence and rigor. After the Alum Rock program has been subjected to the inevitable snap judgments of pundits and critics, the Rand evaluation report may, several years hence, prove to be an invaluable record of an educational system in the throes of change.

Perhaps nothing will come of the OEO's Alum Rock demonstration. Perhaps vouchers will quietly wither and die. But don't bet on it. The American Federation of Teachers, like most professional education groups, has expressed opposition to voucher demonstrations, yet one of its spokesmen said, after the OEO's announcement last April, "Vouchers introduce us to a whole new ball game,. Alum Rock is just the top of the first inning."

James Mecklenburger wrote this article in June before assuming the directorship of research for the National School Boards Association, Evanston, Ill. He is a former Phi Delta Kappa research assistant and author of books and articles on performance contracting.

5. By fall, 4,000 students were to have been enrolled. However, last spring students in kindergarten and in first grade were not placed, nor were special education students. Also, it was anticipated that as many as 500 students would enter the demonstration area during the summer. These exceptions account for the fact that only parents of 2,500 students chose school programs in June.

CREEPING VOUCHERISM

GEORGE LA NOUE

Professor La Noue, a close student of legal questions raised by vouchers, and editor of Educational Vouchers: Concepts and Controversies, a recent anthology from Columbia University Press, spoke to the American Federation of Teachers Quest Conference in April, 1972. He reported that the previous day he had put some hard legal questions to officials at OEO, and found their answers wanting.

The voucher banner has sunk a bit in the last year for several reasons, principally some decisions by the federal courts, but it still exists, and we may see it waved again during the Presidential campaign, if that should become opportune. I would like to tell you where vouchers are at the moment. (I might say that it is going to be the national high-school debate topic next year, and some of you may have a responsibility about vouchers in that regard.)

The history of vouchers is such that it would seem, I think, to any objective observer a rather dubious vehicle for any liberal school reform. In the 19th Century of course, there were various schemes that paid money to parents or students. They really broke down because it proved impossible to have equality of education, so we gave up any methods of financing private schools and moved to the public-school system. Voucher supporters will point to the GI bill as a modern precedent for vouchers, but that's really a false analogy. The GI bill was a device to pay veterans compensation for the deferred income that they lost while being in the armed services. They could use this money for many different kinds of purposes - some went to divinity schools, for example; this money was really considered to belong to them.

There are really two contemporary precedents for educational vouchers in this country. The first is rather sinister. It was, as many of you know, the device that southern state governments finally turned to when all of the other mechanisms that they used to avoid intergtration, failed. In states like Virginia, Alabama, and Louisiana, vouchers became the last hope of the white citizens' councils, and in the tragedy of Prince Edward County, Va., which this union did so much to alleviate when the public schools were abandoned, the device chosen was vouchers, so that white parents could continue the kind of education that they'd had in the past. Everywhere the courts have struck down those kinds of voucher systems. In probably the most significant case, Poindexter vs. Louisiana, Judge Minor Wisdom said this: "Unless this voucher system is destroyed, it will shatter to bits the public-school system of Louisiana and kill the hope that now exists for equal-educational opportunities for all citizens, blacks and whites," and, with that, the federal court unanimously struck it down.

The other modern root for educational vouchers comes from the most conservative wing of the parochial-school movement. It was a theory created by a Jesuit priest at Marquette University that led to the founding of Citizens for Educational Freedom. This is the group that has advocated that the only fair way to distribute educational funds is to create unregulated, noncompensatory vouchers. It comes as no surprise that it is an almost entirely white, middle-class movement, and it is so conservative that it doesn't even have the support of many Catholic bishops. Given this background, you might think that it's very unlikely that an agency of the federal government that is responsible for the education of the deprived, of minority groups, and of the poor, would turn to vouchers, but that's exactly what OEO and the Nixon administration did. They granted a substantial amount of money - several hundred thousand dollars - to Christopher Jencks at the Harvard University Center for the Study of Public Policy — to study this question, but the fact was that Jencks had already committed himself in print to being in favor of educational vouchers, so there was no issue about how the study would come out.

Why did OEO turn to educational vouchers, which are so unlikely a vehicle for educational reform? I think there are probably three reasons. One is that the Nixon administration has looked for several ways to improve education without spending any money, to put it charitably. The voucher philosophy was perfect because it fit in with the traditional Republican view of the superiority of the marketplace to the ballot box in making public policy, it appeased certain parts of the sort of laissez-faire Republican constituency, and it really doesn't cost any more. After all, the Administration has not really committed itself to spend all that much money on vouchers, but only to experiment with it for from five to eight years at which time the incumbent President will no longer be in office for certain, at least, unless there's a constitutional amendment. So it was a sort of a philosophical gimmick.

There is also, I think, a more sinister kind of reason. Kevin Phillips (he was and perhaps still is former Attorney General Mitchell's political advisor), in his book, "The Emerging Republican Macjority," suggested that vouchers could be one of the schemes with which Republicans could unite segregationist parents in the South with parochial-school constituencies in the North, and create the emerging Republican majority. I think that's part of it — the President's speech to the Al Smith Dinner in New York suggested that kind of an approach.

Finally, and we have to recognize this, There are some people in OEO and in the liberal community that really despaired of improving education for the poor with any other system, and they really believe in this. As poorly as the experiment may be designed, they are committed to this as an idealistic kind of approach.

Consequently, then vouchers marry the most cynical kind of reactionary politics with an almost romantic kind of faith in the structural form of education. Jencks, for one, is kind of a realist about this. In his report, he said that an unregulated voucher system could be the most serious setback for education of disadvantaged children in the history of the U.S. That's quite a statement for a supporter of vouchers to make, but Jencks believes that vouchers can be regulated to benefit poor children, and that turns out to be the key to the whole idea. If even its supporters admit that it's extraordinarily dangerous — that it could be the greatest setback in the history of education for poor children — then we must look to the vehicle of regulation that they think would overcome this danger.

The Jencks report lists seven different regulatory rules, including lotteries for student admissions, and compensatory payments for poor children. Jencks' list tends to vary. OEO has a list that's rather similar. The study groups for vouchers in the various cities have slightly altered the list — generally, the lists get longer and longer as people realize the kinds of problems that are involved. But my question is this: If vouchers are to make any difference at all in the competitive aspects of American education, then not much is gained if children simply circulate within the public system. The only real impact that vouchers can make is if there is a substantial movement of children and money from the public sector to the private sector. Another question is: how are these regulations going to be enforced in the private sector? In the OEO approach, there is something called the Educational Voucher Authority — which is supposed to be the body that will enforce all the regulations that will keep this thing from becoming a social disaster. When you try to figure out what an Educational Voucher Authority is going to be, you will see that they haven't really figured it out either, and each time its design has somewhat different components and somewhat different jurisdictions. In Seattle, you have a consortium of parents and representatives of private groups, including a representative appointed by the Archdiocese of Seattle, that would be the management system for this.

In addition, of course, OEO would ride herd on these experiments. And this is the critical factor: OEO regards this money as private money once it's paid to the parents; that is, when the money comes from tax sources and then is paid to the educational voucher authority and the voucher authority gives it to the parents, when the parents then spend that money in the schools, it's private money; the analogy they use is that it is as though it were social-security money.

The consequence, then, is that if this is really considered private money, none of the state or federal constitutional protections any longer apply, just as they don't if you want to spend your social security money. If somebody wants to give their social-security money to the White Citizens' Council, or the John Birch Society, or to a political party, or to a religious group, they can do that any way they want to - that's their money. It's really a government insurance system, or course.

And the fact is that the reason why OEO has created all these regulations is because they intend to do away (this isn't their purpose, but it is the effect) with the whole system of state and federal constitutional regulation of education and, of course, with teacher contracts through collective bargaining as this moves into the private sector.

It will come as no surprise to you that this idea has received enormous criticism from the whole educational establishment. Ironically, it has had the effect of reuniting the public-school coalition of the early '60s. There is not, so far as I know, any educational organization of any consequence at all, that supports educational vouchers. Part of the reason, I think we have to admit, is self-interest. There are good grounds for not wanting to encourage competition among the established educational organizations, but there is also a very real fear that any voucher system in practice, at least when it becomes widespread, would be highly reactionary in terms of racial integration, and economic equality, that it would foster all sorts of new kinds of political and religious sectarian schools, and that the body of law that protects teachers, students, and citizens in dealing with public education would be lost.

I have asked officials at OEO some of the questions that I thought you would like to have the answers to, as teachers. The first question was whether the voucher schools that are in the so-called private sector would be able to discriminate in the hiring of teachers. After all, if we have a district, let's say, in which 70 percent of the teachers were hired by the public system, and you moved to a voucher system and that shift, say, is 50-50, that means these teachers are going to have to find jobs in these privately-controlled voucher schools, and what are the controls on these schools? I was told that the private voucher schools, according to the rules that are created, will not be able to discriminate on the basis of race or economic status but they will be able to discriminate on the basis of the religion of the teacher, the sex of the teacher, or the political philosophy of the teacher.

They have to include the parochial-school constituency, or the politics of the thing fails. They want as great a diversity of schools as possible and, therefore, if they make these restrictions very tight they won't be able to get any private schools to participate.

Secondly, I asked the officials at OEO whether there is any provision for academic freedom for teachers in voucher schools. I have read a great deal about vouchers but I have never seen anything in the provoucher literature that even discusses the question of academic freedom for teachers, the reason being, of course, that the emphasis really is on parent-controlled schools, and I don't have to tell you that there is a certain element of conflict between the parent-controlled schools and academic freedom for teachers. The supporters of vouchers are clearly on the parents' side in this conflict and so they simply have not done anything about protecting academic freedom for teachers.

Finally, I asked about the question of tenure and contract rights. I was informed that the local teachers in Alum Rock have participated in the drawing up of the proposal and had worked out a way to protect contract and tenure rights. (I don't know whether that's true; apparently the announcement will be made in a month that will tell us what the details of this are.) I then said I was a little surprised at that because my understanding was that teachers across the country had pretty much been opposed to vouchers and they said, "No, that OEO had polls in San Francisco, Seattle, and Alum Rock which showed that teachers were overwhelmingly in favor of vouchers. I asked if these had been published and they said, "No, we're thinking about publishing them," and I said I'd like to see them. The fact is that the national polls on this question, which have been printed and look to me to be reasonably valid, show that teachers tend to be about 3½ to 1 against vouchers.

While our attention is diverted to "the voucher experiment," the fact is that such states as Ohio, Pennsylvania, Minnesota, Illinois, and Maryland have passed tax-credit or tuition-grant programs which are, in effect, the worst kinds of vouchers. For one thing, they are almost totally unregulated and they are generally only partially compensatory, so they are really sort of regressive tax schemes and these exist now; they are being challenged in the courts, but that's the real voucher system in the country and that's the real voucher constituency - the kind of people who put those laws through.

Indeed, if we don't do anything about those laws, it will be in effect the most serious setback for the education of disadvantaged children in the history of the country.

But the fact is that vouchers have substantial popular appeal, and I would mislead you and not perform any function as a teacher if I didn't take up the next part of this.

The polls on vouchers show that generally about 50 percent of the citizens or parents support vouchers. Now, there are a lot of reasons for that, and I think the figure may be somewhat inflated. Some people don't understand vouchers and some of the people who support vouchers are doing so for such clearly unconstitutional reasons that they cannot be a part of the policy settlement.

The fact is that there are apparently substantial number of parents who feel so alienated from public education and from those people who have responsibilities for public education, that they are now willing to try a system that would substantially jeopardize the future of public education. And I think that's an indictment on all of us who work with and for public education. There are substantial numbers of people who believe that the public schools are neither responsive nor diverse enough and they are willing to junk the system to get change. And when they do, of course, they will junk the progress that we have made in teacher rights.

We can argue with these people, we can plead with them. If we are lucky, we may win the litigations or beat them in the legislatures, but it seems to me that nothing would be more effective than to actually improve the responsiveness and the diversity within public education.

I am not going back to the rhetoric that one sometimes hears about a monolithic public-school system — that is nonsense. The public-school system is as diverse as American life is itself — anybody who has traveled and looked at schools in different parts of the country knows that.

But there are people, apparently in substantial numbers, who really feel that it does not provide them with the choices that they want provided. So, I have some questions for you: First, does your organization conduct collective bargaining in such a way so that parents and students feel included in the essential issues of educational policy? Secondly, does your school system use any of the modern techniques to find out how citizens in their community feel about public schools and what changes they would like to see? Thirdly, does your system offer as flexible a curriculum as possible? Fourthly, has your system made a serious effort to create alternatives of learning techniques and school cultures within the public sector?

When public education is able to answer those questions with a firm "yes," then I am confident that the American public will answer that the American public will answer with a ringing "no" to vouchers.

VOUCHERS ON THE ROCKS

ROBERT BHAERMAN

The American Federation of Teachers remains vehemently opposed to voucher plans (see "Vouchers--Solution or Sop?" in Part I), and struck most harshly and quickly at the Alum Rock plan.

In Alum Rock, Calif., the voucher plan is tottering on the rocks. Vouchers, as most teachers are aware, is the system whereby parents would be given certificates equal to the cost of educating their children and then they could spend these certificates in any public or private school which agrees to accommodate their children.

Various reports from California have it that the Office of Economic Opportunity's second controversial education program ("performance contracting" was the first) is temporarily bogged down in state legislation. Proposals have been approved by OEO for San Francisco and Seattle as well as for Alum Rock, located near San Jose. According to OEO, the state of Washington is waiting to see what action is taken in Governor Reagan's domain. The California governor, needless to say, is an advocate of the system.

However the report of the feasibility study in Alum Rock discloses that support from other sources is not exactly overwhelming. The feasibility study, conducted by the Center for Planning and Evaluation in San Jose under an OEO grant of $19,230, makes interesting reading.

The item which first caught our attention comes early in the report, in the section describing the Education Voucher Committee which consisted of nine groups: ". . . private schools are placed with the 'teachers' groups because under the 'voucher plan' all schools become 'public' to the extent that they become able to cash vouchers."

As a matter of fact, the entire section dealing with private schools is enlightening. The responses of the non-denominational private schools were reported to be impossible to generalize, for they covered "the whole spectrum from very hostile negative responses to promises to live by any and all EVA (education voucher authority) restrictions." Most of those schools, it was reported, have tuitions greater than the proposed basic voucher and some would "exceed the total of the basic voucher and the proposed increment for 'disadvantaged' students."

The responses of the parochial schools, while very similar, were still more enlightening. These schools have two questions of major concern: "The first involves fears of whether or not they will begin to lose control of their curriculum under a voucher experiment. The second, and perhaps the greater concern, is about admissions policy. The parochial schools all feel a need to give admission preference to members of their own faith. If overapplied, they are willing to use a lottery system, but only to make decisions among church members. All have been willing to admit nonchurch members after church-members needs have been met."

New proprietary schools also would paint themselves into the voucher picture: the omnipresent Behavioral Research Laboratories would begin a school, and the socially concerned Westinghouse Learning Corp. would either sell their materials to existing schools or go the BRL route.

How Do Parents Feel?

A feasibility study would not be complete without a parent survey, and the one by the Center for Planning and Evaluation (CPE) was no exception. While the San Jose Unified School District had a total school population of 37,067 at the time of the study (mid-1971), the parent survey data is based upon approximately 375 responses. Nevertheless, the CPE researchers authoritatively maintain: "The results of the survey are quite clear. While there was a strong favorable reaction to the concepts that underlie the proposed voucher plan, there existed a substantial segment of the community that had no opinion about the term." This "strong favorable reaction" is indicated by data which disclosed that 32 percent felt they were "well informed about the voucher plan," 51 percent were not, and 17 percent were undecided: 26 percent "would want my children to participate," 23 percent would not, and 51 percent were undecided; 23 percent felt "my children would benefit," 21 percent felt they would not, and 56 percent were undecided.

In addition, it was impossible for CPE to generalize about attitudes of parents with children currently in private schools since 363 parents reported zero children in such schools, while only 12 reported children attending them. Also, no breakdown of attitudinal data was undertaken in terms of the religious affiliation of parents.

Other items of interest from the report included:

Expulsion and suspension: (1) The EVA will establish an appeals board for students who are expelled. (2) The appeals board will determine procedures and functions only in contested cases. (3) Expelled students become transfers.

Transfers: Only one transfer per school year is allowable after a reasonable period in attendance. The EVA will establish a court of appeals for second and all other transfer requests. The voucher will be prorated to the new school and OEO will guarantee teacher salaries from contingency funds.

Advertising: The EVA will have the alternative of determining whether or not it would allow individual schools to do their own advertising as part of their recruitment, or to require that all such advertising be done through the central information office only.

Paying Teachers

The preliminary plan for accounting procedures prepared by the C.H. Petersen accounting firm in Mountain View, Calif., also raises some important questions, which, to date, have gone unanswered by the voucher planners. The section of most relevance is this:

"Under the voucher plan, the cost of religious education could be determined and accounted for in a variety of ways, depending on the manner in which religious instruction is integrated with secular instruction at each parochial school. E.g., if religious instruction is conducted only by designated teachers, their salaries and payroll costs could be charged to accounts designated for religious training. If religious instruction were conducted by the same teachers conducting secular instruction, their salaries could be prorated on some equitable basis. E.g., if teachers taught five subjects per day, and one subject was religious, 20 percent of their salaries would be chargeable to religious instruction. Costs of maintaining facilities, utilities, etc,, could be prorated in a similar manner." One cannot help but wonder the extent to which religious instruction will be "integrated" with secular instruction and one cannot help but pity the accountant who might be responsible for observing religious-secular teachers in order to determine if more than 20 percent of their salaries should be chargeable to religious instruction.

What do other Californians think about vouchers in Alum Rock? The appendices of the CPE feasibility study should be read closely to find out. Here are some samples:

The association of teachers raised a number of questions, e.g., "Can non-public schools expect to accept public money without government controls?" and "Would nonpublic schools be subject to legal provisions for student health and safety, minimum teacher-certification qualifications, the minimum-teacher-salary law, minimum class sizes, the minimum school day, curriculum offerings, use of state-adopted textbooks, and academic freedom?"

401

Dr. Wilson Riles, the California superintendent of public instruction, condemned proposed voucher-plan financing as a threat to "destroy public education in this state." The San Jose News of Jan. 21, 1971, reported him as saying that the issue was one of quality education. "If it's inadequate, let's make it adequate."

And, lastly, the San Jose Sun of Feb. 25, 1971, reported the "strong favorable reaction" of a public meeting on vouchers in Alum Rock:

"At one point during testimony . . . a small child babbled several words which appeared to convey a pleasureable connotation.

"This was the only discernible positive note voiced from the audience of several hundred persons during the three-hour public forum at Sheppard school Monday night.

"If there's anyone in the school district who favors the voucher concept, which would allow parents to enroll children at the school of their choice, they are lurking behind the scenes."

The OEO voucher planners doubtlessly mixed a strong drink on the rocks when they read the feasibility study which their $19,230 supported.

VOUCHERS ON THE ROAD

ROBERT BHAERMAN

Last month, we reported on the voucher-feasibility study in Alum Rock, Calif., where, in spite of strong community opposition, the school board is still pushing the plan. A new bill to permit vouchers has been introduced in the California legislature, where a similar one failed last fall. Under this system, federal, state, and local tax aid would go to parochial and private schools through the device of vouchers channeled through parents.

The history of this OEO-sponsored project is based upon a variation of a famous maxim, "If at first you don't succeed, try again; if that doesn't work, try elsewhere." In Alum Rock, they are apparently trying again. In Gary, Ind., the voucher system met a timely death. So recently OEO turned elsewhere: to New Rochelle, N.Y.

OEO has awarded $40,000 to New Rochelle, to conduct a four-month feasibility study, in order to try to determine the practicality of an "internal" voucher system, limited, for the time being, to the city's 12 elementary schools. The New Rochelle superintendent, however, is investigating a plan that would include parochial and private schools in the voucher system. To save his time and the OEO's money, it would be wise for the superintendent to review the notice of the "OEO roadshow" which closed somewhat abruptly in Gary. While the show will open with a new cast of wizards the early advertisements sound as if the same old script will be presented.

The New York City-based Institute for the Advancement of Urban Education (IAUE) wrote the eyecatching Gary script. Eyecatching, to say the least: "Preliminary (sic) Feasibility Study for the Establishment and Use of an Education Voucher System in Gary, Inc." (With a title like that, it might have been written by Thomas Jefferson. But it wasn't. He could spell.)

Various methods were used to test out the concept's desirability (defined by the IAUE as the "stakeholders'" willingness to institute and use the voucher system . . . as opposed to the other term used, i.e., workability, defined as the acceptance of the regulatory mechanisms, the eligibility criteria, the structural requirements, and other programmatic considerations.) The methods included a "public-information campaign composed of the following: use of the media, workshops, forums, in-home meetings, speakers bureau, and a door-to-door campaign."

It is getting harder these days to separate "preliminary" research from honest-to-goodness public-relations jobs. Be that as it may, the report states, "At the outset of the campaign a press conference was held at Gary School City to which representatives of all media were invited." (Knowing other press conferences of the publicity-oriented Gary superintendent, e.g., the one on performance-contracting, in which not-so-hard data was consciously stretched and shaped, the session on vouchers must have been some gathering!) Flyers announcing each workshop and forum were also sent out through each K-6 schoolchild each week and an entire issue of Progress, the Gary School City organ, was devoted to the voucher system.

As with other "preliminary" studies, a parent survey was conducted. It was reported that slightly less than half (46.6 percent) of the parents were "not sure" of the desirability of vouchers. In a similar-personnel survey, 44 percent of the teachers and 31.4 percent of the principals also were "not sure" of the desirability. But 24 percent of the teachers and 22.9 percent of the principals were sure they felt it undesirable.

In terms of the more significant workability questions, for some reason only sketchy data was reported by the IAUE. One of the troubling features of the section on workability is that here "school personnel" all were lumped together:

one cannot tell the teachers' response from the principals', an unlikely occurrence normally. Needless to say, this makes the IAUE data extremely fuzzy, e.g. 37 percent of the school personnel (teachers and principals and "others" combined) agreed and 33.8 percent disagreed with the statement, "If a voucher system were instituted, it should be administered by the existing board of education;" 32.9 percent of the school personnel agreed and 39.1 percent disagreed with the statement. "If a voucher system were instituted, it should be administered by a new agency having complete autonomy from the existing board of education."

Somewhat more definitive is the agreement by 78.4 percent of the school personnel and disagreement by only 2.9 percent with the statement, "The state education department should continue to set up minimum education requirements in all schools, whether they participate in the voucher program or not." Lastly, 63.9 percent of the school personnel disagreed and only 13.1 percent (were they principals?) agreed that "schools participating in an education voucher program should be allowed to hire and fire their teachers independently of the existing school board."

Overall, the types of questions raised by the participants in the various workshops and forums in the "public information campaign" were rather extensive. They dealt with the following issues: structural problems, models and programs, accountability, the target area, feasibility, the value of vouchers, school improvement, the use of public funds, busing, enabling legislation, the church-state problem, and increased costs.

After it was all done, the IAUE concluded that (1) the majority of the respondents felt that voucher schools should not be allowed to depart from minimum state-education requirements, and (b) separation of church and state should be maintained under any voucher plan.

The report ended with the statement that the "study has been limited to an examination of desirability, only one of the components of our operational definition of feasibility, and that additional time and resources would be required in order to test out the workability and advisability of an Education Voucher System for Gary." Nevertheless, because these are puzzling times in which we live, the IAUE recommended that "performance (in voucher schools) be measured in terms of student achievement and/or problem resolution." With the recent history of Gary School City' flirtation with new-style merit pay, the recommendation seemed to fit in with the rest of the schemes proposed by the current superintendent of schools.

To bring the story up to date, not long after the "preliminary" report was submitted, it was learned that the Gary administration dropped out ot what would have been the second-phase feasibility study because, according to school officials, the city already had too many projects going and because public response was largely apathetic to the voucher plan.

"Too many projects" is hardly the word for it: it was at this time that the superintendent and George Stern, former president of Behavioral Research Laboratories (the Banneker School performance contractor) had bigger fish to fry. After receiving a USOE planning grant of $30,000, the Gary administrator and Stern's consulting operation, called the Public Management Corporation, requested from the USOE's Experimental-School program a total of $4,575,000 for a five-year period. This time they were turned down, but that is another story in itself.

So gather up your carpetbags, wandering minstrels of OEO, for the next show will soon begin in New Rochelle. It is time for you to hit the road. The "preliminary" act has ended, but the curtain is ready to lift once again on your little tragicomedy.

Robert Bhaerman is the AFT Director of Educational Research

NO MORE RABBITS OUT OF HATS

PETER JANSSEN

In light of Peter Janssen's insights about OEO, is it possible that OEO's "transitional" program at Alum Rock is actually a face-saving way for OEO to back out of the voucher controversy, rather than (as OEO says) the first bold step in?

The fate of the Office of Economic Opportunity (OEO) is symbolic of society's growing disillusionment with the traditional concept that a great deal of money poured into piecemeal programs will solve social problems. OEO is just one of the myriad programs that were launched with great fanfare in the 1960s, only to wither when it became obvious that all the energy and money expended were not creating lasting change.

OEO discovered, for instance, that the nation's educational system is almost impervious to institutional change. The system is so vast and tradition-oriented that it can absorb a few experiments and just keep grinding along. The bureaucracy still stands, the professional associations and the unions still prevail, the U.S. Office of Education and all the state school boards still control the money and

Reprinted with copyright permission of *Saturday Review*, February 5, 1972.

the apparatus. When challenged by an outsider, members of the club will defend their turf to preserve the status quo.

As a result, though poverty will still be with us in 1976, OEO may not. Today OEO is rapidly running out of money, out of programs, and out of solid, bright ideas.

OEO never had enough money to do the job; now it has barely enough to survive. President Nivon vetoed its appropriation in December because it was in the same bill as money for a new child-care program. In the veto message the President said he wanted to change the direction of OEO itself. Since he took office, the President said, his administration had "sought to redesign, to redirect, indeed, to rehabilitate the Office of Economic Opportunity, which had lost must public acceptance in the five years since its inception." Mr. Nixon added that his aim was to give OEO a "new role" — making it "the primary research and development arm" of the nation's effort to eliminate poverty.

Conducting antipoverty R and D work costs far less, of course, than mounting large new programs; it also is far less upsetting to politicians and the voting public than efforts to give the poor a voice in the system. In any event, the administration plans to fight poverty through income strategy — welfare reform and family assistance — rather than through the OEO programs.

The administration certainly does not want OEO to keep running programs. President Nixon, his first year in office, transferred Head Start and Upward Bound to the Department of Health, Education, and Welfare (HEW), and the Job Corps to the Labor Department. The transplanting has not exactly encouraged their growth. There were almost twice as many preschoolers in Head Start in 1966 (733,000) as there are today; Upward Bound has remained at about the same level (25,000 students). Within OEO, meanwhile, programs are not being renewed as their grants run out. In 1970, for example, the Human Resources Development Division was operating fifty-five programs; this June the total will be down to nine.

OEO also is running out of people. The turnover has been so great that the agency has not printed an organizational chart since the spring of 1970; only three of twenty top officials in place a year also are still there today. Phillip V. Sanchez, named as the new OEO director last September, was the third person to hold the top executive post in a year.

Sanchez was preceded first by Donald Rumsfeld, a former Republican Congressman from Wilmette on Chicago's wealthy North Shore, who actually voted against creating OEO in 1964. Once in OEO himself, Rumsfeld, a graduate of Princeton, a Navy flier, and a Chicago investment banker, ordered the staff to stop referring to

OEO efforts as the "war on poverty"; that, he said, was rhetorical overkill. He also said "the poor" would be known henceforth as "low-income individuals."

When Rumsfeld left to become a counselor to the President (and later director of the Cost of Living Council), he was succeeded by Frank Carlucci, also of Princeton, who had spent fourteen years in the Foreign Service. After eight months Carlucci also moved to the White House, as associate director of the Office of Management and Budget (OMB), and Sanchez, a graduate of California's migrant-labor camps and Fresno State College, took over.

At forty-two, Sanchez is quick and personable, but he has little clout. With his two predecessors setting policy and watching the purse strings at the White House, moreover, he has little room for independent action. Indeed, Sanchez is all dressed up with no place to go. The day he was to be sworn in by President Nixon was the same day that the President vetoed the OEO appropriation bill. The swearing-in ceremony was canceled.

Perhaps most crucial of all, OEO — at least in its programs for education — is about out of new thoughts. "Right now," says Jeffrey Schiller, director of experimental research, "we're kind of looking around for ideas."

In the past, OEO might have had too many ideas. Most were funneled through John Oliver Wilson, a former Yale economics professor, who joined OEO two years ago as director of Planning, Research, and Evaluation. Wilson left in December to set up planning for the family assistance program, should it pass Congress.

"When I arrived at OEO," Wilson says, "I felt strongly that the Office of Education accepted the existing educational framework. We had to move outside that framework. We had to think that nothing was sacrosanct. The old ideas for improving the schools — lower pupil-teacher ratios, higher quality teaching as measured in terms of experience and degrees, higher salaries, better libraries — all were making only marginal changes. So OEO had to get into institutional change, into high-visibility, high-risk operations. We let the Office of Education work with existing institutions. We wanted OEO to look at social issues and the framework of education. With performance contracting and vouchers we got rapidly into the area of institutional change. We tested the water, got new ideas into the arena, forced people to think of alternatives. We went after high visivility. Or course, we didn't want our visibility to be that high."

Actually, the first performance contract was written by the Office of Education with the school district in Texarkana, Arkansas, as part of a program to prevent dropouts. OEO saw the promise of the idea and decided to sponsor a larger test to determine if it would work elsewhere.

In the 1970-71 school year, OEO spent $5.7 million to experiment with performance contracting among six private companies and eighteen school districts. It also financed contracts with teachers associations in Mesa, Arizona, and Stockton, California, and their school boards. As opposed to the "outside firms," the teachers could not lose money if their pupils' performance in reading and mathematics did not improve. The teachers, however, would receive a 5 per cent bonus if pupils' performance did improve.

Education organizations were not terrible pleased with OEO's venture into performance contracting. Some teachers associations and unions viewed it as a move toward merit pay, which they did not want; others complained about insufficient controls over the paraprofessionals and the new materials the companies brought into the classrooms. Many were worried that the contractors were "teaching to the test" or bribing students with small rewards in order to guarantee their performance and the companies' profits.

OEO financed the contracts for only the first year. This year, in line with its new orientation as a research operation, it is studying the results. The Rand Corporation, under a $300,000 contract from HEW, did study some of the districts involved in OEO's performance contracts. Rand gave performance contracting "high marks as an educational change agent but low marks for mean gains on standardized tests." Most pupils, apparently, did not learn much more under performance contracting than they did under the traditional system. For their part, many contractors also were disappointed with the initial results; they did not make as much money as they had expected and they promised to be much tougher in negotiating any new contracts.

If the education establishment was cool to performance contracting, it was downright hostile to vouchers. And while performance contracting at least has been tested in real schools, vouchers are barely off the drawing boards. The basic voucher idea was designed for OEO by Christopher Jencks, director of the Center for the Study of Public Policy in Cambridge, Massachusetts. The system would let parents use a "voucher," representing the amount of money spent per pupil the previous year in their local school district, to attend any school, public or private, participating in the voucher experiment. The school, in turn, would cash in the voucher with the local voucher agency for payment.

Jenck's idea is that the vouchers would expand educational opportunities by giving students and their parents a wide range of schools to choose from, thus allowing a student to overcome the racial boundaries of the neighborhood school. By making the schools responsive to the pupils' needs, the vouchers would drive out the bad schools, since no one would go to them, while retaining the good ones. They would, finally, make the schools accountable for results.

Many school officials did not share Jenck's — and OEO's — enthusiasm. The National Education Association (NEA), the largest organization representing teachers and administrators, passed a resolution saying vouchers "could lead to racial, economic, and social isolation of children and weaken or destroy the public school system." Some educators saw vouchers as a ploy to give tax support to nonpublic schools, while others predicted that competition would only widen the gap between the strong and poor schools, instead of closing it. Initially, civil rights groups also were against vouchers. They remembered the vouchers used by white segregationists in the South to get around the Supreme Court's 1954 *Brown vs. Board of Education* decision, and they didn't want that to happen again.

Despite the opposition, many school systems were interested in vouchers. OEO made planning grants to school boards in Seattle, San Francisco, and Alum Rock, California, a suburb of San Jose. But then it hit a crucial snag. Since vouchers involve giving school tax dollars to private and/or church schools, the plan must be approved by state legislators. In California, enabling legislation to permit a voucher experiment passed the state Assembly, but then was defeated, by one vote, in the Senate finance committee. The bill will be reintroduced this winter, but even if it passes, it will be too late for a trial this fall. California law says that no bill can take effect until sixty days after the legislative session is over, and that usually is not until the summer. Seattle officials, meanwhile, are waiting to see what happens in California.

In dealing with opposition to performance contracting and vouchers, OEO seems almost to have gone out of its way to make enemies. Rumsfeld, for example, in a speech to the San Francisco Chamber of Commerce, launched a counterattack. "Let there be no doubt about it," he said, "a major effort has been mounted by a handful of self-appointed education spokesmen to halt any inquiry into the possibility of education reform." Warming up, he added, that "the critics fear experimentation because it may call into question their dogmas and orthodoxies. A year later, Sanchez also publicly attacked the "educational monopolies" that wage "frantic campaigns replete with wild rhetoric to stave off vouchers and performance contracts."

Such rhetoric hardly cleared the air. Says David Selden, President of the American Federation of Teachers: "I don't mind the people at OEO — they change so often — but I do mind the policies. This voucher thing, for example, is a public boondoggle that serves only political purposes. As a poverty-fighting agency, I think OEO's efforts in education have been disgraceful. Basically, however, I don't think that good ideas, creativity, and innovation are enough. If you are really serious about poverty, you've got to find a way to share the wealth. And that's not something that a hangnail operation like OEO can do." Stanley McFarland, director of federal relations for the NEA, says he basically supported OEO until it proposed vouchers. "They got into an area that had philosophical

and practical difficulties," he says. "They could have gotten into vouchers without the complication of getting into nonpublic schools."

Ultimately, OEO is succumbing more to self-induced problems than to any outside criticism. "Our most fundamental problem," says Thomas K. Glennan, Jr.,
acting director of Planning Research, and Evaluation, "is that we picked off some
pretty glamorous projects, OEO took a position of advocacy, of institutional
change. But when all is said and done, what we need is a lot of hard research. We
still don't understand how children learn, or how to provide accountability in
school systems. So now we need to set some quotas, find a lower profile, find
things without the sex appeal of vouchers or performance contracting, and try to
pay attention to just a few areas."

There seems to be little question that OEO did try to to too many things. For a
while it had so many grants scattered over the social reform landscape that it lost
track of some of them. It did not have enough staff to monitor the grants and it
did not have enough staff to keep them working. For years Congressional committees would call OEO officials up to Capitol Hill to ask questions about a program only to find that the officials knew nothing about it. Now OEO, for fiscal
and management reasons, is turning to a smaller number of programs; officials
hope that the agency can concentrate on them and provide more impact than in
the past.

Still, new programs with impact aren't just lying around. "It's increasingly difficult for OEO to buy involvement in education," says Joseph Howell, director of
OEO's Human Resources Development Division. "Everytime a program is conceived, there's a battle about why some other organization — Congress, HEW,
OMB — shouldn't do it. We have no monopoly on programs. It's getting much
more difficult to find unique ideas that are out there on the cutting edge."

At least a few people believe that the OEO has become a bit rusty and dull. One
OEO program analyst says he was at a conference a few months ago with many
black leaders in government, education, and politics. "They asked what OEO
had in mind next," he said,"and I replied something like we were still on the
cutting edge and they said bullshit. They were right. We used to be on the cutting edge at one time, but not any more."

Regardless of its position, OEO has accomplished one of its major objectives in
education. It has opened debate, it has presented alternatives that had not been
thought of, or had been ignored, before. "OEO," says Christopher Jencks, "is
doing things that, for legislative or political reasons, were not being done elsewhere.
Clearly federal support for experiments such as vouchers would not come from
any other agency. But the budget for experimentation is inadequate. If you have
only eighty million, say, for R and D and you spread it so you budget five million

dollars for vouchers, the way things turn out in appropriations, you'll have one or two million dollars by the time you get going, and you can't do anything on a scale large enough to tell you whether it works or not."

What happens next? Relaxing in his office, with his feet propped on a coffee table, Sanchez takes a pragmatic view. "The bundle of gringo dollars that we get from Congress," he says, "keeps diminishing. We need new ideas – that don't cost much. To get some ideas, I asked the program-development people here to give me answers to five fundamental questions:

"1.   What changes in the American systems – and that's plural – of education will make them more palatable for poor people?

"2.   How can we get more poor people served by educators – not schools, but educators, since not all educators are in schools?

"3.   How can we bring the education processes that are now reserved for middle-class Americans within reach of poor people?

"4.   How can we get the nation to consider basic education a right and not a privilege?

"5.   Finally, what financing systems are necessary to bring these things about? That, of course, is outside the privince of OEO."

Actually, the four othere are outside the province of OEO too, aside from small research projects. Sanchez says that if the President and the OMB want research, "we'll seek it out and give it to anybody who will listen." Handling research papers to OMB, however, is like dropping them down a well. And Sanchez, less than six months on the job, admits that he has more problems with the White House and Congress than he expected, but he adds, "Some people are singing a funeral dirge around here, shedding crocodile tears about the fate of OEO. That's not appropriate, at least not yet."

At the end of the year, OEO issued a list of its "accomplishments" in 1971, including ten items in education. They ranged from completion of the one-year performance contracting experiments and the voucher studies to six New Gate projects for prison inmates, to provide higher education and to lower recidivism rates. OEO still funds things that other agencies do not. It helped start the Navajo Community College, the first Indian-controlled college. in the midst of the Navajo reservation. In the best Upward Bound tradition, it has started an experiment with forty-five fifth-graders from poor families near Hampshire College in Massachusetts. If the fifth-graders perform well academically, the OEO will guarantee them a college education. The pupils attend a special six-week summer course at

Hampshire, plus Wednesday afternoon and Saturday courses there during the school year.

OEO, in short, still is mounting good, solid, badly needed programs. But the programs are not likely to make political waves in an election year, or to change institutions, or to end poverty in the next four years. Meanwhile, other agencies are nibbling at OEO's edges. The new Experimental Schools program in the Office of Education, which has the administration's support, has funded experiments in six school districts through the country to see if they can be turned around.

For its part, OEO is no longer pulling rabbits out of hats. It is consolidating, regrouping, trying to survive. It has no new big plans in education waiting to be launched. "This year," says Joe Howell, "education is not considered a top proprity at OEO."

Peter Janssen is special editor for Editorial Projects for Education, publisher of *The Chronicle of Higher Education*, in Washington, D.C.